VIRGINIA MAXWELL

# İSTANBUL
## C I T Y   G U I D E

# INTRODUCING İSTANBUL

Browse for souvenirs at the sprawling Grand Bazaar (p72)

PHIL WEYMOUTH

First-time visitors often talk about that magical moment when İstanbul becomes fabulous rather than foreign, welcoming rather than overwhelming.

Walking the cobbled streets on either side of the Galata Bridge is a good example. On day one, most of your energy will be spent dodging carpet touts, being jostled by crowds and gaping at the visual magnificence of the minaret-studded skyline. Day two will be different, though. You'll veer away from the well-trodden tourist thoroughfares and find yourself nodding good morning to some friendly locals enjoying a game of backgammon and a glass of tea on the sidewalk. Or you'll walk around a corner and be confronted by the sight of a smiling street vendor dispensing delicious sesame-encrusted *simits* (bread rings) and homespun philosophy to a cluster of headscarfed housewives. On day three, you'll start to anticipate the melodious strains of the call to prayer and be seduced by the scent of apple tobacco issuing from tranquil *çay bahçesis* (tea gardens) on every street corner. Day four could see you sipping cocktails in a Beyoğlu rooftop bar, transfixed by the sight of ferries plying the waters between Europe and Asia. Or maybe you'll be drinking *rakı* (aniseed brandy) and sampling delectable meze dishes in a noisy *meyhane* (tavern) off İstiklal Caddesi. By day five, the die will be well and truly cast: *kısmetse* (the intervention of fate or luck) will have ensured your life-long love affair with this extraordinary city.

# İSTANBUL LIFE

This meeting point of East and West has rarely been as full of confidence and hope for the future as it is today. In its guise as Constantinople the city was powerful and mysterious, but as the 21st century gets into the swing, modern İstanbul is revelling in unprecedented growth and prosperity.

The city's starring role as a European Capital of Culture has led to a massive program of heritage restoration in the Old City. Great monuments such as the imperial mosques have been given loving restorations, as have historically significant but hitherto neglected Byzantine monuments. New museums are opening as regularly as international art exhibitions, and the city's festival circuit is one of the busiest in Europe – İstanbullus are intent on showing the world just how exciting and eclectic their cultural landscape is.

The country's bid to join the European Union (EU) is spearheading much of this activity. Official accession talks kicked off in 2005, but the decision isn't due until 2013 at the earliest. To be honest, İstanbullus aren't all that fussed about the outcome. They know their city has a growing European flavour and they suspect that an EU membership isn't going to change its complexion or their lifestyles to a significant degree. Nor have they surrendered their pride in being inheritors of the glory of the Ottoman Empire, with its deep Islamic sensibility and self-conscious separation from the rest of Europe.

Some changes are inevitable as part of the bid for candidacy. Initiatives to bring the country into line with its European neighbours in the areas of human rights, environmental protection, economic management and freedom of speech are underway, but significant improvements are essential if membership is ever to be attained. There will also need to be a rapprochement between the ruling national Justice and Development Party (AKP), with its soft Islamist agenda, and the staunchly secular National Security Council (NSC).

These weighty issues aside, the city is supremely optimistic about the future that it has in store, and for good reason. Put simply, there's never been a better time to visit.

*So many choices! Sample a variety of dishes at a traditional* meyhane *(tavern; p144)*

# HIGHLIGHTS

JOHN SONES

## SULTANAHMET & AROUND

*Once home to Byzantine emperors and Ottoman sultans, Sultanahmet is now the city's tourism hub. Come here to visit venerable Aya Sofya, uncover the secrets of the seraglio at Topkapı Palace and mingle with the locals in the historic Hippodrome.*

GREG ELMS

MURAT BESLER / SHUTTERSTOCK

GEORGE TSAFOS

IZZET KERIBAR

**❶ Blue Mosque**
İstanbul's most famous landmark (p56) has minarets and visual pizazz galore.

**❷ Aya Sofya**
The massive dome and exquisite mosaics of this building (p49) are guaranteed to impress.

**❸ İstanbul Archaeology Museums**
The Alexander sarcophagus is one of the many highlights of this museum complex (p66).

**❹ Basilica Cistern**
Be sure to visit the watery depths of this Byzantine cistern (p54).

**❺ Topkapı Palace**
Get a glimpse into the sumptuous lives of the sultans at this palace (p59).

**❻ Arasta Bazaar**
Source quality souvenirs in this Ottoman shopping arcade (p132).

PAMELA CHEW / ALAMY

GREG ELMS

# BAZAAR DISTRICT

*Shop till you drop in this sprawling district of ancient shopping malls, hans (caravanserais) and street stalls. When your wallet is empty, enjoy a meditative break in one of the city's magnificent imperial mosques.*

PHIL WEYMOUTH

IZZET KERIBAR

CAGALOGLU HAMAM

### 1 Spice Bazaar
Follow your nose to this bustling Ottoman marketplace (p77).

### 2 Grand Bazaar
This famous shopping mall (p72) has history and atmosphere aplenty.

### 3 Süleymaniye Mosque
This mosque (p76) is the crowing achievement of Ottoman imperial architecture.

### 4 Cağaloğlu Hamamı
Surrender to the steam in this beautiful Turkish bath (p185).

### 5 Mosque of Rüstem Paşa
Precious İznik tiles adorn the walls of this diminutive mosque (p78).

### 6 Nargileh Cafes
Join the locals in one of their favourite pastimes (p168).

IZZET KERIBAR

GREG ELMS

7

**❶ Church of Theotokos Pammakaristos**
Discover exquisite Byzantine mosaics in this recently opened museum (p86).

**❷ Theodosius' Land Walls**
Visit the Byzantine Palace of Constantine Porphyrogenitus while walking Theodosius' walls (p90).

**❸ Chora Church**
This church (p83) is home to extraordinary Byzantine frescoes and mosaics.

NIGEL REED QEDIMAGES / ALAMY

# WESTERN DISTRICTS

*Traditionally home to İstanbul's Jewish, Armenian and Greek communities, these suburbs tucked within the ancient city walls now host the city's AKP power brokers. Wander the residential streets here and you'll discover Byzantine churches, Ottoman mosques and local politicians aplenty.*

RUGGERO VANNI / CORBIS

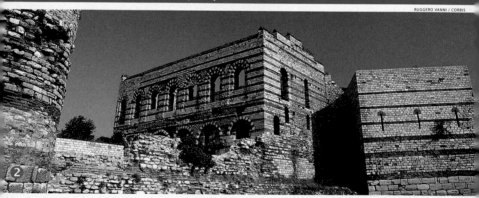

GEORGE TSAFOS

# BEYOĞLU

*Cross the Galata Bridge and you will immediately feel the decidedly feverish pulse of this megalopolis. The main artery of İstiklal Caddesi is at the heart of the action, surrounded by restaurants, bars, cafes, art galleries and boutiques.*

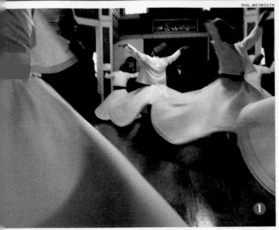

PHIL WEYMOUTH

### ❶ Whirling Dervishes
See the dervishes (p107) whirl their way to a higher plane.

### ❷ Traditional Taverns
Sample the lavish meze spreads served at Beyoğlu's famous *meyhanes* (taverns; p151).

### ❸ İstiklal Caddesi
Promenade the length of the city's most famous boulevard (p109).

GREG ELMS

PHIL WEYMOUTH

# NİŞANTAŞI, BEŞİKTAŞ, ORTAKÖY & KURUÇEŞME

Upmarket shopping and residential districts cascade down the hill from Nişantaşı to the gilded shores of the Bosphorus, where the Ottoman sultans once built lavish pleasure palaces. Today, sybaritic nightclubs and luxury hotels hold court.

MARK AVELLINO

### ❶ Dolmabahçe Palace
Ottoman decorative overkill is the hallmark of this lavish pleasure palace (p114).

### ❷ The Golden Mile
Party the night away in a sophisticated nightclub (p170).

REINA NIGHTCLUB

### ❸ Ortaköy Square
A lively square (p117) right on the Bosphorus shore.

### ❹ Shopping in Nişantaşı
Give your credit card a workout in an upmarket boutique (p140).

TURKEYSHOOT / ALAMY

ALI KABAŞ / ALAMY

**1 Kız Kulesi**
The Maiden's Tower (p121) is one of İstanbul's most distinctive landmarks.

IZZET KERIBAR

# ÜSKÜDAR & KADIKÖY

*A short ferry ride will bring you from Europe to these busy neighbourhoods on the Asian shore, where the skyline is studded with minarets, the headscarf is prominent and the street markets are unrivalled.*

**2 Kadıköy Produce Market**
Savour the sights and smells of this popular street market (p122).

**3 Cross Between Europe & Asia**
Take a ferry trip (p202) between the continents.

JOHN ELK III

STAN GAMESTER / ALAMY

### ➊ The Bosphorus
Sail up the Bosphorus (p202) past ornate wooden mansions and magnificent stone castles.

### ➋ The Golden Horn
Admire the city skyline from the deck of a commuter ferry (p210).

### ➌ The Princes' Islands
A summer retreat (p212) full of gracious wooden mansions.

# FERRY TRIPS

*The city's fabulous flotilla of ferries is waiting to transport you up the mighty Bosphorus, down the evocatively named Golden Horn and across the waters of the Sea of Marmara to the idyllic Princes' Islands.*

# CONTENTS

# THE AUTHOR

## Virginia Maxwell

After working for many years as a publishing manager at Lonely Planet's Melbourne headquarters, Virginia decided that she'd be happier writing guidebooks than commissioning them. Since making this decision she's authored Lonely Planet guides to Turkey, Egypt, Spain, Italy, Lebanon, Morocco, Syria and the United Arab Emirates. Virginia knows İstanbul well, and loves it with a passion. As well as writing the previous two editions of this city guide, she is also the author of Lonely Planet's *İstanbul Encounter* pocket guide and the İstanbul chapter of Lonely Planet's *Turkey* guide. She also writes about the city for a host of international newspapers and magazines. Virginia usually travels with her partner Peter and young son Max, who love the city as much as she does.

### VIRGINIA'S TOP İSTANBUL DAY

After popping into a local *börekçi* for a breakfast of freshly baked *ıspanaklı börek* (pastry stuffed with spinach) and a glass of tea, I saunter past the Blue Mosque (p56) and Aya Sofya (p49), and up Divan Yolu to the Grand Bazaar (p72). After assuring the good-humoured touts that I have no money to spend, I walk through the Sahaflar Çarşısı (Old Book Bazaar; p75) and around İstanbul University to the Süleymaniye Mosque (p76) so that I can marvel at Sinan's most wonderful creation. After this I join the sea of locals on the bustling streets of Tahtakale, making my way past the shops and street vendors down towards Eminönü, where I catch a ferry to Kadıköy in Asia. My first stop there is for lunch at the fabulous Çiya Sofrası (p159), and then I wander for an hour or so around the vibrant fresh-produce market. Catching a ferry back to Karaköy, I recharge over a tea and a piece of the city's best baklava at Karaköy Güllüğlu (p158), before walking up through the narrow streets of Karaköy and Tünel to İstiklal Caddesi for an hour or so of browsing in the book and record stores. Then it's on to meet friends for a drink at Leb-i Derya or Mikla (both p166), followed by dinner at Sofyalı 9 (p154) or Ece Aksoy (p153) in Asmalımescit. Rakı, meze and good friends, all in the best city in the world – life doesn't get any better than this!

# GETTING STARTED

GETTING STARTED WHEN TO GO

## WHEN TO GO

The best times to visit İstanbul are spring (April to May) and autumn (September to October), when skies are clear and temperatures are moderate. In July and August it's hot and steamy; many locals head for the west and south coasts then and some businesses close. Biting winds and snow are common in winter.

Be aware that during the five-day Kurban Bayramı (see p225) banks shut and ATMs can run out of money. During Ramazan (Ramadan; see p225) business hours can be erratic.

Hotel rooms skyrocket in price and are often overbooked during the Formula 1 Grand Prix in June.

## FESTIVALS

In the warmer months İstanbul is awash with arts festivals and music events, giving plenty of choice when it comes to entertainment. Most of the big-name arts festivals are organised by the İstanbul Foundation for Culture and Arts (☎ 212-334 0700; www.iksv.org/english), though Positif (www.pozitif-ist. com) organises some. Tickets to most events are available from Biletix (☎ 216-556 9800; www.biletix. com). For a list of public holidays see p225.

## March
### AKBANK SHORT FILM FESTIVAL
☎ 212-252 3500; www.akbanksanat.com
Beloved by the black-clad Beyoğlu bohemian set, this arty film-culture event is held at the Akbank Culture & Arts Centre.

### NEVRUZ
Locals celebrate this ancient Middle Eastern spring festival on 21 March with jolly goings-on and jumping over bonfires. The streets near the Armada Hotel in Cankurtaran (in the Sultanahmet neighbourhood) host a giant open-air party.

## April
### INTERNATIONAL İSTANBUL FILM FESTIVAL
www.iksv.org/english
If you're keen to view the best in Turkish film and bump into a few local film stars

while doing so, this is the event to attend. Held early in the month in cinemas around town, it's hugely popular. The program includes retrospectives and recent releases from Turkey and abroad.

### İSTANBUL INTERNATIONAL TULIP FESTIVAL
The tulip (lale in Turkish) is one of İstanbul's traditional symbols, and the local government celebrates this fact by planting over three million of them annually. These bloom in late March and early April, endowing almost every street and park with vivid spring colours and wonderful photo opportunities.

## May
### ORTHODOX EASTER
www.ec-patr.org
The celebratory Easter Sunday Mass is the biggest event of the year at the home of the Greek Orthodox community in Fener.

## June
### EFES PILSEN ONE LOVE
www.pozitif-ist.com
This two-day music festival is held at one of İstanbul's hippest art venues, santralistanbul (p179). International headline acts play everything from punk to pop, electronica to disco.

### INTERNATIONAL İSTANBUL MUSIC FESTIVAL
www.iksv.org/english
The city's premier arts festival includes performances of opera, dance, orchestral concerts and chamber recitals. Acts are often internationally renowned and the action takes place in atmosphere-laden venues including Aya İrini (p181) in Sultanahmet.

## July
### INTERNATIONAL İSTANBUL JAZZ FESTIVAL
www.iksv.org/english
This festival was once part of the International İstanbul Music Festival, but branched out on its own over a decade ago and has

16

gone from strength to strength. It usually runs for two weeks and programs a weird hybrid of conventional jazz, electronica, drum 'n' bass, world music and rock. Venues include the Cemil Topuzlu Open-Air Theatre (Cemil Topuzlu Açık Hava Tiyatrosu) in Harbiye, İstanbul Modern (p101), Cemal Reşit Rey Concert Hall (p181) and Nardis Jazz Club (p172).

## September

### INTERNATIONAL İSTANBUL BIENNIAL
www.iksv.org/english
The city's major visual-arts shindig takes place from early September to early November in odd-numbered years. An international curator or panel of curators nominates a theme and puts together a cutting-edge program that is then exhibited in a variety of venues around town.

### ROCK'N COKE
www.pozitif-ist.com
Turkey's largest open-air music festival rocks for two days, with past headliners including The Prodigy, Kaiser Chiefs and Jane's Addiction. It's held in İstanbul Park, the city's Formula 1 track, and crowds can hit 50,000.

## October

### AKBANK JAZZ FESTIVAL
☎ 212-252 3500; www.akbanksanat.com
This older sister to the International İstanbul Jazz Festival is a boutique event, with a program featuring traditional and avant-garde jazz, as well as Middle Eastern fusions and a special program of young jazz. Venues are scattered around town.

## November

### ANNIVERSARY OF ATATÜRK'S DEATH
At 9.05am on 10 November, a minute's silence is held to commemorate the death of the nation's revered founder. Sirens blare and the city comes to a standstill, with people, cars and buses literally stopping in their tracks.

## December

### EFES PILSEN BLUES FESTIVAL
www.pozitif-ist.com
This long-running event tours nationally, keeping blues fans smiling and leaving

an echo of boogie-woogie, zydeco and 12-bar blues from Adana to Trabzon. It stops for a two-day program in İstanbul. The main venue is the Lütfi Kırdar Concert Hall (p181).

# COSTS & MONEY

After years of instability, the Turkish lira is now considered relatively stable. In this book we have given hotel and tour prices in euros, as this is the currency that hotel owners and tour operators work with. All other prices are given in Turkish Lira (TL), and reflect the reality on the ground at the time of research.

Though İstanbul is no longer the bargain travel destination it was in the past, it still offers good value for money. A three-star hotel room for two can cost as little as €60 in Sultanahmet and you can enjoy a decent kebap meal for TL20 to TL25 (without alcohol). Public transport is both efficient and dirt cheap, and many sights – in particular the city's wonderful array of historical mosques – are free. Others are relatively inexpensive, with the average museum entry being TL15.

This isn't to say that everything in the city is a bargain. If you decide to have a night on the town and hit the bars in Beyoğlu and nightclubs along the Bosphorus you'll need to be cashed up – nightclub entries can be as high as TL50 and a drink in these places will cost at least TL20; a glass of wine in one of the glam rooftop bars in Beyoğlu will set you back TL15. And shopping at the new generation of malls such as Kanyon and İstinye Park (boxed text p142) is no different to blowing your budget in Knightsbridge or on Rodeo Drive – this is designer turf and is priced accordingly.

---

### HOW MUCH?
Litre of unleaded petrol TL3.30
Litre of bottled water TL1
Efes Pilsen (bar prices) TL4-8
Ticket on public transport TL1.50
Fish sandwich TL4
Glass of çay (tea) TL1-1.50
Taxi ride from Sultanahmet to Taksim TL12-14
Movie ticket TL9-15
Nargileh (water pipe) TL12-15
English-language newspaper TL1.50

# INTERNET RESOURCES

Cornucopia (www.cornucopia.net) The online site of the glossy 'Connoisseurs of Turkey' magazine has a handy arts diary as well as exhibitions listings and blogs.

Hürriyet Daily News (www.hurriyetdailynews.com) Website of the Opposition-leaning English-language daily newspaper.

İstanbul Şehır Rehberi (http://sehirrehberi.ibb.gov.tr) Online maps of the city.

Lonely Planet (www.lonelyplanet.com) Check out the Thorn Tree bulletin board to find out what city discoveries are being made.

Ministry of Culture and Tourism (www.turizm.gov.tr) Government information on tourism, culture, archaeology and history.

Ministry of Foreign Affairs (www.mfa.gov.tr) Up-to-date visa and security information.

My Merhaba (www.mymerhaba.com) Aimed at expats, but has lots of general information that's of use to visitors too, including entertainment listings.

Time Out İstanbul (www.timeoutistanbul.com/english) The online site of this excellent monthly magazine has a good listings section.

## ADVANCE PLANNING

Two months before you go If you're travelling in spring, autumn or over Christmas, make your hotel booking as far in advance as possible. The good places often book up quickly!

One month before you go İstanbul's big-ticket festivals sell out fast, and for good reason. Check the festival list in this chapter to see what tempts your fancy, and then book ahead.

Two weeks before you go Book a table for dinner at Mikla (p152), Cercis Murat Konağı (boxed text p160), Changa (p152) and other top-end restaurants reviewed in this book.

One week before you go Check the *Time Out* website (see left) for information about openings and events in the city.

Today's Zaman (www.todayszaman.com) Website of the AKP-leaning English-language daily newspaper.

Turism Turkey (www.tourismturkey.org) Government website containing a grab bag of articles and information.

Turkey Travel Planner (www.turkeytravelplanner.com) An ever-growing site about travel throughout Turkey put together by well-known writer and Turkey expert, Tom Brosnahan.

## HISTORY

### EARLIEST TIMES

Semistra, the earliest-known settlement on the site of İstanbul, was probably founded around 1000 BC, a few hundred years after the Trojan War and in the same period that kings David and Solomon ruled in Jerusalem. Semistra was followed by a fishing village named Lygos, which occupied Seraglio Point (Sarayburnu) where Topkapı Palace (Topkapı Sarayı) stands today. Around 700 BC, colonists from Megara (near Corinth) in Greece founded the city of Chalcedon (now Kadıköy) on the Asian shore of the Bosphorus. Chalcedon became one of a dozen Greek fishing colonies along the shores of the Propontis (the ancient name for the Sea of Marmara). The historian Theopompus of Chios, cited in John Freely's *Istanbul: The Imperial City*, wrote in the latter half of the 4th century that its inhabitants 'devoted themselves unceasingly to the better pursuits of life'. Their way of life was apparently in stark contrast to that of the dissolute Byzantines, who founded their settlement across the Bosphorus at Seraglio Point in 657 BC.

### FIRST INCARNATION: BYZANTIUM

Legend tells us that Byzantium was founded by a Megarian colonist named Byzas, the son of the god Poseidon and the nymph Keroessa, daughter of Zeus and Io. Before leaving Greece, Byzas had asked the oracle at Delphi where he should establish his new colony. The enigmatic answer was 'Opposite the blind'. All this made sense when Byzas and his fellow colonists sailed up the Bosphorus and noticed the colony on the Asian shore at Chalcedon. Looking west, they saw the small fishing village of Lygos, built on a magnificent and easily fortified natural harbour of the Golden Horn (Haliç) known to the Greeks as Chrysokeras) on the European shore. Thinking, as legend has it, that the settlers of Chalcedon must have been blind to disregard such a superb position, Byzas and his friends settled here and their new town came to be called Byzantium after its founder.

The new colony quickly prospered, largely due to its ability to levy tolls and harbour fees on ships passing through the Bosphorus, then as now an important waterway. A thriving marketplace was established and the inhabitants lived on traded goods and the abundant fish stocks in the surrounding waters. In all, the early Byzantines were a fortunate lot. They walled their city to ensure its invincibility from attack, enslaved the local Thracian population to do most of the hard work and worshipped the Greek Olympian gods. Theopompus of Chios might have thought that the Chalcedons lived a good clean life when they first established their city on the opposite shore, but he had no such compliment for the Byzantines, writing that they 'accustomed themselves to amours and drinking in the taverns'.

In 512 BC Darius, emperor of Persia, captured the city during his campaign against the Scythians. Following the retreat of the Persians in 478 BC, the town came under the influence and protection of Athens and joined the Athenian League. It was a turbulent relationship, with Byzantium revolting a number of times, only to be defeated by the Athenians. During one of the revolts, the Athenian navy mounted an expedition against Byzantium and Chalcedon and sailed up the Bosphorus to establish a settlement at Chrysopolis ('the City of Gold'), site of the present-day suburb of Üsküdar. From this base they successfully besieged Byzantium.

The Spartans took the city after the end of the Peloponnesian War (404 BC) but were ousted in 390 BC, when Byzantium once again joined the League of Athens. It was granted independence in 355 BC but stayed under the Athenian umbrella, withstanding with Athenian help a siege by Philip, father of Alexander the Great, in 340 BC.

By the end of the Hellenistic period, Byzantium had formed an alliance with the Roman Empire. It retained its status as a free state, which it even kept after being officially incorporated into the Roman Empire in AD 79 by Vespasian, but it paid significant taxes for the privilege. Life was relatively uneventful until the city's leaders made a big mistake: they picked the wrong side in a Roman war of succession following the death of the Emperor Pertinax in AD 193. When Septimius Severus emerged victorious over his rival Pescennius Niger, he mounted a three-year siege of the city, eventually massacring Byzantium's citizens, razing its walls and burning it to the ground. Ancient Byzantium was no more.

The new emperor was aware of the city's important strategic position, and he soon set about rebuilding it. He pardoned the remaining citizens and built a circuit of walls that stretched roughly from where the New Mosque (Yeni Cami) is today (Map pp50–1) to the Bucoleon Palace (Map pp50–1), enclosing a city twice the size of its predecessor. The Hippodrome (p57) was built by Severus, as was a colonnaded way that followed the present path of Divan Yolu. He also erected a gateway known as the Miliarium Aureum or, more simply, the Milion. A weathered marble stellae from this gate can still be seen today (Map pp50–1). Severus named his new city Augusta Antonina and it was subsequently ruled by a succession of emperors, including the great Diocletian (r 284–305).

## DECLINE OF ROME & THE RISE OF CONSTANTINOPLE

Diocletian had decreed that after his retirement, the government of the Roman Empire should be overseen by co-emperors Galerius in the east (Augusta Antonina) and Constantine in the west (Rome). This resulted in a civil war, which was won by Constantine in AD 324 when he defeated Licinius, Galerius' successor, at Chrysopolis.

With his victory, Constantine (r 324–37) became sole emperor of a reunited empire. He also became the first Christian emperor, though he didn't formally convert until he was on his deathbed. To solidify his power he summoned the First Ecumenical Council at Nicaea (İznik) in 325, which established the precedent of the emperor's supremacy in church affairs.

Constantine also decided to move the capital of the empire to the shores of the Bosphorus, where he had forged his great victory and where the line between the Eastern and Western divisions of the Empire had previously been drawn. He built a new, wider circle of walls around the site of Byzantium and laid out a magnificent city within. The Hippodrome was extended and a forum was built on the crest of the second hill, near today's Nuruosmaniye Mosque (Map pp50–1). The city was dedicated on 11 May 330 as New Rome, but soon came to be called Constantinople. First settled as a fishing village over 1000 years earlier, the settlement on Seraglio Point was now the capital of the Eurasian world and would remain so for almost another 1000 years.

Constantine died in 337, just seven years after the dedication of his new capital. His empire was divided up between his three sons: Constantius, Constantien and Constans. Constantinople was part of Constantius' share. His power base was greatly increased in 353 when he overthrew both of his brothers and brought the empire under his sole control.

Constantius died in 361 and was succeeded by his cousin Julian. Emperor Jovian was next, succeeded by Valens (of aqueduct fame; p80).

The city continued to grow under the rule of the emperors. Theodosius I ('the Great'; r 378–95) had a forum built on the present site of Beyazıt Sq and a massive triumphal gate built in the city walls, the Porta Aurea (Golden Gate; p125). He also erected the Obelisk of Theodosius at the Hippodrome. His grandson Emperor Theodosius II (r 408–50) came to the throne as a boy, heavily influenced by his sister Pulcheria, who acted as regent until her brother was old enough to rule

| 1000 BC | 657 BC | 335 BC |
| --- | --- | --- |
| The settlements of Lygos and Semistra are founded by Thracian tribes; Plinius mentions the founding of Semistra in his historical accounts and a few traces of Lygos remain near Seraglio Point | The god Poseidon and the nymph Keroessa, daughter of Zeus and Io, have a son, Byzas, who travels up the Bosphorus and founds Byzantium on the site of Lygos | Byzantium is granted independence but stays under the Athenian umbrella, withstanding with Athenian help a siege by Philip, father of Alexander the Great, in 340 BC |

in his own right. Threatened by the forces of Attila the Hun, he ordered that an even wider, more formidable circle of walls be built around the city. Encircling all seven hills of the city, the walls were completed in 413, only to be brought down by a series of earthquakes in 447. They were hastily rebuilt in a mere two months – the rapid approach of Attila and the Huns acting as a powerful stimulus. The Theodosian walls successfully held out invaders for the next 757 years and still stand today, though they are in an increasingly dilapidated state of repair (see the boxed text p95).

Theodosius II's other achievements were the compilation of the *Codex Theodosianus,* a collection of all of the laws that had been enacted since the reign of Constantine the Great, and the erection of a new cathedral, the Sancta Sophia (Aya Sofya; p49), which replaced an earlier church of the same name that had been burned down during a riot in 404.

## İSTANBUL'S HISTORIAN

This book is littered with mentions of the writings of John Freely (b 1926), an American academic who has been living, working and writing in İstanbul on and off since 1960. Put simply, what Freely doesn't know about the architectural and cultural history of İstanbul probably isn't worth knowing. His eminently readable books include the following:

- *The Byzantine Monuments of Istanbul* (with Ahmet Çakmak; 2004)
- *Inside the Seraglio: Private Lives of the Sultans in Istanbul* (1999)
- *Istanbul: The Imperial City* (1996)
- *Sinan: Architect of Süleyman the Magnificent* (photographs by Ara Guler; 1992)
- *Strolling through Istanbul* (with Hilary Sumner-Boyd; 1972)

## JUSTINIAN & THEODORA

Theodosius died in 450 and was succeeded by a string of emperors, including the most famous of all Byzantine emperors, Justinian the Great.

During the 5th and 6th centuries, as the barbarians of Europe captured and sacked Rome, the new eastern capital grew in wealth, strength and reputation. Justinian (r 527–65) had much to do with this. A former soldier, he and his great general Belisarius reconquered Anatolia, the Balkans, Egypt, Italy and North Africa. They also successfully put down the Nika riots of 532, killing 30,000 of the rioters in the Hippodrome in the process.

Three years before taking the throne, Justinian had married Theodora, a strong-willed former courtesan who is credited with having great influence over her husband. Together, they further embellished Constantinople with great buildings, including SS Sergius and Bacchus, now known as Küçük (Little) Aya Sofya (p76), Haghia Eirene (Aya İrini; p59) and the Basilica Cistern (p54). Justinian's personal triumph was the new Sancta Sophia (Aya Sofya), which was completed in 537.

Justinian's ambitious building projects and constant wars of reconquest exhausted his treasury and his empire. Following his reign, the Byzantine Empire would never again be as large, powerful or rich.

## UNDER SIEGE & IN DECLINE

From 565 to 1025, a succession of warrior emperors kept invaders such as the Persians and the Avars at bay. Though the foreign armies often managed to get as far as Chalcedon, none were able to breach Theodosius' land walls. The Arab armies of the nascent Islamic empire tried

| AD 79 | 330 | 379 |
|---|---|---|
| Byzantium is officially incorporated into the Roman Empire by the soldier-emperor Vespasian, who was described by the Roman senator and historian Tacitus as 'infamous and odious' | Constantine the Great declares Byzantium the capital of the Roman Empire, names it New Rome and commences an ambitious building program; the city soon becomes known as Constantinople in his honour | The emperor Theodosius I (the Great) makes Christianity the official religion of the Roman Empire; he erects the Obelisk of Theodosius, pilfered from Karnak in Egypt, at the Hippodrome in 390 |

## NAMING RIGHTS

Even when it was ruled by the Byzantines, Constantinople was informally known as 'the city' (*polis*). The name İstanbul probably derives from this (the Greek for 'to the city' is *'eis ten polin'*). Though the Turks kept the name Constantinople, they also used other names, including İstanbul and Dersaadet (City of Peace and/or Happiness).

The city's name was officially changed to İstanbul by Atatürk in the early republican years and the use of the name Constantinople was banned for having, it was thought, unfortunate imperial connotations.

in 669, 674, 678 and 717–18, each time in vain. Inside the walls the city was undergoing a different type of threat: the Iconoclastic Crisis. This began in 726 when Emperor Leo III launched his quest to rid the empire of all forms of idolatry. Those who worshipped idols, including the followers of many saints, revolted and a number of uprisings ensued. The emperor was ultimately triumphant and his policy was adopted by his successors. It was first overturned in 780, when the Empress Eirene, mother of the child emperor Constantine VI, set out to restore icons. The issue was finally put to rest by the Empress Theodora, mother of Michael III, another child emperor, in 845.

The powerful emperors of the Bulgarian empire besieged the city in 814, 913 and 924, never conquering it. Under Emperor Basil II (r 976–1025), the Byzantine armies drove the Arab armies out of Anatolia and completely annihilated the Bulgarian forces. For this feat he was dubbed Bulgaroctonus, the 'Bulgar-slayer'.

In 1071 Emperor Romanus IV Diogenes (r 1068–1071) led his army to eastern Anatolia to do battle with the Seljuk Turks, who had been forced out of Central Asia by the encroaching Mongols. However, at Manzikert (Malazgirt) the Byzantines were disastrously defeated, the emperor captured and imprisoned, and the former Byzantine heartland of Anatolia thus thrown open to Turkish invasion and settlement. Soon the Seljuks had built a thriving empire of their own in central Anatolia, with their capital first at Nicaea and later at Konya.

As Turkish power was consolidated in Anatolia to the east of Constantinople, the power of Venice – always a maritime and commercial rival to Constantinople – grew in the West. This coincided with the launch of the First Crusade and the arrival in Constantinople of the first of the Crusaders in 1096.

## THE CRUSADERS: INTERLOPERS FROM THE WEST

Soldiers of the Second Crusade passed through the city in 1146 during the reign of Manuel I, son of John Comnenus II 'the Good' and his empress, Eirene, both of whose mosaic portraits can be seen in the gallery at Aya Sofya. In 1171 Manuel evicted Venetian merchants from their neighbourhood in Galata. The Venetians retaliated by sending a fleet to attack Byzantine ports in Greece.

The convoluted, treacherous imperial court politics of Constantinople have given us the word 'Byzantine'. Rarely blessed with a simple, peaceful succession, Byzantine rulers were always under threat from members of their own families as well as would-be tyrants and foreign powers. This internecine plotting was eventually to lead to the defeat of the city by the Crusaders.

In 1195 Alexius III deposed and blinded his brother, Emperor Isaac II, claiming the throne for himself. Fleeing to the West, Isaac's oldest son, Prince Alexius, pleaded to the pope and

| 408 | 524 | 527 |
|---|---|---|
| Theodosius' grandson Theodosius II inherits the throne as a child; his sister Pulcheria, a devout Christian, takes a vow of virginity to avoid being forced into marriage and acts as her brother's regent | Justinian, who will become the most famous of all of the Byzantine emperors, marries a courtesan called Theodora, the daughter of a bear-keeper at the Hippodrome | Justinian takes the throne and makes Theodora joint ruler; the Imperial Council counsels the Emperor to flee the city during the Nika riots in 532, but Theodora persuades him to stay and fight |

other Western rulers for help in restoring his father to the Byzantine throne. At the time, the Fourth Crusade was assembling in Venice to sail to Egypt and attack the infidel. Knowing this, Prince Alexius sent a message to the Crusaders offering to agree to a union of the Greek and Roman churches under the papacy if the Crusaders could put his father back on the throne. He also promised to pay richly for their assistance. The Crusader leaders agreed, and Enrico Dandolo, Doge of Venice, led the crusaders to Constantinople, arriving in 1203.

Rather than facing the Crusaders, Alexius III fled with the imperial treasury. The Byzantines swiftly restored Isaac II to the throne and made Prince Alexius (Alexius IV) his co-emperor. Unfortunately, the new co-emperors had no money to pay their allies. They were also deeply unpopular with their subjects, being seen as Latin toadies. Isaac fell ill (he died in 1204), and the Byzantines swiftly deposed Alexius and crowned a new emperor, Alexius V. The new emperor foolishly ordered the Crusaders to leave his territory, conveniently ignoring the fact that they believed themselves to be owed a considerable amount of money by the Byzantines. Their patience exhausted, the Crusaders attacked. On 13 April 1204 they broke through the walls, and sacked and pillaged the rich capital of their Christian ally.

When the smoke cleared, Dandolo took control of three-eighths of the city, including Aya Sofya, leaving the rest to his co-conspirator Count Baldwin of Flanders. The Byzantine nobility fled to what was left of their estates and fought among themselves in best Byzantine fashion for control of the shreds of the empire.

After Dandolo's death, Count Baldwin had himself crowned emperor of Romania ('Kingdom of the Romans'), his name for his new kingdom. Never a strong or effective state, Baldwin's so-called empire steadily declined until, just over half a century later in 1261, it was easily recaptured by the soldiers of Michael VIII Palaeologus, formerly the emperor of Nicaea, where the Byzantine Empire in exile sat. The Byzantine Empire was restored.

## THE OTTOMANS: UPSTARTS FROM THE EAST

Two decades after Michael reclaimed Constantinople, a Turkish warlord named Ertuğrul died in the village of Söğüt near Nicaea. He left his son Osman, who was known as Gazi (Warrior for the Faith), a small territory. Osman's followers became known in the Empire as Osmanlıs and in the West as the Ottomans.

Osman died in 1324 and was succeeded by his son Orhan. In 1326 Orhan captured Bursa, made it his capital and took the title of sultan. A victory at Nicaea followed, after which he sent his forces further afield, conquering Ankara to the east and Thrace to the west. His son Murat I (r 1362–89) took Adrianople (Edirne) in 1371 and extended his conquests to Kosovo, where he defeated the Serbs and Bosnians.

Murat's son Beyazıt (r 1389–1402) unsuccessfully laid siege to Constantinople in 1394, then defeated a Crusader army 100,000 strong on the Danube in 1396. Though temporarily checked by the armies of Tamerlane and a nasty war of succession between Beyazıt's four sons that was eventually won by Mehmet I (r 1413–21), the Ottomans continued to grow in power and size. By 1440 the Ottoman armies under Murat II (r 1421–51) had taken Thessalonica, unsuccessfully laid siege to Constantinople and Belgrade, and battled Christian armies for Transylvania. It was at this point in history that Mehmet II 'The Conqueror' (r 1451–81) came to power and vowed to attain the ultimate prize – Constantinople.

| 548 | 565 | 717 |
|---|---|---|
| Theodora dies; during her reign she was known for establishing homes for ex-prostitutes, granting women more rights in divorce cases, allowing women to own and inherit property, and enacting the death penalty for rape | Justinian dies; his lasting memorial is the church of Haghia Sophia (Aya Sofya), which was to be the centre of Eastern Orthodox Christianity for many centuries | Leo III, a Syrian, becomes emperor after deposing Theodosius III; he introduces a series of edicts against the worship of images, ushering in the age of iconoclasm |

# THE CONQUEST

By 1450, the Byzantine emperor had control over little more than Constantinople itself. The first step in Mehmet's plan to take the city was construction of the great fortress of Rumeli Hisarı (see p205), which was completed in 1452. He also repaired Anadolu Hisarı, the fortress on the Asian shore that had been built by his great-grandfather. Between them, the two great fortresses then closed the Bosphorus at its narrowest point, blockading the imperial capital from the north.

The Byzantines had closed the mouth of the Golden Horn with a heavy chain (parts of which are on view in İstanbul's Military Museum, p112, and Naval Museum, p116) to prevent Ottoman ships from sailing in and attacking the city walls on the north side. Mehmet outsmarted them by marshalling his boats at a cove where Dolmabahçe Palace (p114) now stands, and having them transported overland during the night on rollers and slides up the valley (where the İstanbul Hilton now stands) and down the other side into the Golden Horn at Kasımpaşa. As dawn broke his fleet attacked the city, catching the Byzantine defenders by surprise. Soon the Golden Horn was under Ottoman control.

As for the mighty Theodosian land walls to the west, a Hungarian cannon founder named Urban had offered his services to the Byzantine emperor for the defence of Christendom. Finding that the emperor had no money, he conveniently forgot about defending Christianity and went instead to Mehmet, who paid him richly to cast an enormous cannon capable of firing a huge ball right through the city walls.

Despite the inevitability of the conquest (Mehmet had 80,000 men compared with Byzantium's 7000), Emperor Constantine XI (r 1449–53) refused the surrender terms offered by Mehmet on 23 May 1453, preferring to wait in hope that Christendom would come to his rescue. On 28 May the final attack commenced: the mighty walls were breached between the gates now called Topkapı and Edirnekapı, the sultan's troops flooded in and by the evening of the 29th they were in control of every quarter. Constantine, the last emperor of Byzantium, died fighting on the city walls.

# THE CITY ASCENDANT

The 21-year-old conqueror saw himself as the successor to the imperial throne of Byzantium by right of conquest, and he began to rebuild and repopulate the city. Aya Sofya was converted to a mosque; a new mosque, the Fatih (Conqueror) Camii (p85), was built on the fourth hill; and the Eski Saray (Old Palace) was constructed on the third hill, followed by a new palace on Sarayburnu (p59) a few years later. The city walls were repaired and a new fortress, Yedikule, was built. İstanbul, as it was often called, became the new administrative, commercial and cultural centre of the ever-growing Ottoman Empire. Mehmet encouraged Greeks who had fled the city to return and issued an imperial decree calling for resettlement; Muslims, Jews and Christians all took up his offer and were promised the right to worship as they pleased. The Genoese, who had fought with the Byzantines, were pardoned and allowed to stay in Galata, though the fortifications that surrounded their settlement were torn down. Only Galata Tower (p105) was allowed to stand.

Mehmet died in 1481 and was succeeded by Beyazıt II (r 1481–1512), who was ousted by his son, the ruthless Selim the Grim (r 1512–20), famed for executing seven grand viziers and numerous relatives during his relatively short reign.

| 1204 | 1261 | 1453 |
|---|---|---|
| Enrico Dandolo, Doge of Venice, leads the crusaders of the Fourth Crusade in a defeat of Constantinople; after his burial in Aya Sofya his bones are disinterred by locals and thrown to the dogs | Constantinople is recaptured by the soldiers of Michael VIII Palaeologus, formerly the emperor of Nicaea, where the Byzantine Empire in exile sat; the Byzantine Empire is restored | Mehmet's army defeats that of the Byzantine emperor and he takes power in İstanbul, becoming known as El-Fatih, 'The Conqueror'; he commissions the Italian painter Gentile Bellini to paint his portrait in 1479 and dies in 1481 |

The building boom that Mehmet kicked off was continued by his successors, with Selim's son Süleyman the Magnificent (r 1520–66) being responsible for more construction than any other sultan. Blessed with the services of Mimar Sinan (1497–1588), Islam's greatest architect, the sultan and his family, court and grand viziers crowded the city with great buildings. Under Süleyman's 46-year reign, the longest of any sultan, the empire expanded its territories and refined its artistic pursuits at its court. None of the empires of Europe or Asia were as powerful.

## RULE OF THE WOMEN

Süleyman's son Selim II ('the Sot', r 1566–74) and his successors lost themselves in the pleasures of the harem and the bottle, and cared little for the administration of the empire their forebears had built. While they were carousing, a succession of exceptionally able grand viziers dealt with external and military affairs.

Before the drunken Selim drowned in his bath, his chief concubine Nurbanu called the shots in the palace and ushered in the so-called 'Rule of the Women', whereby a series of chief concubines and mothers (*valide sultans*) of a series of dissolute sultans ruled the roost at court. Among the most fascinating of these women was Kösem Sultan, the favourite of Sultan Ahmet I (r 1603–17). She influenced the course of the empire through Ahmet, then through her sons Murat IV (r 1623–40) and Ibrahim ('the Mad', r 1640–48) and finally through her grandson Mehmet IV (r 1648–87). Her influence over Mehmet lasted only a few years and she was strangled in 1651 at the command of the *valide sultan* Turhan Hadice, Mehmet's mother.

For the next century the sultans continued in Selim's footsteps. Their dissolute and often unbalanced behaviour led to dissatisfaction among the people and the army, which would eventually prove to be the empire's undoing.

## DECLINE, THEN ATTEMPTS AT REFORM

The motor that drove the Ottoman Empire was military conquest, and when the sultan's armies reached their geographical and technological limits, decline set in for good. In 1683 the Ottomans laid siege to Vienna for the second time, but failed again to take the city. With the Treaty of Karlowitz in 1699, the Austrian and Ottoman emperors divided up the Balkans, and the Ottoman Empire went on the defensive.

By this time Europe was well ahead of Turkey in politics, technology, science, banking, commerce and military development. Sultan Selim III (r 1789–1807) initiated efforts to catch up to Europe, but was overthrown in a revolt by janissaries (the sultan's personal bodyguards). The modernisation efforts were continued under Mahmut II (r 1808–39). He founded a new army along European lines, provoking a riot among the janissaries, so that in 1826 he had to send his new force in to crush them, which it did. The bodies of janissaries filled the Hippodrome and the ancient corps, once the glory of the empire, was no more.

Sultan Abdül Mecit (r 1839–61) persisted with the catch-up, continuing the Tanzimat (Reorganisation) political and social reforms that had been initiated by his father Mahmut II. But these efforts were too little, too late. During the 19th century, ethnic nationalism, a force more powerful even than Western armies, penetrated the empire's domain and proved its undoing.

| 1520 | 1550-57 | 1556 |
|------|---------|------|
| Selim's son Süleyman, who would come to be known as 'The Magnificent', ascends to the throne; his first acts as sultan are a series of military conquests in Syria, Hungary and Rhodes | Süleyman's chief architect, Mimar Koca Sinan, designs and oversees construction of the great Süleymaniye Mosque complex for his patron; he is buried in a tomb just outside its walls | Süleyman dies while on a military campaign in Hungary; his death is kept secret for days while word is sent to his son Selim so that he can take control in Istanbul before the news arrives |

# ETHNIC NATIONALISM

For centuries, the non-Turkish ethnic and non-Muslim religious minorities in the sultan's domains had lived side by side with their Turkish neighbours, governed by their own religious and traditional laws. The head of each community – chief rabbi, Orthodox patriarch etc – was responsible to the sultan for the community's wellbeing and behaviour.

Ottoman decline and misrule provided fertile ground for the growth of ethnic nationalism among these communities. The subject peoples of the Ottoman Empire rose in revolt, one after another, often with the direct encouragement and assistance of the European powers, who coveted parts of the sultan's vast domains. After bitter fighting in 1831 the Kingdom of Greece was formed; the Serbs, Bulgarians, Romanians, Albanians, Armenians and Arabs would all seek their independence soon after.

As the sultan's empire broke up, the European powers (Britain, France, Italy, Germany and Russia) hovered in readiness to colonise or annex the pieces. They used religion as a reason for pressure or control, saying that it was their duty to protect the sultan's Catholic, Protestant or Orthodox subjects from misrule and anarchy.

The Russian emperors put pressure on the Turks to grant them powers over all Ottoman Orthodox Christian subjects, whom the Russian emperor would thus 'protect'. The result was the Crimean War (1853–56), with Britain and France fighting on the side of the Ottomans against the growth of Russian power. During the war, wounded British, French and Ottoman soldiers were brought to İstanbul for treatment at the Selimiye Army Barracks, now home to the Florence Nightingale Museum (p125), and the foundations of modern nursing practice were laid.

Even during the war, the sultan continued the imperial building tradition. Vast Dolmabahçe Palace and its mosque were finished in 1856, and the palaces at Beylerbeyi (p205), Çırağan (p116) and Yıldız (p116) would be built before the end of the century. Though it had lost the fabulous wealth of the days of Süleyman the Magnificent, the city was still regarded as the Paris of the East. It was also the terminus of the *Orient Express,* which connected İstanbul and Paris – the world's first great international luxury express train.

# ABDÜL HAMIT II & THE YOUNG TURKS

Amid the empire's internal turmoil, Abdül Hamit II (r 1876–1909) assumed the throne. Mithat Paşa, a successful general and powerful grand vizier, managed to introduce a constitution at the same time, but soon the new sultan did away with both Mithat Paşa and the constitution, and established his own absolute rule.

Abdül Hamit modernised without democratising, building thousands of kilometres of railways and telegraph lines and encouraging modern industry. However, the empire continued to disintegrate, and there were nationalist insurrections in Armenia, Bulgaria, Crete and Macedonia.

The younger generation of the Turkish elite – particularly the military – watched bitterly as their country fell apart, then organised secret societies bent on toppling the sultan. The Young Turk movement for Western-style reforms gained enough power by 1908 to force the restoration of the constitution. In 1909 the Young Turk–led Ottoman parliament deposed Abdül Hamit and put his hopelessly indecisive brother Mehmet V on the throne.

When WWI broke out, the Ottoman parliament and sultan made the fatal error of siding with Germany and the Central Powers. With their defeat, the Ottoman Empire collapsed, İstanbul was occupied by the British and the sultan became a pawn in the hands of the victors.

| 1574 | 1826 | 1839 |
|---|---|---|
| Selim II – known as 'The Sot' – drowns after falling in his bath while drunk and is succeeded by his son Murat III, who orders the murder of his five younger brothers to ensure his accession | The Vakayı Hayriye, or 'Auspicious Event' is decreed under which the corrupt and powerful imperial bodyguard known as the Janissary Corps is abolished | Mahmut II implements the Tanzimat reforms, which aim to stop the rise of nationalist movements by integrating non-Muslims and non-Turks into Ottoman society through civil liberties and regulations |

# REPUBLICAN İSTANBUL

The situation looked very bleak for the Turks as their armies were being disbanded and their country was taken under the control of the Allies, but what first seemed a catastrophe provided the impetus for rebirth.

Since gaining independence in 1831, the Greeks had entertained the Megali Idea (Great Plan) of a new Greek empire encompassing all the lands that had once had Greek influence – in effect, the refounding of the Byzantine Empire, with Constantinople as its capital. On 15 May 1919, with Western backing, Greek armies invaded Anatolia in order to make the dream a reality.

Even before the Greek invasion an Ottoman general named Mustafa Kemal, the hero of the WWI battle at Gallipoli, had decided that a new government must take over the destiny of the Turks from the ineffectual sultan. He began organising resistance to the sultan's captive government on 19 May 1919.

The Turkish War of Independence, in which the Turkish Nationalist forces led by Mustafa Kemal fought off Greek, French and Italian invasion forces, lasted from 1920 to 1922. Victory in the bitter war put Mustafa Kemal (1881–1938) in command of the fate of the Turks. The sultanate was abolished in 1922, as was the Ottoman Empire soon after. The republic was born on 29 October 1923.

## DOWNGRADED: NO LONGER THE CAPITAL

After being proclaimed Atatürk (Father Turk) by the Turkish parliament, Mustafa Kemal decided to move away, both metaphorically and physically, from the imperial memories of İstanbul. He established the seat of the new republican government in Ankara, a city that could not be threatened by foreign gunboats. Robbed of its importance as the capital of a vast empire, İstanbul lost much of its wealth and glitter in succeeding decades.

Atatürk had always been ill at ease with Islamic traditions and he set about making the Republic of Turkey a secular state. The fez (Turkish brimless cap) was abolished, as was polygamy; Friday was replaced with Sunday as the day of rest; surnames were introduced; the Arabic alphabet was replaced by a Latin script; and civil (not religious) marriage became mandatory. The country's modernisation was accompanied by a great surge of nationalistic pride, and though it was no longer the political capital, İstanbul continued to be the centre of the nation's cultural and economic life.

Atatürk died in İstanbul in 1938, just before WWII broke out, and was succeeded as president by Ismet İnönü. Still scarred from the calamity of its involvement in the Great War, Turkey managed to successfully stay out of the new conflict until 1945, when it entered on the Allied side.

## THE COUP YEARS

The Allies made it clear that they believed that Turkey should introduce democracy. The government agreed and called parliamentary elections. The first opposition party in Turkey's history – the Democratic Party led by Adnan Menderes – won the first of these elections in 1950.

Though he started as a democrat, Menderes became increasingly autocratic. In 1960 the military staged a coup against his government and convicted him and two of his ministers of treason. All three were hanged in 1961. New elections were held and a government was formed, but it and ensuing administrations were dogged by corruption charges, and constitutional

| 1853-56 | 1915 | 1920-22 |
|---|---|---|
| The Crimean War is fought between Imperial Russia and an alliance that includes the Ottoman Empire; Florence Nightingale arrives at the Selimiye Army Barracks near Üsküdar to nurse the war-wounded | Armenian populations are rounded up and marched into the Syrian desert; Armenians allege that Ottoman authorities were intent on eradicating the Armenian population from İstanbul and Anatolia | Turkish Nationalist forces led by Atatürk fight off Greek, French and Italian invasion forces in the War of Independence |

violations and amendments. In 1971 the military staged another coup, only to repeat the process in 1980 and install a military junta, which ruled for three years before new elections were called. It seemed to many observers that the far left and extreme right factions in the country would never be able to reconcile, and that military coups would be a constant feature of the modern political landscape. However, voters in the 1983 election refused to see this as a *fait accompli* and, rather than voting in the military's preferred candidates, elected the reforming Motherland party of economist Turgut Özal. A new era had begun.

## THE RECENT PAST

Under the presidency of economist Turgut Özal, the 1980s saw a free market–led economic and tourism boom in Turkey and its major city. Özal's government also presided over a great increase in urbanisation, with trainloads of peasants from eastern Anatolia making their way to the cities – particularly İstanbul – in search of jobs in the booming industry sector. The city's infrastructure couldn't cope back then and is still catching up, despite nearly three decades of large-scale municipal works being undertaken.

The municipal elections of March 1994 were a shock to the political establishment, with the upstart religious-right Refah Partisi (Welfare Party) winning elections across the country. Its victory was seen in part as a protest vote against the corruption, ineffective policies and tedious political wrangles of the traditional parties. In İstanbul Refah was led by Recep Tayyip Erdoğan (b 1954), a proudly Islamist candidate. He vowed to modernise infrastructure and restore the city to its former glory.

In the national elections of December 1996, Refah polled more votes than any other party (23%), and eventually formed a government vowing moderation and honesty. Emboldened by political power, Prime Minister Necmettin Erbakan and other Refah politicians tested the boundaries of Turkey's traditional secularism, alarming the powerful National Security Council, the most visible symbol of the centrist military establishment's role as the caretaker of secularism and democracy.

In 1997 the council announced that Refah had flouted the constitutional ban on religion in politics and warned that the government should resign or face a military coup. Bowing to the inevitable, Erbakan did as the council wished. In İstanbul, Mayor Erdoğan was ousted by the secularist forces in the national government in late 1998.

National elections in April 1999 brought in a coalition government led by Bülent Ecevit's left-wing Democratic Left Party. After years under the conservative right of the Refah Partisi, the election result heralded a shift towards European-style social democracy, something highlighted by the country's successful bid to be accepted as a candidate for membership of the European Union. Unfortunately for the new government there was a spectacular collapse of the Turkish economy in 2001, leading to an electoral defeat in 2002. The victorious party was the moderate Adalet ve Kalkınma Partisi (Justice and Development Party, AKP), led by phoenix-like Recep Tayyip Erdoğan who – despite continuing tensions with military hard-liners (see p38) – has run an increasingly stable and prosperous Turkey ever since. In İstanbul, candidates from the AKP have been elected into power in most municipalities, including the powerful Fatih Municipality, which includes Eminönü. The current AKP-endorsed mayor of İstanbul, Kadir Topbaş (b 1945) is one of Erdoğan's former advisors and a former mayor of the Beyoğlu municipality.

| 1922-23 | 1934 | 2005 |
| --- | --- | --- |
| The Grand National Assembly, led by Atatürk, abolishes the Ottoman sultanate and proclaims the Turkish Republic; Atatürk becomes its first president | Women are given the vote; by 1935 4.6% of the national parliament's representatives are female – a percentage that sadly hasn't increased much to this day (it's currently 9.1%) | Europe commences accession talks with Turkey regarding its candidacy bid for the EU; the French aren't keen but the UK is a staunch supporter |

# ARTS

Turks have a unique attitude towards the arts; they're as likely to read, view and listen to works created a century or a decade ago as they are to buy a newly released novel or album. This merging of the old and the new can be initially disconcerting for the foreign observer used to gravitating towards the fresh and new, but it makes for a rich cultural landscape and gives contemporary artists a solid base on which to build their practices. Traditional art forms such as carpet weaving are pretty well bound by tradition and have remained unchanged over the centuries, but there's no lack of innovative contemporary art in İstanbul, particularly within the disciplines of music, the visual arts, literature and cinema.

## CARPETS

Turkish women have been weaving carpets for a very long time. These beautiful and durable floor coverings were a nomadic family's most valuable and practical 'furniture', warming and brightening the clan's oft-moved homes. The oldest known carpet woven in the double-knotted Gördes style (Gördes is a town in the mountains of northwest Turkey) dates from between the 4th and 1st centuries BC.

It is thought that hand-woven carpet techniques were introduced to Anatolia by the Seljuks in the 12th century, so it's not surprising that Konya, the Seljuk capital, was mentioned by Marco Polo as a centre of carpet production in the 13th century.

The general pattern and colour scheme of old carpets was influenced by local traditions and the availability of certain types of wool and colours of dyes. Patterns were memorised and women usually worked with no more than 45cm of the carpet visible. Each artist imbued her work with her own personality, choosing a motif or a colour based on her own artistic preferences, and even events and emotions in her daily life.

In the 19th century, the European rage for Turkish carpets spurred the development of carpet companies. The companies, run by men, would deal with customers, take orders, purchase and dye the wool according to the customers' preferences, and contract local women to produce the finished product. The designs were sometimes left to the women, but more often were provided by the company based on the customers' tastes. Though well made, these carpets lost some of the originality and spirit of the older work.

Carpets made today often use traditional patterns such as the commonly used eye and tree patterns, and incorporate all sorts of symbols that can be 'read' by experts. At a glance, two carpets might look identical, but closer examination reveals the subtle differences that give each Turkish carpet its individuality and charm.

Traditionally, village women wove carpets for their own family's use, or for their dowry. Knowing they would be judged on their efforts, the women took great care over their handiwork – hand-spinning and dyeing the wool, and choosing what they judged to be the most interesting and beautiful patterns. These days the picture is more complicated. Many carpets are made to the dictates of the market rather than according to local traditions. Weavers in eastern Turkey might make carpets in popular styles native to western Turkey. Long-settled villagers might duplicate the wilder, hairier and more naive *yörük* (nomad) carpets.

Village women still weave carpets, but most of them work to fixed contracts for specific shops. Usually they work to a pattern and are paid for their final effort rather than for each hour of work. A carpet made to a fixed contract may still be of great value to its purchaser. However, the selling price should be lower than for a one-off piece.

Other carpets are the product of division of labour, with different individuals responsible for dyeing and weaving. What such pieces lose in individuality and rarity is often more than made up for in quality control. Most silk Hereke carpets (Hereke is a small town near İzmit, about 100km southeast of İstanbul) are mass-produced, but to standards that make them some of the most sought-after of all Turkish carpets.

Fearing that old carpet-making methods would be lost, the Ministry of Culture now sponsors a number of projects to revive traditional weaving and dyeing methods in western Turkey. Some carpet shops will have stocks of these 'project carpets', which are usually of high quality with prices reflecting that fact. Some of these carpets are also direct copies of antique pieces in museums.

Most carpet shops have a range of pieces made using a variety of techniques. Besides the traditional pile carpets, they usually offer double-sided flat-woven mats, such as kilims. Some traditional kilim motifs are similar to patterns found at the prehistoric mound of Çatal Höyük, testifying to the very ancient traditions of flat-woven floor coverings in Anatolia. Older, larger kilims may actually be two narrower pieces of similar, but not always identical, design stitched together. As this is now rarely done, any such piece is likely to be fairly old.

Other flat-weave techniques include *sumak*, a style originally from Azerbaijan, in which intricate details are woven with coloured thread by wrapping them around the warp. The loose weft ends are left hanging at the back of the rug. *Cicims* are kilims with small and lively patterns embroidered on the top.

As well as selling Turkish carpets, many carpet shops in İstanbul sell pieces from other countries, especially from Iran, Afghanistan and from the ex-Soviet Republics of Azerbaijan, Turkmenistan and Uzbekistan. The major difference is that Turkey favours the double-knot technique and Iran favours the single knot. Turkish carpets also tend to have a higher pile, more dramatic designs and more varied colours than their Iranian cousins.

If you're keen to read more about Turkish carpets and rugs, it's worth getting hold of *The Classical Tradition in Anatolian Carpets* by Walter B Denny, *Kilims: The Complete Guide* by Alastair Hull and José Luczyc-Wyhowska, or *Oriental Carpets: A Buyer's Guide* by Essie Sakhai. Most serious collectors eagerly await their bimonthly copy of the excellent magazine *Hali* (www.hali.com), published in the UK. In the city, make sure you visit the Museum of Turkish & Islamic Arts (p58), which has the best collection of antique carpets – including many Turkish examples – in the world.

For information on buying a carpet when in İstanbul, see the boxed text p140.

# LITERATURE

Turkey has a rich but relatively young literary tradition. Its brightest stars are greatly revered throughout the country and bookshop shelves groan under the weight of new local releases, a growing number of which are being translated into English. From its refined Ottoman roots through the flowering of politically driven literary movements in the 19th and 20th centuries, it has progressed to being predominantly concerned with investigating what it means to be a Turk in the modern age, particularly if one is displaced (either by the physical move from country to city or by virtue of one's ethnic background).

## Ottoman Literature

Under the sultans, literature was really a form of religious devotion. Ottoman poets, borrowing from the great Arabic and Persian traditions, wrote sensual love poems of attraction, longing, fulfilment and ecstasy in the search for union with God. Occasionally they wrote about more worldly pleasures and triumphs, as Nabi Yousouf Efendi's 16th-century *Eulogy of Constantinople* (republished in Chronicle Books' *Chronicles Abroad: Istanbul*) attests.

## Early 20th-Century & Nationalist Literature

By the late 19th century the influence of Western literature began to be felt. This was the time of the Tanzimat political and social reforms initiated by Sultan Abdül Mecit, and in İstanbul a literary movement was established that became known as 'Tanzimat Literature'. Its major figures were Sinasi, Ziya Paşa, Namık Kemal and Ahmet Mithat Efendi, all of whom sought to broaden the appeal of literature and bring it into line with developments in the West.

The Tanzimat movement was responsible for the first serious attacks on the ponderous cadences of Ottoman courtly prose and poetry, but it wasn't until the foundation of the republic that the death knell of this form of literature finally rang. Atatürk decreed that the Turkish language should be purified of Arabic and Persian borrowings, and that in the future the nation's literature should be created using the new Latin-based Turkish alphabet. Major figures in the new literary movement (dubbed 'National Literature') included poets Yahya Kemal Beyatli and Mehmet Akıf Ersoy, and novelists Halide Edib Adıvar, Ziya Gokalp, Ömer Seyfettin and Aka Gündüz.

Of these figures, İstanbullu Halide Edib Adıvar (1884–1964) is particularly interesting. A writer and vocal leader of the emerging women's emancipation movement in Turkey, she was an ally of Atatürk and a leading figure in the War of Independence. Her 1926 autobiographical work *Memoir of Halide Edib* recounts her privileged upbringing in Beşiktaş and Üsküdar, progressive education at the American College for Girls in Arnavutköy and subsequent marriage to a noted mathematician, who humiliated her by taking a second wife. After leaving him, she joined the Nationalists, remarried, worked closely with Atatürk and wrote a popular history of the War of Independence called *The Turkish Ordeal* (1928). In later years she worked as a university lecturer, wrote over 20 novels – the most famous of which was probably the 1938 work *Thewn and his Daughter* – and had a brief stint as a member of parliament. A fictionalised account of the early part of this fascinating woman's life can be found in *Halide's Gift*, an enjoyable novel by American writer Frances Kazan.

Though not part of the National Literature movement, İrfan Orga (1908–70) is probably the most famous Turkish literary figure of the 20th century. His 1950 masterpiece *Portrait of a Turkish Family* is his memoir of growing up in İstanbul at the start of the century and is probably the best writing about the city ever published. Exiled from the country of his birth, he also wrote a swathe of nonfiction titles, including the fascinating *The Caravan Moves On: Three Weeks among Turkish Nomads*. English translations of both works are available internationally.

## Late-20th-Century Writers

The second half of the 20th century saw a raft of local writers gain popularity in Turkey. Many were socialists, communists or outspoken critics of the government, and spent long and repeated periods in jail. The most famous of these writers was poet and novelist Nâzım Hikmet (1902–63). Internationally acclaimed for his poetry, Hikmet was in and out of Turkish jails for 30 years due to his alleged communist activity. Released in 1950 after a concerted lobbying effort by the Turkish and international intelligentsia, he left the country and died in exile. His masterwork is the five-volume collection of lyric and epic poetry entitled *Human Landscapes from My Country*. The most readily available English-language translation of his poems is *Beyond the Walls: Selected Poems*.

Yaşar Kemal (b 1923) is another major literary figure whose work has a strong political flavour. A former agricultural labourer and factory worker, he writes highly regarded epic novels dealing with the human condition. Kurdish by birth, his best-known work is probably 1955's *Mehmed, My Hawk*, which deals with the lives of Kurds in Turkey. Two of his novels – *The Birds are Also Gone* and *The Sea-Crossed Fisherman* – are set in İstanbul. Kemal was shortlisted for the Nobel Prize in Literature in 1999.

Aziz Nesin (1915–95) was perhaps the most prolific of all the Turkish political writers of the 20th century. A satirist, he published over 100 books and was jailed several times for his colourful indictments of the country's overly bureaucratic system and social inequalities. *Out of the Way! Socialism's Coming!* is one of the few of Nesin's works to be translated into English.

OZ Livaneli (b 1946) is a political activist, filmmaker and author of three critically acclaimed novels, including the 2003 bestseller *Bliss* (*Mutluluk* in Turkish) Set in a rural village in southeastern Turkey, in İstanbul and on the Aegean coast, it deals with weighty issues such as honour killing and was made into a film in 2007.

Since Halide Edib Adıvar blazed the trail, there have been a number of prominent female writers in Turkey, chief among them Sevgi Soysal, Erendiz Atasü, Buket Uzuner, Latife Tekin and Elif Şafak.

During her short life, Sevgi Soysal (1936–76) was known as the author of strong works promoting women's rights in Turkey. Her 1975 novel *Noontime in Yenişehir* won the most prestigious local literary prize, the Orhan Kemal Novel Award.

Another writer who focuses on the experiences of women in Turkey is Erendiz Atasü (b 1947), a retired professor of pharmacology. Her highly acclaimed 1995 novel *The Other Side of the Mountain* looks at three generations of a family from the end of the Ottoman Empire to the 1990s, focussing on a central female character. It was published in English through a grant from the Arts Council of England. Atasü has also written *That Scorching Season of Youth* (1999) and three volumes of short stories.

# İSTANBUL THROUGH FOREIGN EYES

Writers and filmmakers have long tried to capture the magic and mystery of İstanbul in their work. For a taste of the city, try the following:

- **Aziyadé** Few artists have been as deeply enamoured of the city as the French novelist Pierre Loti (1850–1923). His romantic novel introduced Europe to both Loti's almond-eyed Turkish lover and the mysterious and all-pervasive attractions of the city itself.
- **The Bridge** In this 2007 book, Dutch writer Geert Mak paints the Galata Bridge and its denizens (including anglers and street vendors) as being a microcosm of modern Turkey. Though prematurely dated, it's still a fascinating read.
- **Constantinople** Orhan Pamuk says that this travelogue, written by Italian Edmondo De Amicis in 1878, is the best book ever written about İstanbul.
- **Enlightenment** Though best known as Orhan Pamuk's English translator and John Freely's daughter, Maureen Freely is also a well-regarded novelist. In this work, which is set in İstanbul and has the ostensible structure of a thriller, she writes about truth, repression and the personal and political risks of becoming enmeshed in a foreign culture.
- **The Inspector İkmen Novels** Barbara Nadel investigates İstanbul's underbelly in a suitably gripping style. Whether they're set in Balat or Beyoğlu, her books are always evocative and well researched.
- **James Bond** The sultan of all secret agents pops up twice in İstanbul, first in 1974's *From Russia with Love* and then in 1999's *The World is Not Enough*. The city provides a great backdrop for his suave manoeuvres and sophisticated seductions.
- **Innocents Abroad** Mark Twain's account of his 'grand tour' includes sharp observations of İstanbul.
- **The Janissary Tree** Author Jason Goodwin also wrote the highly regarded *Lords of the Horizon: A History of the Ottoman Empire* (2003). In this 2006 crime novel, he has Yashim Togalu, court eunuch, unravelling intrigue and murder in 1836 İstanbul. The courtly detective reappears in two sequels, *The Snake Stone* (2007) and *The Bellini Card* (2008).
- **L'Immortelle** Alain Robbe-Grillet directed this 1963 film before going on to collaborate with Alain Resnais on *Last Year at Marienbad*, and both films score high on the Esoteric-O-Meter. Here, a man is obsessed with a woman who is being followed around İstanbul (gloriously shot) by a sinister man and his two dogs. Go figure.
- **The Mask of Dimitrios** This 1944 spy thriller directed by James Negulesco is based on an Eric Ambler novel. A ripping yarn, it opens with a body being fished out of the Bosphorus. Sydney Greenstreet and Peter Lorre give great performances.
- **Midnight Express** Alan Parker's 1978 film has three major claims to fame: Giorgio Moroder's insufferable score, Brad Davis' homosexual sex scene and the Turkish tourism industry's virtual demise on the film's release. Mention it to a Turk at your peril.
- **Murder on the Orient Express** Hercule Poirot puts ze leetle grey cells to good use on the famous train in this 1934 novel by Agatha Christie. It was made into a film by Sidney Lumet in 1974 and features a few opening shots of İstanbul.
- **The Rage of the Vulture** Barry Unsworth's 1982 novel is set in Constantinople during the era of Abdül Hamid and the Young Turk movement.
- **Stamboul Train** Graham Green's 1932 thriller focuses on a group of passengers travelling between Ostend and İstanbul on the *Orient Express*. It was filmed in 1934 as *Orient Express*.
- **The Sultan's Seal** This 2006 historical crime novel by Jenny White has Kamil Pasha, a magistrate in one of the new Ottoman secular courts, investigating the murder of an English governess working for Sultan Abdül Aziz's granddaughter. Kamil Pasha also features in White's *The Abyssinian Proof* (2009) and *The Winter Thief* (2010).
- **Sweet Waters** Before he became Mr Vita Sackville-West, Harold Nicolson wrote this extremely moving love story cum political thriller set in İstanbul during the Balkan Wars.
- **Tintin & the Golden Fleece** You'll see the T-shirts everywhere in the Grand Bazaar, but true devotees should check out this 1961 film by Jacques Vierne, which has the Belgian boy detective accompanying Captain Haddock to İstanbul.
- **Topkapi** Melina Mercouri's funky outfits, Peter Ustinov's hilarious performance and great shots of İstanbul make Jules Dassin's 1964 comedy spoof worth a view. It's based on the 1962 novel *The Light of Day* by Eric Ambler.
- **The Turkish Embassy Letters** This 18th-century memoir was written by Lady Mary Wortley Montagu, the observant wife of the British Ambassador to the Sublime Porte. Based on letters she sent during the posting, it's a fascinating account of life in and around the Ottoman court and city.
- **The Vault of Bones** Pip Vaughan-Hughes' 2008 Byzantine thriller has a 13th-century band of international art thieves trying to steal a priceless religious relic from the Pharos Chapel in İstanbul's Bucoleon Palace.

Buket Uzuner (b 1955) writes short stories and novels, the best-known being *Sound of Fish Steps* (1992), which was greatly admired by the local literary set when it was first released, the 2001 novel *The Long White Cloud – Gallipoli* and the 2007 novel *Istanbullu*. All are available in English translations.

Latife Tekin (b 1957) has built a reputation as Turkey's major magic-realist novelist. Her first novel, *Dear Shameless Death* (1983), which told the story of a family's difficult migration to a big city, had a strongly political subtext and was well received by local readers. Tekin's subsequent novels have included 1984's *Berji Kristin: Tales from the Garbage Hills,* another look at the displaced members of society, *Night Lessons* (1986), *Swords of Ice* (1989) and *Signs of Love* (1995).

High-profile writer Elif Şafak was born in Paris in 1971 and has lived and worked in France, Spain, Ankara, İstanbul and the US; she is currently based in İstanbul. Şafak's first novel, *Pinhan (The Sufi)* was awarded the Mevlana Prize for the best work in mystical literature in Turkey in 1998. Since then she has released five novels that have either been written in, or translated into, English: *Mirrors of the City* (1999), which won the Union of Turkish Writers Prize in 2000, *The Gaze* (2000), *The Flea Palace* (2002), *The Saint of Incipient Insanities* (2004) and the controversial *The Bastard of Istanbul* (2006). In 2006, Şafak and her Turkish translator and publisher were charged with 'insulting Turkishness' under the notorious Article 301 of the Turkish Criminal Code for raising the issue of the alleged genocide of the Armenians in *The Bastard of Istanbul* (the Turkish translation of which is 'The Father and the Bastard'). The case was eventually dismissed for lack of evidence. In the novel, Şafak tells the story of two families – one based in İstanbul, the other an exiled Armenian family living in San Francisco – who share a family secret connected with Turkey's turbulent past. Her latest novel is *Aşk* ('Love'; 2009), which is yet to be translated into English.

Turkish-born (but American-based) writer Alev Lytle Croutier, internationally known for her bestselling *Harem: The World Behind the Veil,* has also written a children's book set in İstanbul called *Leyla: The Black Tulip*.

# MUSIC

Turks love music and listen to it in many forms, the most popular of which are the overwrought vocal style called *arabesk* and slick Western-influenced pop. Though many foreigners immediately conjure up the trance-like sounds of Sufi Mevlevi music when they try to categorise Turkey's musical heritage, the reality is worlds away, sitting squarely within the cheerful modern-day vulgarity of Eurovision-style musical romps. These forays into the international scene stem from a solidly populist tradition of *arabesk* and folk, and are packaged with a thickly applied veneer of Western pop. Some local product can't be easily pigeonholed – the fusion sounds of Baba Zulu, for instance – but overall there are four dominant genres today: folk, *arabesk,* fasıl and pop.

## Ottoman, Classical & Sufi Music

The Ottoman court liked to listen to traditional classical music, which utilised a system of *makams* (modalities), an exotic-sounding series of notes similar in function to the familiar Western scales of whole and half-tone intervals. The result was a lugubrious sound that owed a lot to Persian and Arabic classical influences. Usually improvised, it was performed by chamber groups. Though out of favour for over a century, this form has recently undergone a slight revival, largely due to the work of İstanbul-based ensembles such as Al-Kindi. Its *Parfums Ottomans* double album makes great listening, as does Jordi Savall and Hesperion XXI's *Orient-Occident* and *Istanbul: Dimitrie Cantemir 1673–1723*, based on an 18th-century Moldavian prince's transcriptions of Turkish music.

While the court was being serenaded by such music at its soirees, another classical genre, the music of the Sufi Mevlevi, was inspiring followers of the religious sect. Its complex and refined sound was often accompanied by vocal pieces featuring the words of Celaleddin Rumi (Mevlâna), the 13th-century founder of the sect.

After the founding of the republic, the performance of traditional classical music was actively discouraged by Atatürk and his government. The great man considered it to be too redolent of contaminating Arabic influences, and he encouraged musicians and the public to instead turn

## ORHAN PAMUK

When the much-fêted Orhan Pamuk (born 1952) was awarded the 2006 Nobel Prize in Literature, the international cultural sector was largely unsurprised. The writing of the İstanbul-born, now US-based, novelist had already attracted its fair share of critical accolades, including the €100,000 IMPAC Dublin Literary Award, *The Independent* newspaper's Foreign Fiction Award of the Month and every local literary prize on offer. The only prize Pamuk hadn't accepted was the prestigious title of State Artist, which was offered to him in 1999 by the Turkish Government but which he knocked back as, he stated, his protest against the government's incarceration of writers, 'narrow-minded nationalism' and an inability to address the Kurdish problem with anything but force.

In their citation, the Nobel judges said that in his 'quest for the melancholic soul of his native city' (ie İstanbul), Pamuk had 'discovered new symbols for the clash and interlacing of culture'. The only voices heard to criticise their judgment hailed from Turkey. Like Elif Şafak, Pamuk had been charged with 'insulting Turkishness' under Article 301 of the Turkish Criminal Code (the charges were dropped in early 2006), and some local commentators alleged that in his case the Nobel Prize was awarded for political (ie freedom of speech) reasons rather than purely on the merit of his literary oeuvre. Whatever the reason, most Turks were thrilled to hear of the country's very first Nobel Prize win, and rushed to local bookstores to buy copies of his backlist titles.

Most critics describe Pamuk's novels as postmodernist, citing similarities to the work of Umberto Eco and Italo Calvino. He often uses a 'point of view' technique whereby he presents the internal monologues of interdependent characters, splicing them together so as to construct a meticulous overall narrative, often around a murder-mystery theme. Though not the easiest books to read (some critics have called them difficult and self-absorbed), they're meticulously researched and extraordinarily evocative of place. Most are set in his home town, İstanbul.

Pamuk has written eight novels to date. His first, *Cevdet Bey & His Sons* (1982), is a dynastic saga of the İstanbul bourgeoisie. *The Silent House* (1983) and *The White Castle* (1985) both won local literary awards and cemented his reputation, but were nowhere near as successful as his bizarre Beyoğlu detective novel *The Black Book* (1990), which was made into a film (*Gizli Yuz*) by director Omer Kavur in 1992. After this came *The New Life* (1995), followed by his most lauded book to date, *My Name is Red* (1998). A murder mystery set among the calligraphers of the sultan's court in the 16th century, *My Name is Red* took six years to write and was described by the IMPAC judges as 'A rare *tour de force* of literary imagination and philosophical speculation'. Pamuk's most recent novels are *Snow* (2002), which explores issues around the conflict of Western and Islamic ideologies in modern Turkey, and *The Museum of Innocence* (2009), a moving story of love and loss set in İstanbul circa 1975. In 2005, he published a memoir, *Istanbul: Memories of a City*, and in 2007 he published *Other Colours: Essays and Stories*. Of these titles, only *Cevdet Bey & His Sons* and *The Silent House* are not available in English translation.

their attention to Western classical music. The fate of Sufi music under the republic was even more extreme. With the forced closure of the Sufi *tekkes* (lodges) in 1923, the music of the order was in effect banned, only re-emerging when Prime Minister Turgut Özal overturned the ban on Sufi worship after he came to power in 1983. Today there's a healthy recording tradition among Sufi musicians and a whole new genre of Sufi-inspired electronic-techno sounds by musicians such as Mercan Dede, whose albums *Nar*, *Seyahatname*, *Su*, *Sufi Traveller*, *Nefes* and *800* have built a huge international fan base over recent years.

## Anatolian Folk Music

As well as encouraging Western classical music, the republican government began a program of classifying, archiving and promoting *halk müziği* (Anatolian folk music). Spanning 30 years and involving 10,000 songs, the program had its positives and negatives. On the plus side, parts of a rich musical heritage were documented and promoted. Less positively, any music that was deemed 'un-Turkish' (usually due to its roots in the music of ethnic minorities) was struck from the record or forced to conform with the dominant sub-genre.

Until the 1960s and 1970s it was still possible to hear Turkish troubadours (*aşik*) in action around the countryside, playing their particular variety of *halk müziği*. These *aşik* were members of the Alevi sect of central Anatolia and had a set repertoire of mystical songs always featuring the *saz* (Turkish long-necked, stringed instrument) and vocals. Fortunately their music has been revived in studio form, with artists such as Ruhi Su, Arif Sağ, Yavuz Top and Musa Eroğlu reinterpreting the music of the wandering *aşik* for modern audiences.

# Folk Revival: Türkü, Arabesk & Fasıl

In the 1980s traditional *halk müziği* underwent a revival, popularised by musicians such as the soulful Belkis Akkale, who fused it with pop to form a new sub-genre known as *Türkü*. The extremely popular İbrahim Can and Nuray Hafiftaş followed Akkale's lead.

Even before Belkis et al were experimenting with *Türkü*, rock musicians such as Cem Karaca were using folk influences to develop a distinctive form of Anadolu rock featuring politically charged lyrics. Since his death in 2004, Karaca's *Hayvan Terli* album has gained a whole new audience for this type of music. The music of Zülfü Livaneli, a popular singer and *saz* player who incorporates Western instrumentation into his protest songs, clearly shows the influence of Karaca and is best known internationally for his music for Yılmaz Güney's film *Yol* (The Road).

The popularity of some musical genres defied the government's early attempts to promote a national music based solely on *halk müziği*. Two examples were fasıl and *arabesk*, and they're still going strong today.

A mix of folk, classical and fasıl traditions, the name *arabesk* attests to its Arabic influences, specifically Egyptian dance music. First popularised by a local lad, Kaydar Tatliyay, in the 1940s, it was frowned upon by the nationalist government because of its Arabic influences and mournful tone. The government went so far as to first restrict and then ban Arabic musical films and recordings from Egypt and Lebanon to stop further 'contamination' of local musical tastes. Turkish devotees ignored the ban and tuned in to Radio Cairo for regular fixes of their favourite sounds.

*Arabesk* songs have traditionally been geared towards a working-class audience from central and eastern Anatolia and are inevitably about the oppressed – sometimes the singer is oppressed by love, sometimes by his lot in life. Though artists such as Müslüm Gürses have their devoted followers, two singers are the undisputed kings of the genre: İbrahim Tatlıses and Orhan Gencebey. A Turk of Kurdish descent, Tatlıses is from the southeastern town of Urfa and sells truckloads of CDs; Gencebey, who is also an actor, is possibly even more popular – have a listen to his *Akma Gözlerimden* and you'll see why.

As the soulful laments of *arabesk* were building the genre's national following, fasıl (sometimes referred to as Gypsy) music was taking the taverns and nightclubs of İstanbul by storm. Usually performed by Turks of Armenian, Jewish, Greek or Gypsy origin who had no religious scruples preventing them from performing in places where alcohol was served, this lively music usually featured the *klarnet* (clarinet) and *darbuka* (drum played with the hands). Solo improvisations from the stars of the orchestra were commonplace, as were boisterous renditions of emotionally charged songs by vocalists. Today this is the most popular form of music played in the city's many *meyhanes* (see p173).

# Turkish Pop & Rock

On the streets you may hear the plaintive strains of *arabesk*, but they're likely to be overlaid by the powerful sounds of Turkish pop, which is pumped out of shopfronts and cars across the city. Dominated by solo artists rather than bands, pop's pantheon of performers have built their success on a long and rich tradition of popular solo vocal artists trained in *sanat* (art music). Many have also been influenced by *arabesk*.

The first of these vocal stars to build a popular following was the fabulously camp Zeki Müren, Turkey's very own Liberace. Müren released his first album in 1951 and went on to record in classical and *arabesk* styles. Like Liberace, he liked nothing better than frocking up (his stage performances saw him appear in everything from gladiator costumes to sequin-and-feather confections) and was particularly beloved by middle-aged women. He died on stage at a comeback concert in İzmir in 1996 but recordings such as *Kahir Mektubu* still sell like hotcakes.

Following in Müren's cross-dressing footsteps is talented vocalist Bülent Ersoy, whose restrained classical idiom is best heard in her reinterpretation of late-19th-century repertoire, *Alaturka 1995*. Born in 1952, Ersoy is known by her many fans as Abla (Big Sister) as a show of support for her gender change (male to female). Before her operation she was banned from performing because of her 'effeminate ways'; afterwards she managed to successfully lobby Prime Minister Turgut Özal (a big fan) for her right to perform and also for the general civil rights of transsexuals in Turkey.

Though Bülent has attained diva status, her profile comes nowhere near to attaining the royal status given to Sezen Aksu. Aksu's influence on Turkey's popular music industry has been enormous. She's done everything from overseeing the Turkish contributions to the annual Eurovision contest to recording innumerable blockbuster albums of her own, along the way grooming up-and-coming stars such as Tarkan and Sertab Erener. In among her musical accomplishments she's managed to be an outspoken and controversial commentator on feminism and politics. Her most popular album is probably *Deliveren* (2001), though everything she's done since hitting the music scene in the 1970s has been pretty impressive.

Finally, no discussion of contemporary Turkish music would be complete without a mention of the two very different pin-up boys: Tarkan and Ceza.

Tarkan's albums regularly sell millions of copies and his catchy brand of music is the stuff of which recording empires are made. Pretty-boy looks and a trace of attitude are all part of the Tarkan package, and have landed him a mega-lucrative Pepsi contract among other endorsements. His most successful album to date, 1998's *Ölürüm Sana* (I'd Die For You), featured tracks written by former collaborator Sezen Aksu and sold 3.5 million copies in Turkey alone. His *A-acıypsin* (1994) sold over two million copies in Turkey and one million in Europe, making him Turkey's most successful recording artists ever. He even released a self-titled perfume a few years ago (we kid you not).

Ceza is the king of the local rap/hip-hop scene; his fan base is so devoted that he is regularly mobbed in the street. Have a listen to his *Rapstar* (2004) and you'll get an idea about what gets them so excited.

Fatih Akin's popular documentary 2005 film *Crossing the Bridge: The Sound of Istanbul* profiled the city's music scene and its readily available soundtrack makes great listening. It features performances by Ceza, Sezen Aksu, Baba Zula, Orhan Gencebey and Kurdish singer Aynur Doğan.

# CINEMA
## Birth of an Industry

Just a year after the Lumière brothers presented their first cinematic show in 1895, cinema first appeared in Turkey. At first it was only foreigners and non-Muslims who watched movies, but by 1914 there were cinemas run by and for Muslims as well, and the Turks' great love for the art form was up and running.

The War of Independence inspired actor Muhsin Ertuğrul, Turkey's cinema pioneer, to establish a film company in 1922 and make patriotic films. The company's first release was *The Ordeal*, based on a novel about the War of Independence by eminent writer and republican Halide Edib Adıvar. Within a decade Turkish films were winning awards in international competitions, even though a mere 23 films had been made.

After WWII the industry expanded rapidly, with new companies and young directors. Lütfi Akad's *In the Name of the Law* (1952), Turkey's first colour film, brought realism to the screen in the place of melodrama, which had been the main fodder for audiences throughout the 1940s.

## Cinema as Social Commentary

By the 1960s, Turkish cinema was delving deeply into social and political issues. Metin Erksan's *Dry Summer* (1964) won a gold medal at the Berlin Film Festival and another award in Venice. Yılmaz Güney, the fiery actor-director, directed his first film *Horse, Woman, Gun* in 1966 and scripted Lütfi Akad's *The Law of the Borders,* in which he also starred. His 1970 film *Hope* was a turning point for national cinema, kick-starting a trend towards simple neorealist treatments of contemporary social issues that continues today. In this and similar films the commentary about life in modern Turkey was bleak indeed, and the exploration of issues such as the poverty-driven drift from rural areas to congested urban environments introduced a theme that would return again and again. The titles of Güney's subsequent films were representative of the industry's lack of optimism about the future of the country and their industry: after *Hope,* he released *Sorrow* in 1971, followed by *Lament* in 1972. It's not surprising that the government imprisoned him for three years after the 1971 coup.

The 1970s brought the challenge of TV, dwindling audiences, political pressures and union-isation of the industry. This was highlighted at the inaugural İstanbul International Film Festival in 1976, when the jury determined that no film was worthy of the award for best film. Despite the depressed start to the decade, the quality of films improved, and social issues such as the plight of Turkish workers in Europe were treated with honesty, naturalism and dry humour. By the early 1980s, several Turkish directors were well recognised in Europe and the USA, though they were having trouble getting their films shown at home. Despite winning the Palme D'Or at the Cannes Film Festival, Yılmaz Güney's bleak *The Road*, which explores the dilemmas faced by a group of men on temporary release from prison, was banned for 15 years in Turkey before finally being released in 2000. Güney had worked on the film while in jail (his second jail term), passing directions on to co-director Şerif Gören. His last film, *Duvar* (*Enclosure*; 1983), made before his untimely death aged only 46, was a wrist-slashing prison drama.

Though the industry wasn't yet booming, things were looking up by the 1980s, with some excellent films having redemptive themes symbolic of the more optimistic political climate. The most successful film of the decade was probably 1983's *A Season in Hakkâri*, directed by Erdan Kıral, which addressed some of the issues surrounding the plight of Turkey's oppressed Kurdish population.

## Critical Acclaim

The 1990s were an exciting decade for the national cinema, with films being critically and popularly received both in Turkey and internationally. Notable among the many releases were Zeki Demirkubuz's *Innocence* (1997), which followed the story of an ex-con trying to survive in a society that had changed radically since his incarceration a decade before; and Omer Kavur's *Journey on the Hour Hand* (1997), a very different type of film, which can best be described as an existential mystery.

Many of the most highly regarded films of the 1990s were set in İstanbul. These included *Journey to the Sun* by Yeşim Ustaoğlu, which won the top prize at the İstanbul International Film Festival in 1999; the wonderful 1995 *İstanbul Beneath My Wings*; 1998's *Cholera Street* by Mustafa Altıoklar; and *The Bandit* (1996) by Yavuz Turgul. Many of these films explore important social and political themes. *Journey to the Sun*, for instance, is about a boy from the provinces who comes to the big city; he is frequently mistaken for a Kurd due to his dark skin, and is treated appallingly as a result.

## Cinema Today

Turks have taken to cinema-going with alacrity over the past decade, and the industry has gone from strength to strength. Some local releases are accruing box-office receipts from audiences numbering over four million, which is sure to encourage the industry to grow and prosper. Recent local tours de force in both box-office and critical terms have included the controversial *Valley of the Wolves IRAQ* (Serdar Akar, 2004), the dramatic *My Father and My Son* (Çağarn Irmak, 2006), *Ice Cream* (Yüksel Aksu, 2006) and the laugh-one-minute-cry-the-next *The Magician* (Cem Yılmaz, 2006).

Contemporary directors of note include Ferzan Özpetek, whose 1996 film *Hamam*, set in İstanbul, was a big hit on the international festival circuit and is particularly noteworthy for addressing the hitherto hidden issue of homosexuality in Turkish society. His most recent release, *Saturno Contro* (2007), was an enormous success in Italy, where the filmmaker lives and makes most of his films.

Nuri Bilge Ceylan's 2003 film *Distant* received a rapturous response from critics and audi-ences alike when it was released, winning the Jury Prize at the Cannes Film Festival among other accolades. The story of two cousins – played by Muzaffer Özdemir and Mehmet Emin Toprak – who are both alienated from society is in the bleak but visually beautiful tradition of Güney's films. Ceylan's 2008 film *Three Monkeys* won the Best Director award at Cannes.

Turkish-German director Fatih Akın received rave reviews and a screenwriting prize at Cannes for his 2007 film *The Edge of Heaven*, parts of which are set in İstanbul. His film *Head On* won the Golden Bear in Berlin in 2004.

lonelyplanet.com

BACKGROUND ARTS

Yavuz Turgul's wildly popular 2005 film *Heartache* is the story of idealist Nazim, who returns home to İstanbul after teaching for 15 years in a remote village in eastern Turkey and starts a doomed relationship with a single mother who works in a sleazy bar. It's particularly notable for the soundtrack by Tamer Çıray, which features the voice of Aynur Doğan.

## VISUAL ARTS

The visual-arts scene has played second fiddle to that of music, cinema and theatre for years, but all of this is changing with the opening of a swath of top-notch privately funded contemporary art galleries in the city. See the Arts chapter (p178) for more details.

# ENVIRONMENT & PLANNING

İstanbul has been plagued by hyper-growth during the last few decades as villagers move to the city by the tens of thousands in search of a better life. This has placed great pressure on infrastructure and services. On some issues the government is making real progress (see opposite), on others it still faces significant challenges.

Many of the green areas in and around the city have been developed for housing, making open space a rare commodity. Although there are a few protected areas around the city – the Princes' Islands (Kızıl Adalar) and the Beykoz Nature Forests near Polonezköy, for example – a low average of just over 1 sq m of forest reserve is put aside per person; conservationists say the average in Europe is about 40 sq m per person.

Air pollution in the city is a big problem. Though clean-burning Russian natural gas has replaced dirty lignite (soft coal) as the preferred winter heating fuel, air pollution is still significant, largely due to the ever-increasing number of cars jamming city roads. The national Ministry of Environment, established in 1991, is trying to implement programs to reduce smog across the country's large cities, but the International Energy Agency has criticised its efforts, saying that current measures don't go far enough.

The major environmental threat to the city is pollution of its waterways. Increased oil exports from the Caspian Sea region to Russian and Georgian ports and across the Black Sea has led to increased oil-tanker traffic (and risk of accident) through the narrow and winding Turkish Straits, which comprise the Dardanelles, the Sea of Marmara and the Bosphorus. With 50,000 vessels per year using this route, and one in 10 of these carrying oil or liquefied natural gas, the threat of a major spill is very real. Accidents are increasing in frequency, with the worst probably being the March 1994 collision of the Greek tanker *Nassia* with another ship. Thirty seamen were killed in this incident and 20,000 tons of oil were spilled into the Straits a few kilometres north of İstanbul, triggering an inferno that raged for five days. The possibility of this happening closer to the city is very real, as was illustrated in November 2003 when a Georgian-flagged ship ran aground and broke in two – fortunately it was carrying dry goods rather than oil.

Ships using these waters also cause major water pollution by releasing contaminated water as they ballast their holds. Though government has made genuine efforts to flush water through the Bosphorus and Golden Horn (Haliç; the relocation of the current-blocking 19th-century Galata Bridge and municipal rubbish-removal programs being perfect examples), the waters are still highly polluted and have contributed to a major decline of local fish stocks. Overfishing has also been a contributing factor.

# GOVERNMENT & POLITICS

Though the Turks are firm believers in democracy, the tradition of popular rule is relatively short. Real multiparty democracy came into being only after WWII, and has been interrupted several times by military coups, though government has always eventually been returned to civilians.

The historical power of the military is embodied in the make-up of the National Security Council (NSC), which comprises high-level government and military leaders and meets monthly to 'advise' the government. Its relationship with the ruling Justice and Development Party (AKP) national government is extremely uneasy, largely due to the AKP's soft Islamist ideology and the military's firm allegiance to the ideal of the Turkish secular state. In 2007, the

## WAITING FOR THE QUAKE

İstanbul lies over the North Anatolian Fault, which runs for about 1500km between the Anatolian and Eurasian tectonic plates. As the Arabian and African plates to the south push northward, the Anatolian plate is shoved into the Eurasian plate, and squeezed west towards Greece. This movement creates stress along the North Anatolian Fault, which accumulates, and then releases pressure as earthquakes. Thirteen major quakes in Turkey have been recorded since 1939, with the latest in August 1999 devastating İzmit and Adapazarı, about 90km east of İstanbul, leaving nearly 20,000 dead and 100,000 homeless. İstanbul remained relatively unscathed, although the suburb of Avcılar to the west of the city suffered hundreds of deaths when jerry-built dwellings collapsed.

This pattern of earthquakes leaves İstanbul in an unenviable position. Locals are half-panicked, half-fatalistic about the next one, but no-one doubts that it's coming. The city has been hit four times by major earthquakes in the last 500 years and experts predict that the strain placed by İzmit's earthquake on nearby stress segments along the fault could lead to another major quake within the next few decades.

As the destruction at Avcılar illustrated, much of the city's urban development in the last few decades has been poorly built and is unlikely to make it through a major quake. Sadly, the government doesn't seem to be forcing developers to raise their game when it comes to building quality, and when the big one comes the consequences are likely to be catastrophic. Then again, Aya Sofya has made it through more than its fair share of quakes and still crowns the first of the city's hills. Many locals look at it and take heart.

AKP insisted on elevating former foreign minister Abdullah Gül to the position of president, replacing the strongly secular Ahmet Necdet Sezer. The army went into a frenzy, arguing that the fact that Mr Gül's wife wore the headscarf meant that the country's secularist status would be irrevocably compromised on the international stage. The situation was so serious that some Turks feared another military coup. Prime Minister Recep Tayyıp Erdoğan called a general election to sort the issue for once and all, and the election campaign that followed was fought pretty well solely on the Islamist vs secular-state issue, with Mrs Gül's right to wear a headscarf being heatedly debated. The result, when it came, was an enormous shock to the NSC and a ringing endorsement of the government. Over 46% of the electorate was clearly happy with the way in which the prime minister and his government were running the economy and the EU accession process, and had no problem with the AKP's Islamist bias (nor, it can be inferred, were they fussed about whether the first lady wore a headscarf or not). Retreating to lick its wounds, the army was forced to come to terms with the fact that it is no longer the main player on the national political stage and that a pious and increasingly prosperous Anatolian middle class has become the nation's new major power bloc.

The ban on the wearing of the headscarf was overturned by the AKP in early 2008, and became the major trigger of a serious closure case brought against the party by the Chief Public Prosecutor of the Supreme Court of Appeals in the middle of that year. The prosecutor alleged that the AKP was seeking to undermine the secular nature of the state and that its actions were in contravention of Turkey's Political Parties Act. To the relief of most Turks, the case was unsuccessful.

Another interesting outcome from the election was the successful candidacies of 20 members of the pro-Kurdish *Demokratik Toplum Partisi* (DTP; Democratic Society Party), eight of them women. It was the first time since the early 1990s that overtly nationalistic Kurds had taken seats in the 550-member legislature, something that infuriated the far-right *Milliyetçi Hareket Partisi* (MHP; Nationalist Movement Party), which won 71 seats and has called for the DTP to be closed, again citing the Political Parties Act.

## LOCAL GOVERNMENT

İstanbul itself is actually two political entities: the city and the province. The city is organised as a *büyükşehir belediyesi* (metropolitan municipality), with several large sub-municipalities under the overall authority of a metropolitan city government.

The current metropolitan city government is perceived to be doing a pretty good job of coping with the demands on city infrastructure that the continuing influx of migrants from the provinces is making. It's also considered by most to be doing an excellent job with the provision of municipal services such as transport (particularly the huge and visionary Marmaray Project; see the boxed text p218), and with the introduction of environmental programs such as the clean-up of the city's waterways. Accusations of corruption and cronyism are of course made from time to time (particularly about the Fatih Municipality, which includes Eminönü), but overall voter approval is quite high.

# MEDIA

Turkey fell back 20 places in 2009's RSF (International Reporters Without Borders; www.rsf. org) Worldwide Press Freedom Index (sharing 122th place with the Philippines out of a total of 175 countries). This shows that it's going to have to have to lift its game when it comes to the promotion of a free and diverse media if it is to have its bid to join the EU taken seriously. At present 70% of the Turkish media is under the control of only two companies: the Doğan and Çalık groups. Doğan owns eight newspapers, including *Hürriyet, Milliyet, Vatan* and *Radikal*, as well as the CNN Türk, Star TV and Kanal D TV channels. It controls between 40% and 60% of national advertising revenue and 80% of distribution channels, and also has interests in banking, tourism, electricity and fuel distribution. The Çalık group owns *Sabah* newspaper, ATV TV and dozens of periodicals. Like Doğan, it has interests in many other industries.

In 2002, local and international media analysts were outraged when the Ankara government passed legislation smoothing the way for media groups to enter into public tenders and trade on the stock exchange. Seen by many as a move tailor-made for Aydın Doğan, the head of the Doğan Group, the legislation made it possible for Turkish media barons to bid for government contracts and acquire stakes in the many state-owned companies being earmarked for privatisation. Critics feared (and still do) that the media channels owned by these barons would be pressured to present government-friendly media analysis as a way of staying sweet with Ankara and promoting the financial interests of their parent companies. The jury's still out as to whether the demands of the EU for the sanctity and importance of a free press will prevail over the behind-the-scenes machinations of powerful tycoons.

## FREEDOM TO SPEAK

Although Turkey has been implementing a wide range of reforms for its EU membership bid, the country's new penal code still retains the infamous Article 301. In recent years, this article has been the basis for a series of high-profile prosecutions of journalists, writers and artists, exposing what Amnesty International has described as 'a direct threat to freedom of expression, as enshrined in Article 19 of the International Covenant on Civil and Political Rights (ICCPR) and in Article 10 of the European Convention for the Protection of Human Rights and Fundamental Freedoms (ECHR)'.

The most high-profile case to date was that of Turkey's Nobel Prize–winning novelist, Orhan Pamuk, who was tried after the publication of an interview he gave to a Swiss newspaper in which he referred to the ongoing Armenian controversy and the government's heavy-handed response to the Kurdish issue during the 1990s. Charges were dropped in early 2006, but Pamuk became a reluctant political symbol and a target for nationalists.

Lesser-known but just as important cases followed. Journalist and author Perihan Mağden was tried for 'turning people against military service' after she wrote an article in the *Yeni Aktuel* titled 'Conscientious Objection is a Human Right'. The case against her was acquitted in court. Following Mağden's case, author Elif Şafak, her publisher and her Turkish translator were prosecuted for comments made by Armenian characters in her novel *The Bastard of Istanbul* (see p31). Charges against all three were eventually dropped.

Most disturbing of all was the assassination of Turkish-Armenian journalist and editor Hrant Dink in İstanbul in January 2007. The editor-in-chief of the bilingual Turkish-Armenian newspaper *Agos,* who had been charged under Article 301 on three occasions for his outspoken views on what he described as the genocide of Armenians at the hands of Ottoman Turks in 1915, Dink was shot to death by a 17-year-old Turkish nationalist. After the assassination, Orhan Pamuk wrote a piece in the *Hürriyet* newspaper in which he said: 'In a sense, we are all responsible for his death. However, at the very forefront of this responsibility are those who still defend Article 301 of the Turkish Penal Code. Those who campaigned against him, those who portrayed this sibling of ours as an enemy of Turkey, those who painted him as a target, they are the most responsible.'

Concerns within the Turkish and international communities about the law led to its amendment in 2008 – prosecutions now require the permission of the Minister for Justice and must be for insulting 'the Turkish nation' rather than 'Turkishness'. The organisation Human Rights Watch (www.hrw.org) has described these changes as 'cosmetic amendments'.

# FASHION

Fashion in İstanbul is best described as eclectic. Every season the latest trends spotted on the catwalks in Paris, Rome or New York are reworked for and by the local market, hitting the shelves in a remarkably short period of time. Though international chains such as Zara do this supremely well, local chain Yargıcı is the most popular outlet for main-street fashion, and can always be relied upon for a fetching summer frock in the latest colours and style or an accessory *de jour*. Glam areas such as Nişantaşı and Teşvikiye or swish shopping malls such as Kanyon and İstinye Park (boxed text p142) are the places to go to access real European designer items, which are snapped up by the blond-tipped, tanned and immaculately groomed wives of the city's bankers, industrialists and politicians.

At the other extreme are the young suburban women sporting the latest in Islamic chic, invariably a long denim skirt instead of jeans, a fitted (but not too revealing) top and a colour-coordinated headscarf. Cleverly applied makeup to feature the eyes is all part of the demure but modern package. The most popular fashion trend of all is a perennial one: young Turks love their jeans and replace them regularly at local chain store Mavi. And when İstanbul gals want a pretty frock, they look to Machka, which has outlets in Kanyon, İstinye Park and Nişantaşı.

The local designer fashion scene is thriving and does an inspired line in Ottoman-influenced styles created using rich fabrics and embroidery. Gönül Paksoy (described as the 'new Hussein Chalayan') is probably the queen of this trend, but there are plenty of aspirants dotted throughout Nişantaşı and Çukurcuma just waiting to hit the pages of *Wallpaper* or *French Vogue*. Other local designers of note include Umit Ünal, Banu Bora, Özgür Masur, Gul Gurdamar (Eternal Child) and British-based Rifat Ozbek.

The uncompromising Chalayan (known in Turkey as Hüseyin Çağlayan) is, of course, the king of the scene, albeit from a distance. Despite the fact that his clothes are difficult to find in İstanbul – we've seen them at Harvey Nichols at Kanyon but nowhere else – his influence is felt everywhere. After all, he's a local boy who's made it to the big time (well, nearly local – he is in fact a Turkish Cypriot who trained in London), and he's proud of his heritage. More of a conceptual artist than a fashion designer, he undertakes intense historical research as part of his creative process, and has referenced Byzantine, Ottoman, Georgian, Armenian and Greek historical styles in a number of his collections. He freely admits that he likes taking ideas from the past and putting them into contemporary garments, and this appropriation has character-ised most of his collections.

# LANGUAGE

Writing of Constantinople in 1857, Herman Melville said 'You feel you are among the nations', and the city hasn't changed much in this respect. Melville saw this Babel-like reality as a curse, and after taking the reins of government half a century later, Atatürk and his republican colleagues agreed, establishing the modern Turkish language to take over from its 'contaminated' Ottoman predecessor, which was full of Arabic and Persian influences. All Turks were encouraged to learn and speak the new language (and its Latin alphabet) rather than Ottoman Turkish, regional dialects or foreign languages.

Fortunately, contemporary Turkey is reclaiming its polyglot heritage as well as taking pride in its own national language and you'll have no trouble at all communicating in English and, to a lesser extent, French, German or Russian when you're here. Snippets of many foreign languages can be heard throughout Old İstanbul (particularly in the Grand Bazaar) and you'll also notice that the city has particular quarters in which dialects are spoken. Two examples are Ladino, a medieval Spanish dialect that is still used by some descendants of the Sephardic community that migrated here during the Spanish Inquisition; and Aramaic, which is still spoken by many members of the city's Assyrian Church. And after being frowned upon for decades, Kurdish speakers are now being treated more tolerantly.

By learning a few Turkish phrases you'll do your bit to charm the locals; see the Language chapter (p231) for tips.

# NEIGHBOURHOODS

# top picks

# NEIGHBOURHOODS

The 19th-century French writer Pierre Loti once wrote 'Ah Stamboul! Of all the names that can still enchant me, this remains the most magical.' After visiting, you'll know exactly how he felt. Ever since 657 BC, when Byzas first sailed up to the point where the Golden Horn (Haliç), the Bosphorus and the Sea of Marmara meet, this extraordinary city has enchanted travellers and left an indelible stamp on their memories.

'Within the Old City, the most important area for tourists is Sultanahmet'

Each of today's older neighbourhoods hold remnants of ancient Byzantium, Roman Constantinople and Ottoman İstanbul, but have also developed their own modern signatures. By exploring them you'll certainly develop an understanding of the city and its people. You may even, like Loti and so many visitors since, develop a life-long infatuation with their charms.

The district within the boundaries of the Golden Horn, the Sea of Marmara and Theodosius II's monumental city walls is often referred to as the 'Old City' or Historical Peninsula. Within the Old City, the most important area for tourists is Sultanahmet. This is where major historic sights including Topkapı Palace (Topkapı Sarayı) are found, and where the vast majority of the city's midrange and budget accommodation options are located. Standing in Sultanahmet Sq (Sultanahmet Meydanı) and looking one way towards Aya Sofya (p49) and the other towards the Blue Mosque (Sultan Ahmet Camii; p56) is an experience that stays with many people for a lifetime.

West of Sultanahmet is the beguiling Bazaar District, which is home to the famous Grand Bazaar (p72) and Spice Bazaar (p77) as well as a clutch of the city's most significant Ottoman mosques. Its streets run down the hill from the imposing bulk of the Süleymaniye Mosque all the way to the transport hub of Eminönü, picturesquely situated at the mouth of the Golden Horn.

West of the Bazaar District, over the major artery of Atatürk Bulvarı, are the conservative Western Districts, suburbs that were once home to large Jewish and Greek populations. These run down to the shore of the Golden Horn.

Writing about the Galata Bridge (Galata Köprüsü; p78) in the 1870s, Italian novelist Edmondo de Amicis said that though a hundred thousand people crossed it every day, 'not a single idea passes in 10 years'. The difference between the neighbourhoods of the Old City and the European-flavoured neighbourhoods of Beyoğlu, on the other side of the bridge, isn't as stark these days as it was in De Amicis' time, but there is still a decidedly different atmosphere and physical appearance. The bustling but still slightly down-at-heel suburbs of Galata, Karaköy and Tophane are growing more fashionable by the day, and the streets around famous boulevard İstiklal Caddesi, which is crowned by huge Taksim Sq (Taksim Meydanı), are the city's most popular places to eat, drink and indulge in the arts.

Northeast of Taksim Sq is the elegant enclave of Nişantaşı, known for its upmarket shops and restaurants. The streets to the north of its main artery, Teşvikiye Caddesi, are collectively known as Teşvikiye.

At the bottom of the steep hills to the east of Taksim Sq are the Bosphorus suburbs of Beşiktaş, Ortaköy and Kuruçeşme, full of Ottoman palaces and glamorous restaurants and nightclubs. The sultans' buildings here are reminiscent of Coleridge's 'stately pleasure-domes' and are well worth a visit.

These excesses along the Bosphorus stand in stark contrast to the fascinating neighbourhoods of Üsküdar and Kadıköy across the strait on the Asian side of town. They're full of residents shopping in street markets, worshipping in mosques and gossiping on street corners; this is where you'll get a true feel for what it's like to live in this extraordinary megalopolis.

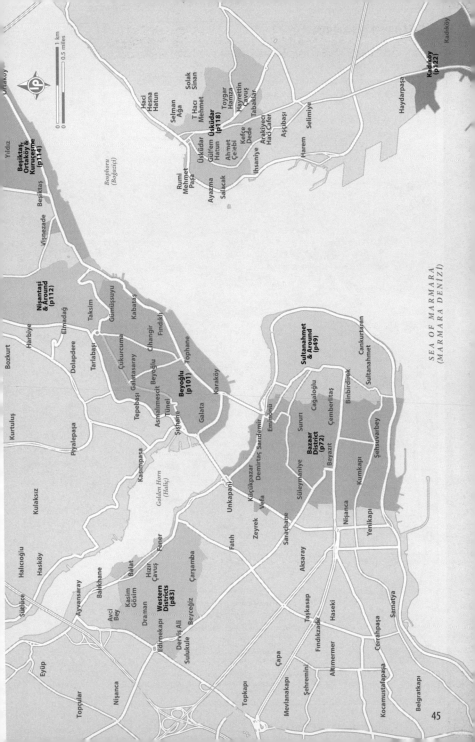

1 km
0.5 miles

Ortaköy

Yıldız

**Beşiktaş, Ortaköy & Kuruçeşme (p114)**

Bosphorus (Boğaziçi)

Vişnezade

Beşiktaş

Harbiye

Bozkurt

**Nişantaşı & Around (p112)**

Elmadağ

Taksim

Gümüşsuyu

Kabataş

Tarlabaşı

Çukurcuma

Cihangir

Fındıklı

Tophane

Dolapdere

Piyalepaşa

Galatasaray

Beyoğlu

Asmalımescit

Tepebaşı

**Beyoğlu (p101)**

Kurtuluş

Tünel

Şişhane

Karaköy

Kasımpaşa

Galata

Kulaksız

Hasköy

Halıcıoğlu

Golden Horn (Haliç)

Unkapanı

Demirtaş Sarıdemir

Eminönü

Küçükpazar

Vefa

Süleymaniye

Sururi

**Sultanahmet & Around (p49)**

Cağaloğlu

Binbirdirek

Çemberlitaş

Sultanahmet

Cankurtaran

Süleymaniye

**Bazaar District (p72)**

Beyazıt

Şehsuvarbey

Kumkapı

Nişanca

Yenikapı

Sütlüce

Ayvansaray

Balıkhane

Kasım Gösim

Hızır Çavuş

Balat

Fener

Zeyrek

Sarıçhane

Fatih

**Western Districts (p83)**

Draman

Avcı Bey

Derviş Ali

Sulukule

Edirnekapı

Beyceğiz

Çarşamba

Aksaray

Eyüp

Nişanca

Topçular

Topkapı

Mevlanakapı

Şehremini

Fındıkzade

Haseki

Çapa

Altımermer

Taşkasap

Cerrahpaşa

Kocamustafapaşa

Samatya

Belgratkapı

Haci Hesna Hatun

Selman Ağa

Solak Sinan

T Hacı Mehmet

**Üsküdar (p118)**

Toygar Hamza

Hayrettin Çavuş

Tabaklar

Gülfem Hatun

Üsküdar

Ahmet Çelebi

Kefce Dede

Arakiyeci Hacı Cafer

Rumi Mehmet Paşa

İhsaniye

Aşçıbaşı

Ayazma

Salacak

Harem

Selimiye

Haydarpaşa

**Kadıköy (p122)**

Kadıköy

*SEA OF MARMARA (MARMARA DENİZİ)*

45

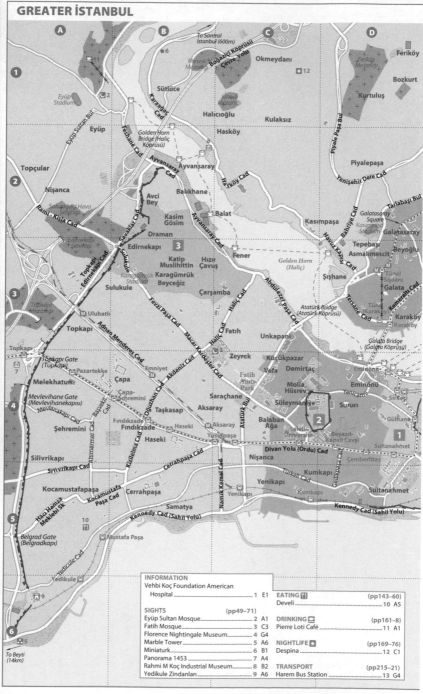

**INFORMATION**
Vehbi Koç Foundation American
Hospital....................................1 E1

SIGHTS (pp49–71)
Eyüp Sultan Mosque..........................2 A1
Fatih Mosque........................................3 C3
Florence Nightingale Museum..........4 G4
Marble Tower........................................5 A6
Miniaturk...............................................6 B1
Panorama 1453....................................7 A4
Rahmi M Koç Industrial Museum.....8 B2
Yedikule Zindanları.............................9 A6

EATING (pp143–60)
Develi....................................................10 A5

DRINKING (pp161–8)
Pierre Loti Café....................................11 A1

NIGHTLIFE (pp169–76)
Despina.................................................12 C1

TRANSPORT (pp215–21)
Harem Bus Station.............................13 G4

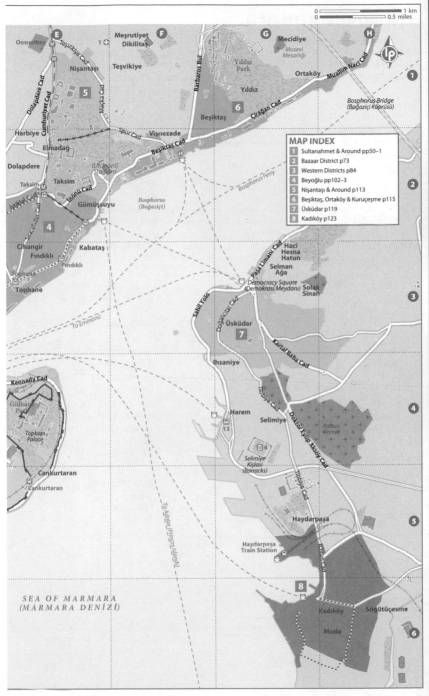

Osmanbey  Teşvikiye Cad  Meşrutiyet  Dikilitaş

Nişantaşı  Teşvikiye

Dolapdere Cad  Macka Cad  5

Cumhuriyet Cad  Spor Cad  Vişnezade

Harbiye  Beşiktaş Cad

Elmadağ

Dolapdere  Büyükdüğ tadargu

Taksim  Taksim  İnönü Cad

İstiklal Cad  Gümüssuyu

Sıraselviler Cad  4

Cihangir  Kabataş

Fındıklı

Tophane  Fındıklı

To Eminönü  Tophane

Kennedy Cad

Gülhane Park

Topkapı Palace

Cankurtaran  Cankurtaran

Barbaros Bul

Yıldız Park

Yıldız

Beşiktaş  Çırağan Cad

Bosphorus Ferry

Bosphorus (Boğaziçi)

Mecidiye

Musevi Mesarlığı

Ortaköy  Muallim Naci Cad

Bosphorus Bridge (Boğaziçi Köprüsü)

**MAP INDEX**

| 1 | Sultanahmet & Around pp50–1 |
| 2 | Bazaar District p73 |
| 3 | Western Districts p84 |
| 4 | Beyoğlu pp102–3 |
| 5 | Nişantaşı & Around p113 |
| 6 | Beşiktaş, Ortaköy & Kuruçeşme p115 |
| 7 | Üsküdar p119 |
| 8 | Kadıköy p123 |

Paşa Limanı Cad  Haci Hesna Hatun

Selman Ağa

Democracy Square (Demokrasi Meydanı)  Solak Sinan

Sahil Yolu  Doğancılar Cad

Üsküdar  7  Kartal Baba Cad

İhsaniye

Tıbbiye Cad

Harem  13  Selimiye

Dokor Eyüp Akboy Cad  Karaca Ahmet

Selimiye Kışlası (Barracks)

Tıbbiye Cad

Haydarpaşa

Haydarpaşa Train Station

8

SEA OF MARMARA (MARMARA DENİZİ)

To Adalar (Princes' Islands)

Kadıköy  Söğütüçeşme

Moda  6

NEIGHBOURHOODS  GREATER ISTANBUL

0 ————— 1 km
0 ————— 0.5 miles

# ITINERARY BUILDER

The table below allows you to plan a day's worth of activities in any area of the city. Simply select which area you wish to explore, and then mix and match from the corresponding listings to build your day. The first item in each cell represents a well-known highlight of the area, while the other items are more off-the-beaten-track gems.

| ACTIVITIES | Sights | Eating & Drinking |
|---|---|---|
| Sultanahmet | Aya Sofya (opposite)<br>Basilica Cistern (p54)<br>Museum of Turkish & Islamic Arts (p58) | Cooking Alaturka (p147)<br>Khorasani (p147)<br>Derviş Aile Çay Bahçesı (p163) |
| Bazaar District | Topkapı Palace (p59)<br>İstanbul Archaeology Museums (p66)<br>Gülhane Park (p68) | Set Üstü Çay Bahçesi (p163)<br>Konyalı Lokantasi (p148)<br>Hafiz Mustafa Şekerlemeleri (p151) |
| Galata | Grand Bazaar (p72)<br>Süleymaniye Mosque (p76)<br>Spice Bazaar (p77) | Hamdi et Lokantası (p149)<br>Şehzade Mehmed Sofrası (p150)<br>Lale Bahçesi (p164) |
| Western Districts | Chora Church (p83)<br>Church of Theotokos Pammakaristos (p86)<br>Gül Mosque (p86) | Asitane (p151)<br>Kömür Lokantası (p211)<br>Ottoman (p211) |
| Üsküdar | İstanbul Modern (p101)<br>Jewish Museum of Turkey (p105)<br>Galata Tower (p105) | Tarıhı Karaköy Balık Lokantası (p153)<br>İstanbul Modern Cafe (p153)<br>Karaköy Güllüoğlu (p158) |
| Kadıköy | Atik Valide Mosque (p118)<br>Florence Nightingale Museum (p125)<br>Kadıköy Produce Market (p122) | Kanaat Lokantesı (p159)<br>Çiya Sofrası (p159)<br>Baylan Pastanesi (p160) |

Drinking p162; Eating p147; Shopping p132; Sleeping p190

Many visitors to İstanbul never make it out of Sultanahmet. And while this is a shame, it's hardly surprising. After all, not many cities have such a concentration of major sights, shopping precincts, hotels and eateries within easy walking distance. The heart of both Byzantium and the Ottoman Empire, it's the area where emperors and sultans built grand places of worship and major public buildings; where court officials lived, schemed and planned advantageous marriages; and where conquering armies declared their victories with obligatory rites of drunken pillage and plunder in the Hippodrome. Today, armies of tourists congregate around this ancient arena, and their only battles are with overenthusiastic carpet touts and postcard sellers.

Occupying a large slab of the promontory that runs from the eastern side of Eminönü on the Golden Horn to Küçük Aya Sofya on the Sea of Marmara, this neighbourhood is where most of İstanbul's major sights and hotels are located. It incorporates a number of small suburbs, including Binbirdirek, which takes its name from the Byzantine cistern and is home to shops and offices; Cankurtaran, where a good percentage of the city's hotels and hostels are located; Çemberlitaş, a shopping district around busy Divan Yolu; Küçük Aya Sofya, a quiet residential area with some significant historical buildings and a few hotels; and Sultanahmet proper, the area around Aya Sofya, Topkapı Palace and the mosque that gives the neighbourhood its name.

This is historical İstanbul, and not the hip East-meets-West city beloved of the current crop of international fashion and travel magazines. Morals and dress are conservative around here, and while there's lots of money being thrown around by tourists there's no trace of the conspicuous local consumption that is the signature over the Golden Horn and along the Bosphorus. Here, people rise early, go to work, have a home-cooked dinner and then go to bed. If you're looking for nightclubs, bars and theatres, don't look here – cross the Galata Bridge instead. On weekends, the tenor of the neighbourhood changes slightly, with residents of other city suburbs visiting to soak up some culture, eat *köfte* at Tarihi Sultanahmet Köftecisi Selim Usta (p148), wander around the Hippodrome and drink coffee in one of the chain outlets along Divan Yolu.

The neighbourhood's major thoroughfares are Divan Yolu Caddesi, which runs from Aya Sofya up towards the Grand Bazaar; and Hüdavendigar Caddesi, which runs north from Divan Yolu down towards Eminönü, the city's major transport hub. Here, Bosphorus and Marmara ferries dock, Galata Bridge traffic from Beyoğlu passes through and buses leave Rüstempaşa/Eminönü Bus Station next to the water for all parts of the city. If you want to observe the city's population in all of its glorious diversity, Eminönü is the place to do it.

There is an excellent tram service that starts at Zeytinburnu in the city's west, passes through the city walls at Topkapı (Gate as opposed to Palace) and follows Adnan Menderes Bulvarı, Ordu Caddesi, Divan Yolu Caddesi and Hüdavendigar Caddesi to Eminönü. It then crosses the Golden Horn and terminates at Kabataş, where passengers can transfer to a funicular travelling up the hill to Taksim Sq in Beyoğlu.

## AYA SOFYA Map p53
Haghia Sofia; ☎ 212-522 0989; Aya Sofya Sq; adult/child under 6yr TL20/free, official guide (45min) TL50; ☺ 9am-7.30pm Tue-Sun summer, 9am-5pm Tue-Sun winter; ⓢ Sultanahmet

Called Haghia Sofia in Greek, Sancta Sophia in Latin and the Church of the Divine Wisdom in English, İstanbul's most famous monument has a history as long as it is fascinating. Built by Emperor Justinian (r AD 527–65), it was constructed on the site of Byzantium's acropolis, which had also been the site of two earlier Aya Sofyas – the first a basilica with a timber roof completed in 360 by Constantine's son and successor, Constantinius, and burned down in a riot

in 404; and the second a building commissioned by Theodosius II (r 408–50) in 415 and destroyed in the Nika riots of 532. Justinian's church, which dwarfed all other buildings in the city, was completed in 537 and reigned as the great church in Christendom until the Conquest of Constantinople in 1453, when Mehmet the Conqueror took possession of it for Islam and immediately converted it into a mosque. As significant to Muslims as it is to Christians, it was proclaimed a museum by Atatürk in 1934. Seemingly interminable restoration work (partly Unesco funded) means that the interior is filled with scaffolding, but not even this can detract from the experience of

# SULTANAHMET & AROUND

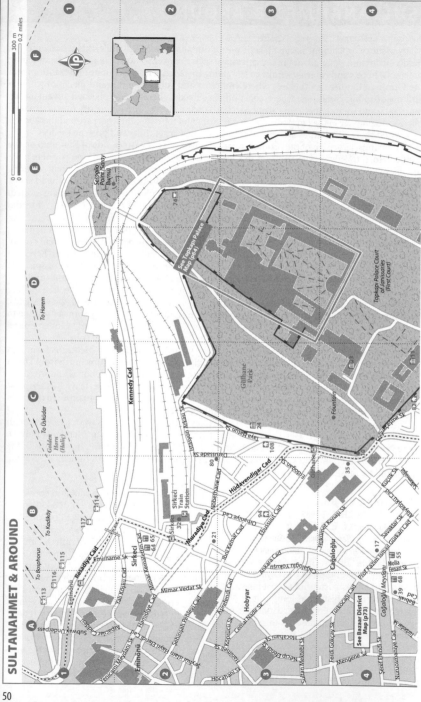

Sea of Marmara
(Marmara Denizi)

Kennedy Cad (Sahil Yolu)

Cankurtaran

İstdemir Paşa
Mosque

Yeni Saraçhane Sk

Cankurtaran

Aya
Sofya

Aya Sofya
Square
(Aya Sofya
Meydanı)

Babıhümayun Cad

Akbıyık
Mosque

Akbıyık Cad

Kabasakal Cad

Alemdar Cad

Million

Sultanahmet
Park

Sultanahmet

Akbıyık Değirmeni Sk

Mimar Mehmet Ağa Cad

Tevkifhane Sk

Yerebatan Cad

Alemdar

Caferiye Sk

İç Kadirga Sk

Akbıyık Sk

Firuz Ağa
Mosque

Finz Ağa
Mosque

Amiral Tafdil Sk

Oyuncu Sk

Blue
Mosque

Tomurcuk Sk

Caferiye Sk

Arasta Bazaar

Sultanahmet

Binbirdirek

Hippodrome

Tavukhane Sk

Gelinlik Sk

Keresteci Hakkı Sk

Atmeydanı Sk

Terzihane Sk

Alemdar

Baş Müsahip Sk

Çatal Çeşme Sk

İşik Sk

Çemberlitaş

Divan Yolu (Ordu) Cad

Kıodfaleri Cad

Sultanahmet Cad

Dr Şevkibey Sk

Küçük
Aya
Sofya

Kaleci Sk

Küçük Aya Sofya Cad

Boyacı Ahmet Sk

Gazi S nan Paşa Sk

Dizdariye Çeşmesi Sk

Nakilbent Sk

Peykhane Cad

Diyar Bekir Cad

Göztaş Sk

Özbekler Sk

Süterazi Sk

Çayiroğlu Sk

Akburçak Sk

Ballı Arkası Sk

# SULTANAHMET & AROUND

visiting one of the world's truly great buildings.

On entering his creation for the first time, Justinian exclaimed, 'Glory to God that I have been judged worthy of such a work. Oh Solomon! I have outdone you!' Entering the building today, it is easy to excuse his self-congratulatory tone. The exterior may be somewhat squat and unattractive but the interior, with its magnificent domed ceiling soaring heavenward, is so sublimely beautiful that many seeing it for the first time are quite literally stunned into silence.

The original achievement of Aya Sofya's architects Anthemeus of Tralles and Isidorus of Miletus, who worked without the benefits of today's technology and materials, remains unequalled. The Byzantines gasped in amazement at the sense of air and space in the nave and the 30 million tesserae (gold mosaic tiles) that covered the dome's interior. Most of all, they marvelled at the apparent lack of support for the enormous dome. How was it possible, they asked? In fact, the original dome lasted only two decades before an earthquake brought it down in 559. It was rebuilt to a slightly less ambitious design, with a smaller base and steeper sides, and the basilica was reopened in 563. Over subsequent centuries it was necessary for succeeding Byzantine emperors and Ottoman sultans to rebuild the dome several times, to add buttresses and other supports and to steady the foundations.

The dome, which is 30m in diameter, is supported by 40 massive ribs constructed of special hollow bricks made in Rhodes from a unique light and porous clay. These ribs rest on four huge pillars concealed in the interior walls. The great Ottoman architect Sinan, who spent his entire professional life trying to design a mosque to match the magnificence and beauty of Aya Sofya, used the same trick of concealing pillars when designing the Süleymaniye Mosque (p76) almost 1000 years later. To truly appreciate what a difference the concealment makes, we suggest that you compare Aya

Sofya's pillar-free central space with that of the nearby Blue Mosque (p56), which features four huge freestanding pillars. You'll find that Aya Sofya shines in comparison.

In Justinian's time, a street led uphill from the west straight to the main door. Today the ticket kiosk is at the southwest side. Past the security check you'll see the sunken ruins of a Theodosian church (404–15) and the low original steps. Entering through the main entrance, visitors are immediately struck by the ethereal beauty of the interior – this is in part due to the innumerable windows with their jewel-like stained glass. It is these windows, with the many arcades, that give the building its famous 'transparency'. Making your way through the outer narthex, you'll walk through the inner narthex and then into the main space. Far ahead of you, in the apse at the other side of the building, is a semidome glowing with a gold mosaic portrait of the Madonna and Child. Above this is another semidome, and above that is the famous main dome.

During its almost 1000 years as a church, only imperial processions were permitted to enter through the central, imperial door.

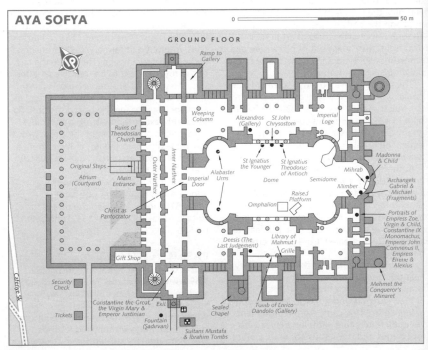

## AYA SOFYA

0 ————————————— 50 m

GROUND FLOOR

You can still notice the depressions in the stone by each door just inside the threshold where imperial guards stood. Also note the matched marble panels in the walls and the breccia (a type of rock made up of angular fragments) columns.

The chandeliers hanging low above the floor are Ottoman additions. Previously, rows of glass oil lamps lined the balustrades of the gallery and the walkway at the base of the dome. Imagine them all lit to celebrate some great state occasion, with the smell of incense and the chants of the Orthodox (and later the Latin) liturgy reverberating through the huge interior space.

The Byzantine emperor was crowned while seated in a throne placed within the omphalion, the square of inlaid marble in the main floor. The nearby raised platform was added by Sultan Murat III, as were the large alabaster urns so that worshippers could perform their ritual ablutions before prayer. During the Ottoman period the mimber (pulpit) and the mihrab (prayer niche indicating the direction of Mecca) were also added.

The large 19th-century medallions inscribed with gilt Arabic letters are the work of master calligrapher Mustafa İzzet Efendi, and give the names of God (Allah), Mohammed and the early caliphs Ali and Abu Bakr. Though impressive works of art in their own right, they seem out of place here and unfortunately detract from the purity of the building's interior form.

The curious elevated kiosk screened from public view is the imperial loge (hünkar mahfili). Sultan Abdül Mecit I (r 1839–61) had it built in 1848 so he could come, pray and go unseen, preserving the imperial mystique. The ornate library behind the omphalion was built by Sultan Mahmut I in 1739.

In the side aisle to the northeast of the imperial door is the weeping column, with a worn copper facing pierced by a hole. Legend has it that the pillar was blessed by St Gregory the Miracle Worker and that putting one's finger in the hole can lead to ailments being healed if the finger emerges moist.

Upstairs in the floor of the south gallery, near the Deesis Mosaic (see the boxed text, opposite), you will see the tomb of Enrico Dandolo (c 1108–1205). Dandolo, who became doge of Venice in 1192, came from a prominent Venetian family that supplied Venice with four doges and numerous admirals. During the Fourth Crusade (1203–4), he diverted the Crusader armies from their goal of defeating the infidels to an assault on the friendly but rival Christian city of Constantinople. The city was ransacked during the assault, and Venice acquired rich spoils as well as numerous Byzantine territories. The victorious Dandolo ruled three-eighths of conquered Constantinople, including Aya Sofya, until his death in 1205, when he was buried here. Tradition tells us that Dandolo's tomb was broken open after the Conquest of the city in 1453, with his bones being thrown to the dogs. Also upstairs (this time in the western gallery) is a large circle of green marble marking the spot where the throne of the empress once stood.

As you exit the building, the şadırvan (fountain) to the right was for ablutions. To your left is the church's baptistry, converted after the Conquest to a tomb for sultans. These are not open to the public. Other tombs are clustered behind it, including those of Murat III (r 1574–95), Mehmet III (r 1595–1603) and Selim 'the Sot' II (r 1566–74). Selim's tomb, which was designed by Sinan and features gorgeous İznik tiles, is particularly poignant as it houses the graves of five of his sons, murdered on the same night in December 1574 to ensure the peaceful succession of the oldest, Murat III. It also houses the graves of 19 of Murat's sons, murdered in January 1595 to ensure Mehmet III's succession. They were the last of the royal princes to be murdered – after this, the younger brothers of succeeding sultans were confined to the kafes (cage) in Topkapı instead (see the boxed text p63). To the southeast of the building a wall hides excavations on a section of the Great Palace (boxed text p69). To the left of the entrance is a small Ottoman primary school built by Mahmut I in 1740.

The first of Aya Sofya's minarets was added by Mehmet the Conqueror (r 1451–81). Sinan designed the others for sultans Beyazıt II (r 1481–1512) and Selim II (r 1566–74).

## BASILICA CISTERN Map pp50–1

Sunken Cistern, Yerebatan Sarnıçı; ☎ 212-522 1259; www.yerebatan.com; Yerebatan Caddesi 13; admission TL10; � 9am-6.30pm Apr-Sep, 9am-5.30pm Oct-Mar; ⬚ Sultanahmet
When those Byzantine emperors built something, they certainly did it properly! This extraordinary subterranean structure,

built by Justinian in 532 (perhaps on the site of an earlier cistern), is the largest surviving Byzantine cistern in İstanbul. Now one of the city's most popular tourist attractions, it's a great place to while away 30 minutes or so, especially during summer when its cavernous depths stay wonderfully cool.

The cistern's roof is 65m wide and 143m long, and is supported by 336 columns arranged in 12 rows. It once held 80,000 cubic metres of water, delivered via 20km of aqueducts from a reservoir near the Black Sea.

The cistern was constructed using columns, capitals and plinths from ruined buildings, and its symmetry and sheer grandeur of conception are quite extraordinary. Don't miss the two columns in the northwestern corner supported by blocks carved into Medusa heads or the column towards the centre featuring a teardrop design – we don't know where these columns originally came from but it's great to speculate.

Walking on the raised wooden platforms, you'll feel the water dripping from the vaulted ceiling and see schools of ghostly carp patrolling the water. Lighting is atmospheric and the small cafe near the exit is certainly an unusual spot to enjoy a glass of tea.

Like most sites in İstanbul, the cistern has an unusual history. Known in Byzantium as

## MOSAICS

Justinian was understandably proud of Aya Sofya's great dome, but he was just as proud of its magnificent mosaic work. Originally, the great dome, the semidomes, the north and south tympana (semicircles) and the vaults of narthex, aisles and galleries were all covered in gold mosaics. Remnants exist and are a highlight of any visit, but one can only imagine what the place must have looked like when the entire interior glittered and gleamed with *tesserae* (small glass tiles incorporating gold leaf). When the Turks took Constantinople and converted Haghia Sofya to a mosque, they decided that the mosaics had to go: fortunately they were covered with plaster rather than destroyed, and some were successfully uncovered and restored by Swiss architects Gaspere and Guiseppe Fossati, working for the sultan, from 1847 to 1849. Though once again covered (this time by paint), they were left in good condition for a final unveiling when the mosque was deconsecrated and the museum opened in 1935. Recent conservation works in the building have led to the uncovering of well-preserved examples, including a seraph (winged biblical angel). Conservators expect to reveal further mosaics before restoration work is completed.

From the floor of Aya Sofya, 9th-century mosaic portraits of St Ignatius the Younger (c 800), St John Chrysostom (c 400) and St Ignatius Theodorus of Antioch are visible high up at the base of the northern tympanum (semicircle) beneath the dome. Next to these three, and seen only from the upstairs east gallery, is a portrait of Alexandros. In the apse is a wonderful mosaic of the Madonna and Child; nearby mosaics depict the archangels Gabriel and Michael, though only fragments of Michael remain. Above the imperial door in the inner narthex there is a striking depiction of Christ as Pantocrator (Ruler of All). He holds a book that carries the inscription 'Peace be with you. I am the Light of the World' and to his right an emperor (probably Leo VI) prostrates himself. As you exit the inner narthex and enter the passage to leave the building, make sure you turn and look up above the door to see one of the church's finest late 10th-century mosaics. This shows Constantine the Great, on the right, offering Mary, who holds the Christ Child, the city of Constantinople; Emperor Justinian, on the left, is offering her Aya Sofya.

The upstairs galleries house the most impressive of Aya Sofya's mosaics and mustn't be missed. They can be reached via a switchback ramp at the northern end of the inner narthex. The magnificent Deesis Mosaic (The Last Judgement) in the south gallery dates from the early 14th century. Christ is at the centre, with the Virgin Mary on the left and John the Baptist on the right.

At the eastern (apse) end of the south gallery is the famous mosaic portrait of Empress Zoe (r 1028–50). When this portrait was done she was 50 years old and newly married to the aged Romanus III Argyrus. Upon Romanus' death in 1034, she had his face excised from the mosaic and that of her virile new husband, Michael IV, put in its place. Eight years later, with Michael dead from an illness contracted on campaign, Zoe and her sister Theodora ruled as empresses in their own right, but did it so badly that it was clear she had to marry again. At the age of 64, Zoe wed an eminent senator, Constantine IX Monomachus, whose portrait remains only because he outlived the empress. The inscription reads 'Constantine, by the Divine Christ, Faithful King of the Romans'.

To the right of Zoe and Constantine is another mosaic depicting characters with less saucy histories: in this scene Mary holds the Christ Child, centre, with Emperor John Comnenus II (Johannes the Good) to the left and Empress Eirene, known for her charitable works, to the right. Their son Alexius, who died soon after this portrait was made, is depicted next to Eirene.

the Basilica Cistern because it lay underneath the Stoa Basilica, one of the great squares on the first hill, it was used to store water for the Great Palace and surrounding buildings. Eventually closed, the cistern seems to have been forgotten by the city authorities some time before the Conquest.

Enter scholar Petrus Gyllius, who in 1545 was researching Byzantine antiquities in the city and was told by locals that they were able to miraculously obtain water by lowering buckets in their basement floors. Some were even catching fish this way. Intrigued, Gyllius explored the neighbourhood and finally discovered a house through whose basement he accessed the cistern. Even after his discovery, the Ottomans (who referred to the cistern as Yerebatan Saray) didn't treat the underground palace with the respect it deserved – it became a dumping ground for all sorts of junk, as well as corpses. Fortunately, later restorations, most notably in the 18th century and between 1955 and 1960, saw it properly maintained. It was cleaned and renovated in 1985 by the İstanbul Metropolitan Municipality and opened to the public in 1987. James Bond fans will recognise the cistern as one of the locations in the film *From Russia With Love* (1963).

## BATHS OF LADY HÜRREM Map pp50–1
**Haseki Hürrem Hamamı; Aya Sofya Sq 4; closed for restoration;** 🚇 **Sultanahmet**
Traditionally, every mosque had a *hamam* (bathhouse) included in or around its complex of buildings. Aya Sofya was no exception and this elegant symmetrical building, designed by Sinan between 1556 and 1557, was built just across the road from the great mosque by Süleyman in the name of his wife Hürrem Sultan, known to history as Roxelana. The *hamam* was one of 32 Sinan designed and is widely thought be his best. It operated until 1910 and until recently functioned as a carpet shop – no-one (including the local heritage authorities) seems to be sure what its future use is going to be after the current restoration is completed.

## BLUE MOSQUE Map pp50–1
**Sultan Ahmet Camii;** 🕾 **212-518 1319; Hippodrome; donation requested;** 🕙 **closed during prayer times;** 🚇 **Sultanahmet**
With this mosque, Sultan Ahmet I (r 1603–17) set out to build a monument that would

rival and even surpass the nearby Aya Sofya (p49) in grandeur and beauty. So enthusiastic was the sultan about his grand project that he is said to have worked with the labourers and craftsmen on site, pushing them along and rewarding extra effort. Ahmet did in fact come close to his goal of rivalling Aya Sofya, and in so doing achieved the added benefit of making future generations of hotel owners in Sultanahmet happy – a 'Blue Mosque view' from the roof terrace being the number-one selling point of the fleet of hotels in the area.

The mosque's architect, Mehmet Ağa, who had trained with Sinan, managed to orchestrate the sort of visual wham-bam effect with the mosque's exterior that Aya Sofya achieved with its interior. Its curves are voluptuous, it has more minarets than any other İstanbul mosque (in fact, there was consternation at the time of its construction that the sultan was being irreverent in specifying six minarets – the only equivalent being in Mecca) and the courtyard is the biggest of all the Ottoman mosques. The interior is conceived on a similarly grand scale: the blue tiles that give the building its unofficial name number in the tens of thousands, there are 260 windows and the central prayer space is huge. No wonder its picture graces a million postcards!

In order to fully appreciate the mosque's design you should approach it via the middle of the Hippodrome rather than walking straight from Sultanahmet Park through the crowds. When inside the courtyard, which is the same size as the mosque's interior, you'll be able to appreciate the perfect proportions of the building. Walk towards the mosque through the gate in the peripheral wall, noting on the way the small dome atop the gate: this is the motif Mehmet Ağa uses to lift your eyes to heaven. As you walk through the gate, your eyes follow a flight of stairs up to another gate topped by another dome; through this gate is yet another dome, that of the ablutions fountain in the centre of the mosque courtyard. As you ascend the stairs, semidomes come into view: first the one over the mosque's main door, then the one above it, and another, and another. Finally the main dome crowns the whole, and your attention is drawn to the sides, where forests of smaller domes reinforce the effect, completed by the minarets, which lift your eyes heavenward.

The mosque is such a popular tourist sight that admission is controlled so as to preserve its sacred atmosphere. In the tourist season (May to September), only worshippers are admitted through the main door; tourists must use the north door. Shoes must be taken off and women who haven't brought their own headscarf or are too scantily dressed will be loaned a headscarf and/or robe. There's no charge for this, but donations for the mosque are requested.

Inside, the stained-glass windows and İznik tiles immediately attract attention. Though the windows are replacements, they still create the luminous effects of the originals, which came from Venice. The tiles line the walls, particularly in the gallery (which is not open to the public). There are so many of these tiles that the İznik workshops producing the finest examples could not keep up with demand, and alternative, less skilled, workshops were called in to fill the gap. The mosque's tiles are thus of varying quality.

You can see immediately why the mosque, which was constructed between 1606 and 1616, over 1000 years after Aya Sofya, is not as daring as its predecessor. Four massive 'elephant's feet' pillars hold up the less ambitious dome, a sturdier solution lacking the innovation and grace of the dome in Justinian's cathedral.

The semidomes and the dome are painted in graceful arabesques. Of note in the main space are the imperial loge, covered with marble latticework, which is to the left of the mihrab; the mihrab itself, which features a piece of the sacred Black Stone from the Kaaba in Mecca; and the high, elaborate mahfil (chair) from which the imam gives the sermon on Friday. The beautifully carved white marble mimber with its curtained doorway at floor level features a flight of steps and a small kiosk topped by a spire.

Mosques built by the great and powerful usually included numerous public-service institutions. Clustered around the Blue Mosque were a medrese (theological college); an imaret (soup kitchen) serving the poor; a hamam so that the faithful could bathe on Friday, the holy day; and shops (the Arasta Bazaar), the rent from which supported the upkeep of the mosque.

The Tomb of Sultan Ahmet I (donation expected; 9.30am-4.30pm), the türbe (tomb) of the Blue Mosque's great patron, is on the north side facing Sultanahmet Park. Ahmet, who had ascended to the imperial throne aged 13, died one year after the mosque was constructed, aged only 27. Buried with Ahmet are his wife, Kösem, who was strangled to death in the Topkapı Harem, and his sons, Sultan Osman II (r 1618–22), Sultan Murat IV (r 1623–40) and Prince Beyazıt (murdered by Murat). Like the mosque, the türbe features fine İznik tiles.

## GREAT PALACE MOSAICS MUSEUM
Map pp50–1

Büyüksaray Mozaik Müzesi; ☎ 212-518 1205; Torun Sokak; admission TL8; 9am-4.30pm Tue-Sun; Sultanahmet

When archaeologists from the University of Ankara and the University of St Andrews (Scotland) dug at the back of the Blue Mosque in the mid-1950s, they uncovered a stunning mosaic pavement dating from early Byzantine times. Restored from 1983 to 1997, it is now preserved in this museum.

Thought to have been added by Justinian to the Great Palace (boxed text p69), the pavement is estimated to have measured from 3500 to 4000 sq m in its original form. The 250 sq m that is preserved here is the largest discovered remnant – the rest has been destroyed or remains buried underneath the Blue Mosque and surrounding shops and hotels.

The pavement is filled with bucolic imagery as well as intricate hunting and mythological scenes. Note the gorgeous ribbon border with heart-shaped leaves surrounding the mosaic. In the westernmost room is the most colourful and dramatic picture, that of two men in leggings carrying spears and holding off a raging tiger.

The museum has informative panels documenting the floor's rescue and renovation. When paying for your ticket, make sure that you receive the correct change in valid currency – on our most recent visit, a ticket seller was attempting to palm off out-of-date notes (see p226).

## HIPPODROME Map pp50–1
Sultanahmet

The Hippodrome (At Meydanı) was the centre of Byzantium's life for 1000 years and of Ottoman life for another 400 years. In its heyday, the arena consisted of two levels of galleries, a central spine, starting boxes and the semicircular southern end known as the Sphendone, parts of which still stand to the south of the Hippodrome. The level of galleries that once topped this stone structure was damaged during the Fourth Crusade and ended up being totally dismantled in the Ottoman period – many of the original columns were used in construction of the Süleymaniye Mosque.

The Hippodrome has been the scene of countless political dramas during the long life of the city. In Byzantine times, the rival chariot teams of 'Greens' and 'Blues' had separate sectarian connections. Support for a team was akin to membership of a political party and a team victory had important effects on policy. Occasionally, Greens and Blues joined forces against the emperor, as was the case in 532 BC when a chariot race was disturbed by protests against Justinian's high tax regime – this escalated into the Nika riots (so called after the protesters' cry of *Nika!*, or Victory!), which led to tens of thousands of protesters being massacred in the Hippodrome by imperial forces. Not unsurprisingly, chariot races were banned for some time afterwards.

Ottoman sultans also kept an eye on activities in the Hippodrome. If things were going badly in the empire, a surly crowd gathering here could signal the start of a disturbance, then a riot, then a revolution. In 1826, the slaughter of the corrupt janissary corps (the sultan's personal bodyguards) was carried out here by the reformer Sultan Mahmut II. And in 1909 there were riots that caused the downfall of Abdül Hamit II.

Though the Hippodrome might be the scene of their downfall, Byzantine emperors and Ottoman sultans outdid one another in beautifying it. Unfortunately, many priceless statues carved by ancient masters have disappeared from their original homes here. Chief among the villains responsible for such thefts were the soldiers of the Fourth Crusade, who invaded Constantinople, a Christian ally city, in 1204. After sacking Aya Sofya, they tore all the plates from the Rough-Stone Obelisk at the Hippodrome's southern end in the mistaken belief that they were solid gold (in fact, they were gold-covered bronze). The crusaders also stole the famous *quadriga*, or team of four horses cast in bronze, a copy of which now sits atop the main door of the Basilica di

San Marco in Venice (the original is inside the basilica).

The level of the Hippodrome rose over the centuries, as successive civilisations piled up their dust and refuse here. A number of its monuments were cleaned out and tidied up by the British troops who occupied the city after the Ottoman defeat in WWI.

Near the northern end of the Hippodrome, the little gazebo in beautiful stonework is actually Kaiser Wilhelm's Fountain. The German emperor paid a state visit to Sultan Abdül Hamit II in 1898 and presented this fountain to the sultan and his people as a token of friendship. The monograms in the stonework are those of Abdül Hamit II and Wilhelm II, and represent their political union.

The impressive granite Obelisk of Theodosius was carved in Egypt around 1450 BC. According to the hieroglyphs, it was erected in Heliopolis (now a Cairo suburb) to commemorate the victories of Thutmose III (r 1479–1425 BC). Theodosius the Great (r 379–95) had it brought from Egypt to Constantinople in AD 390. On the marble billboards below the obelisk, look for the carvings of Theodosius, his wife, sons, state officials and bodyguards watching the chariot-race action from the *kathisma* (imperial box).

South of the obelisk is a strange column coming up out of a hole in the ground. Known as the Spiral Column or Tripod of Plataea, it was once much taller and was topped by three serpents' heads. Originally cast to commemorate a victory of the Hellenic confederation over the Persians in the battle of Plataea, it stood in front of the temple of Apollo at Delphi from 478 BC until Constantine the Great had it brought to his new capital city around AD 330. Though badly damaged in Byzantine times, the serpents' heads survived until the early 18th century. Now all that remains of them is one upper jaw, housed in the İstanbul Archaeology Museums (p66).

## MUSEUM OF TURKISH & ISLAMIC ARTS Map pp50–1
Türk ve İslam Eserleri Müzesi; ☎ 212-518 1805; Hippodrome 46, Atmeydanı Sokak; admission TL10; ⏰ 9am-4.30pm Tue-Sun; Ⓜ Sultanahmet
This impressive museum is housed in the Palace of İbrahim Paşa, built in 1524 on the western side of the Hippodrome.

İbrahim Paşa was Süleyman the Magnificent's close friend and brother-in-law. Captured by Turks as a child in Greece, he was sold as a slave into the imperial household in İstanbul and worked as a page in Topkapı, where he became friendly with Süleyman, who was the same age. When his friend became sultan, İbrahim was made in turn chief falconer, chief of the royal bedchamber and grand vizier. This palace was bestowed on him by Süleyman the year before he was given the hand of Süleyman's sister, Hadice, in marriage. Alas, the fairy tale was not to last for poor İbrahim. His wealth, power and influence on the monarch became so great that others wishing to influence the sultan became envious, chief among them Süleyman's powerful wife, Haseki Hürrem Sultan (Roxelana). After a rival accused İbrahim of disloyalty, Roxelana convinced her husband that İbrahim was a threat and Süleyman had him strangled in 1536.

The museum's exhibits date from the 8th and 9th centuries up to the 19th century. Highlights include the superb calligraphy exhibits, with *müknames* (scrolls outlining an imperial decree) featuring the sultan's *tuğra* (monogram). Look out for the exquisite Iranian book binding from the Safavid period (1501–1786). And whatever you do, don't miss the extraordinary collection of carpets displayed in the *divanhane* (ceremonial hall) – it's generally acknowledged to be the best collection of antique carpets in the world, and includes Holbein, Lotto, Konya, Uşhak, Iran and Caucasia examples.

The lower floor of the museum houses ethnographic exhibits.

Labels are in Turkish and English. The coffee shop in the courtyard of the museum also has tables on the terrace overlooking the Hippodrome.

### TOPKAPI PALACE Map p64

**Topkapı Sarayı; ☎ 212-512 0480; www.topkapisarayi.gov.tr/eng; Babıhümayun Caddesi; admission TL20; ☉ 9am-5pm Wed-Mon; ⓖ Sultanahmet or Gülhane**

This opulent palace is the subject of more colourful stories than most of the world's museums put together. It was the home of Selim the Sot, who drowned in the bath after drinking too much champagne; İbrahim the Crazy, who lost his reason after being locked up for four years in the infamous palace *kafes*; and Roxelana, beautiful and malevolent consort of Süleyman the Magnificent. No wonder it's been the subject of a popular feature film (Jules Dassin's 1963 *Topkapı*), an opera (Mozart's *The Abduction from the Seraglio*) and a blockbuster social history (John Freely's wonderful *Inside the Seraglio*). There's loads to see, so make sure you dedicate at least half a day to exploring.

Mehmet the Conqueror built the first stage of the palace shortly after the Conquest in 1453, and lived here until his death in 1481. Subsequent sultans lived in this rarefied environment until the 19th century, when they moved to ostentatious European-style palaces such as Dolmabahçe

## RAMAZAN IN THE HIPPODROME

The Hippodrome may have been the centre of the city's life in Byzantine and Ottoman times, but this certainly isn't the case these days – that honour is proudly claimed by Taksim Sq (p109) in Beyoğlu. However, for four weeks of every year the Hippodrome regains its symbolic supremacy in the minds of İstanbullus as the host of the city's most popular Ramazan (Ramadan) carnival. Every evening after *iftar* (the breaking of the fast at sunset) the arena is lined with temporary stalls selling fast foods, toys, dried fruits, CDs and sweets to thousands of revellers. Popular snacks include popcorn, roasted corn, *gözleme* (Turkish crepes cooked on a griddle with cheese, spinach or potato) and döner kebaps. Children beg their indulgent parents for *lokma* (a type of fried doughnut in syrup), *macun* (luridly coloured twisted candy on a stick) or fairy floss (cotton candy), and queues form at temporary cafes brewing delicious *közde kahve* (slow-cooked Turkish coffee) on charcoal braziers. Coloured lights and decorations are everywhere, music by the latest darlings of the Turkish airwaves blares from speakers, the stall-owners shout *buyurun!* (an expression meaning welcome) and the crowd smiles and laughs, relieved to have finally eaten and drunk after a long day of fasting. If you're in town over Ramazan (see p225), don't miss it.

Note that the *iftar* tents set up in the Hippodrome and other parts of the city are only for Muslims who have been observing the fast; it is highly inappropriate for non-Muslim tourists to join them. The *iftar* menus offered by restaurants around the city are slightly different – it is best to leave the cheap local places to regulars, but there's nothing wrong in sharing the feast in upmarket or hotel restaurants.

(p114), Çırağan (p116) and Yıldız (p116) that they built on the shores of the Bosphorus. Mahmut II (r 180839) was the last sultan to live in Topkapı.

Buy your tickets to the palace at the main ticket office just outside the gate to the Second Court. Tickets to the Topkapı Harem (p63) are available at the ticket box outside the Harem itself. Guides to the palace congregate next to the main ticket office. A one-hour tour costs €10 per person for large-ish groups; you need to negotiate if you're in a small group or by yourself. Alternatively, an audio guide in English, French, Italian, Spanish or German will cost you TL5. These are available at the audio booth just inside the turnstile entrance to the Second Court. Note that the palace is undergoing a prolonged program of conservation works and its buildings are being closed to the public in turn while they are being restored. A board listing which buildings are currently closed to the public is to the left of the ticket office.

Before you enter the Imperial Gate (Bab-ı Hümayun; Map pp50–1) of Topkapı, take a look at the ornate structure in the cobbled square near the gate. This is the Fountain of Sultan Ahmet III, built in 1728 by the sultan who so favoured tulips. It replaced a Byzantine fountain at the same spring. Typical of architecture during the Tulip Period, it features delicate Turkish rococo decorations (note the floral carvings).

As you pass through the Imperial Gate, you enter the First Court, known as the Court of the Janissaries, also known as the Parade Court. On your left is Aya İrini, also known as Haghia Eirene or the Church of the Divine Peace. There was a Christian church here from earliest times and, before that, a pagan temple. The early church was replaced by the present one, commissioned by Justinian in the 540s. It is almost exactly as old as its close neighbour, Aya Sofya. When Mehmet the Conqueror began building his palace, the church was within the grounds and was most fortunately retained. It was used as an arsenal for centuries, then as an artillery museum and now occasionally as a concert hall (especially during the International İstanbul Music Festival, p16). Its serenely beautiful interior and superb acoustics mean that tickets to concerts here are usually the most sought-after in town. If you're fortunate enough to be here during the festival, think about visiting the temporary box office, located outside Aya İrini, to see if any tickets are available; otherwise book online at Biletix (www.biletix.com). There is talk of the church being used as a museum of Byzantium in the future.

Janissaries, merchants and tradespeople could circulate as they wished in the Court of the Janissaries, but the Second Court was restricted. The same is true today, as you must have a ticket to the palace to enter the Second Court. Just past the ticket windows is a little fountain where the imperial executioner used to wash the tools of his trade after decapitating a noble or rebel who had displeased the sultan. The head of the unfortunate victim was put on a pike and exhibited above the gate you are about to enter.

The Middle Gate (Ortakapı or Bab-üs Selâm) led to the palace's Second Court, used for the business of running the empire. Only the sultan and the valide sultan (queen mother) were allowed through the Middle Gate on horseback. Everyone else, including the grand vizier, had to dismount. The gate was constructed by Süleyman the Magnificent in 1524, utilising architects and workers he had brought back from his conquest of Hungary.

To the right after you enter are models and a map of the palace. Beyond them, in a nearby building, you'll find imperial carriages made in Paris, Turin and Vienna for the sultan and his family.

The Second Court has a beautiful, park-like setting. Unlike typical European palaces, which feature one large building with outlying gardens, Topkapı is a series of pavilions, kitchens, barracks, audience chambers, kiosks and sleeping quarters built around a central enclosure.

The great Palace Kitchens on your right hold a small portion of Topkapı's vast collection of Chinese celadon porcelain, valued by the sultans for its beauty but also because it was reputed to change colour if touched by poisoned food. In a building close by are the collections of European, Russian and Ottoman porcelain, silverware and glassware. Some of the huge pots and pans that were used in the palace's heyday are exhibited in the last of the kitchens, the Helvahane, in which all the palace sweets were made.

On the left (west) side of the Second Court is the ornate Imperial Council Chamber, also called the Divan Salonu. It's beneath the squarish Tower of Justice, the palace's highest point. The Imperial Divan (council) met in the Imperial Council Chamber to discuss matters of state while the sultan eavesdropped through a grille high on the wall. During the great days of the empire, foreign ambassadors were received on days when the janissaries were to get their pay. Huge sacks of silver coins were brought to the Imperial Council Chamber. High-court officers would dispense the coins to long lines of the tough, impeccably costumed and faultlessly disciplined troops as the ambassadors looked on in admiration.

North of the Imperial Council Chamber is the Inner Treasury, which today exhibits Ottoman and European armour.

The entrance to the Harem is beneath the Tower of Justice (Adalet Kulesi) on the left-hand side of the Second Court. The tower is not open to the public.

If you enter the Third Court after visiting the Harem (and thus by the back door), you should head for the main gate into the court and enter again to truly appreciate the grandeur of the approach to the heart of the palace. This main gate, known as the Gate of Felicity or Gate of the White Eunuchs, was the entrance into the sultan's private domain. As is common with oriental potentates, the sultan preserved the imperial mystique by appearing in public very seldom. The Third Court was staffed and guarded by white eunuchs, who allowed only a few very important people in. As you enter the Third Court, imagine it alive with the movements of imperial pages and eunuchs scurrying here and there in their palace costumes. Every now and then the chief white eunuch or the chief black eunuch would appear, and all would bow. If the sultan walked across the courtyard, all activity stopped until the event was over.

An exception to the imperial seclusion was the ceremony celebrating a new sultan's accession to the throne. After girding the Sword of Osman, which symbolised imperial power, the new monarch would sit enthroned before the Gate of Felicity and receive the obeisance, allegiance and congratulations of the empire's high and mighty.

Before the annual military campaigns in summertime, the sultan would also appear before this gate bearing the standard of the Prophet Mohammed to inspire his generals to go out and conquer all for Islam.

Inside the Gate of Felicity is the Audience Chamber, constructed in the 16th century but refurbished in the 18th century. Important officials and foreign ambassadors were brought to this little kiosk to conduct the high business of state. An ambassador, frisked for weapons and held on each arm by a white eunuch, would approach the sultan. At the proper moment, he knelt and kowtowed; if he didn't, the eunuchs would urge him ever so forcefully to do so.

The sultan, seated on the divans whose cushions are embroidered with over 15,000 seed pearls, inspected the ambassador's gifts and offerings as they were passed through the small doorway on the left. Even if the sultan and the ambassador could converse in the same language (sultans in the later years knew French and ambassadors often learned Turkish), all conversation was with the grand vizier. The sultan would not deign to speak to a foreigner and only the very highest Ottoman officers were allowed to address the monarch directly.

Right behind the Audience Chamber is the pretty Library of Ahmet III, built in 1719 by Sultan Ahmet III. Light-filled, it has comfortable reading areas and stunning inlaid woodwork.

To the right of the Audience Chamber (ie on the opposite side of the Harem exit) are the rooms of the Dormitory of the Expeditionary Force, which now house the rich collections of imperial robes, kaftans and uniforms worked in silver and gold thread. Also here is a fascinating collection of talismanic shirts, which were believed to protect the wearer from enemies and misfortunes of all kinds. Textile design reached its highest point during the reign of Süleyman the Magnificent, when the imperial workshops produced cloth of exquisite design and work. Check out the absolutely gorgeous silk kaftan of Süleyman the Magnificent with its appliquéd tulip design.

Next to the Dormitory of the Expeditionary Force is the Imperial Treasury, which features an incredible collection of precious objects made from or decorated with gold, silver, rubies, emeralds, jade, pearls and diamonds. The building itself was constructed by Mehmet the Conqueror in 1460 and has always been used to store works of art and treasure. In the first room, look for the jewel-encrusted sword of Süleyman the

Magnificent and the Throne of Ahmed I, inlaid with mother-of-pearl and designed by Mehmet Ağa, architect of the Blue Mosque. In the second room, the tiny Indian figures, mainly made from seed pearls, are well worth seeking out. These were originally in the possession of the Byzantines and fell into Ottoman hands after the Conquest.

After passing through the third room and having a gawk at the enormous gold and diamond candlesticks, each weighing 48kg, you come to a fourth room and the Treasury's most famous exhibit: the Topkapı Dagger. The object of the criminal heist in Jules Dassin's film *Topkapı*, the dagger features three enormous emeralds on the hilt and a watch set into the pommel. Also here is the Kaşıkçı (Spoonmaker's) Diamond, a teardrop-shaped 86-carat rock surrounded by dozens of smaller stones. First worn by Mehmet IV at his accession to the throne in 1648, it's the world's fifth-largest diamond. It's called the Spoonmaker's Diamond because it was originally found at a rubbish dump in Eğrıkapı and purchased by a street peddler for three spoons.

Opposite the Treasury, on the other side of the Third Court, is another set of wonders: the holy relics in the Suite of the Felicitous Cloak, nowadays called the Sacred Safekeeping Rooms. These rooms, sumptuously decorated with İznik faïence, constitute a holy of holies within the palace. Only the chosen could enter the Third Court, but entry into these special rooms was for the chosen of the chosen, and even then only on ceremonial occasions. During the empire, this suite of rooms was opened only once a year so that the imperial family could pay homage to the memory of the Prophet on the 15th day of the holy month of Ramazan. Even though anyone, prince or commoner, faithful or infidel, can enter the rooms now, you should respect the sacred atmosphere by observing decorous behaviour, as this is still a place of pilgrimage for Muslims.

In the east entry room, notice the carved door and gilded rain gutters from the Kaaba in Mecca.

To the right (north), a room contains a hair of Prophet Mohammed's beard, his footprint in clay, his sword, tooth and more. The felicitous cloak itself resides in a golden casket in a small adjoining room along with the battle standard.

Also in the Third Court are the Quarters of Pages in Charge of the Sacred Safekeeping Rooms,

where the palace school for pages and janissaries was located. These days the building features exhibits of Turkish miniature paintings, calligraphy and portraits of the sultans. Notice the graceful, elaborate *tuğra* of the sultans. The *tuğra*, placed at the top of any imperial proclamation, contains elaborate calligraphic rendering of the names of the sultan and his father, eg 'Abdül Hamit Khan, son of Abdül Mecit Khan, Ever Victorious'.

Other buildings in the Third Court include the Mosque of the Eunuchs and a small library.

Pleasure pavilions occupy the northeastern corner of the palace, sometimes called the Tulip Gardens or Fourth Court. A late addition to Topkapı, the Mecidiye Köşkü, was built by Abdül Mecit (r 1839–61) according to 19th-century European models. Beneath this is the Konyalı restaurant, the palace's only eatery, which serves cafeteria food at restaurant prices.

West of the Mecidiye Köşkü is the sultan's Chief Physician's Room. Interestingly, the chief physician was always one of the sultan's Jewish subjects. Nearby, you'll see the Kiosk of Mustafa Pasha, sometimes called the Sofa Köşkü. Outside the kiosk, during the reign of Ahmet III, the Tulip Garden was filled with the latest varieties of the flower. Little lamps would be set out among the tulips at night.

Up the stairs at the end of the Tulip Garden are two of the most enchanting buildings in the palace, joined by a marble terrace with a beautiful pool. Murat IV built the Revan Kiosk in 1636 after reclaiming the city of Yerevan (now in Armenia) from Persia. In 1639 he constructed the Baghdad Kiosk, one of the last examples of classical palace architecture, to commemorate his victory over that city. Notice the superb İznik tiles, the mother-of-pearl and tortoiseshell inlay, and the woodwork.

Jutting out from the terrace is the golden roof of the İftariye Baldachin, the most popular happy-snap spot in the palace grounds. İbrahim the Crazy built this small structure in 1640 as a picturesque place to break the fast of Ramazan.

On the west end of the terrace is the Circumcision Room (Sünnet Odası), used for the ritual that admits Muslim boys to manhood. Built by İbrahim in 1641, the outer walls of the chamber are graced by particularly beautiful tile panels.

## TOPKAPI HAREM Map p64

**Topkapı Palace; admission TL15; ⊙ 9am-5pm Wed-Mon**

If you decide to tour the Harem at Topkapı Palace – and we highly recommend that you do – you'll need to buy a dedicated ticket from the ticket office outside the Harem's entrance. The fact that there is an extra entry charge means that many stingy tour companies neglect to bring their customers through here – dreadful for people on tours but great for those who aren't, because as a result it has become one of the least crowded areas of the palace. It's a welcome relief after the experience of shuffling through the horrendously crowded Treasury, for instance.

As popular belief would have it, the Harem was a place where the sultan could engage in debauchery at will (and Murat III did, after all, have 112 children!). In more prosaic reality, these were the imperial family quarters, and every detail of Harem life was governed by tradition, obligation and ceremony. The word 'harem' literally means 'private'.

Every traditional Muslim household had two distinct parts: the *selamlık* (greeting room) where the master greeted friends, business associates and tradespeople; and the harem (private apartments), reserved for himself and his family. The Harem, then, was something akin to the private apartments in Buckingham Palace or the White House.

The women of the Harem had to be foreigners, as Islam forbade enslaving Muslims. Girls were bought as slaves (often having been sold by their parents at a good price) or were received as gifts from nobles and potentates. A favourite source of girls was Circassia, north of the Caucasus Mountains in Russia, as Circassian women were noted for their beauty.

Upon entering the Harem, the girls would be schooled in Islam and Turkish culture and language, as well as the arts of make-up, dress, comportment, music, reading, writing, embroidery and dancing. They then entered a meritocracy, first as ladies-in-waiting to the sultan's concubines and children, then to the sultan's mother and finally – if they were particularly attractive and talented – to the sultan himself.

Ruling the Harem was the *valide sultan*, the mother of the reigning sultan. She often owned large landed estates in her own name and controlled them through black eunuch servants. Able to give orders directly to the grand vizier, her influence on the sultan, on the selection of his wives and concubines, and on matters of state was often profound.

The sultan was allowed by Islamic law to have four legitimate wives, who received the title of *kadın* (wife). If a wife bore him a son she was called *haseki sultan; haseki kadın* if it was a daughter. The Ottoman dynasty did not observe primogeniture (the right of the first-born son to the throne), so in principle the throne was available to any imperial son. Each lady of the Harem contrived mightily to have her son proclaimed heir to the throne, to thus assure her own role as the new *valide sultan*.

## LIFE IN THE CAGE

As children, imperial princes were brought up in the Harem, where they were taught and cared for by its women and servants.

In the early centuries of the empire, Ottoman princes were schooled as youths in combat and statecraft by direct experience. They practised soldiering, fought in battles and were given provinces to administer. But as the Ottoman dynasty did not observe primogeniture (succession of the firstborn), the death of the sultan regularly resulted in a fratricidal bloodbath as his sons – often from different mothers – battled it out among themselves for the throne. In the case of Beyazıt II (r 1481–1512), his sons began the battles even before the sultan's death, realising that to lose the battle for succession meant their own death. The victorious son, Selim I (r 1512–20), not only murdered his brothers but even forced Sultan Beyazıt to abdicate and may even have had him murdered as he went into retirement.

Fratricide was not practised by Ahmet I (r 1603–17), who could not bring himself to murder his mad brother Mustafa. Instead, he kept him imprisoned in the Harem, beginning the tradition of *kafes hayatı* (cage life). This house arrest, adopted in place of fratricide by later sultans, meant that princes were prey to the intrigues of the women and eunuchs, kept ignorant of war and statecraft, and thus usually rendered unfit to rule if and when the occasion arose. Luckily for the empire in this latter period, there were able grand viziers.

In later centuries the dynasty adopted the practice of having the eldest male in the direct line assume the throne.

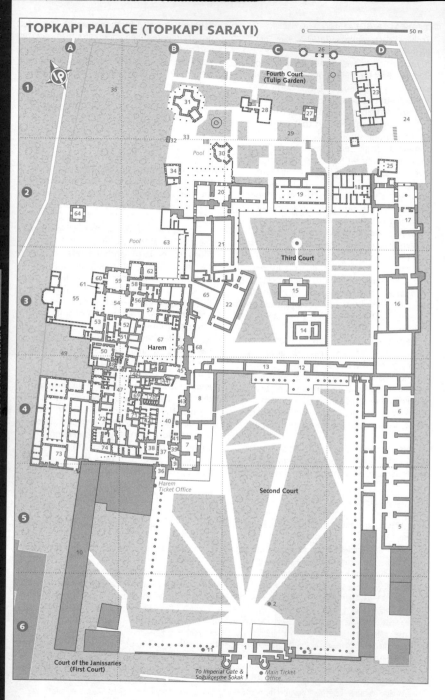

# TOPKAPI PALACE (TOPKAPI SARAYI)

0 _____ 50 m

Fourth Court
(Tulip Garden)

Pool

Pool

Third Court

Harem

Second Court

Harem
Ticket Office

Court of the Janissaries
(First Court)

To Imperial Gate &
Soğukçeşme Sokak

Main Ticket
Office

As for concubines, Islam permits as many as a man can support in proper style. The Ottoman sultans had the means to support many, sometimes up to 300, though they were not all in the Harem at the same time. However, the domestic thrills of the sultans were usually less spectacular. Mehmet the Conqueror, builder of Topkapı, was the last sultan to have four official wives. After him, sultans did not officially marry, but instead kept four chosen concubines without the associated legal encumbrances, thereby saving themselves the embarrassments and inconveniences suffered by another famous Renaissance monarch, King Henry VIII. The exception to this rule was Süleyman the Magnificent (r 1520–66), who famously married his favourite concubine, Roxelana.

The Harem was much like a village with all the necessary services. About 400 or 500 people lived in this section of the palace at any one time. Not many of the ladies stayed in the Harem all their lives. The sultan might grant them their freedom, after which they would often marry powerful men who wanted the company of these well-educated women, not to mention their connections with the palace. And the relationship was twofold: the sultan was also happy to have the women, educated to be loyal, spread throughout the empire to help keep tabs on political affairs via their husbands.

The chief black eunuch, the sultan's personal representative in administration of the Harem and other important affairs of state, was the third most powerful official in the empire, after the grand vizier and the supreme Islamic judge.

The earliest of the 300-odd rooms in the Harem were constructed during the reign of Murat III. In 1665 a disastrous fire destroyed much of the complex, which was rebuilt by Mehmet IV and later sultans.

Although the Harem is built into a hillside and has six levels, you'll only be able to visit one of these. Fortunately, the most important rooms in the complex are here. Interpretive panels in Turkish and English have been placed throughout the building.

You enter the Harem by the Carriage Gate, through which Harem ladies would enter in their carriages. Inside the gate is the Dome with Cupboards. Beyond it is the Hall with Fountain (Hall with Şadırvan), a room decorated with fine Kütahya tiles from the 17th century. This is where the Harem's eunuch guards were stationed; the fountain that gave it its name is now in the Pool of the Privy Chamber of Murad III. To the left is a doorway to the Black Eunuchs' Mosque; on the right is the doorway to the Tower of Justice, which rises above the Imperial Council Chamber. Neither is open to the public.

Beyond the Hall with Fountain is the narrow Courtyard of the Black Eunuchs (Harem Ağaları Taşlığı), also decorated in Kütahya tiles. Behind the marble colonnade on the left are the Black Eunuchs' Dormitories. In the early days white eunuchs were used, but black eunuchs sent as presents by the Ottoman governor of Egypt later took control.

As many as 200 lived here, guarding the doors and waiting on the women of the Harem.

Near the far end of the courtyard on the left, a staircase leads up to the rooms in which imperial princes were given their primary schooling. These are not open to the public. On the right is the Chief Black Eunuch's Room.

At the far end of the courtyard, safely protected by the eunuchs, is the Main Gate (Cümle Kapısı) into the Harem proper, as well as a guard room featuring two gigantic gilded mirrors dating from the 18th century. From this, the Concubines' Corridor (Cariye Koridoru) on the left leads to the Court of the Concubines and the Sultan's Consorts Courtyard (Cariyeler ve Kadınefendiler Taşlığı). This is surrounded by baths, a laundry fountain, a laundry, dormitories and the apartments of the Sultan's chief consorts.

Next you'll go through the pretty Sultan Ahmet's Kiosk, with its tiled chimney, and into the Apartments of the Valide Sultan (Valide Sultan Dairesi), the centre of power in the Harem. These rooms include a large salon, a small bedroom, a room for prayer and other small chambers. From these ornate rooms the valide sultan oversaw and controlled her huge 'family'. After his accession to the throne, a new sultan came here to receive the allegiance and congratulations of the people of the Harem. The later rococo mezzanine was added by the mother of Murat III in the 1580s. Of particular note in these quarters are the charming small hamam designed by Sinan and the lovely 19th-century murals featuring panoramic views of İstanbul.

As he walked these corridors, the sultan wore slippers with silver soles. As no woman was allowed to show herself to the sultan without specific orders, the clatter of the silver soles warned residents of the sultan's approach, allowing them to disappear from his sight. This rule no doubt solidified the valide sultan's control, as she got to choose the most beautiful, talented and intelligent of the Harem girls for her son.

The tour passes through the private hamams and toilets of the valide sultan to the Imperial Hall (Hünkar Fofrası), decorated in Delft tiles. This grand room is the largest in the Harem and was where the sultan and his ladies gathered for entertainment, often being serenaded by musicians in the balcony. Designed perhaps by Sinan during the reign of Murat III, it was redecorated in baroque style by Osman III (r 1754–57).

The tour then enters the Privy Chamber of Murat III (1579), one of the most sumptuous rooms in the palace. Dating from 1578, virtually all of the decoration is original. It is thought to be the work of Sinan. Besides the gorgeous İznik tiles and a copper fireplace, there is a three-tiered marble fountain to give the sound of cascading water and, perhaps not coincidentally, to make it difficult to eavesdrop on the sultan's conversations. The gilded canopied seating areas are later 18th-century additions.

Northeast (to the right) of the Privy Chamber of Murat III are two of the most beautiful rooms in the Harem – the Twin Kiosk/Apartments of the Crown Prince (Çifte Kasırlar/Veliahd Dairesi). These two rooms date from around 1600; note the painted canvas dome in the first room and the fine İznik tile panels above the fireplace in the second. The fabulous stained glass is also noteworthy.

North and east of the Twin Kiosk is the Courtyard of the Favourites (Gözdeler/Mabeyn Taşlığı Ve Dairesi). The Turkish word for 'favourite', gözde, literally means 'in the eye' (of the sultan). Over the edge of the courtyard (really a terrace) you'll see a large pool. Just past the courtyard (but on the floor above) are the many small dark rooms that comprised the Private Prison (kafes) where the unwanted brothers or sons of the sultan were kept (see the boxed text p63).

A corridor leads east to the Golden Road (Altinyol), a passage leading south. A servant of the sultan's would toss gold coins to the women of the Harem here, hence the name. It is among the oldest parts of the palace, having been built by Mehmet the Conqueror.

The Harem tour then re-enters the guardroom with the huge gilded mirrors and exits through the Birdcage Gate into the palace's Third Court.

## İSTANBUL ARCHAEOLOGY MUSEUMS Map pp50–1

Arkeoloji Müzeleri; ☎ 212-520 7740; Osman Hamdi Bey Yokuşu, Gülhane; admission TL10; ☼ 9am-4pm Tue-Sun (last exit 5pm); ☒ Gülhane

It may not attract the number of visitors that flock to nearby Topkapı, but this stunning museum complex is already one of the city's top attractions. It can be easily reached by walking down the slope from Topkapı's First Court, or by walking up the hill from the main gate of Gülhane Park.

The complex is divided into three buildings: the Archaeology Museum (Arkeoloji Müzesi), the Museum of the Ancient Orient (Eski Şark Eserler Müzesi) and the Tiled Pavilion (Çinili Köşk). These museums house the palace collections formed during the late 19th century by museum director, artist and archaeologist Osman Hamdi Bey and added to greatly since the republic. While not immediately as dazzling as Topkapı, they contain a wealth of artefacts from the 50 centuries of Anatolia's history. Excellent interpretive panels are in both Turkish and English. A board at the entrance lists which of the exhibits are open on the day.

The first building on your left as you enter the museum complex is the Museum of the Ancient Orient. Overlooking the park, it was designed by Alexander Vallaury and built in 1883 to house the Academy of Fine Arts. It displays Anatolian pieces (from Hittite empires) as well as pre-Islamic items collected from the expanse of the Ottoman Empire. You can't miss the series of large glazed-brick panels depicting various animals such as lions and bulls. These beautiful blue-and-yellow panels lined the processional street and the Ishtar gate of ancient Babylon from the time of Nebuchadnezzar II (605–562 BC). Other treats here are the amazing 3rd to 1st century BC alabaster statue heads from Yemen and the oldest surviving political treaty: a copy of the Kadesh Treaty drawn up in the 13th century BC between the Egyptians and Hittites.

On the opposite side of the courtyard is the Archaeology Museum, housed in an imposing neoclassical building. The major building in the complex, it features an extensive collection of Hellenic, Hellenistic and Roman statuary and sarcophagi.

A Roman statue of Bes, an impish half-god of inexhaustible power and strength who was thought to protect against evil, greets you as you enter the main entrance of the museum. Turn left and walk into the dimly lit rooms beyond, where the museum's major treasures – sarcophagi from the Royal Necropolis of Sidon and surrounding area – are displayed. These sarcophagi were unearthed in 1887 by Osman Hamdi Bey in Sidon (Side in modern-day Lebanon). As soon as they were discovered, the sarcophagi were swiftly whisked out of the country in a complex operation that involved them being carried on rails laid to the coast and then rafted out to sea, where they were hoisted onto ships and brought to İstanbul. You will see a sarcophagus that is Egyptian in origin; it was later reused by King Tabnit of Sidon. Also here is a beautifully preserved Lycian sarcophagus made from Paros marble dating from the end of the 5th century. It depicts horses, centaurs and human figures with beautifully rendered expressions on their faces. Next to this is the Satrap sarcophagus with its everyday scenes featuring the provincial governor. After admiring these, pass into the next room to see one of the most accomplished of all classical artworks, the famous marble Alexander sarcophagus – so named not because it belonged to the Macedonian general, but because it depicts him among his army battling the Persians (long pants, material headwear), who were led by King Abdalonymos and whose sarcophagus it was. Truly exquisite, it is carved out of Pentelic marble and dates from the last quarter of the 4th century BC. Alexander, on horseback, has a lion's head as a headdress. Remarkably, the sculpture retains remnants of its original red-and-yellow paintwork. At the end of this room the Mourning Women sarcophagus also bears traces of its original paintwork. Its depiction of the women is stark and very moving.

Further on, you'll find an impressive collection of ancient grave cult sarcophagi from Syria, Lebanon, Thessalonica and Ephesus. Beyond that is a room called 'The Columned Sarcophagi of Anatolia', filled with amazingly detailed sarcophagi dating from between 140 and 270 AD. Many of these look like tiny temples or residential buildings; don't miss the Sidamara Sarcophagus from Konya.

Further rooms contain examples of Anatolian architecture from antiquity and Lycian monuments.

Turn back and retrace your steps towards the statue of Bes. The underwhelming 'Anatolia and Troy Through the Ages' and 'Neighbouring Cultures of Anatolia, Cyprus, Syria and Palestine' exhibitions are accessed via a staircase between the rooms housing the Alexander and Satrap sarcophagi; there are also toilets here.

Returning to Bes, you should then enter the first of the museum's statuary galleries. It and the adjacent rooms exhibit a selection of fine works, including a delicate Attic horse's head. Slightly further in, Alexander makes another appearance – you'll see heads and a statue from the Hellenistic period. Other works to look out for include the Ephebos of Tralles, a statue of a young athlete wrapped in a cape and leaning against a pillar; the stunning head of the poetess Sappho, a copy of an original from the Hellenistic period; and the exquisite head of a child from Pergamum.

Artisans at Anatolia's three main sculpture centres – Aphrodisias, Ephesus and Miletus – turned out thousands of beautiful works, some of which have been collected in Room 10. There's a beautiful relief from Aphrodisias showing the struggle of Athena and the Giants, and a statue from Miletus showing Apollo wearing ornate sandals and playing a lyre. The last room has examples of sculpture from throughout the Roman Empire. Check out the delicately carved draperies on the Roman statue of Cornelia Antonia, which dates from the second half of the 2nd century AD.

In the annexe behind the cloak room there is an unimpressive mock-up of the facade of the Temple of Athena at Assos (Behramkale). On the mezzanine level above the Temple of Athena is a dusty but interesting exhibition called İstanbul Through the Ages that traces the city's history through its neighbourhoods during different periods: Archaic, Hellenistic, Roman, Byzantine and Ottoman. The exhibition continues downstairs, where there is an impressive gallery showcasing Byzantine artefacts and a fascinating exhibit entitled In the Light of Day, which focuses on the archaeological excavations associated with the Marmaray transport project (boxed text p218). The section about the excavation of the Byzantine harbour and boats at Yenikapı is particularly interesting.

While children will be bored stiff with the naff dioramas of early Anatolian life in the Children's Museum on the ground floor of the museum, they are likely to enjoy climbing into the large-scale model of the Trojan Horse.

The last of the complex's museum buildings is the Tiled Pavilion (Çinili Köşk) of Sultan Mehmet the Conqueror. Thought to be the oldest surviving nonreligious Turkish building in İstanbul, it was built in 1472 as an outer pavilion of Topkapı Palace and was used for watching sporting events. The re-cessed doorway area is covered with tiles – some with white calligraphy (sülüus) on blue. The geometric patterns and colour of the tiles – turquoise, white and black – on the facade show obvious Seljuk influence. The portico, with its 14 marble columns, was constructed during the reign of Abdülhamid I (1774–89) after the original one burned down in 1737.

On display here is the best collection of Seljuk, Anatolian and Ottoman tiles and ceramics in the country; these date from the end of the 12th century to the beginning of the 20th century. The collection includes İznik tiles from the period between the mid-14th and 17th centuries when that city produced the finest coloured tiles in the world. When you enter the central room you can't miss the stunning mihrab from the İbrahim Bey Mosque in Karaman, built in 1432. Also of note is the pretty peacock-adorned fountain recessed into the wall in the room to the left at the back of the kiosk; this dates from 1590.

## GÜLHANE PARK Map pp50–1
Gülhane Parkı; 🚇 Gülhane
Gülhane Park was once the outer garden of Topkapı Palace. Today crowds of locals come here at weekends to picnic under the many trees, admire the formally planted flowerbeds and enjoy wonderful views over the Golden Horn and Sea of Marmara. Recent beautification works have seen improvements to walkways and amenities, and have included the opening of a new museum, the İstanbul Museum of the History of Science & Technology in Islam (admission TL5; 🕙 9am-5pm Wed-Mon), which is housed in the former palace stables. Its didactic exhibition argues that Islamic advances in science and technology preceded and greatly influenced those in Europe. Most of the exhibits are reconstructions of historical instruments and tools. Rumour has it that the nearby barracks building is being considered as the new home of the Military Museum (Askeri Müze, p112).

Up the hill at the far (north) end of the park is a series of terraces occupied by a tea garden, the Set Üstü Çay Bahçesi (p163). It offers superb water views and is a lovely spot to while away an hour or two.

Next to the south exit is a bulbous little kiosk built into the park wall. Known as the Alay Köşkü (Parade Kiosk), this is where the

## GREAT PALACE OF BYZANTIUM

Constantine the Great built the Great Palace soon after he founded Constantinople in AD 324. Successive Byzantine leaders left their mark by adding to it, and the complex eventually consisted of hundreds of buildings enclosed by walls and set in terraced parklands stretching from the Hippodrome over to Haghia Sofia (Aya Sofya) and down the slope, ending at the sea walls on the Sea of Marmara. The palace was finally abandoned after the Fourth Crusade sacked the city in 1204, and its ruins were pillaged and filled in after the Conquest, becoming mere foundations of much of Sultanahmet and Cankurtaran.

Various pieces of the Great Palace have been uncovered – many by budding hotelier 'archaeologists'. The mosaics in the Great Palace Mosaics Museum (p57) once graced the floor of the complex, and excavations at the Sultanahmet Archaeological Park in Babıhümayun Caddesi, southeast of Aya Sofya, have uncovered other parts of the palace. Controversially, some of these excavations are being subsumed into a new extension of the neighbouring luxury Four Seasons Hotel.

For more information, check out www.byzantium1200.com, which has 3D images that bring ancient Byzantium to life, or purchase a copy of the lavishly illustrated guidebook *Walking Through Byzantium: Great Palace Region*, which was also produced as part of the Byzantium 1200 project. You'll find it in shops around Sultanahmet. Also of interest is the project's exhibition in the Byzantine Binbirdirek Cistern (below).

sultan would sit and watch the periodic parades of troops and trade guilds that commemorated great holidays and military victories. It is now the İstanbul headquarters of the Ministry of Culture and Tourism.

Across the street and 100m northwest of the park's main gate is an outrageously curvaceous rococo gate leading into the precincts of what was once the grand vizierate, or Ottoman prime ministry, known in the West as the Sublime Porte. Today the buildings beyond the gate hold various offices of the İstanbul provincial government (the Vilayeti).

### SOĞUKÇEŞME SOKAK Map pp50–1
Sultanahmet or Gülhane

Soğukçeşme Sokak, or Street of the Cold Fountain, runs between the Topkapı Palace walls and Aya Sofya. In the 1980s, the Turkish Touring & Automobile Association (Turing) acquired a row of buildings on the street and decided to demolish most of them to build nine re-creations of the prim Ottoman-style houses that had occupied the site in the previous two centuries. What ensued was a vitriolic battle played out on the pages of İstanbul's newspapers, with some experts arguing that the city would be left with a Disney-style architectural theme park rather than a legitimate exercise in conservation architecture. Turing eventually got the go-ahead (after the intervention of the Turkish president, no less) and in time opened all of the re-created buildings as Ayasofya Konakları (p191), one of the first boutique heritage hotels

in the city. Conservation theory aside, the colourful buildings and cobbled street are particularly picturesque and worth wandering past.

### CAFERAĞA MEDRESESİ Map pp50–1
212-513 3601; Caferiye Sokak; admission free; 8.30am-7pm; Sultanahmet

This lovely little building, which is tucked away in the shadows of Aya Sofya, was designed by Sinan on the orders of Cafer Ağa, Süleyman the Magnificent's chief black eunuch. Built in 1560 as a school for Islamic and secular education, today it is home to the Turkish Cultural Services Foundation (p223), which runs workshops in traditional Ottoman arts such as calligraphy, *ebru* (traditional Turkish marbling) and miniature painting. Some of the arts and crafts produced here are for sale and there's a pleasant lokanta (see p149) in the courtyard.

### BİNBİRDİREK CISTERN Map pp50–1
Cistern of 1001 Columns, Binbirdirek Sarnıcı; 212-518 1001; www.binbirdirek.com; İmran Öktem Sokak 4, Binbirdirek; admission TL10 incl 1 drink; 9am-7pm summer, 9am-6pm winter; Sultanahmet

Constantine the Great (r 324–37) built Binbirdirek in AD 330. During Ottoman times it was converted into a *han* (caravanserai) for silk manufacturers. Closed for decades, it was restored a few years ago and functions as a cafe and venue for exhibitions, functions and concerts. Nowhere near as impressive as the Basilica Cistern (largely because it has been emptied of its water reserves and has a false floor), it's not really worth the admission price.

## SİRKECİ RAILWAY STATION Map pp50–1

Sirkeci İstasyonu; Ankara Caddesi, Sirkeci; 🚇 Sirkeci

The romance of the *Orient Express* and other locomotives of the era was reflected in the design for this train station, built as the terminus of European routes between 1888 and 1890. Designed by German architect August Jachmund, it is an excellent example of Islamic Eclecticism, an architectural movement introduced into İstanbul by European architects at the end of the 19th century. The structure replaced one of the Topkapı Palace pavilions and it reflects this Ottoman heritage, though its clock tower, arches and large rose windows clearly mirror the neoclassicism popular in Europe at the time. At the time of research the station was still functioning as the city's terminus for European routes, but its future was uncertain.

At the time of writing, dervishes had been conducting a tourism-oriented sema (whirling ceremony; ☎ information & bookings 212-511 4626/36; adult/student under 24yr TL35/25) in the exhibition hall on platform 1 at 7.30pm every Friday and Sunday. The Marmaray project (boxed text p218) may put an end to this, though.

# UNCOVERING BYZANTIUM
## Walking Tour

**1 Aya Sofya** This venerable church (p49) is the most famous Byzantine building in Turkey. The soaring dome, gleaming gold mosaics and innumerable stained-glass windows give it an extraordinary sense of space, mystery and majesty.

**2 Basilica Cistern** There are a number of Byzantine cisterns in the Old City, but this cistern (p54), which was built by order of Justinian, is by far the most impressive. It lay underneath the Stoa Basilica, one of the great squares on the first hill, and was used to store water for the Great Palace (see the boxed text p69).

**3 The Hippodrome** The Byzantine emperors loved nothing more than an afternoon at the chariot races, and this rectangular arena (p57) built by Emperor Septimius Severus (c

## WALK FACTS

Start Aya Sofya
End Sultanahmet Archaeological Park
Duration Four hours
Fuel stops Everywhere you look

145–211 AD) was their venue of choice. Stand in the centre and imagine horse-drawn chariots storming around the perimeter, cheered on by raucous crowds in tiered seating areas.

**4 Kadırga Limanı Meydanı** This large public square is a popular neighbourhood meeting place. Its name means 'Galley Port', a nod to the fact that in Byzantine times it was a seaport. Built by the emperor Julian the Apostate in 362 AD, it silted up in Ottoman times. If you're hungry, consider having a cheap and cheerful meal at İmren Lokantası (p151) on the square's north side.

**5 Little Aya Sofya** After being listed on the World Monument Fund's register of endangered buildings, Little Aya Sofya (p76) has been restored and is looking terrific. Justinian and Theodora, who built it between 527 and 536 BC, would be thrilled if they saw it today. It was converted to a mosque after the Conquest.

**6 Palace of Bucoleon** A vine-covered ruin on the seafront is all that's left of this Byzantine structure, one of the sea-facing buildings of the Great Palace. What you can see is the eastern loggia, with three marble-framed windows and a vaulted room beyond them. These ruins are the only above-ground parts of the palace still in existence.

**7 Constantine's Sea Walls** From the Bucoleon, follow the (sadly deteriorated and partly demolished) Byzantine sea walls east along manic Kennedy Caddesi. Built by Constantine, these fortifications originally stretched from Samatya (where the land walls started) to the Golden Horn and functioned as Byzantium's major maritime defence system. Turn left into the first opening in the walls at Ahırkapı Sokak, turn left and walk up the hill to reach the Arasta Bazaar (p132).

**8 Great Palace Mosaics Museum** Accessed on the east side of the Arasta Bazaar, the huge mosaic on show at this museum (p57) once graced part of the floor of the Great

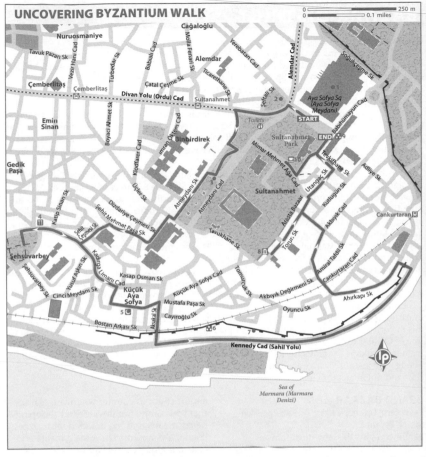

# UNCOVERING BYZANTIUM WALK

Palace. Mosaic images of donkeys, tigers, hunters and landscapes were miraculously preserved under the soil of centuries and are now on show after excavation and restoration work.

**9 Sultanahmet Archaeological Park** This archaeological site behind the Four Seasons Hotel Istanbul encompasses Byzantine ruins including a street with wastewater canal, a small hypocast (centrally heated) bath, a

mosaic floor and the remains of the main entrance to the Great Palace, the Bronze Gate (Khalke Pule).

**10 Tea and Nargileh** Footsore? Relax under the trees at the Derviş Aile Çay Bahçesi (p163), famous for its peerless view of the Blue Mosque (p56). Or if you're in need of something a little stronger, the charming courtyard bar/cafe at the Yeşil Ev Garden Bar/Cafe (p163) is just around the corner.

71

# BAZAAR DISTRICT

Drinking p164; Eating p149; Shopping p134

As well as being home to two world-famous bazaars – one grand and one full of spices – this district is also where you'll find the frantically busy shopping precinct of Tahtakale, located behind and to the west of the Spice Bazaar. Here, vendors with carts full of everything from *simits* (bread rings) to strawberries make their way through narrow streets full of shoppers, delivery vans and tourists valiantly fighting their way through the chaos.

At the top of a hill rising from the Golden Horn is the city's first and most evocative shopping mall – the venerable Grand Bazaar (Kapalı Çarşı, below), established during the rule of Mehmet the Conqueror (r 1451–81) and still going strong. Getting lost in its maze of laneways is obligatory for all first-time visitors; those who have visited previously are quick to gravitate towards their favourite shops and cafes.

Near the bazaar are three great Ottoman mosques: the splendid Süleymaniye Mosque (p76), the dignified Beyazıt Mosque (p79), and the charming Şehzade Mehmet Mosque (p80). All three provide wonderfully contemplative spaces to escape from the mercantile madness of the surrounding streets. The Süleymaniye gives its name to the suburb surrounding it and although the official name for the square on which Beyazıt Mosque is located is Hürriyet Meydanı, everyone in town knows it as Beyazıt Sq.

On the square is İstanbul University, one of the city's premier institutions of learning. This brings lots of students into this neighbourhood and they enliven it considerably, outnumbering the bazaar crowds in the many local *çay bahçesi* (tea gardens) and fast-food joints. If you want to sample the delights of a nargileh (water pipe; the local equivalent of a drink after work), places such as Lale Bahçesi (p164) and Erenler Çay Bahçesi (p164) are where you should head.

The neighbourhood is sliced into north and south halves by Ordu Caddesi, the western continuation of Divan Yolu Caddesi. The tramline between Zeytinburnu and Kabataş runs along this major road, and there are two tram stops: Laleli-Üniversite and Beyazıt. On the southern side of Ordu Caddesi are the residential suburbs leading down to the Sea of Marmara. These include Kumkapı – famous for its fish market and fish restaurants – Gedik Paşa and Kadırga. Though not as conservative as some parts of Sultanahmet, these suburbs are resolutely working class and not at all affluent.

## GRAND BAZAAR  Map p75
**Kapalı Çarşı, Covered Market;** 9am-7pm Mon-Sat; Beyazıt

Before you visit this, the most famous *souq* in the world, make sure you prepare yourself properly. First, make sure you're in a good mood and ready to swap friendly banter with the hundreds of shopkeepers who will attempt to lure you into their establishments. There's no use getting tetchy with the touts here – this is their turf and it would be delusional of you to think that you're anything more than putty in their hands (and liras in their cash registers). Second, allow enough time to look into every nook and cranny, drink innumerable cups of tea, compare price after price and try your hand at the art of bargaining. Shoppers have been doing this here for centuries and, frankly, it would be unbecoming for you to do any less; for tips on bargaining, see p130. And third: never, ever forget your baggage allowance. There's nothing worse than that sinking feeling at the

airport check-in counter when you realise that your Grand Bazaar–induced shopping frenzy means that the dreaded term 'excess baggage' is about to become a reality and test your already sorely abused credit card to its limits.

The bazaar is the heart of the city in much more than a geographical sense and has been so for centuries. With over 4000 shops and several kilometres of lanes, as well as mosques, banks, police stations, restaurants and workshops, it's a covered city all of its own. Though there's no doubt that it's a tourist trap *par excellence,* it's also a place where business deals are done between locals, and where import/export businesses flourish. And it also functions as the nucleus of a large commercial neighbourhood, with most of the surrounding streets (Mahmutpaşa Yokuşu is a good example) catering to every conceivable local shopping need.

Starting from a small masonry *bedesten* (warehouse) built in the time of Mehmet

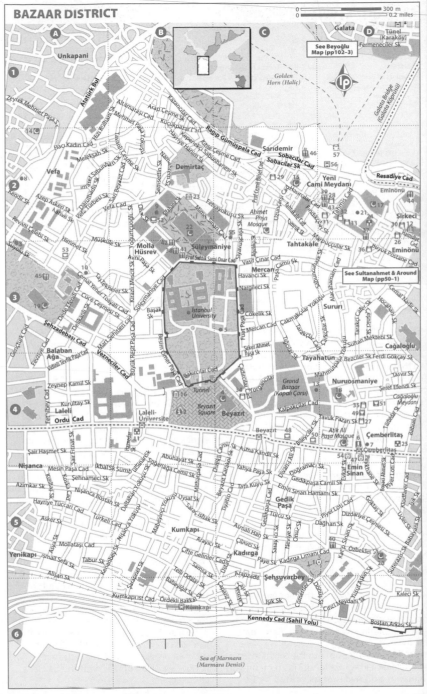

# BAZAAR DISTRICT

the Conqueror, the bazaar grew to cover a vast area as neighbouring shopkeepers decided to put up roofs and porches so that commerce could be conducted comfortably in all types of weather. Finally, a system of locked gates and doors was provided so that the entire mini-city could be closed up tight at the end of the business day. Street names refer to trades and crafts: Kuyumcular Caddesi (Jewellers St) and İnciciler Sokağı (Pearl Merchants St) are two that you're bound to walk down. Large sections of the bazaar have been destroyed by fire and earthquake a number of times in its history (most recently in 1954), but have always been rebuilt.

Just inside the Nuruosmaniye Kapısı (Nuruosmaniye door), on the southeast corner of the market, you'll find a glittering street filled with the stores of gold merchants. This is called Kalpakçılarbaşı Caddesi and it's the closest thing the bazaar has to a main street. Most of the bazaar is on your right (north) in the crazy maze of tiny streets and alleys. You'll inevitably get lost when exploring them, but hey, that's part of the fun!

Make sure you pop into the Sandal Bedesten off Kalpakçılarbaşı Caddesi. This rectangular hall with a domed roof supported by 12

large pillars is also called the Yeni Bedesten (New Warehouse), as it was built after Mehmet's central bedesten, some time in the 17th century.

The Old Bazaar, also known as Cevahir Bedesteni (Jewellery Warehouse), is at the centre of the market. Thought to be the first building Mehmet the Conqueror built, its structure is similar to that of the Sandal Bedesten. Inside, you'll find innumerable small shops selling quality jewellery, silver, ceramics and antiques.

When wandering, seek out north–south Sipahi Caddesi and its famous Şark Kahvesi (p164), a worn-out but charming relic of Old İstanbul whose walls feature quirky images of dervishes on flying carpets. This is a great place to linger over a game of backgammon and a few glasses of tea. Other places that make good coffee and tea stops in the bazaar are Fes Café (p164) and Ay Café (p164).

In the bazaar itself, the most comfortable dining spot is Havuzlu Restaurant (p150), located in a han near the PTT in Gani Çelebi Sokak; for a quick snack, join the locals in claiming a stool and noshing on a quick kebap at Burç Ocakbaşı (p151). Two nearby lokantas – Subaşı Lokantası (p150) and Sefa Restaurant (p148) – are also popular with the bazaar's shopkeepers.

# GRAND BAZAAR (KAPALI ÇARŞI)

0 ⊏══════ 50 m

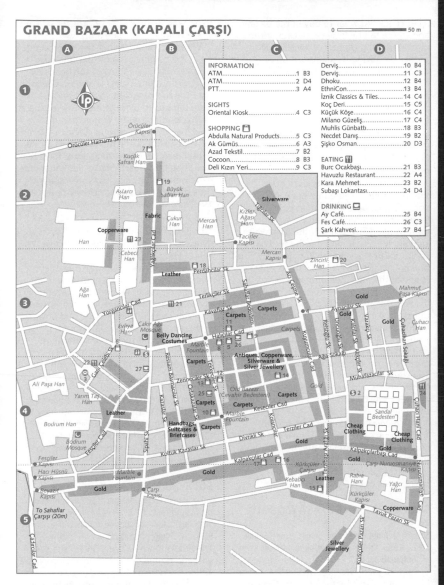

| INFORMATION | |
|---|---|
| ATM...........................1 B3 |
| ATM...........................2 D4 |
| PTT............................3 A4 |
| | |
| SIGHTS | |
| Oriental Kiosk..................4 C3 |
| | |
| SHOPPING | |
| Abdulla Natural Products.......5 C3 |
| Ak Gümüş.....................6 A3 |
| Azad Tekstil...................7 B2 |
| Cocoon........................8 B3 |
| Deli Kızın Yeri.................9 C3 |

| | |
|---|---|
| Derviş........................10 B4 |
| Derviş........................11 C3 |
| Dhoku.......................12 B4 |
| EthniCon....................13 B4 |
| İznik Classics & Tiles........14 C4 |
| Koç Deri.....................15 C5 |
| Küçük Köşe..................16 C4 |
| Milano Güzeliş...............17 C4 |
| Muhlis Günbattı.............18 B3 |
| Necdet Danış................19 B2 |
| Şişko Osman.................20 D3 |
| | |
| EATING | |
| Burc Ocakbaşı...............21 B3 |
| Havuzlu Restaurant..........22 A4 |
| Kara Mehmet.................23 B2 |
| Subaşı Lokantası.............24 D4 |
| | |
| DRINKING | |
| Ay Café......................25 B4 |
| Fes Café.....................26 C3 |
| Şark Kahvesi.................27 B4 |

Near the junction of Halıcılar Caddesi and Kuyumcular Caddesi you'll find the crooked Oriental Kiosk, which was built as a coffee house and now functions as a jewellery shop. North from here, up Acı Çeşme Sokak, is the gorgeous pink Zincirli Han, home to one of the bazaar's most famous carpet dealers, Şişko Osman (p136).

Bibliophiles will want to head towards Sahaflar Çarşısı (Old Book Bazaar; Map p73), which is found in a shady little court-yard west of the bazaar at the end of Kalpakçılarbaşı Caddesi. The book bazaar dates from Byzantine times. Its stallholders sell wares both new and old, and though it's unlikely you'll uncover any underpriced antique treasures, you'll certainly be able to find old engravings, a curiosity or two, phrasebooks and books on İstanbul and Turkish culture in several languages.

To check out what to buy in the bazaar and where to buy it, see p134. One of the most intriguing aspects of a visit to the bazaar is noticing its juxtaposition of tourist tat and precious objects, proving the point that the place really does cater to every possible shopping desire!

## LITTLE AYA SOFYA Map p73

Küçük Aya Sofya Camii, SS Sergius & Bacchus Church; ☎ 212-458 0776; Küçük Aya Sofya Caddesi; donation requested; 🚇 Sultanahmet or Çemberlitaş

Justinian and his wife Theodora built this little church sometime between 527 and 536 (just before Justinian built Aya Sofya) and you can still see their monogram worked into some of the frilly white capitals. It was named after the two patron saints of Christians in the Roman army. The building, which has recently been restored, is one of the most beautiful in the city. Its dome is architecturally noteworthy and its plan – an irregular octagon – is quite unusual. Like Aya Sofya (p49), its interior was originally decorated with gold mosaics and featured columns made from fine green and red marble. The mosaics are long gone, but the impressive columns remain. The church was converted into a mosque by the chief white eunuch Hüseyin Ağa around 1500; his tomb is to the north of the building.

The *medrese* cells, arranged around the mosque's forecourt, are now used by second-hand booksellers and bookbinders. In the leafy forecourt there is a tranquil çay bahçesi (tea garden) where you can relax over a glass of tea.

## SOKOLLU MEHMET PAŞA MOSQUE
Map p73

Sokollu Mehmet Paşa Camii; Şehit Çeşmesi Sokak 20-22, Küçük Aya Sofya; donation requested; 🚇 Sultanahmet

Sinan designed this mosque in 1571, at the height of his architectural career. Though named after the grand vizier of the time, it was really sponsored by his wife Esmahan, daughter of Sultan Selim II. Besides its architectural harmony, typical of Sinan's greatest works, the mosque is unusual because the *medrese* is not a separate building but actually part of the mosque structure, built around the forecourt. If the mosque isn't open, wait for the guardian

to appear; he may offer photos for sale and will certainly appreciate a tip.

When you enter, notice the harmonious form, the coloured marble and the spectacular İznik tiles – some of the best ever made. The stained glass is also particularly fine. The mosque contains four fragments from the sacred Black Stone in the Kaaba at Mecca: one above the entrance framed in gold, two in the *mimber* and one in the mihrab. Interestingly, the marble pillars by the mihrab revolve if the foundations have been disturbed by an earthquake – an ingenious early warning device – though apparently they didn't move during the earthquake of 1999 as one was 'out of order'!

## NURUOSMANİYE MOSQUE Map p73

Nuruosmaniye Camii, Light of Osman Mosque; Vezir Hanı Caddesi; 🚇 Beyazıt

Facing Nuruosmaniye Kapısı, one of several doorways into the Grand Bazaar, this mosque was built in Ottoman baroque style between 1748 and 1755. Construction was started by Mahmut I and finished by his successor Osman III. Though it was meant to exhibit the sultans' 'modern' taste, the baroque building has very strong echoes of Aya Sofya, specifically the broad, lofty dome, colonnaded mezzanine galleries, windows topped with Roman arches and the broad band of calligraphy around the interior. Despite its prominent position on the busy pedestrian route from Cağaloğlu Sq and Nuruosmaniye Caddesi to the bazaar, it is surprisingly peaceful and contemplative inside.

## SÜLEYMANİYE MOSQUE Map p73

Süleymaniye Camii, Mosque of Sultan Süleyman the Magnificent; ☎ 212-514 0139; Prof Sıddık Sami Onar Caddesi; donation requested; 🕙 tombs 9.30am-5.30pm; 🚇 Beyazıt

The Süleymaniye crowns one of the seven hills and dominates the Golden Horn, providing a landmark for the entire city. It was commissioned by the greatest, richest and most powerful of Ottoman sultans, Süleyman I (r 1520–66), known as 'The Magnificent', and was the fourth imperial mosque built in İstanbul, following the Fatih, Beyazıt and Selim I complexes.

Though it's not the largest of the Ottoman mosques, the Süleymaniye is certainly the grandest. It was designed by Mimar Sinan, the most famous and talented of all imperial architects. Though Sinan described the smaller Selimiye Camii in Edirne as his best work, he chose to be buried here in the Süleymaniye complex, probably knowing that this would be the building that he would be best remembered for. His *türbe* is just outside the mosque's walled garden, next to the *medrese* building.

The mosque was built between 1550 and 1557; records show that 3523 craftspeople worked on its construction. Though it's seen some hard times, being damaged by fire in 1660 and having its wonderful columns covered by cement and oil paint at some point after this, restorations in 1956 and 2009 mean that it's in great shape these days. It's also one of the most popular mosques in the city, with worshippers rivalling the Blue and New Mosques in number.

The mosque's setting and plan are particularly pleasing, featuring gardens and a three-sided forecourt with a central domed ablutions fountain. Its four minarets with their beautiful balconies are said to represent the fact that Süleyman was the fourth of the Osmanlı sultans to rule the city.

Inside, the mosque is breathtaking in its size and pleasing in its simplicity. It is also remarkably light. Sinan's design is particularly ingenious due to the fact that the buttresses used to support the four columns are incorporated into the walls of the building, masked by galleries with arcades of columns running between the buttresses. Put simply, the architect, ever challenged by the technical accomplishments of Aya Sofya, took the floor plan of that church and here perfected its adaptation to the requirements of Muslim worship.

There is little interior decoration other than some very fine İznik tiles in the mihrab, gorgeous stained-glass windows done by one İbrahim the Drunkard, and four massive columns – one from Baalbek in modern-day Lebanon, one from Alexandria and two from Byzantine palaces in İstanbul. The painted arabesques on the dome are 19th-century additions. If you visit when the stairs to the gallery on the northeast side (ie facing the Golden Horn) are open, make sure you go upstairs and out to the balcony. The views from this vantage point are among the best in the city.

The *külliye* (mosque complex) of the Süleymaniye, which is outside the walled garden, is particularly elaborate, with the full complement of public services: soup kitchen, hostel, library, hospital etc. Today the *imaret* (soup kitchen), with its charming garden courtyard, houses the Dârüzziyafe Restaurant, which is a lovely place to enjoy a *çay* (tea). Lale Bahçesi (p164), located in a sunken courtyard next to Dârüzziyafe, is an atmospheric venue for *çay* and nargileh. Both it and the nearby Erzincanı Alı Baba Fasulyeci (p151) are extremely popular with students and locals. Those in need of an energy boost could make the short trip to Vefa Bozacısı (p164), the most famous place in the city to sample *boza*, the İstanbullu tonic drink made with fermented grain.

The mosque's *hamam* still functions.

Near the southeast wall of the mosque is the cemetery, home to the tombs of Süleyman and his wife Haseki Hürrem Sultan (Roxelana). The tilework in both is superb. In Süleyman's tomb, little jewel-like lights in the dome are surrogate stars. In Roxelana's tomb, the many tile panels of flowers and the delicate stained glass produce a serene effect. You are required to take off your shoes, cover your heads and shoulders (women only) and give a donation to enter both.

## SPICE BAZAAR Map p73
Mısır Çarşısı, Egyptian Market; ⊗ 8.30am-6.30pm Mon-Sat; Ⓜ Eminönü

Need a herbal love potion or natural Turkish Viagra? This is the place to find them, although we won't vouch for the efficacy of either! As well as *baharat* (spices), nuts, honey in the comb and olive-oil soaps, the bustling spice bazaar sells truckloads of *incir* (figs), *lokum* (Turkish delight) and *pestil* (fruit pressed into sheets and dried). The number of shops selling tourist trinkets increases annually, yet this remains a great place to stock up on edible souvenirs, share a few jokes with the vendors and marvel at the well-preserved building. It's also home to one of the city's oldest restaurants, Pandeli, and an attractive competitor, Bab-i Hayat (p150).

The market was constructed in the 1660s as part of the New Mosque (Yeni Cami) complex (p78); the rent from the shops supported the upkeep of the mosque and its charitable activities, which included a school, baths, hospital and public fountains. The name 'Egyptian Market' comes from the fact that the building was initially endowed with taxes levied on goods imported from Egypt. In its heyday, the market was the last stop for the camel caravans that travelled the Silk Routes from China, India and Persia.

Between the market and the New Mosque is the city's major outdoor market for flowers, plants, seeds and songbirds. There's a toilet *(tuvalet)* down a flight of stairs, subject to a small fee.

On the west side of the market there are outdoor produce stalls selling fresh foodstuff from all over Anatolia. Also here is the most famous coffee supplier in İstanbul, Kurukahveci Mehmet Efendi Mahdumları (p134), established over 100 years ago. It is located on the corner of Hasırcılar Caddesi, which is full of shops selling foodstuffs and kitchenwares.

## MOSQUE OF RÜSTEM PAŞA Map p73
Rüstem Paşa Camii; ☎ 212-526 7350; Hasırcılar Caddesi; ⓡ Eminönü

Plonked in the middle of the busy Tahtakale district, this little-visited mosque is a gem. Built in 1560 by Sinan for Rüstem Paşa, son-in-law and grand vizier of Süleyman the Magnificent, it is a showpiece of the best Ottoman architecture and tilework, albeit on a small scale. It is thought to have been the prototype for Sinan's greatest work, the Selimiye in Edirne.

At the top of the two sets of entry steps there is a terrace and the mosque's colonnaded porch. You'll notice at once the panels of İznik faïence set into the mosque's facade. The interior is covered in similarly gorgeous tiles and features a lovely dome, supported by four tiled pillars.

The preponderance of tiles was Rüstem Paşa's way of signalling his wealth and influence – İznik tiles being particularly expensive and desirable. It may not have assisted his passage into the higher realm, though, because by all accounts he was a loathsome character. His contemporaries dubbed him Kehle-i-Ikbal (the Louse of Fortune) because he was found to be infected with lice on the eve of his marriage to Mihrimah, Süleyman's favourite daughter. He is best remembered for plotting with Roxelana to turn Süleyman against his favourite son, Mustafa. They were successful and Mustafa was strangled in 1553 on his father's orders.

The mosque is easy to miss because it's not at street level. There's a set of access stairs on Hasırcılar Caddesi and another on the small street that runs right (north) off Hasırcılar Caddesi to the Golden Horn.

## NEW MOSQUE Map p73
Yeni Cami; ☎ 212-527 8505; Yenicami Meydanı Sokak, Eminönü; donation requested; ⓡ Eminönü

Only in İstanbul would a 400-year-old mosque be called 'New'. The Yeni Camii was begun in 1597, commissioned by Valide Sultan Safiye, mother of Sultan Mehmet III (r 1595–1603). The site was earlier occupied by a community of Karaite Jews, radical dissenters from Orthodox Judaism. When the *valide sultan* decided to build her grand mosque here, the Karaites were moved to Hasköy, a district further up the Golden Horn that still bears traces of their presence.

Safiye lost her august position when her son died and the mosque was completed six sultans later in 1663 by Valide Sultan Turhan Hadice, mother of Sultan Mehmet IV (r 1648–87).

In plan, the New Mosque is much like the Blue Mosque (p56) and the Süleymaniye Mosque (p76), with a large forecourt and a square sanctuary surmounted by a series of semidomes crowned by a grand dome. The interior is richly decorated with gold, coloured İznik tiles and carved marble. It also has an impressive mihrab.

The mosque was created after Ottoman architecture had reached its peak. Consequently, even its tiles are slightly inferior products, the late 17th century having seen a diminution in the quality of the products coming out of the İznik workshops. You will see this if you compare these tiles with the exquisite examples found in the nearby Rüstem Paşa Mosque (left), which are from the high period of İznik tilework. Nonetheless, it is a popular working mosque and a much-loved adornment to the city skyline.

Across the road from the mosque is the tomb of Valide Sultan Turhan Hadice, the woman who completed construction of the New Mosque. Buried with her are no fewer than six sultans, including her son Mehmet IV, plus dozens of imperial princes and princesses. Further east, on Hamidiye Caddesi, are two of the best places in town to buy fresh Turkish delight, Hafız Mustafa Şekerlemeleri (p134) and Ali Muhiddin Hacı Bekir (p134).

## GALATA BRIDGE Map p73
Galata Köprüsü; ⓡ Eminönü or Karaköy

Nothing is quite as evocative as walking across the Galata Bridge at sunset, when the Galata Tower (p105) is surrounded by shrieking seagulls and the mosques atop the seven hills of the city are thrown into relief against a soft red-pink sky. During the day, the bridge carries a constant flow of İstanbullus crossing to and from Beyoğlu and Eminönü, a handful or two of hopeful anglers trailing their lines into the waters below, and a constantly changing procession of street vendors hawking everything from fresh-baked *simits* to Rolex rip-offs. This is İstanbul at its most magical.

Underneath the bridge, touristy restaurants and cafes serve drinks and food all day and night. Come here to inhale the evocative scent of apple tobacco wafting out of the nargileh cafes and to watch the passing parade of ferries zooming past. There's even a shop selling fishing equipment for those who aspire to emulate the anglers up on the bridge.

The present, quite ugly, bridge was built in 1992 to replace an iron structure dating from 1909 to 1912, which in turn had replaced two earlier structures. The iron bridge was famous for the ramshackle fish restaurants, teahouses and nargileh joints that occupied the dark recesses beneath its roadway, but it had a major flaw: it floated on pontoons that blocked the natural flow of water and kept the Golden Horn from flushing itself free of pollution. In the late 1980s the municipality started to draw up plans to replace it with a new bridge that would allow the water to flow. A fire expedited these plans in the early 1990s and the new bridge was built a short time afterwards. (The remains of the old, much-loved bridge were moved further up the Golden Horn near Hasköy.)

## ÇEMBERLİTAŞ Map p73
### Çemberlitaş
Close to the Çemberlitaş tram stop, in a plaza packed with pigeons, you'll find one of the city's most ancient and revered monuments: a derelict column known as Çemberlitaş (also known as the Hooped, Banded Stone or Burnt Column). Erected by Constantine to celebrate the dedication of Constantinople as capital of the Roman Empire In 330, the column was placed in what was the grand Forum of Constantine and was topped by a statue of the great emperor himself. The column lost its crowning statue of Constantine in 1106 and

was damaged in the 1779 fire that ravaged the nearby Grand Bazaar. It was covered in hoardings at the time of research (and had been for many years), but restoration works were underway.

Also in this vicinity is the historic Çemberlitaş Hamam (p185).

## BEYAZIT SQUARE Map p73
### Beyazıt
Beyazıt Sq is officially called Hürriyet Meydanı (Freedom Sq), though everyone knows it simply as Beyazıt. Under the rule of the Byzantines it was called the Forum of Theodosius. Sections of the forum's columns decorated with stylised oak-knot designs were dug up from the square during the 1950s and can be seen on the other side of Yeniçeriler Caddesi. Today the square is home to street vendors, students from İstanbul University and plenty of pigeons, as well as a few policemen who like to keep an eye on student activities.

The square is backed by the impressive portal of İstanbul University. After the Conquest, Mehmet the Conqueror built his first palace here, a wooden structure called the Eski Sarayı (Old Seraglio). After Topkapı was built the Eski Sarayı became home to women when they were pensioned out of the main palace – this was where *valide sultans* came when their sultan sons died and they lost their powerful position as head of the harem. The original building was demolished in the 19th century to make way for a grandiose Ministry of War complex designed by Auguste Bourgeois; this now houses the university. The stone Beyazıt Tower, visible from most of Old İstanbul, was built as a lookout for fires. Both the university and tower are off limits to travellers.

## BEYAZIT MOSQUE Map p73
**Beyazıt Camii, Mosque of Sultan Beyazıt II;**
☎ 212-519 3644; Yeniçeriler Caddesi; Beyazıt
Dating from 1501 to 1506, this was the second imperial mosque to be built in the city after Mehmet the Conqueror's Fatih Mosque (p85), and was the prototype for other imperial mosques. In effect, it is the link between Aya Sofya (p49), which obviously inspired its design, and the great mosques such as Süleymaniye (p76), which are realisations of Aya Sofya's design fully adapted to Muslim worship.

## İSTANBUL'S SEVEN HILLS

The famous minaret-studded skyline of the Old City is made distinctive by its seven hills, each of which is topped by a significant Byzantine structure or Ottoman Mosque:

| | |
|---|---|
| First Hill | Aya Sofya |
| Second Hill | Nuruosmaniye Mosque |
| Third Hill | Süleymaniye Mosque |
| Fourth Hill | Fatih Mosque |
| Fifth Hill | Sultan Selim Mosque |
| Sixth Hill | Mihrimah Sultan Mosque |
| Seventh Hill | Constantine's land walls |

Of note is the mosque's exceptional use of fine stone: marble, porphyry, verd antique and rare granite. The mihrab is simple, except for the rich stone columns framing it, and the courtyard, with its 24 small domes and central fountain, is pretty. Some of the other buildings of Beyazıt's *külliye* (mosque complex) have been well utilised. The soup kitchen has been turned into a library, while the *medrese* now houses the Museum of Turkish Calligraphic Art (closed for restoration at the time of research). Unfortunately the once-splendid *hamam* is still waiting to be restored. Beyazıt's *türbe* is behind the mosque.

### ŞEHZADE MEHMET MOSQUE Map p73

Şehzade Mehmet Camii, Mosque of the Prince; Şehzadebaşı Caddesi; Ⓜ Laleli-Üniversite

Süleyman the Magnificent built this mosque between 1543 and 1548 as a memorial to his son, Mehmet, who died of smallpox in 1543 at the age of 22. It was the first important mosque to be designed by Mimar Sinan. Although not one of his best works, it has two beautiful minarets and attractive exterior decoration. Among the many important people buried in tile-encrusted tombs here are Prince Mehmet, his brothers and sisters, and Süleyman's grand viziers, Rüstem Paşa and İbrahim Paşa. After you've visited the mosque, consider stopping for a tea or lunch at Şehzade Mehmed Sofrası (p150), housed in one of the *külliye* buildings behind the mosque.

### AQUEDUCT OF VALENS Map p73

Bozdoğan Kemeri; Ⓜ Aksaray

Rising majestically over the traffic on busy Atatürk Bulvarı, this limestone aqueduct is one of the city's most distinctive landmarks.

Commissioned by the Emperor Valens and completed in AD 378, it was part of an elaborate system sourcing water from the north of the city and linking more than 250km of water channels, some 30 bridges and over 100 cisterns within the city walls, making it one of the greatest hydraulic engineering achievements of ancient times. The aqueduct linked the third and fourth hills and carried water to a cistern at Beyazıt Sq before finally ending up at the Great Byzantine Palace. After the Conquest it supplied the *Eski* (Old) and Topkapı Palaces with water.

### MOLLA ZEYREK MOSQUE Map p73

Molla Zeyrek Camii, Church of the Pantocrator; İbadethane Sokak; Ⓜ Laleli-Üniversite

This mosque complex was originally an important Byzantine sanctuary comprising a monastery (church, library and hospital), second church and chapel joining the two churches. Empress Eirene had the monastery built between 1118 and 1124 (she features in a mosaic at Aya Sofya with her husband Emperor John II Comnenus) and her husband built the second church and chapel on the site after her death; the mosque occupies the church that Eirene built. The complex is the second-largest still-standing church built by the Byzantines (after Aya Sofya) and was until recently included on the World Monument Fund's List of the world's 100 most endangered cultural heritage sites – it's now undergoing a slow restoration funded in part by the Koç Foundation, which runs the adjacent restaurant, Zeyrekhane (p149).

# MOSQUES & MARKETS WALK
## Walking Tour

**1 Nuruosmaniye Mosque** This Ottoman baroque building (p76) stands at the Nuruosmaniye Gate, one of the main entrances to the Grand Bazaar. It's always busy at prayer time, but is wonderfully peaceful at other times. The gold emblem above the gateway into the bazaar is the Ottoman armorial emblem with the sultan's monogram.

**2 Grand Bazaar** When Mehmet the Conqueror laid the foundation stone for this bazaar (p72), he set off a craze for shopping malls that İstanbullus have cultivated ever since. His original *bedesten* (covered market) now an

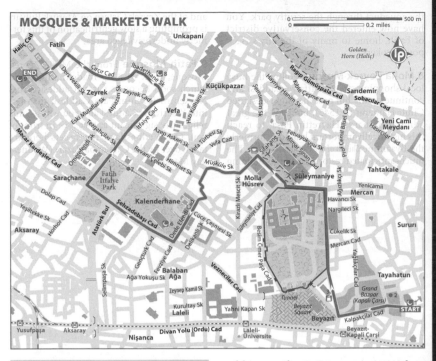

## MOSQUES & MARKETS WALK

## WALK FACTS

**Start** Nuruosmaniye Mosque
**End** Fatih Mosque
**Duration** Four hours
**Fuel stops** Dârüzziyafe Restaurant, Lale Bahçesi (p164), the *fasulye* (bean) restaurants opposite Süleymaniye Mosque (p76) or Şehzade Mehmed Sofrası (opposite), in the grounds of Şehzade Mehmed Mosque

antiques and curios hall, spread and engulfed surrounding *han*s, creating the chaotic shopping crush you see today.

**3 Book Bazaar** Walk through the bazaar along Kalpakçılar Caddesi and exit through the Beyazıt Kapısı (Beyazít Doorway). Turn sharp right into Çadırcılar Caddesi and then take the first turn left to enter the historic Sahaflar Çarşısı, which dates from Byzantine times.

**4 Süleymaniye Mosque** Backtrack to Çadırcılar Caddesi, turn left and follow this street north, continuing along Fuat Paşa Caddesi, which hugs the walls of İstanbul University. Turn left into Professor Siddık Sami Onar Caddesi and you will see the minarets

of this magnificent religious complex (p76) in front of you.

**5 An atmospheric tea break** After visiting the mosque, enjoy a glass of tea at Dârüzziyafe restaurant, housed in the mosque's former soup kitchen, or do as the locals do and order tea and nargileh at Lale Bahçesi (p164). Alternatively, opt for a plate of tasty beans and rice at one of the *fasülyeci* (slow-cooked bean joints) opposite the mosque's southern entrance.

**6 Şehzade Mehmet Mosque** Follow Şifahane and Molla Şemsettin Cami Sokaks down into the residential streets of the Molla Hüsrev district, passing the Ekmekçızade Ahmet Paşa Medresesi (c 1618) and then accessing this peaceful and attractive complex (opposite) via Dede Efedi Caddesi or (as is sometimes possible) the gate off Vefa Caddesi behind the mosque.

**7 Aqueduct of Valens** Leave the mosque and head west; you'll see remnants of this majestic Byzantine piece of infrastructure (opposite) to your right. Cross Atatürk Bulvarı using the underpass and then head towards the aqueduct through the scruffy park. You have now entered the conservative district of Fatih, home to many of the city's AKP powerbrokers.

**8 Molla Zeyrek Mosque** Follow the busy local shopping street of İtfaiye Caddesi and continue up the hill past the Sinan-designed Çinili Hamamı (c 1545), built for the great admiral Barbaros Hayrettin Paşa, to reach this historically important building, formerly the Byzantine Church of the Pantocrator (p80). The much-anticipated restoration of this building

and of the Zeyrek Cistern on Atatürk Bulvarı is prompting a slow gentrification of this formerly underprivileged area.

**9 Fatih Mosque** From the Molla Zeyrek Mosque, walk west up İbadelthane Sokak, which soon becomes Çırçır Caddesi. Cross Nevşehirli İbrahim Paşa Caddesi, turn left into Yeserizade Caddesi and you will see this religiously significant building (p85) in front of you. On Wednesdays, the streets here are taken over by the Çarşamba Pazarı (Wednesday Market).

Eating p151

This part of the city is one of the least visited by visitors and that's a shame, because it's one of the most interesting. Those travellers interested in veering off the tourist track and exploring will find that spending a day here is extremely rewarding.

As İstanbul grew over the centuries, its boundaries moved westward and a series of successive city walls were put up to protect the city. In these western suburbs, populations of two major ethnic groups settled – the Jews in Balat and the Greeks in Fener. Though remnants of these and other population groups still live around here, most of the current inhabitants are from the east of Turkey and are more conservative than the rest of the city's population. You'll notice, for instance, that headscarves are *de rigueur* here, with some women even wearing *çarşafs* (chadors or burkas). These areas are also conspicuously less affluent than the suburbs around Beyoğlu, the Bosphorus or even Sultanahmet, although the inexorable progression of gentrification is starting to make itself felt.

The major through-roads are Mürsel Paşa Caddesi (at various points also called Abdülezel Paşa Caddesi and Sadrazam Ali Paşa Caddesi), which follows the shore of the Golden Horn, and Fevzi Paşa Caddesi (the continuation of Macar Kardeşler and Şehzadebaşı Caddesis), which runs from Beyazıt and punches through the land walls at Edirnekapı. Major transport is provided by bus along Fevzi Paşa Caddesi and by the Eminönü–Eyüp ferry along the Golden Horn.

## CHORA CHURCH Map p86

**Kariye Müzesi; ☎ 212-631 9241; Kariye Camii Sokak, Edirnekapı; admission TL15; ☽ 9am-4.30pm Thu-Tue; ◉ Edirnekapı**

Chora literally means 'country', reflecting the fact that when this church (also known as the Church of the Holy Saviour Outside the Walls) was built in AD 527–65 it was located outside the original city walls built by Constantine the Great. However, within a century it was engulfed by Byzantine urban sprawl and enclosed within a new set of walls built by Emperor Theodosius II.

The environs of the church weren't the only thing to change over the years – after centuries of use as a mosque, Kariye Camii, after the Conquest and it now functions as a museum. And what you see today is not the original church-outside-the-walls. Rather, this one was built in the late 11th century, with reworking in the succeeding centuries. Virtually all of the interior decoration – the famous mosaics and the less renowned but equally striking frescoes – dates from 1312 and was funded by Theodore Metochites, a man of letters who was auditor of the Treasury under Andronikos II (between 1282 and 1328). One of the museum's most wonderful mosaics (map item 48), found above the door to the nave in the inner narthex, depicts Theodore offering the church to Christ.

The mosaics, which depict the lives of Christ and Mary, are stunning; see the plan

on p86. Look out for the Khalke Jesus (map item 33), which shows Christ and Mary with two donors – Prince Isaac Comnenos and Melane, daughter of Mikhael Palaiologos VIII. This is under the right dome in the inner narthex. On the dome itself is a stunning depiction of Jesus and his ancestors (the Genealogy of Christ; map item 27). On the narthex's left dome is a serenely beautiful mosaic of Mary and the Child Jesus surrounded by her ancestors (map item 34).

In the nave are three mosaics: of Christ (map item 50c), of Mary and the child Jesus (map item 50b) and of the Dormition (Assumption; map item 50a) of the Blessed Virgin – turn around to see this, as it's over the main door you just entered. The 'infant' being held by Jesus is actually Mary's soul.

To the right of the nave is the parecclesion, a side chapel built to hold the tombs of the church's founder and his relatives, close friends and associates. It is decorated with frescoes that deal with the themes of death and resurrection, depicting scenes taken from the Old Testament. The striking painting in the apse known as the Anastasis (map item 51) shows a powerful Christ raising Adam and Eve out of their sarcophagi, with saints and kings in attendance. The gates of hell are shown under Christ's feet. Less majestic but no less beautiful are the frescoes (map item 65) adorning the dome, which show Mary and 12 attendant angels.

# WESTERN DISTRICTS

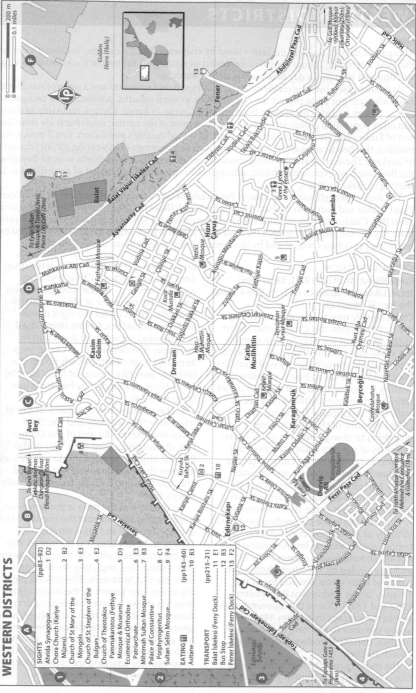

**SIGHTS** (pp83–92)
| | |
|---|---|
| Ahrida Synagogue | 1 D2 |
| Chora Church (Kariye Müzesi) | 2 B2 |
| Church of St Mary of the Mongols | 3 E3 |
| Church of St Stephen of the Bulgars | 4 E2 |
| Church of Theotokos Pammakaristos (Fethiye Mosque & Museum) | 5 D3 |
| Ecumenical Orthodox Patriarchate | 6 E3 |
| Mihrimah Sultan Mosque | 7 B3 |
| Palace of Constantine Porphyrogenitus | 8 C1 |
| Sultan Selim Mosque | 9 F4 |

**EATING** (pp143–60)
| | |
|---|---|
| Asitane | 10 B3 |

**TRANSPORT** (pp215–21)
| | |
|---|---|
| Balat İskelesi (Ferry Dock) | 11 E1 |
| Bus Stop | 12 B3 |
| Fener İskelesi (Ferry Dock) | 13 F2 |

To Eyüp Sultan Mosque & Tomb (2km); Pierre Loti Café (1.6m)

Golden Horn (Haliç)

Balat

Fener

Greek Orthodox College of the Fener

Çarşamba

Kasım Gösim

Draman

Katip Musluhittin

Avcı Bey

Karagümrük

Beyceğiz

Edirnekapı

To Emir Buhari Tekkesi; Anemas Dungeons; Dervis Efendi Mosque (60m)

Sulukule

Derviş Ali

Fevzi Paşa Cad

To Fatih Mosque (tomb of Mehmet the Conqueror) & Gülbahar (1.1m)

To Topkapı Gate & Panorama 1453 (1km)

0 200 m
0 0.1 miles

Though no one knows for certain, it is thought that the frescoes were painted by the same masters who created the mosaics. Theirs is an extraordinary accomplishment, as the paintings, with their sophisticated use of perspective and exquisitely portrayed facial expressions, are reminiscent of those painted by the Italian master Giotto, the painter who more than any other ushered in the Italian Renaissance.

Between 1948 and 1959 the decoration was carefully restored under the auspices of the Byzantine Society of America. Plaster and whitewash covering the mosaics and frescoes was removed and the works were cleaned.

This is one of the city's best museums and deserves an extended visit. On leaving, we highly recommend sampling the delectable Ottoman menu at the restaurant Asitane (p151), which is in the basement of the next-door Kariye Oteli; access it via the stairs on the left-hand side of the hotel.

Finally, a plea: despite signs clearly prohibiting the use of flashes in the museum, many visitors wilfully ignore this rule. Please don't be one of them.

## FATİH MOSQUE Map pp46–7
Mosque of the Conqueror, Fatih Camii; Fevzi Paşa Caddesi; ☼ tombs 8.30am-4.30pm; 🚌 Fatih
The Fatih was the first great imperial mosque built in İstanbul following the Conquest. For its location Mehmet the Conqueror chose the hilltop site of the ruined Church of the Apostles, burial place of Constantine and other Byzantine emperors. The mosque complex, finished in 1470, was enormous; set in extensive grounds, it included in its külliye 15 charitable establishments such as religious schools, a hospice for travellers and a caravanserai. Unfortunately, the mosque you see today is not the one Mehmet built. The original stood for nearly 300 years before toppling in an earthquake in 1766. Though rebuilt, it was destroyed by fire in 1782. The present mosque dates from the reign of Abdül Hamit I and is on a completely different plan. Though traces of Mehmet's mosque remain – the courtyard and its main entrance portal – the interior of the Fatih is relatively unimpressive.

Directly behind the mosque are the tombs of Mehmet the Conqueror and his wife Gülbahar. Confusingly, Mehmet isn't buried here, but rather under the *mimber*

in the mosque. Muslims consider Mehmet's tomb a very holy site, so it's inevitably filled with worshippers.

The grassed outer courtyard of the mosque is a favourite place for locals to congregate and for families to picnic, especially on Sunday. On Wednesday the streets behind and to the sides of the mosque host the Fatih Pazarı (Çarşamba Pazarı), a weekly market selling everything from saucepans to shoes.

## MİHRİMAH SULTAN MOSQUE Map p84
Mihrimah Sultan Camii; Ali Kuşçu Sokak, Edirnekapı; 🚌 Edirnekapı
The great Sinan put his stamp on the entire city and this mosque, constructed in the 1560s next to the Edirnekapı section of the historic land walls, is one of his best works. Commissioned by Süleyman the Magnificent's favourite daughter, Mihrimah, it was reaching the end of a long restoration when this book went to print. The mosque is known for its delicate stained-glass windows and its large interior space, made particularly light by its 19 windows in each arched tympanum. Occupying the highest point in the city, its dome and one slender minaret are major adornments to the city skyline; they are particularly prominent on the road from Edirne. Remnants of the *külliye* include a still-functioning *hamam* on the corner of Ali Kuşçu and Eroğlu Sokaks.

## PALACE OF CONSTANTINE PORPHYROGENITUS Map p84
Palace of the Sovereign, Tekfur Sarayı; Hocaçakır Caddesi; 🚌 Edirnekapı
Sacred buildings often endure because they continue to be used, even though they may be converted for use in another religion. Put simply, there's something a bit dodgy about razing a place of worship, and not too many people want to do it. No such squeamishness surrounds secular buildings such as palaces, though, and history shows that these are often torn down and rebuilt to cater to the tastes and needs of different generations. İstanbul is no different – the Byzantine palaces that once crowded Sultanahmet Sq are all gone, and so is most of the Great Palace of Blachernae, which was also in this neighbourhood. Only the Tekfur Sarayı remains.

Though the building is only a shell these days, it is remarkably preserved considering

## CHORA CHURCH (KARİYE MÜZESİ)

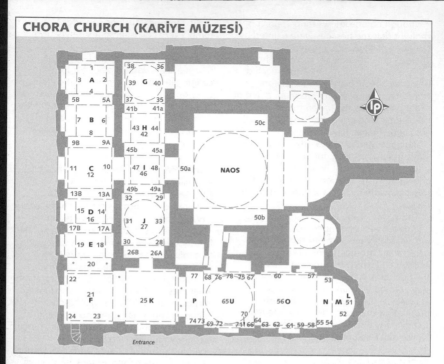

Entrance

its great age. Built in the late 13th or early 14th century and located close to the end of Theodosius II's wall, it was a large three-storeyed palace that may have been an annex of the Palace of Blachernae. Later uses were not so regal: after the Conquest it functioned in turn as a menagerie for exotic wild animals, a brothel and a poorhouse for destitute Jews.

To see it, wander into the sportsground next door (on Sundays, this hosts the city's largest meet of pigeon fanciers). The site itself is fenced.

### CHURCH OF THEOTOKOS PAMMAKARISTOS Map p84

Fethiye Camii & Müzesi; admission TL5; ☺ 9am-4.30pm Thu-Tue; Fethiye Kapısı; ☝ Fener or ☐ Fener

Built between 1292 and 1294, the Church of the Theotokos Pammakaristos, or Church of the all-praised Mother of God, briefly served as the headquarters of the Ecumenical Orthodox Patriarch (1455–1587). Not long after the Conquest, Mehmet the Conqueror visited here to discuss theological questions with Patriarch Gennadios. They talked in the southern side chapel known as the pareċclesion, which was built to a cross-shaped plan and has a small dome, a gallery and a narthex. Though not as splendid as those in the nearby Chora Church, the paracclesion's Byzantine-era mosaics have been beautifully restored and are well worth seeing, particularly the Pantocrator and 12 Prophets adorning the dome, and the Deesis (Christ with the Virgin and St John the Baptist) in the apse.

The church was added to several times over the centuries before being converted to a mosque in 1573 and named Fethiye (Conquest) to commemorate Sultan Murat III's victories in Georgia and Azerbaijan.

### GÜL MOSQUE Off map p84

Gül Camii; cnr Gül Camii Sokak & Şerefiye Sokak, Fener; ☝ Fener or ☐ Fener

Rarely visited by anyone other than local worshippers, this cross-domed church building dates from the 11th century. Originally known as Church of St Theodosia, it is now called the Gül (Rose) Mosque. Legend has it that on Theodosia's saint day (29 May) preceding the Conquest, worshippers filled the church with rose petals in her honour and prayed that the Ottomans wouldn't be successful in breaching the city's walls. Their prayers went unanswered, but when soldiers of Mehmet's army entered they saw the petals and renamed the building Gül Mosque. In fact, the building was used as a shipyard warehouse after the Conquest and wasn't converted into a mosque until the reign of Beyazıt II (r 1481–1512). The central, extremely high, dome is an Ottoman addition and the pretty minaret dates from the rule of Selim II (r 1512–20).

## CHURCH OF ST MARY OF THE MONGOLS Map p84
**Church of Theotokos Panaghiotissa, Kanlı Kilise; Tevkii Cafer Mektebi Sokak, Fener; ⚫ Fener or ⛟ Fener**
History buffs will find a visit here more satisfying than those specifically interested in architecture, as this squat red-brick church is quite unprepossessing from the outside and an unfortunate exercise in ecclesiastical decorative overkill inside. Historically, though, it is extremely signifi-

cant, being the only Byzantine church in İstanbul which has not, at some stage or another, been converted into a mosque. It was consecrated in the 13th century and saved from conversion by the personal decree of Mehmet the Conqueror. If you ring the bell on the outside gate you may attract the attention of the caretaker, who is usually happy to show visitors the church in exchange for a tip.

## AHRIDA SYNAGOGUE Map p84
**Ahrida Sinagogu; Vodina Sokak 9, Balat; ⚫ Balat or ⛟ Balat**
Sephardic Jews, driven from Spain by the judges of the Inquisition, found refuge in the Ottoman Empire in the late 15th and early 16th centuries and many settled in this quarter of the city. Some of their descendants still live here and speak the native Spanish dialect of Ladino. Like all other religious 'nations' within the empire, the Jewish community was governed by its supreme religious leader, the Chief Rabbi, who oversaw its adherence to religious law

## SAVING SULUKULE

Architect and artisan Aslı Kıyak İngin is a member of the Human Settlements Association ( ☎ 542 347 6241), a group of local architects and urban planners who work to promote the IAHH (International Association of Humane Habitat) goal of ensuring adequate shelter for all and making human settlements safer, healthier and more liveable, equitable, sustainable and productive. In recent years, the association has been fighting to save the urban and cultural fabric of the historic neighbourhood of Sulukule, behind the Miramah Sultan Mosque in Edirnekapı. This extremely poor area has traditionally been the home of the city's Roma or Rom (Gypsy) minority, but since 2006 the local Fatih Municipality has been actively pursuing a program of 'urban renewal' whereby it has declared most of the neighbourhood's traditional courtyard houses uninhabitable and demolished them, forcing Rom residents to relocate to suburbs on the outskirts of the city (the only neighbourhoods where rents are as low as they were in Sulukule before the intervention). As Aslı says, 'The municipality has said that Sulukule was a slum area with illegal recent housing, but in fact the Rom have been living there for 1000 years. Until the 1990s, there were famous entertainment houses in Sulukule offering music and dance performances but then the Fatih police started to hassle locals and patrons and forced the houses to close down – destroying the livelihoods of the local residents. Now it's awful – full of drugs and prostitutes – but it didn't used to be like that at all. Then, it was a poor but proud community.'

After visiting İstanbul in 2007, a Unesco delegation highlighted the treatment of Sulukule's Rom residents and the threat to its historical fabric, and called on local authorities to act before it was too late; more recently, the *Hürriyet Daily News* alleged that local politicians and their business associates had been privately acquiring the rezoned land in Sulukule for bargain-basement prices. As a result, a founding member of the ruling Justice and Development Party (AKP) Fatih branch was forced to resign from the party for 'unethical acts'.

Aslı and her fellow Human Settlement Association members are trying to keep the issue alive in the media and are working to document the neighbourhood's heritage structures, which include houses, cisterns and aqueducts. They are also in the midst of restoring six traditional courtyard houses with the financial support of likeminded sponsors. It sometimes seems like an uphill battle, though: 'Sulukule isn't the only area in İstanbul where these injustices are being carried out', Aslı says. 'Similar threats are being faced by residents in Balat, Fener, Süleymaniye and Tarlabaşı.'

and who was responsible to the sultan for the community's good conduct. Today, you'll need to contact the current Chief Rabbinate of Turkey (fax 212-244 1980; info@musevicemaati.com) at least 24 hours in advance if you wish to visit this synagogue, which was built by Macedonian Jews in the 15th century.

### CHURCH OF ST STEPHEN OF THE BULGARS Map p84

Sveti Stefan Church; ☎ 212-521 1121; Mürsel Paşa Caddesi 85, Fener; 🚢 Fener or 🚌 Fener

These days we're accustomed to kit homes and assemble-yourself furniture from Ikea, but back in 1871, when this Gothic Revival cast-iron church was constructed from pieces shipped down the Danube and across the Black Sea from Vienna on 100 barges, the idea was extremely novel.

It's hard to say which is the more unusual: the building and its interior fittings – all made completely of cast iron – or the history of its congregation.

During the 19th century, ethnic nationalism swept through the Ottoman Empire, with each of the empire's many ethnic groups – who identified themselves on the basis of language, religion and racial

heritage – wanting to rule its own affairs. This sometimes led to problems; this is what happened with the Bulgars.

Originally a Turkic-speaking people, the Bulgars came from the Volga in about AD 680 and overwhelmed the Slavic peoples living in the area today known as Bulgaria. They adopted the Slavic language and customs, and founded an empire that threatened the power of Byzantium. In the 9th century they were converted to Christianity.

The Orthodox patriarch, head of the Eastern church in the Ottoman Empire, was an ethnic Greek; in order to retain as much power as possible, the patriarch was opposed to any ethnic divisions within the Orthodox church. He put pressure on the sultan not to allow the Bulgarians, Macedonians and Romanians to establish their own religious groups.

The pressures of nationalism became too great, however, and the sultan was finally forced to recognise some sort of religious autonomy for the Bulgars. He established not a Bulgarian patriarchate, but an 'exarchate', with a leader supposedly of lesser rank, yet independent of the Greek Orthodox patriarch. In this way the Bulgarians would achieve their desired ethnic recognition and would escape the dominance of the Greeks, but the Greek patriarch would allegedly suffer no diminution of his glory or power. St Stephen's functioned as the main church of the Bulgarian exarch.

Architectural historians believe that the cast-iron building, based on a design by the Ottoman architect Housep Aznavour (1853–1935), replaced an earlier timber church on the site that was destroyed by fire. The interior features screens, a balcony and columns all cast from iron; it is extremely beautiful, with the gilded iron glinting in the hazy light that filters in through stained-glass windows.

The church is rarely open, so see if you can find the caretaker who lives on the grounds – he's usually happy to open the gate in exchange for a tip. Otherwise, your best bet is to try before or after Sunday-morning services or during the International İstanbul Music Festival, when it functions as an occasional venue.

## ECUMENICAL ORTHODOX PATRIARCHATE Map p84

Patrikhane; ☎ 212-531 9670; www.ec-patr.org; Sadrazam Ali Paşa Caddesi, Fener; donation requested; 🕙 9am-5pm; 🚢 Fener or 🚌 Fener
The Ecumenical patriarch is a ceremonial head of the Orthodox Church, though most of the churches in Greece, Cyprus, Russia and other countries have their own patriarchs or archbishops who are independent of İstanbul. Nevertheless, the symbolic importance of the patriarchate, here in the city that saw the great era of Byzantine and Orthodox influence, is considerable. The patriarchate has been located in this district since 1600 and the patriarch's official title is the Archbishop of Constantinople, New Rome and Ecumenical Patriarch.

To the Turkish government, the patriarch is a Turkish citizen of Greek descent nominated by the church and appointed by the government as an official in the Directorate of Religious Affairs. In this capacity he is the religious leader of the country's Orthodox citizens and is known officially as the Greek Patriarch of Fener (Fener Rum Patriği). The relationship of the patriarchate and the wider Turkish community has been strained in the past, no more so than when Patriarch Gregory V was hanged for treason after inciting Greeks to overthrow Ottoman rule at the start of the Greek War of Independence (1821–32). The lingering antagonism over

this and the Greek occupation of parts of Turkey in the 1920s no doubt explains the elaborate security around the patriarchate, including a security checkpoint at the main entrance.

The Church of St George within the patriarchate compound is a modest structure built in 1720. Its main glory is the ornate patriarchal throne that is thought to date from the last years of Byzantium. In 1941 a disastrous fire destroyed many of the buildings but fortunately spared the church.

## SULTAN SELIM MOSQUE Map p84

Sultan Selim Camii, Mosque of Yavuz Selim; Yavuz Selim Caddesi; 🚢 Fener or 🚌 Fener
By all accounts the sultan to whom this mosque was dedicated (Süleyman the Magnificent's father, Selim I, known as 'the Grim') was a nasty piece of work. He is famous for having his father poisoned and for killing two of his brothers, six of his nephews and three of his own sons. Odd, then, that his mosque is one of the most loved in the city. The reason becomes clear when a visit reveals the mosque's position on a lawned terrace with spectacular views of the Golden Horn – picnic spots don't come much better than this. The building itself, constructed in 1522, was undergoing a major renovation when this book was going to print. Inside, its tilework and painted woodwork provide the most distinctive features.

## EYÜP SULTAN MOSQUE & TOMB Map pp46–7

Eyüp Sultan Camii, Mosque of the Great Eyüp; Camii Kebir Sokak, Eyüp; 🕙 tomb 9.30am-4.30pm; 🚢 Eyüp or 🚌 Eyüp
This mosque complex occupies what is reputedly the burial place of Ayoub al-Ansari (Eyüp Ensari in Turkish), a friend of the Prophet's and a revered member of Islam's early leadership. Eyüp fell in battle outside the walls of Constantinople while carrying the banner of Islam during the Arab assault and siege of the city from 674 to 678. He was buried outside the walls and, ironically, his tomb later came to be venerated by the Byzantine inhabitants of the city.

When Mehmet the Conqueror besieged Constantinople in 1453, he built a grander and more fitting tomb. The mosque that he built on the site became the place where the Ottoman princes came for the Turkish

## MAŞALLAH!

If you visit Eyüp on a Friday, Sunday or holy day, you will see young boys in white suits being carried by their proud fathers and followed by a circle of relatives. These apprehensive yet excited young chaps are about to undergo one of the most important Muslim rites – *sünnet* (circumcision). Their white suit is supplemented with a spangled hat and red satin sash emblazoned with the word *Maşallah* (May God Protect Him).

Circumcision, or the surgical removal of the foreskin on the penis, is performed on a Turkish Muslim boy when he is between five and 11 years old (odd-numbered years are thought to be luckier), and marks his formal admission into the faith.

On the day of the operation the boy is dressed in the special suit, visits relatives and friends, and leads a parade – formerly on horseback, now in cars – around his neighbourhood or city, attended by musicians and merrymakers.

The simple operation, performed in a hospital or in a clinic during the afternoon, is followed by a celebration with music and feasting. The newly circumcised boy attends, resting in bed, as his friends and relatives bring him special gifts and congratulate him on having entered manhood.

equivalent of coronation: to gird the Sword of Osman, signifying their power and their title as *padişah* (king of kings), or sultan. In 1766 Mehmet's building was levelled by an earthquake; a new mosque was built on the site by Sultan Selim III in 1800.

If you arrive by ferry (the best way), cross the road from the ferry stop and walk up İskele Caddesi, the main shopping street, until you reach the mosque complex. From the plaza outside the complex, enter the great doorway to a courtyard shaded by a huge plane tree; the mosque is to your right and the tomb, rich with silver, gold and crystal chandeliers and coloured İznik tiles, is to your left. Even though women pray in a separate room to the right of the mosque, females can usually enter the mosque itself and stand at the rear if they are properly covered.

Be careful to observe the Islamic proprieties when visiting, as this is an extremely sacred place for Muslims, ranking fourth after the big three: Mecca, Medina and Jerusalem. It's always busy on Fridays and religious holidays.

During your visit you may see boys dressed up in white satin suits with spangled caps and red sashes emblazoned with the word 'Maşallah'. These lads are on the way to their circumcision and have made a stop beforehand at this holy place; see the boxed text above.

After visiting the mosque, many visitors head north up the hill to the Pierre Loti Café (Map pp46–7; ☎ 212-581 2696; Gümüşsuyu Balmumcu Sokak 1, Eyüp; ☼ 8pm-midnight), where the famous French novelist is said to have come for inspiration. Loti loved İstanbul, its decadent grandeur and the late-medieval customs of a society in decline. When he

sat in this cafe, under a shady grapevine sipping tea, he saw a Golden Horn busy with *caïques* (long, thin rowboats), schooners and a few steam vessels. The water in the Golden Horn was still clean enough to swim in and the vicinity of the cafe was given over to pasture. The cafe that today bears his name offers views similar to the ones he must have enjoyed. It's in a warren of streets on a promontory surrounded by the Eyüp Sultan Mezarlığı (Cemetery of the Great Eyüp) where many important Ottomans are buried.

To find the cafe, walk out of the mosque's main gate and turn right. Walk around the complex (keeping it to your right) until you see a set of stairs and a steep cobbled path going uphill into the cemetery. Hike up the steep hill for 10 to 15 minutes to reach the cafe. Alternatively, a cable car (TL1.50 each way, Akbil accepted) joins the waterfront with the top of the hill. In the cafe, be sure to check your bill – we have found unexpected and unwarranted additions on ours in the past. There's also a souvenir store here that sells postcards featuring historical views of the city.

## A WALK ALONG THE WALLS
### Walking Tour

**1 Emir Buhari Tekkesi** Take the Haliç ferry from Eminönü to Ayvansaray. Disembark and you will see remnants of Theodosius II's land walls in front of you. Cross busy Ayvansaray Caddesi and enter the gate punched into this section of the walls. Walk uphill into Ayvansaray Kuyusu Sokak and then veer right into Dervişzade Sokak (Street of the Dervis' Son). On your left you will see this recently restored tekke (Derviş lodge).

**2 Anemas Dungeons** Opposite the *tekke* are the remains of the vast Anemas Zindanları (Anemas Dungeons), once part of the Blachernae Palace built by the Emperor Anastasius (491–518). A number of deposed emperors were imprisoned and tortured in this prison, and two (Isaac Angelus and his son Alexius IV) were murdered here. Restoration of the dungeons and walls here commenced in 2001 but has stalled in recent years.

**3 İvaz Efendi Mosque** Some architectural historians attribute this mosque to Sinan, but others disagree. Built in the shadow of the walls in c 1581–85, its diminutive form is certainly elegant enough to be the work of the great architect. Inside, the mihrab is decorated with fine İznik tiles.

**4 Palace of Constantine Porphyrogenitus** Continue walking uphill and then veer right to reach Şişhane Caddesi. Veer left (still uphill) and follow the walls until you reach the ruins of this Byzantine palace (p85).

**5 Chora Church** Turn off Hoca Çakır Caddesi (the extension of Şişhane Caddesi) into

## WALK FACTS

Start Ayvansaray İskelesi
End Sulukule or the Marble Tower
Time Three hours (to Sulukule), six hours (to the Marble Tower)
Fuel stops Enjoy an Ottoman lunch fit for a sultan at Asitane (p151)

# A WALK ALONG THE WALLS

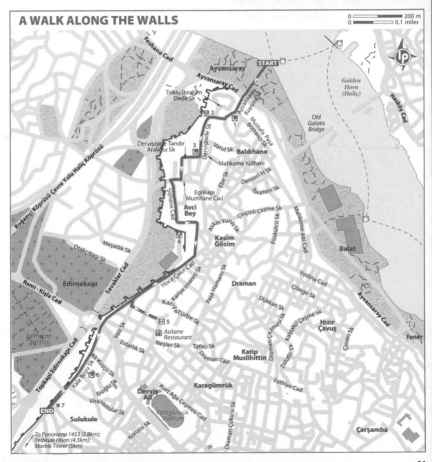

Vaiz Sokak and then turn sharp left into Kariye Camii Sokak to arrive at this museum (p83), one of the finest in the city. The exquisite Byzantine mosaics and frescoes were funded by Theodore Metochites, the auditor of the imperial treasury, and he certainly got lots of bang for his buck. Refuel near here at the delightful Asitane restaurant (p151).

**6 Mihrimah Sultan Mosque** Backtrack to Hoca Çakır Caddesi. This stretch of the walls has been restored, so you can climb up and enjoy a magnificent view. Continue uphill to busy Fevzi Paşa Caddesi, cross the road and you will arrive at the Edirnekapı (Edirne Gate) and this lovely Sinan-designed building (p118).

**7 Sulukule** Stand next to or atop the walls next to the mosque and you will be able to observe their monumental progress towards Topkapı Gate. On your left is the traditional *Rom* (Gypsy) neighbourhood of Sulukule, site of a controversial urban regeneration program (see the boxed text p88).

**8 To the Sea of Marmara** It's possible to follow the walls from Edirnekapı all the way past the Panorama 1453 exhibit (p126) near the Topkapı Gate and the massive fortress of Yedikule Zindanları (p125) to the Marble Tower on the shore of the Sea of Marmara, which was thought to have been part of an imperial sea pavilion in Byzantine times. The walls are in various states of disrepair in these stretches, and you'll need sturdy shoes to climb over tumbled masonry and various obstacles. It's not wise to do this walk by oneself, both for safety reasons (in case you trip or fall) and due to the fact that vagrants and stray dogs live in the wall cavities. This stretch takes about three hours.

# ARCHITECTURE

The massive dome belonging to one of the world's great buildings – Aya Sofya (p49)

MARK AVELLINO

# ARCHITECTURE

Marvel at the sheer beauty of the Blue Mosque (p56) at dawn

DIEGO LEZAMA

Urban designers wanting to study the world's best practice when it comes to putting together a city skyline need go no further than İstanbul. Forget Chicago and New York with their overwhelming skyscraper canyons, or London with its gimmicky Eye and squat clock tower – İstanbul is the real thing. Here you'll find delicate minarets reaching towards the heavens, distinctive domes crowning hills, and austere and elegant medieval towers commanding views across the waters.

This imperial city is the architectural equivalent of a chocolate box with the best possible mixed assortment of treats. Byzantine churches sit beside Ottoman mosques, *medreses* (theological schools) and *hamams* (steam baths); 19th-century timber *yalıs* (seaside villas) adorn the Bosphorus shore; and neoclassical embassies are dotted along Beyoğlu's boulevards. There's little of note from the second half of the 20th century, so the city is consolidating its time-capsule status, undergoing a continuous program of restoration and attempting to legislate to protect its revered skyline. Time capsule doesn't mean Disney-like, though: İstanbullus still worship in historic mosques and churches, live in the timber houses, run restaurants in *medreses*, sweat out their anxieties in *hamams* and attend cocktail parties in the embassies. Today's İstanbul is a living testimonial to the architects and patrons who have contributed to its contemporary form. It's also proof that back in the old days, they sure knew how to build great buildings.

The oldest surviving buildings are in Old İstanbul, with a number of Byzantine structures remaining, including churches, cisterns, fortresses and fortified walls. Urban spaces such as the Hippodrome and ceremonial boulevards such as Divan Yolu also date from this era. In Beyoğlu, traces of the Genoese presence dating back to the final years of the Byzantine Empire can be found, as can buildings from every stage of Ottoman rule. Early essays in the development of a national architectural movement in the early 20th century are found on both sides of the Golden Horn (Haliç). These areas are where most visitors spend their time, but there are discoveries galore through every part of the city. In fact, that's what makes the place so fascinating – the layers of history have a physical manifestation here. There might be stellae from a Roman ceremonial way on one corner and an Ottoman *han* (caravanserai) on another…you'll end up acting like an archaeologist, looking to make new discoveries each time you leave your hotel room.

# BYZANTINE ARCHITECTURE

The city spent 1123 years as a Christian metropolis and there are a surprising number of structures surviving from this era. The big-ticket items are churches, but there are also examples of Byzantine walls, cisterns and aqueducts.

When Mehmet the Conqueror descended on İstanbul in 1453 many churches were converted into mosques; despite the minarets, you can usually tell a church-cum-mosque by the distinctive red bricks, characteristic of all İstanbul's Byzantine churches.

During Justinian's reign, architects were encouraged to surpass each other's achievements when it came to utilising the domed, Roman-influenced basilica form. Aya Sofya (p49), built in 537 and with a dome diameter of over 30m, is the supreme example of this.

From the outside, Byzantine churches lacked ornamentation and were often dull, with the dome being the only striking external feature. For example, both Aya Sofya and the Chora Church (Church of the Holy Saviour, Kariye Müzesi; p83) display relatively drab exteriors, giving no hint of the mosaics inside, which glint, gleam and make the soul soar.

Early Byzantine basilica design used a centralised polygonal plan with supporting walls and a dome set on top, inside rectangular external walls. The lovely Little Aya Sofya (Küçük Aya Sofya Camii; p76), built around 530, is an example. Later, a mixed basilica and centralised polygonal plan developed. This was the foundation for church design from the 11th century until the Conquest and many Ottoman mosques were inspired by it. The Molla Zeyrek Mosque (Molla Zeyrek Camii, Church of the Pantocrator; p80) is a good example of this.

## HERITAGE IN DANGER

Every two years, the World Monuments Fund (WMF) releases its high-profile list of the 100 most endangered cultural heritage sites in the world. In recent years, a number of İstanbul's buildings and structures have featured, including Aya Sofya (1996 and 1998), the Molla Zeyrek Mosque (2000) and Little Aya Sofya (2002, 2004, 2006). The enormous international attention that a listing elicits has helped to preserve both Aya Sofya and Little Aya Sofya, with the big church receiving funding for a painstaking and seemingly interminable Unesco-supervised restoration and the little church recently being unveiled after similarly meticulous but faster conservation works. Restoration work on the shockingly dilapidated Molla Zeyrek Mosque commenced in 2009.

The 2008 list featured another of the city's heritage treasures, and this time the fund's citation for its inclusion was blunt. Justinian's fortified city walls are, according to the WMF, in extreme danger due to exposure to the elements and urban environment, as well as lack of an effective conservation management plan. Indeed, so poorly have authorities protected the walls (and other city buildings in the past) that the WMF committee considered placing the whole of Historic İstanbul – a Unesco World Heritage Site – on the list. The lack of conservation work on the walls since the warning was given means that the Turkish government and local heritage authorities must be awaiting the unveiling of the 2010 list with a fair degree of trepidation.

IZZET KERIBAR

GEORGE TSAFOS

*Molla Zeyrek Mosque (p80)*

*Mosaics, Chora Church (p83)*

The Byzantines also had a yen to build fortifications. The greatest of these is the still-standing land wall. Twenty kilometres long, it protected the city during multiple sieges until it was finally breached in 1453. Constructed in the 5th century by the order of Emperor Justinian II, the wall remained relatively intact until the 1950s, when parts were removed. Consisting of a moat, an outer wall and towers, it has a monumental appearance befitting its purpose.

Constantine the Great, the first Byzantine Emperor, named his city 'New Rome'. Chief among its great public works was the stone aqueduct (p80) built by Emperor Valens between 368 and 378. The aqueduct fed a series of huge cisterns built across the city, including the Basilica Cistern (p54) and Binbirdirek (Cistern of 1001 Columns; p69).

Like Rome, the city was built on seven hills and to a grid pattern that included ceremonial thoroughfares such as Divan Yolu. Every emperor wanted a major public space carrying his name. These punctuated the ceremonial ways and acted as sites for celebrations and great public gatherings. The greatest of all the Byzantine public spaces is the Hippodrome (p57).

The extraordinary subterranean Basilica Cistern (p54)

GEORGE TSAFOS

# OTTOMAN ARCHITECTURE

After the Conquest, the sultans wasted no time in putting their architectural stamp on the city. Mehmet didn't even wait until he had the city under his control, building the monumental Rumeli Hisarı (Fortress of Europe; p205) on the Bosphorus. The fortress was the first of many

DIANA MAYFIELD

The Bosphorus glistens in the sunlight while Rumeli Hisarı (p206) looms overhead

Ottoman structures built in elevated positions commanding extraordinary views and contributing to the skyline.

Once in the city, Mehmet kicked off a centuries-long Ottoman building spree, constructing a number of buildings including a mosque on the fourth hill.

After these he started work on the building that attracts more visitors to visit İstanbul than any other, the Topkapı Palace (p59).

Mehmet had a penchant for palaces, but his great-grandson, Süleyman the Magnificent, was more of a mosque man. With his court architect, Mimar Sinan (see the boxed text, right), he built the greatest of the city's Ottoman imperial mosques. Sinan's prototype mosque form had a forecourt with a şadırvan (fountain) and domed arcades on three sides. On the fourth side was the mosque, with a two-storey porch. The main prayer hall was covered by a central dome surrounded by smaller domes and semidomes. There was usually one minaret, though imperial mosques had either two or four; one imperial mosque, the later Blue Mosque (Sultan Ahmet Camii; p56), has six.

Each imperial mosque had a külliye (mosque complex) clustered around it. This was a philanthropic complex including a medrese, hamam, dar-üş-şifa (hospital), imaret (soup kitchen), kütüphane (library) and cemetery with türbes (tombs). Over time, many of these külliyes were demolished; fortunately, many of the buildings in the magnificent Süleymaniye (p76) and Atik Valide (p118) complexes are intact.

Later sultans continued Mehmet's palace-building craze. No palace would rival Topkapı, but Sultan Abdül Mecit I tried his best with the grandiose Dolmabahçe Palace (p114). Abdül Aziz I

## THE GREAT SINAN

None of today's star architects come close to having the influence over a city that Mimar Koca Sinan had over Constantinople during his 50-year career.

Born in 1497, Sinan was a recruit to the devşirme, the annual intake of Christian youths into the janissaries, becoming a Muslim (as all such recruits did) and eventually taking up a post as a military engineer in the corps. Süleyman the Magnificent appointed him the chief of the imperial architects in 1538.

Sinan designed a total of 321 buildings, 85 of which are still standing in İstanbul. He died in 1588 and is buried in a self-designed türbe (tomb) located in one of the corners of the Süleymaniye Mosque (p76), the building that many believe to be his greatest work.

Visit the grand Dolmabahçe Palace (p114), standing proudly on the shores of the Bosphorus

built the extravagant Çırağan Palace (p116) and Beylerbeyi Palace (p205). These and other buildings of the era have been collectively dubbed 'Turkish baroque'.

These mosques and palaces dominate the landscape and skyline of the city, but there are other quintessentially Ottoman buildings: the *hamam* and the Ottoman timber house. *Hamams* were usually built as part of a *külliye,* and provided an important point of social contact as well as facilities for ablutions. Architecturally significant *hamams* include Sinan's exquisite Baths of Lady Hürrem (p56), and the still-functioning *hamams* of Çemberlitaş (p186) and Cağaloğlu (p185).

The Ottomans built many timber houses, called *yalıs,* along the shores of the Bosphorus for the Ottoman nobility and foreign ambassadors; city equivalents were sometimes set in a garden but were usually part of a crowded, urban streetscape. Unfortunately, not too many of these houses survive, a result of the fires that regularly raced through the Ottoman city.

*Kanyon (p142) – a newbie to the architectural scene*
ALI KABAS / ALAMY

## OTTOMAN REVIVALISM & MODERNISM

In the late 19th and early 20th centuries, architects created a blend of European architecture alongside Turkish baroque, with some concessions to classic Ottoman style. This style has been dubbed 'Ottoman Revivalism' or First National Architecture. Its main proponents were architects Vedat Tek (1873–1942) and Kemalettin Bey (1870–1927). Tek is best known for his Central Post Office in Sirkeci (1909), Haydarpaşa iskelesi (ferry dock; 1915–17) and home in Nişantaşı (1913, now the Zihni bar and

PHIL WEYMOUTH

*The romance of the Orient Express was reflected in the design of the Sirkeci Railway Station (p70)*

restaurant; p168). Kemalettin Bey's Bebek Mosque (1913; p205) and Fourth Vakıf Han (1912–26), a bank building in Eminönü that now houses the World Park Hotel, are his best-known works.

During the same period, art nouveau hit the city. Raimondo D'Aronco, an Italian architect, designed a number of elegant buildings, including the Egyptian consulate (p205) and the gorgeous but sadly dilapidated Botter House (p110).

When Atatürk proclaimed Ankara the capital of the republic, İstanbul lost much of its glamour and investment capital. Modernism was played out on the new canvas of Ankara, while İstanbul's dalliances went little further than the İstanbul City Hall, designed by Nevzat Erol and built in 1953; the İstanbul Hilton Hotel, designed by SOM and Sedad Hakkı Eldem and built in 1952; and the much-maligned Atatürk Cultural Centre (p181) by Hayati Tabanlıoğlu, built in 1956–57.

Recent architecture in the city can hardly be called inspiring. One building of note is Kanyon (see the boxed text, p142), a mixed residential, office and shopping development designed by the LA-based Jerde Partnership with local architects Tabanlıoğlu Partnership. Also noteworthy are new art museums, some of which feature impressive new wings or inspired architectural conversions of industrial spaces. The best are İstanbul Modern (p101), by Tabanlıoğlu Partnership; the Sakıp Sabancı Museum (p207), by Savaş, Erkel and Çırakoğlu; and santralistanbul (p179), by Emre Arolat, Nevzat Sayın and Han Tümertekin. There has been much talk about prominent international architects including Frank Gehry and Zaha Hadid designing buildings here, but no projects have as yet come to fruition.

The decorated dome of the Blue Mosque (p56)

ANDERS BLOMQVIST

TIM HUGHES

Take a stroll along the popular Nevizade Sokak (p93) and check out the restaurants and clubs

An ornate doorway in the charming suburb of Ortaköy (p114)

TIM HUGHES

# BEYOĞLU

Drinking p165; Eating p151; Shopping p137; Sleeping p196

Though challenging to define geographically, the sprawling district of Beyoğlu (bey-oh-loo) roughly follows the shores of the Golden Horn and Bosphorus from Atatürk Bridge (Atatürk Köprüsü) to Kabataş, extends northwest up the hill to Taksim Sq and then follows Tarlabaşı Bulvarı and Refik Saydam Caddesi southwest back to the Atatürk Bridge.

The district's backbone is the famous boulevard of İstiklal Caddesi. Known to locals simply as İstiklal, the street runs east–west between Taksim Sq and Tünel Sq (Tünel Meydanı). A historic tram rattles along its length every 30 minutes or so – you'll need a ticket from the Tünel station or a transport card (see the boxed text p220).

South of Tünel Sq, in the area running down to the Galata Bridge, are the suburbs of Galata (around the tower of the same name) and Karaköy (around the shores of the Golden Horn). There was a settlement in this area before the birth of Christ, and by the time of Theodosius II it was large enough to become an official suburb of Constantinople. Theodosius built a fortress here to complete the defence system of his great land walls, and he called it Galata, as the suburb was then the home of many Galatians (Celtic people from Asia Minor). The neighbouring suburb of Tophane, which stretches along the banks of the Bosphorus, dates from a slightly later period and has historically been known as a maritime suburb where boats docked and offloaded cargo to huge warehouses. Its name comes from the cannon foundry (*tophane*) that was built there during the reign of Mehmet the Conqueror and is now a campus of the Mimar Sinan Fine Arts University.

To the northwest of Tünel Sq is the area known as Asmalımescit, filled with *meyhanes* (taverns) and stylish Western-style brasseries. Tepebaşı, the pocket that is home to the famous Pera Palace Hotel (Pera Palas Oteli, p108), is behind Asmalımescit.

Midway along İstiklal Caddesi is Galatasaray Sq, occupied since 1868 by its namesake, the Galatasaray Lycée. On the opposite side of the street are the busy Balık Pazar (Fish Market) and Nevizade Sokak, one of the busiest restaurant strips in the city.

Behind the lycée to the east are the areas known as Çukurcuma and Cihangir. Çukurcuma is where you'll find many of the city's best antique shops, and Cihangir is an upmarket residential area where trendy bars and cafes are found and where much of the city's Western expat community lives.

Beyoğlu is one of the city's major transport hubs. Buses to every part of the city leave from the bus station at Taksim Sq and a modern metro system travels between Şişhane near Tünel Sq to Taksim and on to the ritzy residential and shopping suburbs to its north, terminating at the Atatürk Oto Sanayi Station in Maslak. The line is divided into three separate sections: Şişhane–Taksim, Taksim–Levent 4 and Levent 4–Atatürk Oto Sanayi. Funiculars run between Taksim Sq and the terminus of the Zeytinburnu–Kabataş tramline and between Tünel Sq and Evren Caddesi near the Galata Bridge, making access between Beyoğlu and the Old City extremely easy.

## İSTANBUL MODERN Map pp102–3

☎ 212-334 7300; www.istanbulmodern.org; Meclis-I Mebusan Caddesi, Tophane; adult/student/child under 12yr TL7/3/free, free entry on Thu; ☉ 10am-6pm Tue-Wed & Fri-Sun, 10am-8pm Thu; ⍟ Tophane

In recent years İstanbul's contemporary-art scene has boomed. Facilitated by the active cultural philanthropy of the country's industrial dynasties – many of which have built extraordinary arts collections – museum buildings are opening nearly as often as art exhibitions. İstanbul Modern, funded by the Eczcıbaşı family, is the big daddy of them all. Opened with great fanfare in

2005, this huge converted shipping terminal has a stunning location right on the shores of the Bosphorus at Tophane and is easily accessed by tram from Sultanahmet.

The museum's curatorial program is two-fold: the 1st floor highlights the Eczcıbaşı family's collection of Turkish 20th-century and contemporary art using a thematic approach; and the downstairs spaces host temporary exhibitions from local and international artists. While the 1st floor exhibits are interesting – look for works by Şekere Ahmet Ali Paşa (1841–1907), Orhan Peker (1926–78), İsmet Doğan (1957–), Ömer Kaleşi (1932–), Cihat Burak (1918–94),

# BEYOĞLU

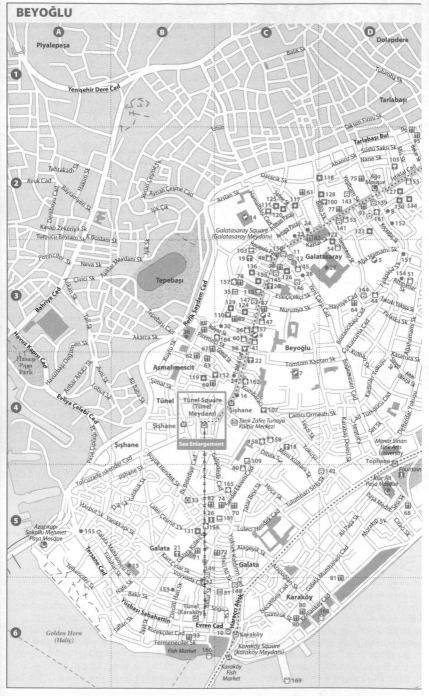

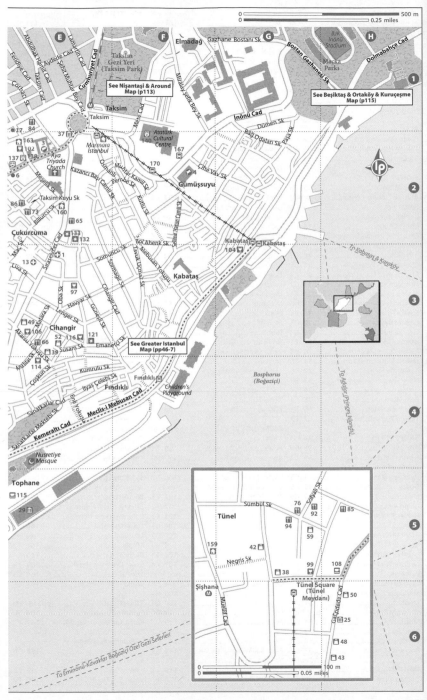

0           500 m
0          0.25 miles

Elmadağ   Gazhane Bostanı Sk

BJK İnönü Stadium

Bostan Gazhanesi Sk

Maçka Parkı

Dolmabahçe Cad

Abdülhak Hamit Cad

Aydede Cad

Şehit Muhtar Bey Cad

Cumhuriyet Cad

Feridiye Cad   Çorbacı Sk   Topçu Sk

Taksim Gezi Yeri (Taksim Park)

**See Nişantaşı & Around Map (p113)**

Miralay Şefik Bey Sk

İnönü Cad

Dümen Sk

**See Beşiktaş & Ortaköy & Kuruçeşme Map (p115)**

Taksim

Taksim

17   84

163   3

102

137   138

6

Meşelik Sk

Mete Cad

Atatürk Cultural Centre   140

167

Bağ Odaları Sk

Tarla Başı Cad

Marmara İstanbul

Aya Triyada Church

Kazancı Başı Camii Sk

Muhtar Kamil Sk

Pembe Sk

170

Cihangir Camii Sk

**Gümüşsuyu**

Çifte Vav Sk

4

Taksim Kuyu Sk

86

73   160

65

Selime Hatun Camii Sk

Kurtul Sk

**Çukurcuma**

133

132

Sıraselviler Cad

Bol Ahenk Sk

Somuncu Sk

Sıraağacı Sk

Büyük Hendek Sk

Fındıklı Camii Sk

**Kabataş**

104

**Kabataş**

To Kabataş & Karaköy

13   1

97

Oba Sk

Havyar Sk

Lenger Sk

Güneşli Sk

Cihangir Cad

**Kabataş**

Mebusan Yokuşu

 Büyük Ucmaz Sk

**Cihangir**

49

106

52   116

66

121

Emanetçi Sk

39   Susam Sk

114

Akarsu Yokuşu Sk

Matara Sk

Malta Sk

Coşkun Sk

Kumrulu Sk

İlyas Çelebi Sk

**Fındıklı**

**See Greater Istanbul Map (pp46-7)**

Fındıklı

*Children's Playground*

*Bosphorus (Boğaziçi)*

To Adalar (Prince's Islands)

Sanatkarlar Cad

**Kemeraltı Cad**

Sanatkar Mektebi Sk

Emir Yokuşu

**Meclis-i Mebusan Cad**

4

**Tophane**

Nusretiye Mosque

115

29

**Tünel**

Sümbül Sk

76

92

85

94

Sofyalı Sk

159

42

59

Negris Sk

38

99

108

**Şişhane**

Mumhane Cad

Tünel Square (Tünel Meydanı)

50

25

Galipdede Cad

48

43

0        100 m
0       0.05 miles

To Eminönü-Kavaklar Boğaziçi Özel Gezi Seferleri

**NEIGHBOURHOODS BEYOĞLU**

İhsan Cemal Karaburçak (1897–1970), Avni Arbaş (1919–2003), Selma Gürbüz (1960–), Alaaddin Aksoy (1942–), Fahreinissa Zeid (1901–91), Nurullah Berk (1906–82) and Adnan Çoker (1927–) – it's the temporary exhibitions and permanent installations in the downstairs spaces that really stand out.

Of these, don't miss Richard Wentworth's *False Ceiling* (1995–2005), an installation of Turkish and Western books floating overhead that plays with ideas of cultural closeness and difference. Make sure you check out what is showing in the main temporary gallery (it's always good), the photography gallery and two video projection rooms.

The museum also has a dedicated interactive exhibition space for children called Genç (Young). Conceived and designed in association with the Centre Georges Pompidou in Paris, it runs education programs for children aged between six and 12. This is hands-on fun that also bolsters arts awareness – great stuff. Also of note are the museum's cafe (p153) and gift shop (p139).

### JEWISH MUSEUM OF TURKEY Map pp102–3
500 Yil Vakfi Türk Musevileri, The Quincentennial Foundation Museum of Turkish Jews; ☎ 212-292 6333; www.muze500.com; Perçemli Sokak, Karaköy; admission TL5; ⏰ 10am-4pm Mon-Thu, 10am-2pm Fri & Sun

In the late 15th century, Isaac Sarfati, Chief Rabbi of Edirne, wrote the following to brethren in Germany: 'Brothers and teachers, friends and acquaintances! I, Isaac Sarfati, proclaim to you that Turkey is a land wherein nothing is lacking, and

where, if you will, all shall yet be well with you…Here, every man may dwell at peace under his own vine and fig tree.' At around the same time, Sultan Beyazıt II proclaimed '…the Jews of Spain should not be refused, but rather be welcomed with warm feelings'. Alas, this enlightened state didn't last through the centuries, and Jewish Turks were made to feel considerably less welcome when racially motivated 'wealth taxes' were introduced in 1942 and violence against Jews and other minorities was unleashed in 1955, prompting many families to flee the country. More recently, Islamist terrorists bombed synagogues on a number of occasions. This museum, housed in the ornate 19th-century Zullfaris synagogue near the Galata Bridge, chooses to focus on the positive rather than the negative, tracing the rich 700-year-history of Jews in Turkey and documenting their mostly harmonious coexistence with the Muslim majority. The displays, though modest, are as fascinating as they are well-intentioned.

### GALATA TOWER Map pp102–3
Galata Kulesi; ☎ 212-293 8180; www.galatatower.net; Galata Meydanı, Galata; admission TL10; ⏰ 9am-8pm; 🚇 Karaköy

The cylindrical Galata Tower stands sentry over the approach to 'new' İstanbul. For centuries the tallest structure in Beyoğlu, it dominates the skyline north of the Golden Horn.

Galata was home to traders from Genoa and Venice during both Byzantine and

---

## İSTANBUL'S CONTEMPORARY ART SCENE

Turkish-born, American-educated Lora Sarıaslan knows that she has a great job. Since 2005, she has been working as a curator at the İstanbul Modern, helping to put together the major exhibitions that the institution is known for. She gets very animated when talking about her workload.

'Since starting in my position, I've worked on shows featuring highlights from both the Venice and İstanbul Biennales, an Andreas Gursky exhibition, a show celebrating the 60th anniversary of Magnum Photos, a Cihat Burak retrospective, a major retrospective of Turkish-born American conceptual artist Sarkis and a 'Design Cities' collaboration with London's Design Museum that was the first design exhibition ever to be shown in a Turkish museum. At the moment I'm working on a show that will spotlight five major Turkish realist painters and on another that will highlight Turkish artists working here and overseas. This is titled 'Modernity and Tradition' and will include works by Hüseyin Chalayan, Ayse Erkmen, Selim Birsel, Hale Tenger, Leyla Gediz, Serhan Özkaya and Sarkis.'

Asked to sum up the museum's curatorial ambition, Lora says that it aims to be a 'house for Turkish and international art of our time', with an acquisitions program and top-drawer exhibition program to match. Away from her workplace, Lora likes to visit the Galerist (p178), Galeri Nev (p178) and Galeri Apel (p178) commercial galleries to see the work of young and upcoming local artists: 'There's a great contemporary art scene here that all visitors should check out, particularly when the İstanbul Biennial (see p17) is on.'

Ottoman times, and functioned almost like a separate colony, with distinct architecture, a preponderance of taverns and a decidedly European flavour. Originally constructed in 1348, this tower was the highest point in the Genoese fortifications of the suburb, and has been rebuilt many times. It has survived a number of earthquakes, as well as the demolition of the rest of the Genoese walls in the mid-19th century.

The paved public square surrounding the tower was created by the municipality as part of the ongoing Beyoğlu Beautification Project and it's been a big hit with locals of all ages, who gather each day to play football and backgammon, drink tea on the outdoor terrace of Café Gündoğdu, buy food from the street vendors and swap local news.

There is a cafeteria on the 8th floor of the tower where you can enjoy a drink, and a vertiginous panorama balcony offering 360-degree views of the city. To be frank, we don't think the view (as spectacular as it is) justifies the steep admission cost.

## ARAB MOSQUE Map pp102-3
Arap Camıı; Galata Mahkemesi Sokak, Galata; 🚇 Karaköy or 🚋 Tersane Caddesi

This mosque is the only surviving place of worship built by the Genoese; it was the largest of the Latin churches in the city. Dating from 1337, it was converted to a mosque by Spanish Moors in the 16th century. It has an impressive stone exterior and wooden ceiling, a simple plan – long hall, tall square belfry-cum-minaret – and ornate flourishes such as the pretty porch and the galleries added in the 20th century.

## KAMONDO STAIRS Map pp102-3
Galata; 🚇 Karaköy or 🚋 Tersane Caddesi

The curvaceous 18th-century Kamondo Stairs, one of Beyoğlu's most distinctive pieces of urban design, run south from Kart Çınar Sokak. Around the corner from the stairs you'll find the Schneidertempel Art Centre (p179). This art gallery, which is housed in a modest former synagogue, hosts shows of Jewish art, usually contemporary and local in origin.

## CHURCH OF SS PETER & PAUL Map pp102-3
SS Pierre et Paul; 🕾 212-249 2385; Galata Kulesi Sokak 44, Galata; ☯ 7-8am Mon-Fri, 3.30-5.30pm Sat, 10am-noon Sun; 🚇 Karaköy

Tucked away in one of the steep streets below Galata Tower you'll find the small grey-and-white doorway to the courtyard of the Church of SS Peter and Paul. A Dominican church originally stood on this site, but the building you see today dates from the mid-19th century. It's the work of the Fossati brothers who also designed the Dutch and Russian consulate buildings (both in Beyoğlu). Like many other Latin churches in the city, its courtyard design reflects the Ottoman ruling that Latin churches could not be built directly fronting onto a road or on top of a hill (the Church of St Mary Draperis on İstiklal Caddesi is another example of this). The church backs onto a section of the Genoese fortifications.

## NEVE SHALOM SYNAGOGUE Map pp102-3
🕾 212-292 0386; www.nevesalom.org/english; Büyük Hendek Caddesi 61, Galata; 🚇 Karaköy

During the 19th century, Galata had a large Sephardic Jewish population and a number of synagogues. Most of this community has now moved to other residential areas in the city, but the synagogues remain. Tragically, this building (which dates from the 1930s) seems to have become a target for anti-Jewish extremists and it has suffered three attacks in recent decades – a brutal massacre by Arab gunmen during the summer of 1986, a bomb attack in 1992 and a 2003 car-bomb attack carried out by a motley group of Turkish Muslims inspired by Osama bin Laden. In a tragic irony, the name Neve Shalom means Oasis or Valley of Peace. To visit, fax a request including your name, address and phone number in İstanbul and passport number to 212-292 0385.

## GALATA MEVLEVİHANESİ Map pp102-3
Museum of Court Literature, Divan Edebiyatı Müzesi; 🕾 212-245 4141; Galipdede Caddesi 15, Tünel; 🚇 Karaköy, then funicular to Tünel

If you thought the Hare Krishnas or the Harlem congregations were the only religious orders to celebrate their faith through music and movement, think again. Those sultans of spiritual spin known as the 'whirling dervishes' have been twirling their way to a higher plane ever since the 13th century and show no sign of slowing down soon.

The Mevlevi *tarika* (order), founded in Konya during the 13th century, flourished throughout the Ottoman Empire. Like several other orders, the Mevlevis stressed the unity of humankind before God regardless of creed.

Taking their name from the great Sufi mystic and poet, Celaleddin Rumi (1207–73), called Mevlana (Our Leader) by his disciples, Mevlevis seek to achieve mystical communion with God through a *sema* (ceremony) involving chants, prayers, music and a whirling dance.

Dervish orders were banned in the early days of the Turkish republic because of their ultraconservative religious politics. Although the ban has been lifted, only a handful of functioning *tekkes* (dervish lodges) remain in İstanbul, including this one. Konya remains the heart of the Mevlevi order. For more information check www.emav.org.

This Mevlevihanesi (whirling-dervish hall) was erected by a high officer in the court of Sultan Beyazıt II in 1491. It was part of a complex including dervish cells, sheik's room, library, drinking fountain and kitchen. Its first *şeyh* (sheik) was Mohammed Şemai Chelebi, a grandson of the great Mevlana. The building burned down in 1776, but was repaired that same year by Sultan Mustafa III.

The building, which is currently closed for restoration, is fronted by a graveyard full of stones with graceful Ottoman inscriptions, including the tomb of Galip Dede,

the 17th-century Sufi poet whom the street is named after. The shapes atop the stones reflect the headgear of the deceased, each hat denoting a different religious rank.

### CHRIST CHURCH Map pp102–3
☎ 212-251 5616; Serdari Ekrem Sokak 52, Karaköy; Ⓜ Karaköy, then funicular to Tünel
Designed by GE Street (who also did London's Law Courts), the cornerstone of this Anglican church was laid in 1858 by Lord Stratford de Redcliffe, known as 'The Great Elchi' (*elçi*, meaning ambassador) because of his paramount influence in mid-19th-century Ottoman affairs. The church, dedicated in 1868 as the Crimean Memorial Church, is the largest of the city's Protestant churches. It was restored and renamed in the mid-1990s.

### PATISSERIE MARKİZ Map pp102–3
İstiklal Caddesi 360-362; Ⓜ Karaköy, then funicular to Tünel
In Pera's heyday, there was no more glamorous spot to be seen than Patisserie Lebon in the Grand Rue de Pera (now İstiklal Caddesi). *The* place to enjoy gateaux and gossip, it was favoured by the city's European elite, who dressed to kill when they popped in for afternoon tea. Noting this, tailors, furriers and milliners opened shops in the adjoining Passage Orientale and did a brisk trade, making it the city's most exclusive retail precinct.

## SEEING THE DERVISHES WHIRL
Even in Ottoman times, Galata's Mevlevihanesi was open to all who wished to witness the *sema* (ceremony), including foreign, non-Muslim visitors. Though banned for a short period in the 1920s by Atatürk, the tradition remained strong and continues today. It is a highlight for many visitors to the city.

When this book went to print, the Mevlevihanesi was closed for restoration, so no *sema* was being performed there. When you arrive in town, check with your hotel as to whether the situation has changed.

At the time of writing, dervishes had been conducting a tourism-oriented *sema* (whirling ceremony; ☎ information & bookings 212-511 4626/36; adult/student under 24yr TL35/25) in the exhibition hall on platform 1 of Sirkeci Railway Station at 7.30pm every Friday and Sunday. The Marmaray project (see the boxed text p218) may put an end to this, though. On Wednesday and Saturday at 7.30pm, this *sema* moves to the Hocapaşa Cultural Centre (Map pp50–1; Hocapaşa Hamamı Sokak 5), housed in a beautifully restored 15th-century *hamam* near the train station.

The most authentic *semas* can be seen most Monday nights at the Fatih *tekke* in the Western Districts of the Old City or on Thursday nights at a *tekke* in Silivrikapi. These are the real deal, not performances put on for tourists, and are highly recommended. Note, though, that chanting – rather than whirling – is the main event. The easiest way to attend is to go with Les Arts Turcs (Map pp50–1; ☎ 212-520 7743; www.lesartsturcs.com; 3rd fl, İncili Çavuş Sokak 37, Sultanahmet), a cultural tourism company that charges €25 per person to give you a briefing about the meaning of the ceremony, take you to the *tekkes* from its office near Aya Sofya and bring you back after the ceremony.

Remember that the ceremony is a religious one – by whirling, the adherents believe that they are attaining a higher union with God – so don't talk, leave your seat or take flash photographs while the dervishes are spinning or chanting.

Part of the patisserie's attraction was its gorgeous art nouveau interior. Four large tiled wall panels had been designed around the theme of the four seasons by Alexandre Vallaury, the architect of the Pera Palace Hotel (below), and were created in France. Unfortunately, only two (Autumn and Spring) survived the trip from France – they have adorned the walls ever since. With chandeliers, fragile china, gleaming wooden furniture and decorative tiled floor, the place was as stylish as its clientele.

In 1940 the Lebon was taken over by Avedis Çakır, who renamed it Patisserie Markiz. It continued to trade until the 1960s, when Pera's decline and a lack of customers led to its closure. Fortunately, closure didn't mean destruction – the building was boarded up and left just as it had been, fittings and all. In the 1970s, local artists and writers lobbied the authorities to have the patisserie and passage added to the country's register of historical buildings; this occurred in 1977, ensuring the entire building's preservation.

In late 2003 the magnificently restored patisserie re-opened to great acclaim. It had a short-lived and much-lamented second life as an upmarket patisserie, but has recently been reinvented as a fast-food joint called Yemek Kulubu, serving cheap coffee and food. Still, the glorious interior means that a stop here remains well worthwhile.

## PERA PALACE HOTEL Map pp102–3
Pera Palas Oteli; ☎ 212-243 0737; Meşrutiyet Caddesi 52, Tepebaşı; 🚇 Karaköy, then funicular to Tünel

The Pera Palas was built by Georges Nagelmackers, the Belgian entrepreneur who founded the Compagnie Internationale des Wagons-Lits et Grands Express Européens in 1868. Nagelmackers, who had succeeded in linking Paris and Constantinople by luxury train with his famed Orient Express, found that once he had transported his esteemed passengers to the Ottoman imperial capital there was no suitable place for them to stay. What was Nagelmackers to do? Why, build a new luxury hotel of course!

The hotel opened in 1892 and advertised itself as having 'a thoroughly healthy situation, being high up and isolated on all four sides', and 'overlooking the Golden Horn and the whole panorama of Stamboul'. Its guests included Agatha Christie, who sup-

posedly wrote Murder on the Orient Express in Room 411; Mata Hari, who no doubt frequented the elegant bar with its lovely stained-glass windows and excellent eavesdropping opportunities; and Greta Garbo, who probably enjoyed her own company in one of the spacious suites.

As this book went to print the hotel was undergoing a total renovation and was scheduled to reopen in early 2010. Some consternation was being aired around town as to how sympathetic the renovation will be to the building's rich cultural and architectural history.

## PERA MUSEUM Map pp102–3
Pera Müzesi; ☎ 212-334 9900; www.peramuzesi. org.tr; Meşrutiyet Caddesi 65, Tepebaşı; adult/ student & child over 12yr/child under 12yr TL7/3/ free; ⏱ 10am-7pm Tue-Sat, noon-6pm Sun; 🚇 Karaköy, then funicular to Tünel

The most beloved painting in the Turkish canon – Osman Hamdı Bey's The Tortoise Trainer (1906) – sold at auction in late 2004 for a massive US$3.5 million, making it the most expensive art purchase of recent times. Turks were worried that the painting might be lost to the nation, so there was rejoicing when this new, privately funded museum announced that it had been the successful bidder and that the painting would be the focal point of its wonderful Orientalist painting collection. Acquired by Suna and İnan Kıraç over decades, this collection consists of more than 300 paintings with Turkish Orientalist themes. Its canvasses by Turkish and European artists provide fascinating glimpses into the Ottoman world from the 17th to the early 20th century. Sometimes these treatments are realistic, at other times they are highly romanticised – what's consistent is their focus on the rich costumes, fascinating domestic settings and varied individuals of the period.

The museum has conceived a program of long-term thematic exhibitions to showcase these Orientalist paintings, and has been loaned important Orientalist works from the Sevgi and Erdoğan Gönül Collection to supplement its holdings.

The museum also has two permanent exhibits: a top-notch collection of Kütahya tiles and ceramics, and a somewhat esoteric collection of Anatolian weights and measures. The top three floors are devoted to temporary exhibitions, mostly of local contemporary works in mixed media.

## FLOWER PASSAGE Map pp102–3

**Çiçek Pasaji; İstiklal Caddesi;** 🚇 **Kabataş, then funicular to Taksim**

Back in the days when the *Orient Express* was rolling into Old Stamboul and promenading down İstiklal Caddesi was the height of fashion, the Cité de Pera building was the most glamorous address in town. Built in 1876 and decorated in Second Empire style, it housed a shopping arcade as well as apartments. As Pera declined, so too did the building, its stylish shops giving way to cheap restaurant-taverns where in good weather beer barrels were rolled out onto the pavement, marble slabs were balanced on top, wooden stools were arranged and enthusiastic revellers caroused the night away. Renamed Çiçek Pasajı (Flower Passage), it continued in this vein until the late 1970s, when parts of the building collapsed. When it was reconstructed, the passage was 'beautified'. That is, its makeshift barrels and stools were replaced with comfortable and solid wooden tables and benches, and its broken pavement was covered with smooth tiles. The passage also acquired a glass canopy to protect pedestrians from foul weather. These days its raffish charm is nearly gone and locals in the know bypass the touts and the mediocre food on offer here and instead make their way behind the passage to Nevizade Sokak if they are seeking a great night on the town.

Next to the Çiçek Pasajı you'll find the Fish Market (Balık Pazar) in Sahna Sokak, where small stands sell *midye* (skewered mussels) fried in hot oil (get a skewer that's been freshly cooked). You'll also find stalls selling fruit, vegetables, pickles and other produce.

At 24A Sahne Sokak, look for the gigantic black doors to the courtyard of the Üç Horan Ermeni Kilisesi (Armenian Church of Three Altars). Visitors can enter the church providing the doors are open. Opposite the church are the neoclassical European Passage (Avrupa Pasajı aka Aynalı Pasajı or Arcade of Mirrors), a small gallery with marble paving and shops selling tourist wares and some antique goods, and Aslıhan Passage (Aslıhan Pasajı), an arcade jam-packed with second-hand book and record stalls.

## TAKSİM SQUARE Map pp102–3

🚇 **Kabataş, then funicular to Taksim**

The symbolic heart of modern İstanbul, this busy square is named after the stone

reservoir on its western side, once part of the city's old water-conduit system and now home to the unassuming Taksim Republic Art Gallery (Taksim Cumhuriyet Sanat Galerisi; admission free; ⏰ variable). The main water line from the Belgrade Forest, north of the city, was laid to this point in 1732 by Sultan Mahmut I (r 1730–54). Branch lines then led from the *taksim* to other parts of the city.

Hardly a triumph of urban design, the square has a chaotic bus terminus on one side, a slightly pathetic garden laid out in its centre and the tracks of the İstiklal Caddesi tram circumnavigating this garden. The mayor of İstanbul, Kadir Topbaş has publicly announced plans to beautify the square and integrate it with neighbouring Gezi Park, moving the bus station and redirecting traffic in the process; however no timeline for works had been announced when this book went to print.

The prominent modern building at the eastern end of the plaza is the Atatürk Cultural Centre (Atatürk Kültür Merkezi, sometimes called the Opera House; p181). Designed by Hayati Tabanlıoğlu in 1956–57, it appears to best advantage at night, when its elegant steel mesh is illuminated. In the summertime, during the International İstanbul Music Festival, tickets for festival events are on sale in the ticket office here, and some performances are staged in the centre's halls.

At the western end of the square is the Republic Monument (Cumhuriyet Anıtı), created by Canonica, an Italian sculptor, in 1928. It features Atatürk, his assistant and successor, İsmet İnönü, and other revolutionary leaders. The monument's purpose was not only to commemorate revolutionary heroes, but also to break down the Ottoman-Islamic prohibition against the making of 'graven images'.

# İSTIKLAL CADDESI PROMENADE
## Walking Tour

**1 Taksim Square** Start this walk at Beyoğlu's nerve centre (left). This is where locals meet before setting off to promenade down İstiklal Caddesi, formerly known as the Grand Rue de Pera.

**2 Galatasaray Lycée** This prestigious public school was established in 1868 by Sultan

Abdül Aziz, who was keen to have the sons of the Ottoman court schooled in both Turkish and French. Today, İstanbul's establishment still sends its sons here to be educated. The Galatasaray Football Club was founded here in 1905.

**3 Flower Passage** The picturesque Çiçek Pasajı (p109) opposite the Lycée has been hosting

raucous crowds of drinkers since the late 1800s, and shows no sign of changing its ways any time soon. The Fish Market (Balık Pazar) on its western side is a great place to stock up on groceries or grab a fishy street snack.

**4 European Passage** Of the many covered arcades in this area, the Avrupa Pasajı (off the Flower Passage, p109) is the most attractive.

**5 British Consulate General** This neoclassical hulk was designed in the 1840s by Sir Charles Barry, architect of London's Houses of Parliament, and was originally known as Pera House. Home to the British Consul General ever since, it underwent major restoration after a shocking bomb attack in 2003 that killed 16 people, 10 of whom were consulate staff.

## WALK FACTS

Start Taksim Sq
End Galata Kulesi Sq
Time 2½ hours
Fuel stops İstanbul Culinary Institute (p154), Pera Palace Hotel (p108), Galata Konak Patisserie Café (p157)

**İSTİKLAL CADDESI PROMENADE**

0 — 300 m
0 — 0.2 miles

**6 Pera Museum** Fans of Orientalist painting should make a beeline for the 3rd floor of this impressive museum (p108). Afterwards, consider stopping for lunch at the İstanbul Culinary Institute (p154) or, when it reopens, a drink at the famous Pera Palace Hotel (p108).

**7 Netherlands Consulate General** This handsome building dating from 1855 was designed by the Swiss-born Fossati brothers, who had been architects to the Russian tsar before they arrived in İstanbul to take the town by architectural storm.

**8 Church of St Mary Draperis** Built c 1772, this Franciscan church is behind an iron fence and down a flight of steps. It occupies the site of its previous building, which was built in 1678 but was largely destroyed in the 1767 great fire of Beyoğlu. During the Ottoman period, there was a law that prevented non-Muslim spires from appearing on the city skyline – no doubt the reason for this 'sunken' location.

**9 Russian Consulate** Another grand embassy designed by the Fossati brothers. This building dates from 1837 and replaced an earlier Russian embassy (now known as the Narmanlı Han), which is a bit further down İstiklal Caddesi on the opposite side of the road.

**10 Botter House** Designed by Raimondo D'Aronco for the chief tailor to the imperial court of Sultan Abdül Hamit II, this was the first art nouveau building in Pera. It's currently in a deplorable state of repair and has been scaffolded for safety reasons.

**11 Royal Swedish Consulate** Yep, it's another grand embassy building. This one was built by the Swedes at the end of the 17th century.

**12 Galata Kulesi Square** Turn off İstiklal Caddesi at Tünel Sq, walk down Galipdede Caddesi, with its many music shops, and veer right into this well-used public space, presided over by the distinctive Galata Tower (p105). From here, you can explore the streets of Galata, enjoy the Bosphorus view from the Galata Konak Patisserie Café (p157) or make your way across the Galata Bridge to the Old City.

# NİŞANTAŞI & AROUND

Drinking p168; Eating p158; Shopping p140; Sleeping p199

If you're a dab hand at air-kissing and striking a pose over a caffè latte, you'll feel totally at home here. Serious shoppers, visiting celebs, PR professionals and the city's gilded youth gravitate towards this upmarket enclave, which is located about 2km north of Taksim Sq. Bars, restaurants, boutique hotels and international fashion and design outlets are found in the streets surrounding the man artery, Teşvikiye Caddesi, prompting some locals to refer to that area as Teşvikiye. Closer to Taksim are the suburbs of Elmadağ and Harbiye, accessed via frantically busy Cumhuriyet Caddesi, where many of the city's airline offices are located. To get here, walk or catch a metro from Taksim Sq (metro stop Osmanbey).

## MILITARY MUSEUM Map p113

**Askeri Müze;** ☎ 212-233 2720; Vali Konağı Caddesi, Harbiye; adult/student TL3/1; ☾ 9am-5pm Wed-Sun; ☐ Kabataş, then funicular to Taksim

For a rousing museum experience, present yourself at this little-visited museum located 1km north of Taksim. Try to visit in the afternoon so that you can enjoy the concert given by the Mehter, which occurs most days between 3pm and 4pm.

The large museum is spread over two floors. On the ground floor are displays of weapons and Turkish military uniforms through the ages, as well as glass cases holding battle standards, both Turkish and captured. These include Byzantine, Greek, British, Austro-Hungarian, Italian and Imperial Russian standards.

Also on show are an old-fashioned diorama of the Conquest and a tapestry woven by Ottoman sailors (who must have had lots of time on their hands) showing the flags of all of the world's important maritime nations.

The upper floor has a Çannakale (Gallipoli) diorama and a room devoted to

Atatürk, who was, of course, a famous Ottoman general before he became founder and commander-in-chief of the republican army and first president of the Turkish Republic.

Perhaps the best reason to visit this museum is to view the short concert by the Mehter. Turkish historians argue that the Mehter was the world's first true military band. Its purpose was not to make pretty music for dancing, but to precede the conquering Ottoman *paşas* (governors) into vanquished towns, impressing upon the defeated populace their new, subordinate status. Children in particular will love watching them march with their steady, measured pace, turning all together to face the left side of the line of march, then the right side.

The easiest way to get to the museum is to walk up Cumhuriyet Caddesi from Taksim Sq. This will take around 15 minutes. When this book went to print, there were rumours that the museum would relocate to the stables building in Gülhane Park (p68) near Topkapı Palace.

# NİŞANTAŞI & AROUND

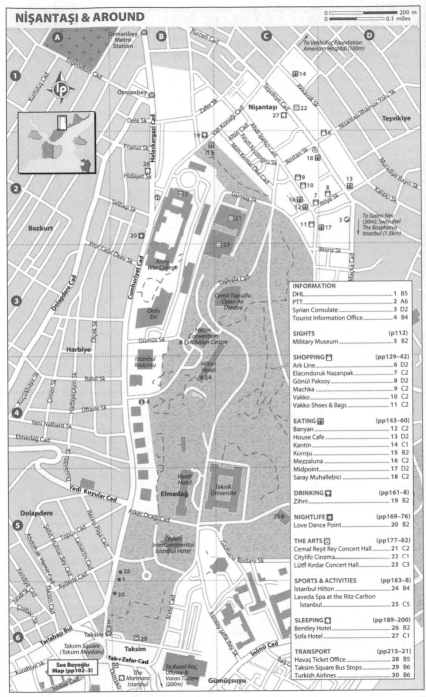

**INFORMATION**

| | |
|---|---|
| DHL | 1 B5 |
| PTT | 2 A6 |
| Syrian Consulate | 3 D2 |
| Tourist Information Office | 4 B4 |

**SIGHTS** (p112)

| | |
|---|---|
| Military Museum | 5 B2 |

**SHOPPING** (pp129–42)

| | |
|---|---|
| Ark Line | 6 D2 |
| Elacındoruk Nazanpak | 7 C2 |
| Gönül Paksoy | 8 C2 |
| Machka | 9 C2 |
| Vakko | 10 C2 |
| Vakko Shoes & Bags | 11 C2 |

**EATING** (pp143–60)

| | |
|---|---|
| Banyan | 12 C2 |
| House Cafe | 13 D2 |
| Kantin | 14 C1 |
| Komşu | 15 B2 |
| Mezzaluna | 16 C2 |
| Midpoint | 17 D2 |
| Saray Muhallebici | 18 C2 |

**DRINKING** (pp161–8)

| | |
|---|---|
| Zihni | 19 B2 |

**NIGHTLIFE** (pp169–76)

| | |
|---|---|
| Love Dance Point | 20 B2 |

**THE ARTS** (pp177–82)

| | |
|---|---|
| Cemal Reşit Rey Concert Hall | 21 C2 |
| Citylife Cinema | 22 C1 |
| Lütfi Kırdar Concert Hall | 23 C3 |

**SPORTS & ACTIVITIES** (pp183–8)

| | |
|---|---|
| İstanbul Hilton | 24 B4 |
| Laveda Spa at the Ritz-Carlton İstanbul | 25 C5 |

**SLEEPING** (pp189–200)

| | |
|---|---|
| Bentley Hotel | 26 B2 |
| Sofa Hotel | 27 C1 |

**TRANSPORT** (pp215–21)

| | |
|---|---|
| Havaş Ticket Office | 28 B5 |
| Taksim Square Bus Stops | 29 B6 |
| Turkish Airlines | 30 B6 |

# BEŞİKTAŞ, ORTAKÖY & KURUÇEŞME

Drinking p168; Eating p158; Shopping p142; Sleeping p199

As well as being a major transport hub and the home of one of the 'Big Three' football teams (see the boxed text p188), Beşiktaş has the largest concentration of Ottoman pleasure palaces and pavilions in İstanbul. French writer Pierre Loti described the shoreline here as a '…line of palaces white as snow, placed at the edge of the sea on marble docks' and the description is still as accurate as it is evocative. This is where the unrepentantly over-the-top Dolmabahçe Palace (below) and the ritzy Çırağan Palace Kempinski İstanbul (p199), a former Ottoman royal palace, are located.

A slightly more restrained tone is evident at Yıldız Şale, a palace set in leafy Yıldız Park (p116). While its designer didn't go as far as eschewing the ornate and ostentatious (heaven forbid!), this building has a more human scale than its waterside equivalents.

The nearby suburb of Ortaköy is nowhere near as grand as Beşiktaş, but has considerable charm, particularly on warm summer nights when its main square is crowded with locals dining at its waterside restaurants or enjoying an after-dinner coffee and ice cream by the water. Later in the evening, the clubbing set hits the nearby venues on the Bosphorus, most of which are located on or near Muallim Naci Caddesi. Known as the 'Golden Mile', this sybaritic stretch finishes at the next-door suburb of Kuruçeşme.

It can be difficult to access Yıldız and Ortaköy, as narrow Çırağan/Muallim Naci Caddesi provides the only vehicular access and is inevitably jammed bumper-to-bumper with commuters making their way to or from the Bosphorus suburbs. This means that taxi rides here can be slow and expensive. Buses also get caught in the traffic jam and can be unpleasantly crowded. As a result, many people choose to catch a ferry or bus to Beşiktaş and walk the kilometre or so to Ortaköy rather than driving, bussing or catching a taxi.

If you're visiting Dolmabahçe only, this is easily accessed by foot (15 minutes) from the Kabataş tram stop and the lower stop of the Taksim Sq–Kabataş funicular.

## DOLMABAHÇE PALACE Map p115

Dolmabahçe Sarayı; ☎ 212-236 9000; www.dolmabahce.gov.tr; Dolmabahçe Caddesi, Beşiktaş; admission TL20, camera TL6, video camera TL15; ⊕ 9am-4pm Tue, Wed & Fri-Sun summer, to 3pm winter; 🚌 Beşiktaş or 🚋 to Kabataş & then walk
These days it's fashionable for architects and critics influenced by the less-is-more aesthetic of the Bauhaus masters to sneer at buildings such as Dolmabahçe. The crowds that throng to this imperial pleasure palace with its neoclassical exterior and over-the-top interior fit-out clearly don't share their disdain, though.

More rather than less was certainly the philosophy of Sultan Abdül Mecit I, who, deciding that it was time to give the lie to talk of Ottoman military and financial decline, decided to move from Topkapı to a lavish new palace on the shores of the Bosphorus. For a site he chose the *dolma bahçe* (filled-in garden) where his predecessors Sultans Ahmet I and Osman II had filled in a little cove in order to create a royal park complete with wooden pleasure kiosks and pavilions. Other wooden buildings succeeded the original kiosk, but all burned to the ground in 1814. In 1843 Abdül Mecit

commissioned imperial architects Nikoğos and Garabed Balyan to construct an Ottoman-European palace that would impress everyone who set eyes on it. Traditional Ottoman palace architecture was eschewed – there are no pavilions here, and the palace turns its back to the splendid view rather than celebrating it. The designer of the Paris Opera was brought in to do the interiors, which perhaps explains their exaggerated theatricality. Construction was finally completed in 1854 and the Sultan and his family moved in two years later. Though it had the wow factor in spades, Abdül Mecit's project also did more to precipitate the empire's bankruptcy than to dispel rumours of it, and signalled the beginning of the end for the Osmanlı dynasty. During the early years of the republic, Atatürk used the palace as his İstanbul base. He died here in 1938.

The palace, which is set in well-tended gardens and entered via its ornate imperial gate, is divided into two sections, the Selamlık (Ceremonial Suites) and the Harem-Cariyeler (Harem and Concubines' Quarters). Entry is via a compulsory guided tour (around 35 people per group), which focuses on the Selamlık but visits parts of the harem as well.

# BEŞİKTAŞ & ORTAKÖY & KURUÇEŞME

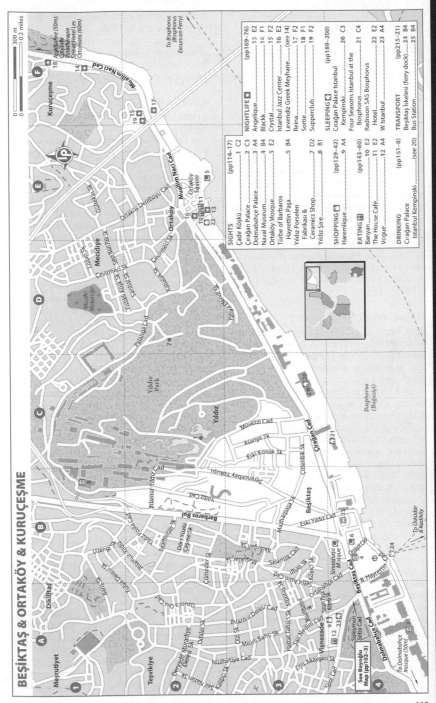

| SIGHTS | (pp114-17) |
|---|---|
| Çadir Köşkü | 1 C2 |
| Çırağan Palace | 2 C3 |
| Dolmabahçe Palace | 3 A4 |
| Naval Museum | 4 B4 |
| Ortaköy Mosque | 5 E2 |
| Türbe of Barbaros | |
| Hayrettin Paşa | 5 B4 |
| Yıldız Porselen | |
| Fabrikası & | |
| Ceramics Shop | 7 D2 |
| Yıldız Şale | 8 B1 |

| SHOPPING | (pp129-42) |
|---|---|
| Haremlique | 9 A4 |

| EATING | (pp143-60) |
|---|---|
| Banyan | 10 E2 |
| The House Café | 11 E2 |
| Vogue | 12 A4 |

| DRINKING | (pp151-8) |
|---|---|
| Çırağan Palace | |
| Istanbul Kempinski | (see 20) |

| NIGHTLIFE | (pp169-76) |
|---|---|
| Angelique | 13 E2 |
| Blackk | 14 F1 |
| Crystal | 15 F2 |
| Istanbul Jazz Center | 16 E2 |
| Levendiz Greek Meyhane | (see 14) |
| Reina | 17 F2 |
| Sortie | 18 F1 |
| Supperclub | 19 F2 |

| SLEEPING | (pp189-200) |
|---|---|
| Çırağan Palace Istanbul | |
| Kempinski | 20 C3 |
| Four Seasons Istanbul at the | |
| Bosphorus | 21 C4 |
| Radisson SAS Bosphorus | |
| Hotel | 22 E2 |
| W Istanbul | 23 A4 |

| TRANSPORT | (pp215-21) |
|---|---|
| Beşiktaş İskelesi (ferry dock) | 24 B4 |
| Bus Station | 25 B4 |

300 m
0.2 miles

In busy periods the tours leave every five minutes; during quiet times every 25 minutes is more likely. Be warned that queues at the ticket office can be very long (waits of up to two hours) and there is no shade. The tourist entrance to the palace is near the palace's ornate clock tower, designed by Sarkis Balyan between 1890 and 1895 for Sultan Abdül Hamid II (r 1876–1909). There is an outdoor cafe near here with premium Bosphorus views.

Don't set your watch by any of the palace clocks, all of which are stopped at 9.05am, the moment at which Kemal Atatürk died in Dolmabahçe on 10 November 1938. When touring the harem you will be shown the small bedroom he used during his last days. Each year on 10 November, at 9.05am, the country observes a moment of silence in commemoration of the great leader.

The nearby Dolmabahçe Mosque (Dolmabahçe Camii) on Muallim Naci Caddesi was designed by Nikoğos Balyan and completed in 1853.

## NAVAL MUSEUM Map p115

Denız Müzesı ☎ 212-327 4345; www.dzkk.tsk.tr; cnr Cezayir & Beşiktaş Caddesis, Beşiktaş; adult/student TL3/1; ☉ 9am-12.30pm & 1.30-5pm Wed-Sun; ☒ Beşiktaş or ☒ to Kabataş & then walk
Landlubbers and salty seadogs alike will enjoy a visit to this museum of Turkish naval history, which is located on the Bosphorus shore close to the Beşiktaş ferry terminal.

Though the Ottoman Empire is most remembered for its conquests on land, its maritime power was equally impressive. During the reign of Süleyman the Magnificent (r 1520–66), the eastern Mediterranean was virtually an Ottoman recreational lake. The sultan's navies cut a swathe in the Indian Ocean as well. Sea power was instrumental in the conquests of the Aegean coasts and islands, Egypt and North Africa. Discipline, logistics and good ship design contributed to Ottoman victories.

Exhibits focus on two great Turkish sailors: the 16th-century cartographer Piri Reis; and the admiral of Süleyman the Magnificent's fleet, Barbaros Heyrettin Paşa (1483–1546), better known as Barbarossa. The admiral's tomb, designed by Sinan, is in the square opposite the museum.

Highlights include a coloured 1461 map on antelope skin, and a portion of the great chain that the Byzantines stretched across the mouth of the Golden Horn to keep out the sultan's ships during the battle for Constantinople in 1453.

The museum's indoor and outdoor spaces were being renovated when this book went to print, but the main exhibits were still open to the public.

## ÇIRAĞAN PALACE Map p115

Çırağan Sarayı; Çırağan Caddesi 84, Beşiktaş; ☒ Yıldız Parkı
Not satisfied with the architectural exertions of his predecessor at Dolmabahçe, Sultan Abdül Aziz (r 1861–76) built his own grand residence at Çırağan, on the Bosphorus shore only 1.5km away from Dolmabahçe. The architect was Nikoğos Balyan, one of the designers of Dolmabahçe, and here he created an interesting building melding European neoclassical with Ottoman and Moorish styles.

Abdül Aziz's extravagance may have been one of the reasons why he was deposed in 1876, to be replaced by his mentally unstable and alcoholic nephew, Murat. Abdül Aziz later died in Çırağan under mysterious circumstances, probably suicide. Murat was in turn swiftly deposed by Abdül Hamit II, who kept his predecessor and brother a virtual prisoner in Çırağan. Murat died in the palace in 1904. In 1909 it became the seat of the Ottoman Chamber of Deputies and Senate, but in 1910 it was badly damaged by fire under suspicious circumstances.

The palace is now part of the Çırağan Palace Kempinski İstanbul (p199).

## YILDIZ PARK Map p115

Yıldız Parkı; ☎ 212-261 8460; Çırağan Caddesi; admission free; ☉ 9am-6pm summer, 9am-5.30pm winter; ☒ Yıldız Parkı
Sultan Abdül Hamit II (r 1876–1909) didn't allow himself to be upstaged by his predecessors. He built his own fancy palace by adding considerably to the structures built by earlier sultans in Yıldız Park, continuing the Ottoman tradition of palace pavilions that had been employed so wonderfully at Topkapı. It was to be the last sultan's palace built in İstanbul.

The park began life as the imperial reserve for the Çırağan Sarayı, but when Abdül Hamit built Yıldız Şale, largest of the park's surviving structures, the park then served that palace and was planted with rare and exotic trees, shrubs and flowers. It also gained carefully tended paths and superior electric lighting and drainage systems. The landscape designer, G Le Roi, was French.

The park and its kiosks became derelict during the early years of the Republic, but in the 1980s it was restored by the Turkish Touring & Automobile Association (Turing) under lease from the city government. In 1994 the newly elected city government declined to renew the lease and took over operation of the park. Today it's a pretty, leafy retreat alive with birds, picnickers and couples enjoying a bit of hanky-panky in the bushes.

Near the top of the hill (to the left of the road if you enter by Çırağan Caddesi), you'll see the Çadır Köşkü. Built between 1865 and 1870, the ornate kiosk is nestled beside a small lake and now functions as a cafe.

At the top of the hill, enclosed by a lofty wall, is the Yıldız Şale (Yıldız Chalet Museum; ☎ 212-259 4570; admission TL4, still/video camera TL6/15; ☪ 9.30am-5pm Tue-Wed & Fri-Sun, until 4pm winter), a 'guesthouse' built in 1875 and expanded in 1889 and 1898 by Abdül Hamit – both times for the use of Kaiser Wilhelm II of Germany during state visits. As you enter the palace, a Turkish-speaking guide will take you on a compulsory half-hour tour through the building. The chalet isn't as plush as Dolmabahçe, but it's far less crowded (in fact, it's often empty), so you get more time to feast your eyes on the exhibits.

It would seem the Kaiser had enough space to move in, as the chalet has 64 rooms. After his imperial guest departed, the sultan became quite attached to his 'rustic' creation and decided to live here himself, forsaking the palaces on the Bosphorus shore.

Abdül Hamit was paranoid, and for good reason. When eventually deposed, he left this wooden palace in April 1909 and boarded a train that took him to house arrest in Ottoman Salonika (today Thessaloniki, Greece). He was later allowed by the Young Turks' government to return to İstanbul and live out his years in Beylerbeyi Palace, on the Asian shore of the Bosphorus.

The first room on the tour was used by Abdül Hamit's mother for her religious devotions; the second was her guest reception room, with a very fine mosaic tabletop. Then comes a women's resting room and afterwards a tearoom with furniture marked with a gold star on a blue background, which reminds one that this is the 'star' (yıldız) chalet.

During the 1898 works the chalet was expanded, and the older section became the harem (with steel doors), while the new section functioned as the selamlık (ceremonial suites). In the selamlık is a bathroom with tiles from the Yıldız Porcelain Factory and several reception rooms, one of which has furniture made by Abdül Hamit himself. The grand hall of the selamlık is vast, its floor covered by a 7½-tonne Hereke carpet woven just for this room. The rug is so huge that it had to be brought in through the far (north) wall before the building was finished.

Around 500m past the turn-off to Yıldız Şale, you'll come to the Malta Köşkü, now a restaurant and function centre. Built in 1870, this was where Abdül Hamit imprisoned the deposed Murat V and his family. With its views of the Bosphorus, the terrace here makes a great place for a light lunch, tea or coffee.

If you continue walking past the Malta Köşkü for 10 minutes you'll arrive at the Yıldız Porselen Fabrikası (Yıldız Porcelain Factory; ☎ 212-260 2370; ☪ 9am-3pm). The factory is housed in a wonderful building designed by Italian architect Raimondo D'Aronco, who was to introduce art nouveau to İstanbul. Constructed to manufacture dinner services for the palace, it still operates and is open to visitors. There's a small ceramics shop (☪ 9am-7pm) at the entrance.

The steep walk uphill from Çırağan Caddesi to the Şale takes 15 to 20 minutes. If you come to the park by taxi, have it take you up the steep slope to the Şale and visit the other kiosks on the walk back down the hill. A taxi from Taksim Sq to the top of the hill should cost around TL8.

## ORTAKÖY MOSQUE Map p115
### Ortaköy Camıı; Büyük Mecidiye Camii, Ortaköy; 🚋 Ortaköy

Right on the water's edge, this mosque is the work of Nikoğos Balyan, one of the architects of Dolmabahçe Palace (p114). It was built for Sultan Abdül Mecit I between 1853 and 1855. With the modern Bosphorus Bridge now looming behind it, the mosque provides a fabulous photo opportunity for those wanting to illustrate İstanbul's 'old meets new' character. Within the mosque hang several masterful examples of Arabic calligraphy executed by the sultan, who was an accomplished calligrapher.

The mosque fronts onto Ortaköy Sq, the hub of this former fishing village and home to a pretty fountain and waterfront cafes.

Eating p159

Üsküdar (pronounced 'ooh-skoo-dar') is the Turkish form of the Byzantine name, Scutari, which dates from the 12th century. It comes from the imperial palace of Scutarion, once located on the point of land near Kız Kulesi (p120). The first colonists lived in Chalcedon (modern-day Kadıköy), to the south, and Chrysopolis (now Üsküdar) became its first major suburb; both towns existed about two decades before Byzantium was founded. The harbour at Chrysopolis was superior to that of Chalcedon so that, as Byzantium blossomed, Chrysopolis outgrew Chalcedon to become the largest suburb on the Asian shore. Unwalled and therefore vulnerable, it became part of the Ottoman Empire at least 100 years before the Conquest of 1453.

Judging that Scutari was the closest point in İstanbul to Mecca, many powerful Ottoman figures built mosques here to assist their passage to Paradise. Every year during the Empire a big caravan left from here en route to Mecca and Medina for the hajj, further emphasising its reputation for piety. Even today, Üsküdar is one of İstanbul's more conservative suburbs. Home to many migrants from rural Anatolia, the mosques are busier here, the families are larger and the headscarf is more obvious than elsewhere in the city. Like Kadıköy and the Western Districts, it's a fascinating and totally un-touristy place to explore.

The suburb's major streets radiate from Democracy Sq (Demokrasi Meydanı), the square opposite the ferry docks. There were major works occurring around the main square when this book went to print, all of which were associated with the Marmaray project (see the boxed text p218). These included archaeological excavations at the site of an ancient arasta (shops of the same trade built in a row), a tannery and a Byzantine pier – all discovered when the Marmaray works got underway. The main bus station is currently just north of the ferry docks, on Paşalimanı Caddesi, but this may change. The nearby suburbs of Harem and Kadıköy are to the south. Buses to Harem and Kadıköy travel along the shoreline along Sahil Yolu (find them south of the Şemşi Paşa Mosque); dolmuşes (minibuses) to Kadıköy leave from outside the Yeni Valide Mosque on Hakimiyet-i Milliye Caddesi and take the longer route through the hills.

## ATİK VALİDE MOSQUE Map p119
Atik Valide Camii; Valide Imaret Sokak; Üsküdar

This is one of the grandest of Sinan's İstanbul mosques, second only to his Süleymaniye Mosque (p76). Experts rate it as one of the most important Ottoman mosque complexes in the country. It was built in 1583 for Valide Sultan Nurbanu, wife of Selim II and mother of Murat III. Nurbanu had been captured by Turks on the Aegean island of Paros when she was 12 years old, ending up as a slave in Topkapı. The poor woman had a lot to bear – first being kidnapped and then taking the fancy of Selim the Sot – but she was his favourite concubine and became a very clever player in Ottoman political life. The Kandınlar Sultanatı (Rule of the Women) under which a succession of powerful women influenced the decisions made by their sultan husbands and sons began with her. Murat adored his mother and on her death commissioned Sinan to build this monument to her on Üsküdar's highest hill. Like the Süleymaniye, it has an impressive courtyard and extensive külliye.

The tile-adorned mihrab is particularly attractive.

The mosque is located in the neighbourhood of Tabaklar, up Hakimiyet-i Milliye and Dr Fahri Atabey Caddesis.

## ÇİNİLİ MOSQUE Map p119
Çinili Camii, Tiled Mosque; Çinili Mescit Sokak; Üsküdar

This little mosque is fairly unprepossessing from the outside, but the interior is a totally different story. The walls are brilliant with İznik faïence, the bequest of Mahpeyker Kösem (1640), wife of Sultan Ahmet I and mother of sultans Murat IV and İbrahim (known as 'İbrahim the Crazy'). It's a 10-minute walk to get here from the Atik Valide Mosque.

## MİHRİMAH SULTAN MOSQUE Map p119
Mihrimah Sultan Camii; Demokrasi Meydanı; Üsküdar

Sometimes called the İskele (Dock) Camii, this mosque was built between 1547 and 1548 by Sinan for Süleyman the Magnificent's daughter. Though imposing on the

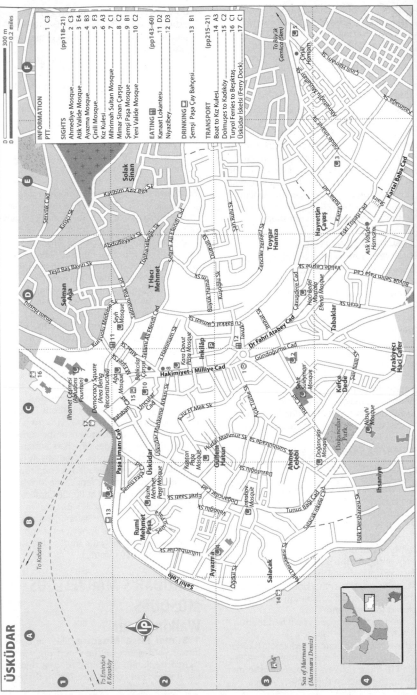

outside, it's a bit claustrophobic and dull inside and is need of restoration and a good clean. You'll find it northeast of the Demokrasi Meydanı. Look out for its ablutions fountain in the traffic island, which is particularly attractive.

## MİMAR SİNAN ÇARŞISI Map p119
**Hakimiyet-i Milliye Caddesi; admission free; 9am-6pm; Üsküdar**

Built by Nurbanu Sultan, mother of Sultan Murat III, between 1574 and 1583, this *hamam* is thought to have been the first designed by Sinan. Having fallen into ruins, part of it was torn down to accommodate construction of the avenue; the remaining half was restored in 1966 and is now cramped and crowded with shops.

## YENİ VALİDE MOSQUE Map p119
**Yeni Valide Camii, New Queen Mother's Mosque; Demokrasi Meydanı; Üsküdar**

Unusual because of the striking 'birdcage' tomb in its overgrown garden, the Yeni Valide Mosque was built by Sultan Ahmet III between 1708 and 1710 for his mother, Gülnuş Emetullah. After being captured as a child on Crete and brought to Topkapı, Gülnuş became the favourite concubine of Mehmet IV, and bore him two sons who would become sultan: Mustafa II and his younger brother, Ahmet. Built late in the period of classical Ottoman architecture, it lacks the architectural distinction of many of the suburb's other mosques.

## ŞEMSİ PAŞA MOSQUE Map p119
**Şemsi Paşa Camii, Kuskonmaz Camii; Sahil Yolu; Üsküdar**

This charming mosque complex right on the waterfront was designed by Sinan and built in 1580 for grand vizier, Şemsi Ahmet Paşa. It is modest in size and decoration, reflecting the fact that its benefactor (whose tomb has an opening into the mosque) only occupied the position of grand vizier for a couple of months under Süleyman the Magnificent. When this book went to press, the mosque and its adjoining *medrese* were closed for restoration.

Next to the mosque you'll find the run-down Şemsi Paşa Çay Bahçesi, a decent place to recover from a hectic schedule of Üsküdar mosque viewing if the weather is fine. Behind it, there's always a posse of fishermen trying their luck in the choppy waters.

## BÜYÜK ÇAMLICA off Map p119
**Turistik Çamlıca Caddesi; admission free; 9am-11pm; Üsküdar, then Turistik Çamlica Tes or taxi**

The term megalopolis is bandied about a fair bit to describe İstanbul, but it's only when you come to a spot like this that it becomes meaningful. Larger than many sovereign states, the city sprawls further than the eye can see, even when afforded this bird's-eye view. And what a view it is! A hilltop park with a crown of pine trees, Büyük Çamlıca is the highest point in the city and can be seen from miles away (you'll see it as you ferry down the Bosphorus, for example). It's beloved by İstanbullus, who flock here to relax, picnic in the pretty gardens, enjoy a snack or glass of tea at the Çamlıca Restaurant ( 9am-midnight) and gaze upon their fine city. From the terraces you'll see the minaret-filled skyline of Old İstanbul, as well as the Bosphorus winding its way to the Black Sea.

Once favoured by Sultan Mahmut II (r 1808–39), by the late 1970s the park was an unkempt car park threatened by illegal and unplanned construction. In 1980 the municipal government leased the land to the Turing group, which landscaped the hilltop and built a restaurant that Mahmut might have enjoyed. The municipal government took over management of the park in 1995.

To reach the hilltop from Demokrasi Meydanı, you can take a taxi (about TL9) all the way to the summit or bus 9UD from the bus station to the bus stop near the corner of Turistik Çamlica Caddesi; the park entrance is only a short walk north. Alternatively, you can take a Ümraniye-headed *dolmuş* from the rank in front of the Yeni Valide Mosque and ask to be dropped at Büyük Çamlica; this will pass the entrance to Küçük Çamlica and drop you off shortly thereafter in a district called Kısıklı. The walk uphill (pleasant but no great views) following the signs to the summit takes 20 to 30 minutes.

# ÜSKÜDAR'S MARVELLOUS MOSQUES
## Walking Tour
**1 Şemsi Paşa Mosque** This cute-as-a-button building (left) on the waterfront was designed by Sinan. It's more modest than his usual work, but no less pleasing for that fact.

**2 Kız Kulesi** İstanbul is a maritime city, so it's appropriate that this tower, one of its most distinctive landmarks, is on the water. In ancient times a predecessor of the current 18th-century structure was used as a tollbooth and defence point; the current building has functioned as a lighthouse, quarantine station and customs control point. In 1999, the tower featured in the Bond film *The World is Not Enough*.

**3 Ayazma Mosque** One of the most prominent sights on the Üsküdar skyline, this baroque-style mosque, built in 1760–61 by Sultan Mustafa III, is accessed via a courtyard and graceful set of entry stairs.

**4 Ahmediye Mosque** Eminzade Hacı Ahmet Paşa, comptroller of the Arsenal under Ahmet III, commissioned this unusual mosque and attached *medrese* in 1722. Its design features a main gate with a *dershane* (lecture hall) and library built over it.

**5 Atik Valide Mosque** This is one of the two great İstanbul mosque complexes designed by Sinan. Though not as spectacular as the Süleymaniye, this mosque (p118) was designed to a similar plan and built in a similarly commanding location. Its extensive *külliye* includes a now-decommissioned *hamam* on Dr Fahri Atabey Caddesi and, closer to the mosque, an *imaret, medrese,* hospital (*darüş-şifa*) and *han*.

**6 Çinili Mosque** Yes, it's a modest and run-down little mosque (p118) but wow, how about those İznik tiles?! These were the bequest of Mahpeyker Kösem (1640), wife of Sultan Ahmet I. Though run-down, the mosque's twin *hamam* is still used by locals.

**7 Take a Break** At the end of the walk, treat yourself to lunch or a glass of tea and a traditional dessert at Üsküdar's best-known eatery, Kanaat Lokantası (p159).

## WALK FACTS

Start Şemsi Paşa Mosque
End Çinili Mosque
Time 2½ hours
Fuel stop Kanaat Lokantası (p159)

NEIGHBOURHOODS ÜSKÜDAR

### ÜSKÜDAR'S MARVELLOUS MOSQUES

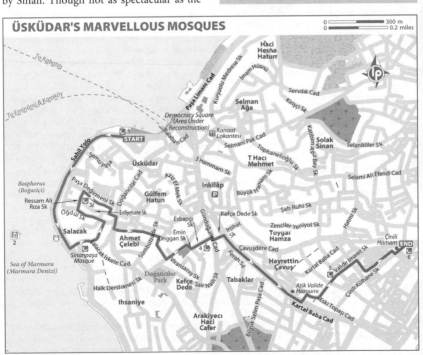

Drinking p159; Eating p168

Legend has it that the first colonists established themselves at Chalcedon, the site of modern Kadıköy. Byzas, bearing the oracle's message to found a colony 'Opposite the blind', thought the Chalcedonites blind to the advantages of Seraglio Point (Sarayburnu) as a town site when he arrived in the area, and founded his colony (Byzantium) on the European shore, opposite.

Though there's nothing to show of these historic beginnings and no headline sights, Kadıköy is a neighbourhood well worth visiting, particularly as the half-hour trip here by ferry from Eminönü or Karaköy is so enjoyable. There's fabulous fresh produce available in the market precinct near the ferry terminal; cafes and bars galore around Kadife Sokak; and one of the city's largest street markets, the Salı Pazarı (Tuesday Market; see the boxed text p142).

The two main ferry docks – Eminönü & Karaköy and Kızıl Adalar – face a plaza running along the south side of Kadıköy's small harbour. To the north is Haydarpaşa train station, a 15-minute walk from the ferry terminals. In the early 20th century, when Kaiser Wilhelm of Germany was trying to charm the sultan into economic and military cooperation, he presented

## İSTANBUL: EUROPEAN CAPITAL OF CULTURE

In his role as Director of Cultural Tourism for İstanbul, Professor Ahmet Emre Bilgili oversees the day-to-day functioning of more than his fair share of the city's heritage assets. He is also responsible for managing the biggest cultural hoedown in the city's history – İstanbul's starring role as one of the 2010 European Capitals of Culture. The scope of this event is enormous – and extremely expensive. The department's usual annual budget of US$500 million was set to increase by 50% in 2010, with 70% of the funds going to restoration of historically and architecturally significant monuments and 30% towards staging an eclectic program of cultural events that will underpin the Turkish government's ambition to use the event to reinforce İstanbul's status as 'a global city'. Fortunately, Professor Bilgili hasn't been seduced by the bread-and-circuses mentality that often characterises this type of event. The major project his department is funding is a heritage masterplan of the Topkapı Palace precinct, looking at the future of this priceless cultural asset and assessing the viability and suitability of future projects – including the possibility of expanding the İstanbul Archaeology Museums (p66), converting Aya İrini (p60) into a Byzantine Museum, and reopening the Baths of Lady Hürrem (p56) as either a functioning tourist *hamam* or a museum of the *hamam*. He believes the masterplan will 'give more importance to the historical peninsula' and says that it is unlikely to be completed until the end of 2010. Like many locals and visitors to the city, he is frustrated at how slowly many major restoration projects occur – Aya Sofya (p49) and Çemberlitaş (p79) being perfect examples – but he is quick to emphasise that the major priority must be conducting the restorations properly. Otherwise, botched jobs such as the infelicitous interventions in the historic land walls could again occur: 'I am particularly interested in the future of the city walls and have been working to develop strategies to conserve rather than restore them. We need to remove the unfortunate modern interventions and make the walls safe so that people can walk along and on top of them. Perhaps we could build cafes, hotels and museums along the way.' Queried about the dangers inherent in commercialising heritage assets such as the walls and Haydarpaşa and Sirkeci railway stations, Professor Bilgili nods, but then says, 'It is a huge challenge when you have as many assets as İstanbul has. At the moment, the İstanbul Vakıflar Bölge Müdürlüğü (Directory of the Pious Foundations, responsible for the maintenance of religious buildings in the city) is undertaking an ambitious program to restore all of the imperial mosques in the Old City in time for 2010, but there are so many projects for us all to work on and so many buildings that could potentially be museums...'

Other restoration projects being carried out under the 2010 banner include the restoration of the Atatürk Cultural Centre (p181), Galata Mevlevihanesi (p106) and Süleymaniye Kütüphanesi (theological library; p76). New museums are also being funded, including an archaeological park at Yenikapı, where 24 Byzantine wooden ships were discovered in an ancient silted-up harbour during excavations for the Marmaray transport project (boxed text p218).

In 2008, İstanbul hosted 7 million tourists, which significantly contributed to the local economy. The government is hoping to increase this figure to 10 million during 2010 and is confident that these projects will play a central role in attracting these extra visitors. For more information on the 2010 projects, see www.en.istanbul2010.org.

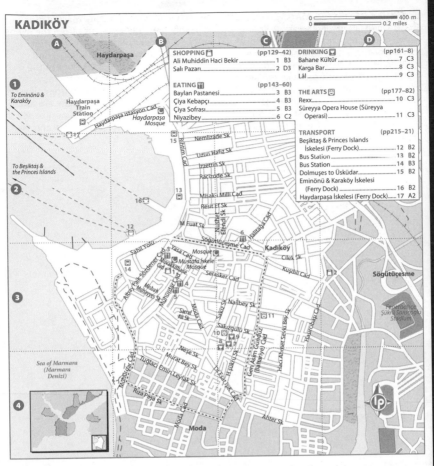

the station as a small token of his respect. Resembling a German castle, the neoclassical exterior is a prominent part of Kadıköy's skyline as you approach by ferry. It also has a very pretty, small ferry terminal designed by Vedat Tek. Works associated with the Marmaray project will see the terminal for trains to Anatolia move from this building to a new station at Söğütlüçesme; plans for this building's future had not been determined at the time of writing, although conversion to a hotel and shopping mall has been suggested.

Kadıköy's main street, Söğütlüçesme Caddesi, runs eastward uphill from the docks into Kadıköy proper; another main road, Serasker Caddesi, runs parallel to it. Busy Bahariye Caddesi runs perpendicular to both of them, around 300m inland, and is where the over-the-top Süreyya Operası (Süreyya Opera House) is located. The street continues on to the posh residential suburb of Moda.

Near the street market is Rüştü Saraçoğlu Stadium (the home of Fenerbahçe Football Club), and further on from this is the glamorous shopping and cafe precinct of Bağdat Caddesi, İstanbul's equivalent of Rodeo Drive.

## KADIKÖY PRODUCE MARKET p123

**Streets around Güneslibahçe Sokak;** 🚇 Kadıköy

Arriving by ferry, cross over Deniz Sokak in front of the ferry terminal and then walk up Muvakkıthane Sokak. Kadıköy's highly regarded fresh-produce market occupies the streets to the left (north), around the unassuming Mustafa İskele Mosque. You'll see fish glistening on beds of crushed ice, carts of seasonal fruits and vegetables, combs of amber-coloured honey and bins of freshly roasted nuts. Freshly baked bread issues from the ovens of Eser Ekmek Fabrikasi on Mühürdar Caddesi, and *simits* (bread rings) and *macarons* (macaroons) race out of the door of popular Bayaz Fırın on Yasa Caddesi. Delis selling everything from olive oil to pungent sheeps' milk cheese are found on both Yasa Caddesi and Güneşlibahçe Sokak. A feast for the eyes, nose and soul.

## YEDİKULE ZİNDANLARI Map pp46–7

**Yedikule Dungeon, Fortress of the Seven Towers;**
☎ 212-584 4012; Kule Meydanı 4, Fatih; admission
TL5, camera TL5; ☺ 9am-6.30pm; 🚈 Yedikule or
🚇 Yedikule

If you arrived in İstanbul by train from
Europe, or if you rode in from the airport
along the seashore, you will probably have
noticed this fortress looming over the
southern approaches to the city. One of the
city's major landmarks, it has a history as
substantial as its massive structure.

In the late 4th century Theodosius the
Great built a triumphal arch here. When
the next Theodosius built his massive
land walls, he incorporated the arch in the
structure. Four of the fortress' seven towers
were built as part of Theodosius II's walls;
the other three, which are inside the walls,
were added by Mehmet the Conqueror.
Under the Byzantines, the great arch
became known as the Porta Aurea (Golden
Gate) and was used for triumphal state
processions into and out of the city. For
a time its gates were indeed plated with
gold. The doorway was sealed in the late
Byzantine period.

In Ottoman times the fortress was used
for defence, as a repository for the Imperial Treasury, as a prison and as a place of
execution. In times of war, ambassadors of
'enemy' countries were thrown in prisons;
foreign ambassadors to the Sublime Porte
often ended up incarcerated in Yedikule.
Latin and German inscriptions still visible in
the Ambassadors' Tower bring the place's
eerie history to light. It was also here that
Sultan Osman II, a 17-year-old youth, was
executed in 1622 during a revolt of the
janissary corps. The kaftan he was wearing
when he was murdered is now on display
in Topkapı Palace's costumes collection.

The spectacular views from the battle-
ments are the highlight of a visit here. Note
that the lack of handrails or barriers on the
steep stone staircases can be offputting for
some visitors.

While you're in the neighbourhood,
consider a trip to İstanbul's best kebapçı,
Develi (boxed text p150), one station east at
Mustafa Paşa. You can also walk along the
historic land walls all the way to the Golden
Horn from here; see the Üsküdar Walking
Tour on p120.

## FLORENCE NIGHTINGALE MUSEUM
Map pp46–7

☎ 216-556 8161; fax 216-310 7929; Burhan Felek
Caddesi, Selimiye; admission free; ☺ 9am-5pm
Mon-Fri; 🚢 Harem or 🚇 12H, 16, 139 or 320 from
Üsküdar

The experience of visiting the Selimiye
Army Barracks, where this museum is
housed, is actually better than the museum
itself. The barracks, built by Mahmut II in
1828, is on the site of a barracks originally
built by Selim III in 1799 and extended by
Abdül Mecit I in 1842 and 1853. It is the
headquarters of the Turkish First Army, the
largest division in the country, and is an
extremely handsome building, with 2.5km
of corridors, 300 rooms and 300 windows.
During the Crimean War (1853–56) the barracks became a military hospital where the
famous lady with the lamp and 38 nursing
students worked. It was here that Nightingale put in practice the innovative nursing
methods that history has remembered her
for. Though they seem commonsensical
from a modern perspective, it is hard to
overstate how radical they seemed at the
time. It really is amazing to hear that before
she arrived, the mortality rate was 70% of
patients and when she left it had dropped
to 5%.

The museum is spread over three levels
in the northwest tower of the barracks.
Downstairs there is a display charting the
history of the First Army and concentrating
on the Crimean War. On the two upstairs
levels you see Nightingale's personal
quarters, including her surgery room with
original furnishings (including two lamps)
and her living room, with extraordinary
views across to Old İstanbul. Here there are
exhibits such as an original letter explain-
ing how the lady herself defined being a
good nurse.

To visit, you need to fax a letter requesting to visit and nominating a time. Include
a photocopy of your passport photo page.
Do this 48 hours before you wish to visit
and make sure you include your telephone
number in İstanbul so that someone can
respond to your request. The recruits, who
vet your papers at the entrance, show you
from the security check to the museum and
take you on a guided tour, are almost all
young conscripts counting down the days

until their military service is finished. They may not all speak English (although the tour is always in that language) but they are without exception charming and helpful. Their mothers would be proud!

The museum is about half way between Üsküdar and Kadıköy, near the fairytale-like clock towers of the TC Marmara University. If you arrive at Harem on the ferry from Eminönü, walk to the right (south) until you arrive at the Selimiye Kıslası Harem Kapısı (the barracks' Harem Gate); it only takes 10 minutes or so. To get here from Üsküdar, catch a bus from the bus stand south of the Şemsi Paşa Mosque and alight at the Gümrük stop; from Kadıköy, take a bus from Rıhtım Caddesi.

## PANORAMA 1453 Map pp46–7

☎ 212-467 0700; Topkapı Gate; adult/student TL5/3; ☼ 8.30am-7pm

Opened in 2009, this nationalistic display is a huge 360-degree painted panorama of the Conquest of Constantinople on 29 May 1453. It's oddly old-fashioned, with no multimedia elements save a soundtrack, and only a few fake-looking props. Still, it's worth a visit if only to witness the reverence with which Turks approach anything to do with this hugely significant event. The panorama is located outside the Topkapı Gate, where Mehmet the Conqueror had placed the giant cannon (topkapı) that was instrumental in his victory.

## RAHMI M KOÇ INDUSTRIAL MUSEUM
Map pp46–7

Rahmı M Koç Müzesı; ☎ 212-369 6600; www.rmk-museum.org.tr; Hasköy Caddesi 5; adult/child & student TL10/5, submarine adult/child & student TL5/4; ☼ 10am-5pm Tue-Fri, 10am-7pm Sat & Sun; 🚢 Hasköy or 🚍 54HT or 36T to Taksim Sq (Hasköy Parkı stop)

Hasköy, located on the Beyoğlu side of the Golden Horn, was for centuries a small, predominantly Jewish, village. In the Ottoman period it also became home to a naval shipyard and a sultan's hunting ground. Today, its main claim to fame is this splendid museum dedicated to the history of transport, industry and communications in Turkey. Founded by the head of the Koç industrial group, one of Turkey's most prominent conglomerates, it exhibits artefacts from İstanbul's industrial past. The collection is highly eclectic, giving the

impression of being a grab-bag of cool stuff collected over the decades or donated to the museum by individuals, organisations or companies who didn't know what else to do with it. This might sound like we're damning the place with faint praise, but this is far from the case – in fact, we highly recommend a visit here, particularly if you are travelling with children.

The museum is in two parts: a new building on the Golden Horn side of the road and a superbly restored and converted Byzantine stone building opposite. Exhibits are largely concerned with forms of transport: Bosphorus ferry parts and machinery; a horse-drawn tram; an Amphicar (half car, half boat) that crossed the English Channel in 1962; Sultan Abdül Aziz's ornate railway coach with its duck-egg-blue stain upholstery; cars (everything from ugly Turkish Anadol models to fabulous pink Cadillacs); a 1960 Messerschmitt; and the fuselage of 'Hadley's Harem', a US B-24D Liberator bomber that crashed off Antalya in August 1943. There's even a working railway that takes visitors on a short trip in a period carriage behind a 1960s Ruston and Hornsby diesel locomotive or a 1970s Baguley-Drewy every hour on Saturday and Sunday. Other exhibits look at how appliances and electronic devices work – the exhibition of how whitegoods work is particularly fascinating.

Wheelchair access is offered throughout the complex. What's more, excellent interpretive panels in Turkish and English are provided. There are buttons galore to push, a lovely cafe right on the water, a convivial bar and an upmarket French brasserie. The submarine exhibit, from which children under eight years of age are barred, requires an extra ticket.

The museum is near the northern end of the old Galata Bridge (near where Hasköy Caddesi changes into Kumbarahane Caddesi). The Haliç ferry from Eminönü stops right next to the museum.

## MINIATURK Map pp46–7

☎ 212-222 2882; www.miniaturk.com.tr; İmrahor Caddesi, Sütlüce; adult/child TL10/3; ☼ 9am-6pm; 🚢 Sütlüce or 🚍 36T from Taksim (Miniatürk stop)

We can't explain why this new museum has been such a hit with locals. Marketed as a miniature park that showcases 'all times and locations of Anatolia at the same place at the same time', it's a bizarre tiny town stocked with models of Turkey's great buildings – everything from the Celsus Library at Ephesus to Atatürk International Airport – set in manicured lawns dotted with fake rocks blasting a distorted recording of the national anthem. Children aren't interested in the models but love the miniature train that traverses the paths and the playground equipment. It's tacky and only really interesting as a demonstration of how greatly Turks revere their heritage, even when it's kitsch-coated.

The museum is a five-minute bus ride further on from the Rahmi M Koç Industrial Museum (opposite). It's easily accessed via the Haliç ferry from Eminönü.

# top picks

- Cocoon (p133)
- Design Zone (p135)
- Mehmet Çetinkaya Gallery (p133)
- Ali Muhiddin Hacı Bekir (p134)
- Abdulla Natural Products (p135)
- Necdet Danış (p136)
- Doors (p138)
- Gönül Paksoy (p141)
- Haremlique (p142)
- İstinye Park (boxed text p142)

# SHOPPING

Over centuries, İstanbullus have perfected the practice of shopping and then shopping some more. Trading is in their blood and they've turned making a sale or purchase into a true art form. Go into any carpet shop and you'll see what we mean – there's etiquette to be followed, tea to be drunk, conversation to be had. And, of course, there's money to be spent and made.

Whether you're after a cheap souvenir or a family-heirloom-to-be, you'll find it in İstanbul. Rugs (carpets and kilims), textiles, fashion, homewares, ceramics, olive-oil soap and jewellery are just a few of the temptations laid out in more arcades, bazaars and stores than you could ever hope to flash a credit card in.

## ANTIQUITIES & THE LAW

When shopping for antiques, it's important to remember that antiquities – objects from Turkey's Hittite, Greco-Roman, Byzantine and early Ottoman past – may not be sold, bought, or taken out of the country under penalty of law. A century-old painting, bowl or carpet usually poses no problems, but a Roman statuette, Byzantine icon or 17th-century İznik tile means trouble and quite possibly time in jail.

## BARGAINING

Traditionally, when customers enter a Turkish shop to make a significant purchase, they're offered a comfortable seat and a drink (coffee, tea or soft drink). There is some general chitchat, then discussion of the shop's goods (carpets, apparel, jewellery etc), then of the customer's tastes, preferences and requirements. Finally, a number of items in the shop are displayed for the customer's inspection.

The customer asks the price; the shop owner gives it; the customer looks doubtful and makes a counteroffer 25% to 50% lower. This procedure goes back and forth several times before a price acceptable to both parties is arrived at. It is considered very bad form to offer an amount, have the shopkeeper agree and then change your mind. If no price is agreed upon, the customer has absolutely no obligation and may walk out at any time.

To bargain effectively you must be prepared to take your time, and know something about the items in question, not to mention their market price. The best way to do this is to look at similar goods in several shops, asking prices but not making counteroffers. Shopkeepers will give you a quick education about their wares by demonstrating to you what's good about them and telling you what's bad about

their competitors' goods. Soon you will discover which shops have the best quality for the lowest asking prices and you can then proceed to bargain. Always stay good-humoured and polite when you are bargaining – if you do this, the shopkeeper will too. And remember: shopkeepers know their own bottom line and will only bargain up to a certain point.

When bargaining, you can often get a discount by offering to buy several items at once,

## CLOTHING SIZES

### Women's clothing

| | | | | | | |
|---|---|---|---|---|---|---|
| Aus/UK | 8 | 10 | 12 | 14 | 16 | 18 |
| Europe | 36 | 38 | 40 | 42 | 44 | 46 |
| Japan | 5 | 7 | 9 | 11 | 13 | 15 |
| USA | 6 | 8 | 10 | 12 | 14 | 16 |

### Women's shoes

| | | | | | | |
|---|---|---|---|---|---|---|
| Aus/USA | 5 | 6 | 7 | 8 | 9 | 10 |
| Europe | 35 | 36 | 37 | 38 | 39 | 40 |
| France only | 35 | 36 | 38 | 39 | 40 | 42 |
| Japan | 22 | 23 | 24 | 25 | 26 | 27 |
| UK | 3½ | 4½ | 5½ | 6½ | 7½ | 8½ |

### Men's clothing

| | | | | | | |
|---|---|---|---|---|---|---|
| Aus | 92 | 96 | 100 | 104 | 108 | 112 |
| Europe | 46 | 48 | 50 | 52 | 54 | 56 |
| Japan | S | | M | M | | L |
| UK/USA | 35 | 36 | 37 | 38 | 39 | 40 |

### Men's shirts (collar sizes)

| | | | | | | |
|---|---|---|---|---|---|---|
| Aus/Japan | 38 | 39 | 40 | 41 | 42 | 43 |
| Europe | 38 | 39 | 40 | 41 | 42 | 43 |
| UK/USA | 15 | 15½ | 16 | 16½ | 17 | 17½ |

### Men's shoes

| | | | | | | |
|---|---|---|---|---|---|---|
| Aus/UK | 7 | 8 | 9 | 10 | 11 | 12 |
| Europe | 41 | 42 | 43 | 44½ | 46 | 47 |
| Japan | 26 | 27 | 27½ | 28 | 29 | 30 |
| USA | 7½ | 8½ | 9½ | 10½ | 11½ | 12½ |

Measurements approximate only; try before you buy

or by paying in cash and not requesting a receipt.

If you don't have sufficient time to shop around, follow the age-old rule: find something you like at a price you're willing to pay, buy it, enjoy it and don't worry about whether or not you received the world's lowest price.

## OPENING HOURS

The most common shopping hours are from 9am to 6pm Monday to Saturday, but this is by no means always the case. We have indicated specific hours in all reviews.

## WHAT TO BUY

### Antiques

The grand Ottoman-era houses of İstanbul are still surrendering fascinating stuff left over from the empire. You'll find these treasures – furniture in the Ottoman baroque style, jewellery, crockery, paintings and more – in the antique shops of Çukurcuma and at the Horhor Antique Market (boxed text p134).

### Ceramics

After rugs, ceramics are Turkey's most popular souvenirs. This is for good reason: the ceramics are beautiful and the standard fare fits within most budgets. Many of the tiles you see in the tourist shops have been painted using a silkscreen printing method and this is why they're cheap. Hand-painted bowls, plates and other pieces are one step up; these are made by rubbing a patterned carbon paper on the raw ceramic, tracing the black outline and filling in the holes with colour. The most expensive ceramics for sale are hand-painted – without the use of a carbon-paper pattern – and derived from an original design.

### Glassware

İstanbul produces some unique glasswork, a legacy of the Ottoman Empire's affection for this delicate and intricate art. The Paşabahçe factory on the upper Bosphorus has been producing glass for over 70 years and still churns out some good stuff. If you're after tea sets, the Grand Bazaar (Kapalı Çarşı) has many shops selling plain, colourful and gilded options. Note that most of the ornate, curvy perfume bottles you see in the touristy shops are Egyptian, despite what the seller might say.

### Inlaid Wood

Local artisans make jewellery boxes, furniture, and chess and backgammon boards that are inlaid with different coloured woods, silver or mother-of-pearl. Make sure the piece really does feature inlay. These days, alarmingly accurate decals exist. Also, check the silver: is it really silver, or does it look like aluminium or pewter? And what about that mother-of-pearl – is it in fact 'daughter-of-polystyrene'?

### Jewellery

İstanbul is a wonderful place to buy jewellery, especially pieces inspired by Ottoman and Byzantine designs. Gold shops should have a copy of the newspaper that bears the daily price for unworked gold of so many carats. Serious gold buyers should check this price, watch carefully as the jeweller weighs the piece in question, and then calculate what part of the price is for gold and what part for labour. Silver will also be weighed. There is sterling-silver jewellery (look for the hallmark), but nickel silver and pewterlike alloys are much more common. Serious dealers don't try to pass off alloy as silver. Some tourist shops will pass off plastic, glass and other stones as real gemstones – if you don't know what you're looking for, steer clear.

## Leather

On any given Kurban Bayramı (Sacrifice Holiday; see p225), more than 2½ million sheep are slaughtered throughout Turkey. Add to that the normal day-to-day needs of a cuisine based on mutton and lamb and you have a massive amount of raw material to be made into leather items, hence the country's thriving leather industry. If you've always wanted that leather coat or jacket, İstanbul may be the place to purchase it, but be wary of shoddy workmanship.

## Old Books, Maps & Prints

Collectors will have a field day with İstanbul's wealth of antique books – some immaculate, some moth-eaten. The city and its inhabitants have been immortalised in maps, illustrations and engravings throughout the years, and many of these are available as prints, which make excellent souvenirs. You'll also see illuminated pages, supposedly from Ottoman manuscripts. These are usually modern reproductions, but they're attractive nevertheless and, again, make excellent souvenirs. The best places to look are the Sahaflar Çarşısı (Old Book Bazaar; Map p73) near the Grand Bazaar and in Beyoğlu shops such as Denizler Kitabevi (p138) and Artrium (p137).

## Rugs

Asking locals for a recommendation when it comes to rug shops can be something of a knotty subject. This industry is rife with commissions, fakes and dodgy merchandise, so you need to be very careful when making a purchase. Don't fall for the shtick of touts on the street – these guys never, ever work for the truly reputable dealers. We've recommended a few long-standing and reputable businesses in this chapter but counsel you very strongly to always do your research before making a purchase, particularly if it involves a significant amount of money. See the boxed text p140.

## Spices, Potions & Turkish Delight

The Spice Bazaar (Mısır Çarşısı; p77) was once the centre of the spice and medicinal herb trade in İstanbul. It's still an important outlet, though these days locals are just as likely to shop for spices, tea, dried fruits, nuts and herbs in surrounding streets such as Hasırcılar Caddesi (Map p73). The city's most famous *lokum* (Turkish delight) shop is Ali Muhiddin Hacı Bekir (p134), which has an outlet close to the Spice Bazaar.

## Textiles

Turkey's southeast region is known for its textiles, and there are examples aplenty on show in the Grand Bazaar (p72). You can find top-quality cotton, linen and silk here – for the best range and quality, enter the veritable Aladdin's Cave that is Necdet Danış (p136).

Collectors of antique textiles will be in seventh heaven when inspecting both the decorative tribal textiles that have made their way here from Central Asia and the gold-embroidered velvet textiles beloved of the Ottoman gentry. In the Grand Bazaar, visit Muhlis Günbattı (p136) and in Sultanahmet go to Cocoon (opposite), Khaftan (below) and Mehmet Çetinkaya Gallery (opposite).

# SULTANAHMET & AROUND

The best shopping in Sultanahmet is found in and around the Arasta Bazaar. This historic arcade of shops was once part of the *külliye* (mosque complex) of the Blue Mosque (Sultan Ahmet Camii) and rents still go towards the mosque's upkeep. Some of Turkey's best-known rug and ceramic dealers have shops in the surrounding streets.

**KHAFTAN** Map pp50–1     Art, Antiques & Jewellery
☎ 212-458 5425; www.khaftan.com; Nakilbent Sokak 33; ☼ 9am-8pm; 🚇 Sultanahmet
Owner Adnan Cakariz sells antique Kütahya and İznik ceramics to collectors and museums here and overseas, so you can be sure that the pieces he sells in his own establishment are top-notch. Gleaming Russian icons, delicate calligraphy (old and new), ceramics, Karagöz puppets and contemporary paintings are all on show in this gorgeous shop.

## JENNIFER'S HAMAM Map pp50–1    Bathwares

☎ 212-518 0648; www.jennifershamam.com;
135 Arasta Bazaar, Sultanahmet; ⏰ 9am-10.30pm
Apr-Sep, 9am-7.30pm Oct-Mar; 🚇 Sultanahmet
Owned by Canadian Jennifer Gaudet, this
recently opened shop stocks *hamam* items
including towels, robes and *peştemals*
(bath wraps) produced on old hand looms
or hand/motor looms. It also sells natural
soaps, *kese* (coarse cloth mittens used for
depilation) and *rosense* products (natural
rose hand and body products from Isparta).

## GALERİ KAYSERİ Map pp50–1    Books

☎ 212-512 0456; Divan Yolu Caddesi 11 & 58;
⏰ 9am-9pm; 🚇 Sultanahmet
Twin shops almost opposite each other
offer a modest range of English-language
fiction and glossy books on İstanbul. The
range looks larger and better than it actually is, but it's the best English-language
bookshop this side of the Galata Bridge.

## İZNİK CLASSICS & TILES Map pp50–1 Ceramics

☎ 212-517 1705; www.iznikclassics.com; Arasta
Bazaar 67, 73 & 161, Cankurtaran; ⏰ 9am-8pm;
🚇 Sultanahmet
İznik Classics is one of the best places in
town to source hand-painted collector-item
ceramics made with real quartz and using
metal oxides for pigments. Admire the
range in the two shops and gallery in the
Arasta Bazaar, in the Grand Bazaar store or
in the outlet at 17 Utangaç Sokak.

## VAKKO İNDİRİM

Map pp50–1    Clothing & Accessories
Vakko Sale Store; ☎ 212-522 8941; Yenicami
Caddesi 13, Eminönü; ⏰ 9.30am-6pm Mon-Sat;
🚇 Eminönü
This remainder outlet of İstanbul's most
glamorous department store should be on
the itinerary of all bargain hunters. Top-
quality men's and women's clothing –
often stuff that's been designed and made
in Italy – is sold here for a fraction of its
original price.

## CAFERAĞA MEDRESESİ

Map pp50–1    Handicrafts
☎ 212-513 3601; Caferiye Sokak, near Topkapı Palace; ⏰ 8.30am-7pm; 🚇 Gülhane or Sultanahmet
The rooms around this pretty *medrese*
(Islamic school; p69) are used as art-teaching
studios and some of the products – jewel-

lery, miniatures, *ebru* (marbled paper) – are
sold here for reasonable prices. There isn't a
lot to choose from, but it's certainly worth
wandering in for a peek at what's on offer.

## İSTANBUL HANDICRAFTS MARKET

Map pp50–1    Handicrafts
İstanbul Sanatlar Çarşısı; ☎ 212-517 6782; Kabasakal Caddesi 23; ⏰ 9am-6.30pm; 🚇 Sultanahmet
Set in the small rooms surrounding the
leafy courtyard of the 18th-century Cedid
Mehmed Efendi Medresesi, this handicrafts
centre next door to the Yeşil Ev hotel is
unusual in that local artisans sometimes
work here and don't mind if visitors watch.
Their creations are available for purchase;
it's a great place to source beautiful calligraphy, glassware, hand embroidery, miniature
paintings, ceramics and fabric dolls.

## NAKKAŞ Map pp50–1    Rugs, Jewellery & Ceramics

☎ 212-458 4702; Mimar Mehmet Ağa Caddesi 39;
⏰ 9am-7pm; 🚇 Sultanahmet
As well as pricey rugs and jewellery, Nakkaş
stocks an extensive range of ceramics made
by the well-regarded İznik Foundation.
One of the reasons the place is so beloved
of tour groups is the beautifully restored
Byzantine cistern that's in the basement –
make sure you have a peek.

## COCOON Map pp50–1    Rugs & Textiles

☎ 212-638 6271; www.cocoontr.com; Küçük Aya
Sofya Caddesi 13; ⏰ 8.30am-7.30pm;
🚇 Sultanahmet
There are so many rug and textile shops in
İstanbul that choosing individual shops to
recommend is incredibly difficult. We had no
problem whatsoever in singling this one out,
though. Felt hats, antique costumes and textiles from central Asia are artfully displayed
in one store, while rugs from Persia, central
Asia, the Caucasus and Anatolia adorn the
other. There's a third shop in the Arasta
Bazaar and another in the Grand Bazaar.

## MEHMET ÇETİNKAYA GALLERY

Map pp50–1    Rugs & Textiles
☎ 212-517 6808; www.cetinkayagallery.com;
Tavukhane Sokak 7, Küçük Aya Sofya; ⏰ 9.30am-
7.30pm; 🚇 Sultanahmet
Described by an editor at *Halı* Publications
as 'Turkey's leading dealer of antique textile
art', Mehmet Çetinkaya is also known as
one of the country's foremost experts on
antique oriental carpets. His flagship store

## ANTIQUES, ANYONE?

Those seeking out authentic Ottoman souvenirs should visit the Horhor Antikacılar Çarşısı (Horhor Antique Market; ☺ varies according to shop; ⓡ Aksaray), where the city's serious collectors congregate. This decrepit building in Aksaray is home to five floors of shops selling antiques, curios and bric-a-brac of every possible description, quality and condition.

is full of treasures, but remember – quality never comes cheaply. There's a second shop selling textiles and objects in the Arasta Bazaar and a third in the Four Seasons Istanbul at the Bosphorus (p199).

### YÖRÜK COLLECTION
Map pp50–1      Rugs & Textiles
☎ 212-511 7766; Yerebatan Caddesi 35-37, Sultanahmet; ☺ 9am-9pm; ⓡ Sultanahmet
It's worth entering this shop to see the building, which formerly housed an Ottoman library and has been beautifully restored. Stock includes rugs, silk, miniatures, textiles, ceramics, jewellery and quirky handmade glass light fittings. For a bit of fun, ask to go upstairs and check out 'Mike's Museum', which is filled with a colourful jumble of rugs, pottery, costumes, tassels, jewellery and textiles.

### YILMAZ İPEKÇİLİK
Map pp50-1      Textiles & Soap
☎ 212-638 4579; Ishakpaşa Caddesi 36; ☺ 9am-9pm Mon-Sat, 3-9pm Sun; ⓡ Sultanahmet
Hand-loomed textiles made in a family-run factory in Antakya are on sale in this out-of-the-way shop. Good-quality silk, cotton and linen items at reasonable prices make it worth the short trek.

# BAZAAR DISTRICT
The city's two most famous marketplaces are here: the Grand and Spice Bazaars. It's also worth investigating Hasırcılar Sokak next to the Spice Bazaar.

### SOFA Map p73      Art, Antiques & Jewellery
☎ 212-520 2850; www.kashifsofa.com; Nuruosmaniye Caddesi 85, Cağaloğlu; ☺ 9.30am-7pm Mon-Sat; ⓡ Çemberlitaş
What a treasure-trove of a shop! As well as its eclectic range of prints, textiles, calligraphy and Ottoman miniatures, Sofa sells contemporary Turkish art. The pricey jewellery made out of antique Ottoman coins and 24-carat gold is particularly alluring.

### ALİ MUHİDDİN HACI BEKİR
Map p73      Food & Drink
☎ 212-522 0666; www.hacibekir.com.tr/eng; Hamidiye Caddesi 83, Eminönü; ☺ 8am-8pm Mon-Sat; ⓡ Eminönü
It's obligatory to sample lokum while in İstanbul, and one of the best places to do so is at this historic shop, which has been operated by members of the same family for over 200 years. As well as enjoying sade (plain) lokum, you can buy it made with cevizli (walnut) or şam fıstıklı (pistachio), or flavoured with portakal (orange), badem (almond) or roze (rose-water). Try a çeşitli (assortment) to sample the various types. There are also branches in Beyoğlu and Kadıköy.

### HAFİZ MUSTAFA ŞEKERLEMELERİ
Map p73      Food & Drink
☎ 212-526 5627; Hamidiye Caddesi 84-86, Eminönü; ☺ 8am-8pm Mon-Sat, 9am-8pm Sun; ⓡ Eminönü
Opposite Ali Muhiddin Hacı Bekir, this shop sells excellent Turkish delight. You can buy a small bag of freshly made treats to sample, plus gift boxes to take home. Best of all, they're happy to let you taste before buying (within reason, of course). There's also a small cafe/börekçi upstairs.

### KURUKAHVECİ MEHMET EFENDİ
MAHDUMLARI Map p73      Food & Drink
☎ 212-511 4262; www.mehmetefendi.com/eng; cnr Tahmis Sokak & Halıcılar Caddesi, Rüstempaşa; ☺ 9am-6.30pm Mon-Fri, 9am-2pm Sat; ⓡ Eminönü
Caffeine addicts are regularly spotted queuing outside this, the flagship store of İstanbul's most famous coffee purveyor. You can join them in getting a fix of the freshest beans in town, and also purchase a cute little set of two signature coffee cups and saucers, a copper coffee pot and a jar of coffee – it's a great gift to take back home.

### MALATYA PAZARİ Map p73      Food & Drink
☎ 212-520 0440; Mısır Çarşısı 44 (Spice Bazaar), Eminönü; ☺ 8.30am-6.30pm Mon-Sat; ⓡ Eminönü
The city of Malatya in central-eastern Turkey is famed for its apricots, and these

three shops on the intersection (all with the same owner) stock the cream of the crop, dried both naturally and chemically. Its other quality dried fruit and nuts eclipse all others in this bazaar.

## AK GÜMÜŞ Map p75    Handicrafts & Jewellery
☎ 212-526 0987; Gani Çelebi Sokak 8, Grand Bazaar; ⏰ 9am-7pm Mon-Sat; Ⓜ Beyazıt
Specialising in Central Asian tribal arts, this delightful store stocks an array of felt toys and hats, as well as jewellery and other objects made using coins and beads.

## DELİ KIZIN YERİ Map p75    Handicrafts
☎ 212-511 1914; Halıcılar Caddesi 42, Grand Bazaar; ⏰ 9am-7pm Mon-Sat; Ⓜ Beyazıt
Don't let the name – the Crazy Lady's Place – put you off. With a cute line of handmade Turkish teddies, dolls and puppets on offer, this is a great place to pick up gifts for the little ones in your life.

## ABDULLA NATURAL PRODUCTS
Map p75    Homewares
☎ 212-527 3684; Halıcılar Caddesi 62, Grand Bazaar; ⏰ 9am-7pm Mon-Sat; Ⓜ Beyazıt
The first of the Western-style designer stores that are now appearing in this ancient marketplace, Abdulla sells cotton bed linen, handspun woollen throws from Eastern Turkey, cotton peştemals and pure olive-oil soap. It's all top-quality, but it's not cheap. There's another store in the Fes Café (p164) in Cağaloğlu.

## DERVİŞ Map p75    Homewares
☎ 212-514 4525; www.dervis.com; Keseciler Caddesi 33-35, Grand Bazaar; ⏰ 9am-7pm Mon-Sat; Ⓜ Beyazıt
Gorgeous raw cotton and silk peştemals share shelf space here with traditional Turkish dowry vests and engagement dresses. If these don't take your fancy, the pure olive-oil soaps and old hamam bowls are sure to step into the breach. There's another store at Halıcılar Caddesi 51.

## DESIGN ZONE Map p73    Jewellery & Homewares
☎ 212-527 9285; www.designzone.com.tr; Alibaba Türbe Sokak 21, Nuruosmaniye; ⏰ 10am-6pm Mon-Sat; Ⓜ Beyazıt
Contemporary Turkish designers show and sell their work in this attractive boutique. Look out for the super-stylish jewellery and hand-crafted hamam-bowl sets created by owner Özlem Tuna. The varied stock caters to all budgets

## MILANO GÜZELIŞ Map p75    Jewellery
☎ 212-527 6648; Kalpakçılar Caddesi 103, Grand Bazaar; ⏰ 9am-7pm Mon-Sat; Ⓜ Beyazıt
When this family-run business started trading here in 1957, it was one of only 10 or so jewellery shops in the Grand Bazaar. The Güzelış family have been making jewellery to order using every gold grade and every

## MADE IN THE KAPALI ÇARŞI

Özlem Tuna has been working as a jewellery designer since 1996. In 2007, she opened her store Design Zone (above) in the Nuruosmaniye neighbourhood to the immediate east of the Grand Bazaar (Kapalı Çarşı), breaking into what was a staunchly traditional and male-dominated local industry. She loves the Nuruosmaniye area, describing it as '...full of lively energy and rich with culture', and she spends a lot of time in the Grand Bazaar visiting ustas (masters) in their ateliers to learn the secrets of their trades and garner inspiration for her acclaimed collections of Turkish-themed contemporary jewellery and homewares.

Özlem is one of a group of artisans involved in a project called MIKC (Made In the Kapalı Çarşı), which is working to retain artisans' ateliers in and around the Grand Bazaar. MIKC members are concerned that ateliers – which traditionally occupy the upstairs floors of historic hans (caravansaries) – are being moved out of the area, replaced by hotels and tourist services that can afford to pay higher rents for their traditional workspaces. The group is currently working on a project that will spotlight 10 ustas working in or around the Grand Bazaar, particularly those working in hans. If the project goes ahead (when this book went to print MIKC was negotiating with The Grand Bazaar Association for funding and a space in the bazaar in which to set up an office and exhibition space), it will offer tours of the bazaar and the ateliers of these ustas. As Özlem says: 'İstanbul's artisan traditions and training are intangible heritage; if we don't do something to protect them, they will soon disappear. The big jewellery manufacturers and many others have already moved out of this area to the city's outskirts and cheap, mass-produced product manufactured outside Turkey is starting to dominate the local market. We must not lose this important part of our culture.'

conceivable gem ever since, and have built a trusted reputation in the process.

### KOÇ DERİ Map p75 — Leather
☎ 212-527 5553; Kürkçüler Çarşısı 22-46, Grand Bazaar; ☷ 8.30am-8pm; ☷ Beyazıt
If you fancy a leather jacket or coat, Koç is bound to have something that suits. It's one of the bazaar's busiest stores and certainly the most stylish of the leather outlets here.

### KÜÇÜK KÖŞE Map p75 — Leather Handbags
Little Corner; ☎ 212-513 0335; Kalpakçılar Caddesi 89-91, Grand Bazaar; ☷ 9am-7pm Mon-Sat; ☷ Beyazıt
If you've always wanted a Kelly or Birkin but can't afford Hermès, this place is for you. Its copies of the work of the big-gun designers are good quality and they're a lot more affordable than the originals. The next-door store, Pako, is owned by the same people.

### GÜVEN TİCARET Map p73 — Metalwork
☎ 212-526 0307; Kutucular Caddesi 26, Rüstempaşa; ☷ 6am-6pm Mon-Sat, 8am-6pm Sun; ☷ Eminönü
Cheap *hamam* bowls, cooking pans and coffee pots are sold at this simple shop at the end of Hasırcılar Caddesi near the Spice Bazaar. You'll pay approximately a quarter of the price of their Grand Bazaar equivalents.

### DHOKU Map p75 — Rugs
☎ 212-527 6841; Tekkeciler Sokak 58-60, Grand Bazaar; ☷ 9am-7pm Mon-Sat; ☷ Beyazıt
One of the new generation of rug stores opening in the bazaar, Dhoku (meaning texture) sells artfully designed wool kilims in resolutely modernist designs. Its sister store, EthniCon (www.ethnicon.com), opposite this store, sells similarly stylish rugs in vivid colours and can be said to have started the current craze in contemporary kilims.

### ŞİŞKO OSMAN Map p75 — Rugs
☎ 212-528 3548; Zincirli Han 15, Grand Bazaar; ☷ 9am-7pm Mon-Sat; ☷ Beyazıt
The Osmans have been in the rug business for four generations and are rated by many as the best dealers in the bazaar. Certainly, their stock is a cut above many of their competitors. Most of the rugs on sale

are dowry pieces and all have been hand woven and coloured with vegetable dyes. There's another store at Halıcılar Caddesi 49.

### ARSLAN BAHARAT Map p73 — Spices & Tonics
☎ 212-522 9589; Mısır Çarşısı 39, Spice Bazaar; ☷ 8.30am-6.30pm Mon-Sat; ☷ Eminönü
A good range of spices keeps most travellers happy, but serious shoppers know that this spot has the city's best range of rare natural aromatics such as musk and amber. It also stocks saffron at good prices.

### MEHMET KALMAZ BAHARATÇI
Map p73 — Spices & Tonics
☎ 212-522 6604; Spice Bazaar 41, Eminönü; ☷ 8am-7pm Mon-Sat; ☷ Eminönü
One of the few shops in the Spice Bazaar that specialises in potions and lotions, this old-fashioned place sells remedies to make women younger, others to make men stronger, and a royal love potion that, we guess, is supposed to combine the two. It also stocks spices, bath accessories, teas and medicinal herbs.

### AZAD TEKSTİL Map p75 — Textiles
☎ 212-512 4202; Yağlıkçılar Caddesi 16, Grand Bazaar; ☷ 9am-7pm Mon-Sat; ☷ Beyazıt
If you're after simple but stylish 100% cotton bedspreads, tablecloths or *peştemals,* this place is worth checking out. The products aren't quite as nice as those sold at Derviş or Abdulla Natural Products, but they're certainly cheaper.

### MUHLİS GÜNBATTI Map p75 — Textiles
☎ 212-511 6562; Parçacilar Sokak 48, Grand Bazaar; ☷ 9am-7pm Mon-Sat; ☷ Beyazıt
One of the most famous stores in the bazaar, Muhlis Günbattı specialises in *suzani* fabrics from Uzbekistan. These beautiful bedspreads, tablecloths and wall hangings are made from fine cotton embroidered with silk. As well as the textiles, it stocks top-quality carpets, brightly coloured kilims and a small range of antique Ottoman fabrics richly embroidered with gold. Its second shop at Tevkifhane Sokak (Map pp50–1) in Sultanahmet sells a wider range of costumes at truly stratospheric prices.

### NECDET DANIŞ Map p75 — Textiles
☎ 212-526 7748; Yağlıkçılar Caddesi 57, Grand Bazaar; ☷ 9am-7pm Mon-Sat; ☷ Beyazıt

## QUEEN OF FASHION

Fashion guru Ferhan İstanbullu has plenty to say when it comes to discussing the local scene. A style columnist with the liberal-leaning *Radikal* newspaper and presenter of the popular '5 x 5' lifestyle program on the NTV network, she is one of the city's major style setters and is, of course, herself formidably fashionable. Asked to nominate her favourite local designers, she doesn't hesitate: 'Ümit Ünal, Banu Bora, Gönül Paksoy and Özgür Masur'. Her favourite cafes and eateries? 'I like the İstanbul Culinary Institute in Tepebaşı (p154) and Kantin in Nişantası (p158), but my favourite places are in Bebek, where I live. The scene at the Bebek Bar (In the Bebek Hotel on Cevdet Paşa Caddesi) is fun, as are those at Happily Ever After, a cafe on the same street, and Bebek Kahve, on the waterfront next to the Bebek Mosque.' As to boutiques, she is unequivocal: 'Banu Bora's Midnight Express (p139) is the only true boutique in İstanbul. It has a strong concept and a modern sensibility – there's none of the horrible faux-Oriental stuff that is seen in the Grand Bazaar.'

Fashion designers and buyers from every corner of the globe know that when in İstanbul, this is where to come to source top-quality textiles. It's crammed with bolts of fabric of every description – shiny, simple, sheer and sophisticated – as well as *peştemals,* scarves and clothes. Next-door Murat Danış is part of the same operation

### EKİNCİOĞLU TOYS & GIFTS Map p75  Toys
☎ 212-522 6220; Kalçın Sokak 5, Eminönü; ✆ 9am-7pm; ⓡ Eminönü
If your junior travelling companion's behaviour is on the downward spiral and some urgent bribery is called for, this place should provide the answer.

# BEYOĞLU

İstiklal Caddesi has a long history as the city's most glamorous shopping strip but has lost its sheen in recent years, probably due to the phenomenal popularity of the sleek shopping malls opening in the affluent suburbs north of Beyoğlu (see the boxed text p142). You'll find the city's best book and music shops here, but not much else worthy of comment.

Next to Flower Passage (Çiçek Pasajı; p109), along Şahne Sokak, is Beyoğlu's Fish Market (Balık Pazar), with stalls selling fruit, vegetables, caviar, pickles and other produce. Leading off the Fish Market is the neoclassical Avrupa Pasajı (European Passage), a pretty passageway with a handful of shops selling tourist wares and antique prints. Aslıhan Pasajı, nearby, is a two-storey arcade bursting with second-hand books.

The streets around Tünel Sq and Galata Kulesi Sq are being colonised by the city's avant-garde fashion designers and make for exciting shopping. Between the two squares is Galipdede Caddesi, home to a major concentration of musical-instrument shops.

Antique stores can be found dotting the narrow winding streets of Çukurcuma and small fashion ateliers are scattered across the expat enclave of Cihangir. Both areas are well worth a wander.

### ARTRIUM Map pp102–3  Art & Antiques
☎ 212-251 4302; Tünel Sq 7; ✆ 9am-7pm Mon-Sat; ⓡ Karaköy then funicular to Tünel
This Aladdin's cave of a shop is crammed with antique ceramics, maps, prints and jewellery. Make sure you check out both the gorgeous felt clothing and the exquisite miniatures by Iranian artist Haydar Hatemi. If you're after anything in particular, ask the owner, and she'll rummage upstairs in the storage area where excess stock is kept.

### GALERİ ALFA Map pp102–3  Art & Antiques
☎ 212-251 1672; www.galerialfa.com in Turkish; Faikpaşa Sokak 43, Çukurcuma; ✆ 11am-5.30pm; ⓡ Kabataş then funicular to Taksim
What makes this store special is its range of charming toy Ottoman soldiers and court figures – even Süleyman the Magnificent has been shrunk to 10cm tall. It also stocks old maps and prints.

## CONTEMPORARY TURKISH HOMEWARES

The traditional homewares sold in the Grand Bazaar and other tourist areas are often poorly designed and shoddily made. To source well-made contemporary homewares inspired by traditional Turkish designs, make your way to Hiref (www.hiref.com.tr), where alluring items designed by Ebru Çerezci are on offer. The collection includes copper bowls and serving plates, glassware, silver cutlery and candles. There are stores at Kanyon and İstinye Park (for both see the boxed text p142).

## DENIZLER KİTABEVİ

Map pp102–3                     Antique Books, Maps & Prints

☎ 212-249 8893; İstiklal Caddesi 395; ☉ 9.30am-7.30pm; ⓢ Kabataş then funicular to Taksim
A charmingly eccentric shop specialising in old maps and books, Denizler Kitabevi also stocks antique prints.

## HOMER KİTABEVİ Map pp102–3            Books

☎ 212-249 5902; www.homerbooks.com; Yeniçarşı Caddesi 12A, Galatasaray; ☉ 10am-7.30pm Mon-Sat, 12.30-7.30pm Sun; ⓢ Kabataş then funicular to Taksim
Come here for an unrivalled range of Turkish fiction, plus an enviable collection of nonfiction covering everything from Sufism and Islam to Kurdish and Armenian issues. It stocks children's books too.

## İSTANBUL KİTAPÇISI Map pp102–3        Books

☎ 212-292 7692; İstiklal Caddesi 379; ☉ 10am-6.45pm Mon-Sat, noon-6.45pm Sun; ⓢ Karaköy then funicular to Tünel
This bookshop is run by the municipality and as a consequence prices are very reasonable. It stocks some English-language books about İstanbul, and a good range of maps, CDs, postcards and prints.

## PANDORA Map pp102–3                   Books

☎ 212-243 3503; Büyükparmakkapı Sokak 8B; ☉ 10am-8pm Mon-Wed, 10am-9pm Thu-Sat, 1-8pm Sun; ⓢ Kabataş then funicular to Taksim
This long-standing independent bookshop has recently opened a new store dedicated solely to English-language books. It has great crime fiction and travel sections, as well as loads of books about Turkey.

## ROBINSON CRUSOE Map pp102–3          Books

☎ 212-293 6968; İstiklal Caddesi 389; ☉ 9am-9.30pm Mon-Sat, 10am-9.30pm Sun; ⓢ Karaköy then funicular to Tünel
There are few more pleasant fates than being marooned here for an hour or so. With its classy decor, good magazine selection and wide range of English-language novels and books about İstanbul, it's one of the best bookshops around. Staff speak English and know their books.

## SIR Map pp102–3                       Ceramics

☎ 212-293 3661; www.sircini.com; Serdar Ekrem Sokak 66, Galata; ☉ 11am-7pm Mon-Sat; ⓢ Karaköy then walk or funicular to Tünel

Ceramics produced in İstanbul can be pricey, but the attractive hand-painted plates, platters, bowls and tiles sold at this small atelier are exceptions to the rule.

## BERRIN AKYÜZ Map pp102–3             Clothing

☉ 212-251 4125; www.berrinakyuz.com; Akarsu Yokuşu Sokak 22, Cihangir; ☉ 10.30am-7pm Mon-Sat; ⓢ Kabataş then funicular to Taksim
Local lasses love the reworked vintage clothing on offer at this Cihangir boutique, and no wonder. It's well priced and extremely stylish. There's another branch in Üsküdar ( ☎ 216-334 9296; 2nd fl, Dr Fahri Atabey Caddesi 98).

## BUILDING FOOD LAB & APPAREL

Map pp102–3                             Clothing

☎ 212-243 0717; www.building.com.tr; Serder-ı Ekrem Caddesi 27; ☉ 10am-midnight Mon-Sat, noon-7pm Sun; ⓢ Karaköy then walk or funicular to Tünel
It may be 50% boutique and 50% bar, but Building is definitely 100% fashionable. Men's and women's designer threads from Turkey and overseas are on show at the rear of the space; young fashionistas are on display in the front bar area. It's hard-edged and just a teeny bit hard to take seriously.

## DOORS Map pp102–3                     Clothing

☎ 212-245 7886; www.umitunal.com; Ensiz Sokak 1B, Tünel; ☉ 9am-8pm Mon-Sat & noon-6pm Sun; ⓢ Karaköy then funicular to Tünel
Local fashion designer Ümit Ünal is rapidly acquiring an international profile, with stores in New York, Hong Kong and London stocking his striking pieces. His women's clothes, which use natural fabrics in muted colours, are best described as wearable art. Prices are surprising reasonable considering the originality and quality on offer.

## LEYLA SEYHANLI Map pp102–3           Clothing

☎ 212-293 7410; Altıpatlar Sokak 6, Çukurcuma; ☉ 11am-5.30pm; ⓢ Kabataş then funicular to Taksim
If you love old clothes, you'll adore Leyla Seyhanlı's boutique. Filled to the brim with piles of Ottoman embroidery and outfits, it's a rummager's delight. It stocks everything from 1890s cashmere and velvet coats to 1950s taffeta party frocks to silk-embroidery cushion covers that would've been at home in the Dolmabahçe Palace linen cupboard.

## MARIPOSA Map pp102–3 — Clothing

212-249 0483; Şimşirci Sokak 11A, Cihangir; 10am-8.30pm Mon-Fri, 11am-8.30pm Sat & Sun; Kabataş then funicular to Taksim

The Mariposa atelier turns out a particularly fetching line in floral frocks. Fashionistas will adore the fact that it not only makes to order, but also designs and tailors unique ensembles. As well as the dresses, coats and jackets on the racks, it makes pretty bedspreads and pillowslips.

## MIDNIGHT EXPRESS

Map pp102–3 — Clothing

212-251 1968; www.midnightexpress.com.tr; 2nd fl, Mısır Apt, İstiklal Caddesi 163, Galatasaray; 10am-8.30pm Mon-Fri, 11am-8.30pm Sat & Sun; Karaköy then funicular to Tünel

Local designer Banu Bora chose the ultra-chic Mısır Apartment Building on İstiklal Caddesi as the Beyoğlu location for her business, reinforcing its status as the city's most sophisticated fashion boutique. It stocks Bora's own labels (there are two) plus clothes and accessories from local and international designers. If the door is closed, ring the bell. There's another store in Bebek ( 212-257 9514; Bebek Palas Apt, Gemencik Sokak 1) that sells both fashion and homewares.

## TEZGAH ALLEY Map pp102–3 — Clothing

Terko 2 Caddesi; Karaköy then funicular to Tünel

Put your elbows to work fighting your way to the front of the *tezgah* (stalls) in this alleyway, off İstiklal Caddesi, which are heaped with T-shirts, jumpers, pants and shirts on offer for a mere TL3 to TL6 per piece. Turkey is a major centre of European clothing manufacture, and the items here are often factory run-ons from designer or high-street-chain orders.

## LA CAVE WINE SHOP

Map pp102–3 — Food & Drink

La Cave Şarap Evi; 212-243 2405; Sıraselviler Caddesi 207, Cihangir; 9am-9pm; Kabataş then funicular to Taksim

Its enormous selection of local and imported wine makes La Cave a good stop for tipplers. The staff can differentiate a Chablis from a Chardonnay and will be happy to give advice on the best Turkish bottles to add to your cellar.

## İSTANBUL MODERN GIFT SHOP

Map pp102–3 — Gifts

212-334 7300; www.istanbulmodern.org; Meclis-i Mebusan Caddesi, Tophane; 10am-6pm Tue, Wed & Fri-Sun, 10am-8pm Thu; Tophane

It's often difficult to source well-priced souvenirs and gifts to take home, but this stylish shop in the İstanbul Modern gallery sells suitable items aplenty. Check out the niftily designed T-shirts, CDs, coffee mugs, CDs, homewares, jewellery and cute gifts for kids.

## PAŞABAHÇE Map pp102–3 — Glassware

212-244 0544; www.pasabahce.com; İstiklal Caddesi 314; 10am-8pm; Karaköy then funicular to Tünel

Established in 1934, this local firm manufactures excellent glassware from its factory on the Bosphorus. Three floors of glassware, vases and decanters feature here and prices are very reasonable. Styles are both traditional and contemporary. There's another branch on Teşvikiye Caddesi in Nişantaşı.

## MOR TAKI Map pp102–3 — Jewellery

212-292 8817; Turnacıbaşı Sokak 16, off İstiklal Caddesi; 10.30am-8.30pm Mon-Sat; Kabataş then funicular to Taksim

The gals of this city love their jewellery, and this funky little store keeps many of their collections topped up with costume pieces by local designers.

## TAKIL PERA Map pp102–3 — Jewellery

212-292 1792; www.takilpera.com; General Yazgan Sokak 10, Tünel; 10am-8pm Mon-Sat, 1-7pm Sun; Karaköy then funicular to Tünel

Full to the brim with the work of young Turkish jewellers, this store just off Tünel Sq offers tempting contemporary designs as well as more-traditional pieces. Musa Özer's coin-and-stone pieces and Şenay Akın's sleek silver creations are particularly tempting.

## LALE PLAK Map pp102–3 — Music

212-293 7739; Galipdede Caddesi 1, Tünel; 9am-7pm Mon-Sat; Karaköy then funicular to Tünel

This small shop is crammed with CDs of jazz, Western classical and Turkish classical and folk music. It's a popular hang-out for local bohemian types.

## A CARPET-BUYER'S PRIMER

There's no right or wrong way to go about buying a carpet when you're in Turkey. There are only two hard-and-fast rules. The first is that you should never feel pressured by anyone to buy – the decision is yours and yours alone. The second is to only ever pay a price that you feel comfortable with. When you return home, you want to do so with a piece that you love and that isn't going to bankrupt you.

A good-quality, long-lasting carpet should be 100% wool (*yüz de yüz yün*): check the warp (the lengthwise yarns), weft (the crosswise yarns) and pile (the vertical yarns knotted into the matrix of warp and weft). Is the wool fine and shiny, with signs of the natural oil? More expensive carpets may be of a silk and wool blend. Cheaper carpets may have warp and weft of mercerised cotton. You can tell by checking the fringes at either end; if the fringe is of cotton or 'flosh' (mercerised cotton) you shouldn't pay for wool. Another way to identify the material of the warp and weft is to turn the carpet over and look for the fine, frizzy fibres common to wool, but not to cotton. But bear in mind that just being made of wool doesn't guarantee a carpet's quality. If the dyes and design are ugly, even a 100% woollen carpet can be a bad buy.

Check the closeness of the weave by turning the carpet over and inspecting the back. In general, the tighter the weave and the smaller the knots, the higher the quality and durability of the carpet. The oldest carpets sometimes have thick knots, so consider the number of knots alongside the colours and the quality of the wool.

Compare the colours on the back with those on the front. Spread the nap with your fingers and look at the bottom of the pile. Are the colours brighter than on the surface? Slight colour variations could occur in older carpets when a new batch of dye was mixed, but richer colour deep in the pile is often an indication that the surface has faded in the sun. Natural dyes don't fade as readily as chemical dyes. There is nothing wrong with chemical dyes, which have a long history of their own, but natural dyes and colours tend to be preferred and therefore fetch higher prices. Don't pay for natural if you're getting chemical.

New carpets can be made to look old, and damaged or worn carpets can be rewoven (good work but expensive), patched or even painted. There is nothing wrong with a dealer offering you a patched or repainted carpet, of course, provided they point out these defects and price the piece accordingly. And note that some red Bukhara carpets (Bukhara is a city region in Uzbekistan) will continue to give off colour, even though they're of better quality than cheap woollen carpets that don't.

When you are examining the carpet, look at it from one end, then from the other. The colours will differ because the pile always leans one way or the other. Take the carpet out into the sunlight and look at it there. Imagine where you might put the carpet at home and how the light will strike it.

It's all very well taking measures such as plucking some fibres and burning them to see if they smell like wool, silk or nylon, or rubbing a wet handkerchief over the carpet to see if the colour comes off, but unless you know what

---

### MEPHISTO Map pp102–3 Music
☎ 212-249 0687; www.mephisto.com.tr in Turkish; İstiklal Caddesi 197; 🕘 9am-midnight; 🚋 Kabataş then funicular to Taksim
If you manage to develop a taste for local music while you're in town, this popular store is the place to indulge it. As well as a huge CD collection of Turkish popular music, there's a select range of Turkish folk, jazz and classical music.

### ELVIS Map pp102–3 Musical Instruments
☎ 212-293 8752; Galipdede Caddesi 35; Tünel; 🕘 10am-6pm; 🚋 Karaköy then funicular to Tünel
If you thought Elvis was hiding in the Bahamas, you're wrong. He's here, selling a good range of traditional stringed instruments. Nearby İstanbul Müzik Merkezi (☎ 212-2445885; Galipdede Caddesi 21) also stocks a good range.

### İPEK Map pp102–3 Silk
☎ 212-249 8207; İstiklal Caddesi 120; 🕘 9am-6pm; 🚋 Kabataş then funicular to Taksim

The silk ties and scarves sold at this long-established store make great presents, as they don't take up much of your baggage allowance and are keenly priced. Check out the colourful scarves featuring Ottoman calligraphy.

# NİŞANTAŞI & AROUND

The city's serious shoppers gravitate towards the upmarket suburbs of Teşvikiye and Nişantaşı, about 2km north of Taksim Sq. This is where international fashion and design labels have traditionally set up shop (though some are now decamping to the malls; see the boxed text p142) and where top-drawer local designers show off their creations.

### ARK LINE Map p113 Clothing
☎ 212-225 9456; www.ark-istanbul.com; Ihlamur Yolu 5, Teşvikiye; 🕘 10am-7pm Mon-Sat; 🚋 Kabataş then funicular to Taksim then Ⓜ Osmanbey

you're doing you're unlikely to learn much from the exercise – and you may well end up with an irate carpet-seller to deal with!

In the end the most important consideration should be whether or not you like the carpet.

## Pricing & Payment

When it comes to buying, there's no substitute for spending time developing an 'eye' for what you really like. You also need to be realistic about your budget. These days carpets are such big business that true bargains are hard to come by unless there's something (like gigantic size) that makes them hard to sell for their true value. Prices are determined by age, material, quality, condition, demand, the enthusiasm of the buyer and the debt load of the seller. Bear in mind that if you do your shopping on a tour or when accompanied by a guide, the price will have been inflated to include a commission of up to 35% for the tour operator or guide.

It may be wiser to go for something small but of high quality rather than for a room-sized cheapie. And it's worth remembering that kilims (pileless woven rugs) are usually cheaper than carpets. Another way to make your money stretch further is to opt for one of the smaller items made from carpet materials: old camel bags and hanging baby's cradles opened out to make rugs on which food would be eaten, decorative grain bags, even the bags that once held rock salt for animals.

Most dealers prefer to be paid with cash. Most will accept credit cards, but some require you to pay the credit-card company's fee and the cost of the phone call to check your credit-worthiness. A few dealers will let you pay in instalments.

All of this is a lot to remember, but it will be worth it if you get a carpet you like at a decent price. You'll have something to take home that will give you pleasure for the rest of your life.

## Beware of the Carpet Bait & Switch

Here's the scenario: you make friends with a charming Turk, or perhaps a Turkish-American/European couple. They recommend a friend's shop, so you go and have a look. There's no pressure to buy. Indeed, your new friends wine and dine you (always in a jolly group with others). Before you leave İstanbul you decide to buy a carpet. You go to the shop, choose one you like and ask the price. So far so good; if you can buy that carpet at a good price, everything's fine. But if the owner strongly urges you to buy a 'better' carpet, more expensive because it's 'old' or 'Persian' or 'rare' or 'makes a good investment', beware. You may return home to find you've paid many times more than it is worth. If the shopkeeper ships the carpet for you, the carpet that arrives may not be the expensive carpet you bought; instead it could be a cheap copy.

To avoid this rip-off, you should choose a carpet, inspect it carefully, then shop around. Compare prices for similar work at other shops, then buy the best-value one: not necessarily the one from your friends' shop. Finally take the carpet with you or ship it yourself; don't have the shopkeeper ship it.

One of the motifs of contemporary Turkish fashion is the inspiration local designers take from their Ottoman heritage. Ark Line has followed Gönül Paksoy (below) in referencing the sartorial style of the sultans and their entourages in its collections. The clothes here are nowhere near as assured and desirable as Paksoy's, but they are considerably cheaper, meaning that they sit within most budgets.

### GÖNÜL PAKSOY Map p113 Clothing
☎ 212-261 9081; Atiye Sokak 6A, Teşvikiye; ◷ 10am-7pm Mon-Sat; Ⓜ Osmanbey
Gönül Paksoy creates and sells pieces that transcend fashion and step into art. In fact, her work was the subject of a 2007 exhibition at İstanbul's Rezan Haş Gallery. These two shops showcase her distinctive clothing, which is made using naturally dyed fabrics and is often decorated with vintage beads. She also creates and sells delicate silk and cotton knits and exquisite jewellery based on traditional Ottoman designs.

### VAKKO Map p113 Clothing & Accessories
☎ 212-219 9660; Adbilpekçi Caddesi, Nişantaşı; ◷ 10.30am-7.30pm Mon-Sat; Ⓜ Osmanbey
İstanbul's most famous boutique department store stocks a quality range of men's and women's clothing at its store on Nişantaşı's major shopping street. It's best known for high-quality silk scarves and ties. There are also stores at Kanyon, İstinye Park and Akmerkez (for all see the boxed text p142) and there's a small outlet in the international departures lounge at Atatürk International Airport.

### ELACİNDORUK NAZANPAK
Map p113 Jewellery
☎ 212-219 6292; www.elacindoruknazanpak.com; Atiye Sokak 14, Teşvikiye; ◷ 2-7pm Mon, 10.30am-7pm Tue-Sat; Ⓜ Osmanbey
It may be small in size, but Elacindoruk Nazanpak is certainly well endowed when it comes to style. It showcases contemporary pieces in silver, gold, felt, paper and

other materials created by Turkish and international designers.

# BEŞİKTAŞ, ORTAKÖY & KURUÇEŞME

**HAREMLIQUE** Map p115          Homewares
☎ 212-236 3843; www.haremlique.com; Şair Nedim Bey Caddesi 11, Akaretler; ⊗ Mon-Sat; 🚋 Kabataş then walk

The shops around the fashionable W Istanbul (p200) are among the most glamorous in the city. Marni, Chloé, Marc Jacobs and Jimmy Choo are just a few of the labels that draw the city's moneyed elite here to shop. Among these international labels is this local business, which sells top-drawer bed linen and bathwares. Come here to source items such as boudoir cushion-covers featuring Ottoman rococo prints – they're certain to wow your guests back home.

## MARKETS & MALLS

With one foot planted in the East and another in the West, İstanbul's shopping has more than its fair share of contradictions: ritzy shopping plazas dot posh suburbs, while the mass of shoppers elbow for goods at the weekly street markets.

### Street Markets

On Tuesday there is a massive market in Kadıköy, on the Asian side: the Salı Pazarı (Map p123). The cheapest clothes in town are on sale here, so if you've been on the road for a while and your underwear needs replenishing, this is the place to do it! To get there, get off the ferry and move straight ahead along the major boulevard of Söğütlüçeşme Caddesi for about 500m until you come to a busy intersection, Altıyol Sq. Cross over, take the right fork and continue eastward along Kuşdili Caddesi for another 250m (three cross streets). At Hasırcıbaşı Caddesi turn left and you'll see the tent-city market spread out before you. It's open between 8am and 6pm.

On Saturday and Sunday the laneways around the waterfront mosque in Ortaköy host a flea market. Merchandise is tacky – most seems to come from the Subcontinent and Africa and is found in flea markets worldwide – and the handicrafts on offer are firmly in the hippy camp, but it's still a pleasant spot to while away a weekend hour or two.

On Wednesday the streets surrounding the Fatih Mosque (p85) in the Western Districts host the Fatih Pazarı, a great market selling fresh produce, clothes and household items.

### Malls

Western-style mall culture has well and truly taken off on İstanbul.

The ritzy Kanyon (off Map pp46–7; ☎ 212-353 5300; www.kanyon.com.tr; Büyükdere Caddesi 185, Levent; ⊗ 10am-10pm; Ⓜ Levent) is home to multinational names such as Harvey Nichols, Wagamama, Georg Jensen, Le Pain Quotidien, Birkenstock, Mango and Mandarina Duck. It also has a few locally based stores, including Vakko, Ottoman Empire (funky T-shirts screen-printed with Ottoman-influenced motifs) and Remzi Kitabevi (an excellent chain bookstore with a big English-language selection).

Next door is Metrocity (off Map pp46–7; ☎ 212-344 0660; www.metrocity.com.tr in Turkish; Büyükdere Caddesi 171, Levent; ⊗ 10am-10pm; Ⓜ Levent), which isn't anywhere near as glam as Kanyon but is still extremely popular. It hosts high-street labels such as Zara, Benetton, Nike, Levi's and Mavi Jeans.

These two malls are large, but they're nowhere near the size of the massive Cevahir (off Map pp46–7; ☎ 212-380 0893/4; www.istanbulcevahir.com in Turkish; Büyükdere Caddesi 22, Şişli; ⊗ 10am-10pm; Ⓜ Şişli), which advertises itself as Europe's largest mall. It's home to many of the same stores that you'll find in Metrocity and Akmerkez, as well as familiar UK-based outlets such as Topshop and Miss Selfridge.

Perhaps the best of the city's malls is İstinye Park (off Map pp46–7; ☎ 212-345 5555; İstinye Bayın Caddesi, İstinye; www.istinyepark.com.tr; ⊗ 10am-10pm; Ⓜ İTÜ Ayazağa), located in the upper Bosphorus suburb of İstinye. You'll find classy department stores Beymen and Vakko here, a slew of prestige international designers, and high-street chains including Banana Republic, Marks & Spencer, Mavi and Zara. Eateries include branches of Mezzaluna and The House Café.

Once the jewel in the city's shopping crown, Akmerkez (off Map pp46–7; ☎ 212-282 0170; www.akmerkez.com.tr; Nispetiye Caddesi, Etiler; ⊗ 10am-10pm; Ⓖ 43R, 58A or 58N to Akmerkez) has lost some of its shine, but it still boasts an impressive array of shops, including Beyman, Vakko, Zara, Mothercare and Remzi Kitabevi.

# top picks

- Cooking Alaturka (p147)
- Develi (p150)
- Karaköy Güllüoglu (p158)
- Mikla (p152)
- Ece Aksoy (p153)
- Sofyalı 9 (p154)
- Tarıhı Karaköy Balık Lokantası (p153)
- Zübeyir Ocakbaşi (p154)
- Çiya Sofrası (p159)
- Cercis Murat Konağı (boxed text p160)

İstanbullus love to eat. For them, food is much more than mere fuel. Instead, it's a celebration of community. Here, meals unfurl with great ceremony – they are joyful, boisterous and almost inevitably communal.

The national cuisine has been refined over centuries and is treated more reverently than any museum collection in the country. That's not to say it's fussy, because what differentiates Turkish food from other national noshes is its rustic and honest base. Here meze are simple, kebaps uncomplicated, salads unstructured and seafood unsauced. Flavours explode in your mouth because ingredients are used when they are in season – being a locavore is something taken for granted by Turks.

The dishes served in restaurants throughout İstanbul are the same as those in eateries around the country in all but one important respect – they're better. This is where the country's best chefs come to perfect their art and where the greatest number of cuisines are showcased. In Beyoğlu, you're as likely to encounter an innovative take on an Italian pasta dish as you are a classic meze selection or a fabulously fresh grilled fish. Feel like sushi or a Thai red curry? You'll get it here. Have a yen to challenge your tastebuds with an edgy fusion dish conceived and prepared by a European- or Australasian-trained master of the kitchen? No problem – the city has plenty of options.

The city's best eateries are in Beyoğlu. This is where you should come to sample a progression of hot and cold meze dishes in a *meyhane* (tavern), watch your meat being grilled over charcoal in an *ocakbaşı* (barbecue restaurant) or take your pick from a scrumptious array of Anatolian dishes on display in a *lokanta* (restaurant serving ready-made food). It's also where you should come to eat at top Western-style restaurants.

Away from Beyoğlu, you should seek out the national dish – kebaps – in Eminönü or further afield, or investigate a *balık restoran* (fish restaurant) along the Bosphorus. For recommendations of places to eat on the Bosphorus and Golden Horn (Haliç), see the Ferry Trips chapter.

As the Turks say, *afiyet olsun!* (bon appétit!).

## LOCAL CUISINE

The day starts with *sabahları* (morning food) or *kahvaltı* (breakfast), usually eaten between 6am and 8am; one of the most popular breakfast snacks is *börek* (sweet or savoury pastry), which comes in versions stuffed with cheese, meat, potato or spinach. *Öğle yemeği* (lunch) kicks off around noon and is usually consumed quickly, often in a *lokanta*, *kebapçı* (kebap joint) or *pideci* (Turkish pizza parlour). *Akşam yemeği* (dinner) is eaten any time after 6pm and is where the *meyhane*, *ocakbaşı* and *restoran* (restaurant) come into their own; in İstanbul many of these places

serve until midnight and meals can be drawn out over a long period.

### Bread

Bread *(ekmek)* is an essential part of any Turkish meal. The day will start with a sesame-encrusted *simit* (bread ring) or crusty white loaf to accompany cheese and olives. Lunch may be a pide or *lahmacun* – both are Turkish versions of the pizza: *lahmacun* has a thin, crispy base; pide has a standard pizza base. Dinner is always served with baskets of bread to mop up meze and wrap around morsels of meat. Light and airy *lavaş* (thin crispy bread) is often served with the house speciality at kebap restaurants.

### Meze

Meze isn't just a type of dish, it's an eating experience. In a household, your host may put out a few lovingly prepared dishes to nibble on before the main meal. If you choose to spend a few hours in a Beyoğlu *meyhane*, beckoning the waiter over so that you can choose 'just a

### PRICE GUIDE

Our guide to the per-person price of a meal consisting of meze/starter and main dish without alcohol is as follows:

| | |
|---|---|
| €€€ | more than TL50 |
| €€ | TL16 to TL50 |
| € | TL15 or under |

few more' inevitably means that the meze will comprise most of your meal.

Turks credit Süleyman the Magnificent with introducing meze into the country. While campaigning in Persia, Süleyman learned from the Persian rulers that food tasters were a good idea for every sultan who wanted to ensure his safety. Once home, Süleyman decreed that *çesnici* (taste) slaves be given small portions of his meals before he tucked in. These portions became known as meze, the Persian word for 'pleasant, enjoyable taste'. Popular mezes include *çacik* (yogurt with cucumber and mint), *enginar* (cooked artichoke), *haydari* (yogurt with roasted eggplant/aubergine and garlic) and *yaprak sarma* (vine leaves stuffed with rice, herbs and pine nuts).

## Meat Dishes

There are more *et* (meat) dishes in the Turkish culinary repertoire than you can poke a *şiş* (skewer) at. The most famous of these is the kebap – *şiş* and *döner* – but *köfte* (meatballs), *saç kavurma* (stir-fried cubed-meat dishes), *güveç* (meat and vegetable stews) and *tandır* (meat cooked in a clay oven) dishes are just as common. Offal dishes are also popular, particularly *çiğer* (grilled liver) – if you're a bit squeamish about the yucky bits steer clear of *işkembe* (tripe), *kelle* (head) and *koç yumurtası* (ram's balls). The most popular sausage is the spicy beef *sucuk*. Chicken is extremely popular; you'll find it roasted, boiled, stewed and skewered.

Kebaps come in many forms. In İstanbul you'll find the following dishes everywhere:

**Döner kebap** Compressed meat (usually lamb) cooked on a revolving upright skewer and thinly sliced.

**Fıstıklı kebap** Minced suckling lamb studded with pistachios.

**İskender (Bursa) kebap** Döner lamb served on crumbled pide and yoghurt, topped with tomato and butter sauces.

**Patlıcan kebap** Cubed or minced meat grilled with eggplant.

**Şiş kebap** Small pieces of lamb grilled on a skewer and usually served with a side of grilled peppers.

**Tokat kebap** Lamb cubes grilled with potato, tomato, eggplant and garlic.

**Tavuk şiş** Chicken pieces grilled on a skewer.

Tasty *köfte* are nearly as common, and are mainly in the following forms:

**Adana kebap** A spicy version of *şiş köfte*, with paprika and chillies.

**Çiğ köfte** Raw ground-lamb mixed with pounded bulgur, onion, spices and pepper.

**İçli köfte** Ground lamb and onion with a bulgur coating, often served as a meze.

**Şiş köfte** Wrapped around a flat skewer and barbecued.

**Tekirdağ köftesi** Köfte served with rice and peppers.

## Seafood

İstanbullus have always made the most of the city's seaside position, falling hook, line and sinker for fresh fish (*balık*) in any form. There are a number of excellent but pricey fish restaurants along the Bosphorus, and in town the army of *meyhanes* in Beyoğlu, Kumkapı, Florya and Yeşilköy are often run by restaurateurs from the Black Sea, where the quality of fish is famous. These serve up lightly fried *kalamares* (calamari) as a meze; mains are usually simply grilled fresh fish of the day served with salad.

*Kalkan* (turbot) and *uskumru* (mackerel) are best consumed between March and June. Mid-July to August is the best time to feast on *levrek* (sea bass), *lüfer* (bluefish), *barbunya* (red mullet) and *istravrit* (horse mackerel), while winter means the delectable and slightly oily *hamsi* (European anchovy).

EATING LOCAL CUISINE

### THE FISH SANDWICH – AN İSTANBUL INSTITUTION

The cheapest way to enjoy fresh fish from the waters around İstanbul is to buy a *balık ekmek* (fish sandwich) from a boatman. Go to the Eminönü end of the Galata Bridge (Map pp50–1) and you'll see bobbing boats tied to the quay. In front of each boat, men tend to a cooker loaded with fish fillets. The quick-cooked fish is crammed into a quarter loaf of fresh bread and served with salad and a squeeze of lemon. It will set you back a mere TL5 or so.

Other simple fishy snacks are on offer at Fürreyya Galata Balıkçısı (Map pp102–3), a cute hole-in-the-wall cafe near the Galata Tower (fish soup TL4, fish sandwich TL5) or at the ramshackle Furran Balıkçısı, an open-air fish restaurant next to the Fish Market at Karaköy. Here you can order a serve of freshly caught fish (TL6 to TL10) and have the cooks grill it to perfection over coals. Look for the plastic furniture and bright-red tablecloths.

## Vegetables

If it weren't for the Turks' passionate love affair with the kebap, they'd probably all be vegetarians. They're sensible about their vegetables, too. There's none of the silly Western fixation with preparing vegetables that are out of season – here tomatoes are eaten when they're almost bursting out of their skins and peppers are stewed when they're so ripe they're downright sexy. Look for what's on the vendors' carts when you're walking around town – you'll see the same produce featuring on that season's restaurant menus. There are two particularly Turkish ways of preparing vegetables: the first is *zeytinyağlı* (sautéed in olive oil) and the second *dolma* (stuffed with rice or meat).

## Salad

Simplicity is the key to Turkish *salata* (salads), with crunchy fresh ingredients being caressed by a shake of oil and vinegar at the table and eaten with gusto as a meze or as an accompaniment to a meat or fish course. The most popular salad in İstanbul's restaurants in summer is *çoban salatası* (shepherd's salad), a colourful mix of chopped tomatoes, cucumber, onion and pepper.

## Desserts & Sweets

If you have a sweet tooth, prepare to put it to good use when in İstanbul. Though the locals aren't convinced of the idea of dessert to finish a meal, they love a mid-afternoon sugar hit and will pop into a *baklavacı, pastane* (patisserie) or *muhallebici* (pudding shop) for a piece of baklava, a plate of chocolate-drenched profiteroles or a *fırın sütlaç* (rice pudding) tasting of milk, sugar and just a hint of exotic spices. Turkish specialities worth sampling are *fırın sütlaç; dondurma* (the local ice cream); *kadayıf*, dough soaked in syrup and topped with a layer of *kaymak* (clotted cream); and *künefe*, layers of *kadayıf* cemented together with sweet cheese, doused in syrup and served with a sprinkling of pistachio.

## VEGETARIANS & VEGANS

Though it's normal for Turks to eat a vegetarian meal, the concept of vegetarianism is quite foreign. Say you're a vegan and Turks will either look mystified or assume that you're 'fessing up to some strain of socially aberrant behaviour. There is a sprinkling of vegetarian restaurants in Beyoğlu, a couple of which serve some vegan meals, but the travelling vegetarian certainly can't rely on specialist restaurants.

Meze is usually vegetable-based, and meat-free salads, soups, pastas, omelettes and *böreks*, as well as hearty vegetable dishes are all readily available. Ask '*etsiz yemekler var mı?*' (is there something to eat that has no meat?) to see what's on offer.

The main source of inadvertent meat eating is *et suyu* (meat stock), which is often used to make otherwise vegetarian *pilavs*, soups and vegetable dishes. Your hosts may not even consider *et suyu* to be meat, so they will reassure you that the dish is vegetarian; ask '*et suyu var mı?*' (is there meat stock in it?) to check.

## COOKING COURSES

**Cooking Alaturka** (Map pp50–1; ☎ 212-458 5919, 0536 338 0896; www.cookingalaturka.com; Akbiyik Caddesi 72a, Sultanahmet; classes €60) runs excellent, hands-on Turkish cooking classes in English. The delicious results are enjoyed over lunch in the school's restaurant (see opposite).

**The İstanbul Culinary Institute** (Enstitü; Map pp102–3; ☎ 212-2512214; www.istanbulculinary.com; Meşrutiyet Caddesi 59, Tepebaşı) offers three-hour workshops in Turkish aimed at mastering local dishes (TL100), as well as tours of the Kadıköy Produce Market and the fish and spice markets. It also offers a three-hour street-food tour. All tours are priced according to the number of participants; you'll need to specify your language requirements.

## SELF-CATERING

İstanbul has many small supermarkets (DIA, Gima, Makro) sprinkled through the streets around Beyoğlu, with giant cousins (such as Migros) in the suburbs. These sell most of the items you will need if you plan to self-cater. Then there is the ubiquitous *bakkal* (corner shop), which stocks bread, milk, basic groceries and usually fruit and vegetables. Some of these also sell *süt* (fresh milk) – look for the term 'pasteurised' on the label and you'll know it's fresh rather than long-life.

The best places to purchase fresh produce are undoubtedly the street markets. Down in Eminönü, the streets around the Spice Bazaar (Mısır Çarşısı; Map p73) sell fish, meats, vegetables, fruit, spices, sweets and much more.

The best stuff is available at the street stalls on Tahmis Caddesi on the market's west wall and in the shops on Hasırcılar Sokak – the Namlı delicatessens on Hasırcılar Sokak and over the bridge in Rıhtım Caddesi, Karaköy, sell an alluring range of local and imported products including cheese, *pastırma* (pastrami), tea and ready-made meze. In Beyoğlu, the Balık Pazar (Fish Market) next to the Flower Passage (Çiçek Pasajı; Map pp102–3) on İstiklal Caddesi is a great, if expensive, little market. As well as its many fish stalls, it has small shops selling freshly baked bread, greengrocers selling a wide range of fruit and vegetables, and delicatessens (*şarküteri*) selling cheeses, *pastırma*, pickled fish, olives, jams and preserves. Larger produce markets are found opposite the ferry terminals in Kadıköy and Beşiktaş – Kadıköy is known for its delicatessens and bakeries, and Beşiktaş for its fruit and vegetable stalls.

# SULTANAHMET & AROUND

It really is a shame that the quality of food served up in Sultanahmet's eateries is so mediocre. Some of the local restaurants have lovely settings and great views, but the food is too often disappointing (disgraceful is a word that frequently comes to mind). We've eaten our way through the neighbourhood, and are forced to limit our recommendations to those below. Around here places close early and there is no food strip as such.

**BALIKÇI SABAHATTIN** Map pp50-1    Fish €€€
☎ 212-458 1824; Seyit Hasan Koyu Sokak 1, Cankurtaran; meze TL3-25, mains TL28-50; 😋 noon-midnight; 🚇 Sultanahmet
The limos outside Balıkçı Sabahattın pay testament to its enduring popularity with the city's establishment, who join hordes of cashed-up tourists in enjoying its limited menu of meze and fish. The food here is excellent, though the service can be harried. You'll dine in a wooden Ottoman house or under a leafy canopy in the garden. It's wise to book.

**TERAS RESTAURANT**
Map pp50–1    Modern Turkish €€€
☎ 212-638 1370; Hotel Armada, Ahırkapı Sokak, Cankurtaran; degustation menu TL68, starter tray TL27-29, mains TL24-37; 😋 7-11pm; 🚇 Sultanahmet

The chef at this upmarket hotel restaurant came up with an inspired idea when he devised his Turkish degustation menu. Sampling courses of 'İstanbul cuisine' feature, and they are wonderfully complemented by an excellent (and affordable) wine list. Alternatively, order a starter tray to begin and follow with an à la carte main – the fish is particularly good. With a killer view of the Blue Mosque and Sea of Marmara, as well as very comfortable seating and occasional live Turkish music, this place is quite possibly the best eating option in Sultanahmet.

**COOKING ALATURKA** Map pp50–1 Anatolian €€
☎ 212-458 5919; www.cookingalaturka.com; Akbıyık Caddesi 72A, Sultanahmet; set lunch or dinner TL40; 😋 lunch Mon-Sat & dinner by reservation; 🚇 Sultanahmet
This great little restaurant is run by Dutch-born foodie Eveline Zoutendijk, who both knows and loves Anatolian food. She serves a set four-course menu that changes daily according to what produce is in season and what's best at the local markets. Eveline says that she aims to create a little haven in the midst of carpet-selling frenzy and she has indeed done this. She also sells unusual and authentic produce such as homemade jams, pomegranate vinegar and *pekmez* (grape molasses), as well as cookbooks and Turkish cooking utensils.

**MOZAİK**
Map pp50–1    Modern Turkish & International €€
☎ 212-512 4177; www.mozaikcaferestaurant.com; İncirli Çavuş Sokak 1; pastas TL14-19, mains TL18-55; 😋 9am-midnight; 🚇 Sultanahmet
Over the years Mozaik has built a reputation as the most stylish restaurant in this part of town. Housed in a romantic Ottoman building dating from 1878 and with plenty of streetside tables, it has a huge menu that offers pastas and other international food as well as dishes from different regions of Turkey. Prices are far too high considering the quality of the food (average at best), but the surrounds are welcoming and the service is excellent.

**KHORASANİ** Map pp50–1    Kebaps €€
☎ 212-519 5959; www.khorasanirestaurant.com; Ticarethane Sokak 39-41; starters TL5-6.50, kebaps TL16-26; 😋 9am-11.30pm; 🚇 Sultanahmet
When considering *ocakbaşıs*, the word stylish doesn't often come to mind.

succulent, yes. Smoky, sometimes. But stylish? Hmm. The owners of this new place off Divan Yolu are aiming to challenge preconceptions with Khorasani, and it seems to be working for their predominantly tourist clientele. Here, the meat plays second fiddle to the surrounds, which are extremely attractive. The chef hails from Antakya, and the kebap style is that of southeastern Anatolia, meaning that a few spicy dishes adorn the menu. A welcome addition to the Sultanahmet eating scene.

### ALBURA KATHİSMA Map pp50–1 Anatolian €€
☎ 212-517 9031; www.alburakathisma.com; Akbıyık Caddesi 26, Cankurtaran; starters TL4-18, salads TL10-13, mains TL14-24; ☺ 9am-2am; ☷ Sultanahmet
Albura Kathisma is a welcome addition to the otherwise mediocre array of restaurants along Akbıyık Caddesi. Its streetside tables are usually occupied by tourists sampling Turkish dishes such as *hünkar beğendi* (lamb or beef goulash served on a mound of rich aubergine puree) or *mantı* (Turkish ravioli topped with yoghurt, tomato and butter). The food is decent, with lots of vegetarian options.

### SEFA RESTAURANT Map pp50–1 Anatolian €
☎ 212-520 0670; Nuruosmaniye Caddesi 17, Cağaloğlu; soup TL3, portion TL5-7, kebaps TL7-17; ☺ 7am-5pm Mon-Sat; ☷ Sultanahmet
Locals rate this place near the bazaar highly, and after sampling the dishes on offer you'll realise why. It describes its cuisine as Ottoman, but what's really on offer here are *lokanta* dishes and kebaps at extremely reasonable prices. You can order from an English menu or choose from the bain marie – the vegetable dishes are particularly appetising. Try to arrive early-ish for lunch because many of the dishes run out by 1.30pm.

### BUHARA RESTAURANT & OCAKBAŞI
Map pp50–1 Kebaps €
☎ 212-527 5133; Nuruosmaniye Caddesi 7A, Cağaloğlu; kebaps TL10-17; ☺ 11am-10pm; ☷ Sultanahmet
If you're craving a kebab and haven't the time or inclination to walk down the hill to Eminönü's Hamdi Et Lokantası (opposite) or Zinhan (opposite), this unassuming eatery might be the solution. Management can be gruff and the servings are on the small side, but the

quality of the meat is good. You can order an Efes to accompany your meal.

### TAMARA RESTAURANT & CAFE
Map pp50–1 Anatolian €
☎ 212-518 4666; www.tamararestaurant.com; Küçük Ayasofya Caddesi 14; kebaps TL7-10, pide TL6-7; ☺ 6am-10pm; ☷ Sultanahmet
Located on one of Sultanahmet's most interesting shopping strips, Tamara serves good-quality kebaps, *lokanta* dishes and pides. Appearing for the prosecution: the cavernous and somewhat soulless interior. For the defence: good prices and attractively presented food. It's better for lunch than dinner.

### KONYALİ LOKANTASİ Map pp50–1 Anatolian €
☎ 212-527 1935; Mimar Kemalettin Caddesi 5, Sirkeci; soups TL5-8, portion TL8-17, kebaps TL12-17; ☺ 7am-9.30pm Mon-Sat; ☷ Sirkeci
The bustle of the Eminönü docks is replicated inside this popular *lokanta* every lunchtime, when crowds of shoppers, workers and commuters pop in here to choose from the huge range of soups, *böreks*, kebaps and stews on offer. This isn't a place where lingering over one's meal is encouraged (it's far too busy for that), but you can move on to the next-door *pastanesi* for a glass of tea and a delicious pastry if you so choose.

### TARİHİ SULTANAHMET KÖFTECİSİ SELİM USTA Map pp50–1 Köfte €
☎ 212-520 0566; www.sultanahmetkoftesi.com; Divan Yolu Caddesi 12; köfte, beans & salad TL15; ☺ 11am-11pm; ☷ Sultanahmet
This is one of the most famous eateries in the city, and to be frank, we're at a total loss to understand why. The ever-present queues of locals obviously adore its rubbery *ızgara köfte* (grilled meatballs) served with bread, white beans, salad and pickled chillies, but we have always been underwhelmed. Why not try it yourself, though? The place has been serving since 1920 and is certainly clean, cheap and cheerful.

### KARADENİZ AİLE PİDE VE KEBAP SALONU Map pp50–1 Pide & Kebaps €
☎ 212-528 6290; Hacı Tahsınbey Sokak 1, off Divan Yolu Caddesi; pides TL7-9; ☺ 11am-11pm; ☷ Sultanahmet
This long-timer off Divan Yolu serves a delicious *mercimek* (lentil soup) and is also a

EATING SULTANAHMET & AROUND

favourite for its pide. You can claim a table in the utilitarian interior, but most people prefer those on the cobbled lane. The Karadeniz Aile Pide & Kebap Sofrası ( ☎ 212-526 7202; Dr Emin Paşa Sokak 16; ⏰ 11am-11pm; ▣ Sultanahmet) opposite is equally welcoming and cheap.

## CAFERAĞA MEDRESESİ

Map pp50–1                                    Anatolian €

☎ 212-513 3601; Caferiye Sokak; soup TL3, köfte TL10; ⏰ 8.30am-6pm; ▣ Sultanahmet
In Sultanahmet, it's rare to nosh in stylish surrounds without paying through the nose for the privilege. That's why this teensy *lokanta* in the gorgeous courtyard of this Sinan-designed *medrese* near Topkapı Palace is such a find. The food isn't anything to write home about, but it's fresh and inexpensive.

## ÇİĞDEM PASTANESİ Map pp50–1        Cafe €

☎ 212-526 8859; Divan Yolu Caddesi 62A; cappuccino TL5, tea TL2, pastries TL1-4; ⏰ 8am-11pm; ▣ Sultanahmet
Çiğdem Pastanesi has been serving locals since 1961, and it's still going strong. The *ay çöreği* (pastry with walnut, sultana and spice filling) is the perfect accompaniment to a cappuccino, and a cheese *börek* goes wonderfully well with a cup of tea or fresh juice.

# BAZAAR DISTRICT

Generations of shoppers have worked up an appetite around the Grand Bazaar (Kapalı Çarşı). Fortunately there have always been eateries to meet this need, including a range of good *lokantas* such as Havuzlu and Subaşı. A little further away is the tranquil Şehzade Mehmed Sofrası, one of our favourite spots in the Old City. Down near the water there aren't too many choices – a delicious fish sandwich on the quay at Eminönü is probably your best bet. At night, enjoy a meal served with magnificent views at Hamdi Et Lokantası or Zinhan Kebap House.

## ZEYREKHANE Map p73            Ottoman €€

☎ 212-532 2778; www.zeyrekhane.com; İbedethane Arkası Sokak 10, Zeyrek; meze TL14-18, mains TL22-31; ⏰ 9am-10pm Tue-Sun; ▣ Aksaray
This fine-dining establishment in the restored former *medrese* of Molla Zeyrek Mosque (see p80) also has an outdoor garden and terrace with magnificent views

of the Golden Horn and back to the Süleymaniye Mosque. It serves beautifully presented and well executed Ottoman-influenced food in elegant surrounds. Better for lunch than dinner.

## ZİNHAN KEBAP HOUSE AT STORKS

Map p73                        Kebaps & International €€

☎ 212-512 4275; rezervasyon@zinhan-kebap -house.com; Ragıpgümüşpala Caddesi 2-5, Eminönü; meze TL4-8, kebabs TL13-23; ⏰ noon-11pm; ▣ Eminönü
Zinhan's regal position next to the Galata Bridge (p78) means that every İstanbullu knows it. Unfortunately (for them, that is) most haven't eaten here. If you buck this trend, you'll enjoy an excellent meal on one of the most impressive roof terraces in the city – the views from here are simply sensational. Best is the fact that there are lots of tables in prime positions, meaning that you won't have to book weeks ahead as is often the case at places such as Hamdi Et Lokantası (below). You'll sit on comfortable chairs at huge, well-spaced tables to enjoy tasty mezes such as *hummus pastırmalı* (hummus with *pastırma*) and sophisticated kebap dishes such as *ali nazik* (spicy kebap on a bed of broiled eggplant salad with garlic yoghurt). Also on offer are international dishes such as Tournados Rossini and a well-priced wine list. Book ahead and request a table with a view.

## HAMDİ ET LOKANTASI Map p73      Kebaps €€

Hamdi Restaurant; ☎ 212-528 0390; www. hamdirestorant.com.tr; Kalçın Sokak 17, off Tahmis Caddesi, Eminönü; meze TL4-12, kebabs TL15-22; ⏰ noon-11pm; ▣ Eminönü
A favourite İstanbullu haunt since 1970, Hamdi has phenomenal views overlooking the Golden Horn and Galata that are matched by great food, professional service and a bustling atmosphere. Try the *haydari* (yoghurt with roasted eggplant and garlic), the *içli köfte* (meatballs rolled in *bulgur*) and the *patıcanlı kebab* (lamb kebab with eggplant) and you'll see what we mean. Any place this good is always going to be busy, so make sure you book, and don't forget to request a rooftop table with a view (outside if the weather is hot). If you get there early (around 6pm), you might be able to score one of these without booking. Enter through the ground-floor baklava shop.

## ŞEHZADE MEHMED SOFRASI
Map p73           Anatolian €€

☎ 212-526 2668; www.sehzademehmed.com.tr;
Şehzadebaşı Caddesi, Fatih; kebaps & mains TL10-19,
pides TL8-12; ⏱ 9am-11pm; 🚇 Laleli-Üniversite
Locations don't come any better than
this. You'll find this welcoming restaurant
and *çay bahçesi* in the magnificent *külliye*
(mosque complex) of the Şehzade Mehmed
Mosque (p80). After a simple but tasty meal
of *köfte, tavuk kavurma* (roast chicken),
kebap or pide you can settle back on one
of the Turkish couches and relax over a *Türk
kahvesi* (Turkish coffee) and nargileh (water
pipe). Enter from the garden at the rear of
the mosque. No alcohol.

## BAB-I HAYAT
Map p73           Anatolian €

☎ 212-520 7878; www.babihayat.com; Mısır
Çarşısı 47; pides TL7-8, kebaps TL8-14; ⏱ 7.30am-
7.30pm; 🚇 Eminönü
It took seven months for a team headed
by one of the conservation architects from
Topkapı Palace (Topkapı Sarayı) to restore
and decorate this vaulted space over the
eastern entrance to the Spice Bazaar. Hand-
painted ceilings and tiled window frames
provide an atmospheric setting in which to
sample decent kebaps and adequate pides
and *hazır yemek* dishes. The ultra-friendly
service stands in stark contrast to that at
neighbouring Pandeli (which we've elected
not to review), and you can even get a beer
if you ask discreetly. Enter through the
Serhadoğlu fast-food shop.

## HAVUZLU RESTAURANT
Map p75           Anatolian €

☎ 212-527 3346; Gani Çelebi Sokak 3, Grand
Bazaar; portions TL10-14; ⏱ 8am-7pm Mon-Sat;
🚇 Beyazıt
After a morning spent shopping, many
visitors to the Grand Bazaar choose to park
their shopping bags at this well-known
*lokanta*. A lovely space with a vaulted ceiling, pale lemon walls and an ornate central
light fitting, Havuzlu (named after the small
fountain at its entrance) serves up tasty fare
to hungry hordes of tourists and shopkeepers – go early when the food is freshest. It
also has a clean toilet, something quite rare
in the bazaar.

## SUBAŞI LOKANTASI
Map p75           Anatolian €

☎ 212-522 4762; Kiliçcilar Sokak 48; portions
TL6-14; ⏱ 11am-5pm Mon-Sat; 🚇 Çemberlitaş
This place first opened its doors in 1959
and it's been feeding a constant stream
of the Grand Bazaar's shopkeepers and
customers ever since. Choose from the
spread of good-quality hot food in the
kitchen on the right as you enter and then
grab a seat at a table on one of the two
floors. Don't let the waiters cajole you into
ordering an expensive mixed plate (they
have a tendency to do this to unsuspect-
ing tourists, who then end up with hefty
bills); instead check out the price list at
the door and order by the portion (opt for
one plus rice). You'll find it north of the
Nuruosmaniye gate.

## KEBAP KINGS

Turkey's signature dish is undoubtedly the kebap. Turks will tuck into anything cooked on a stick with gusto, and if asked where they would like to celebrate a special event, they will inevitably nominate one of the city's two most-famous *kebapçıs*, Develi and Beyti.

Develi (Map pp46–7; ☎ 212-529 0833; www.develikebap.com; Gümüşyüzük Sokak 7, Samatya; meze TL5-9, kebaps TL13-25; ⏱ noon-midnight; 🚇 Koca Mustafa Paşa) opened its first restaurant in Kuruluş in 1912, but its most popular outlet is located at Samatya, in the shadow of Theodosius' Great Wall. The succulent kebaps here come in many guises and often reflect the season – the *keme kebabi* (truffle kebab) is only served for a few weeks each year, for instance. Prices here are extremely reasonable for the quality of food that is on offer and the service is exemplary – request a table on the roof terrace, which has great sea views. To get here from Sultanahmet, catch a taxi along Kennedy Caddesi (approximately TL10) or take the train from Cankurtaran Station (get off at Kocamustafapaşa Station). You'll find Develi inland from the station on a plaza filled with parked cars.

Beyti (off Map pp46–7; ☎ 212-663 2990; Orman Sokak 8, Florya; mains TL27-34; ⏱ noon-midnight Tue-Sun; 🚇 Florya) is located in an affluent suburb way out near the airport, but serious meat lovers know that it's worth the trip. Mr Beyti's famous *kuzu şiş* (skewered lamb kebab) and other meat dishes are extraordinarily good and worth every *kuruş* (cent) of their relatively hefty price tags. Catch the train from Sirkeci or Cankurtaran, exit the station and walk up the hill. A taxi from Sultanahmet will cost approximately TL25.

## BURÇ OCAKBAŞI Map p75      Kebaps €

☎ 212-527 1516; Terlikçiler Sokak, off Yağlıkçılar Caddesi, Grand Bazaar; kebaps TL8-12; ⏰ 8am-7pm Mon-Sat; Ⓜ Beyazıt

We promised a shopkeeper friend that listing this unassuming *ocakbaşı* in the Grand Bazaar wouldn't lead to it being overrun by tourists. Now we're worried that we may have been overly optimistic. He was concerned that the *usta* (master cook) at his favourite lunch spot – a previously well-guarded secret – would end up being too busy to pay proper attention to the juicy cuts of Gaziantep-style meats and delicious dolmas that he serves to the locals (the southeastern region of Gazientep is considered one of Turkey's culinary hotspots). We sincerely hope this won't be the case. You can pull up a stool or ask for your kebap to be a *durum* (wrapped in bread) to go. Another bazaar *ocakbaşı* worth considering is Kara Mehmet (Cebeci Hanı 92) – try its Adana kebap.

## ERZİNCANLI ALI BABA FASULYECİ
Map p73      Anatolian €

☎ 212-513 6219; www.kurufasulyeci.com; Prof Sıddık Sokak 11, Süleymaniye; beans with pilaf & pickles TL9.50; ⏰ 7am-7pm; Ⓜ Laleli-Üniversite

Join the crowds of hungry locals at this long-time institution in the former *kütüphanesi medrese* (theological-school library) of the Süleymaniye Mosque (p76). It's been dishing up its signature *kuru fasulye* (Anatolian-style haricot beans cooked in a spicy tomato sauce) since 1924. Try some with side dishes of pilaf (rice) and pickles, and wash it all down with an *ayran* (yoghurt drink). Next-door Kanaat Fasulyeci is nearly as old and serves up more of the same.

## İMREN LOKANTASI Map p73      Lokanta €

☎ 212-638 1196; Kadırga Meydanı 143, Kadırga; soup TL3, portions TL4-7; ⏰ 7am-10.30pm; Ⓜ Çemberlitaş

A tiny neighbourhood *lokanta* with extremely friendly staff, İmren is off the tourist trail but is worth the walk. It serves excellent, dirt-cheap dishes such as peppery lamb *guveç* (stew) or *musakka* (baked aubergine and mincemeat). Go for lunch rather than dinner.

## HAFIZ MUSTAFA ŞEKERLEMELERİ
Map p73      Sweets & Börek €

☎ 212-526 5627; Hamidiye Caddesi 84-86, Eminönü; ⏰ 11am-7pm Mon-Sat; Ⓜ Eminönü

Choosing between the delicious baklava, tasty *börek* or indulgent *meshur tekirdağ peynir helvası* (a cheese-based sweet prepared with sesame oil, cereals and honey or syrup) is the challenge that confronts customers at this popular place. You can enjoy your choice with a glass of tea in the upstairs cafe.

# WESTERN DISTRICTS

There aren't too many eateries of note in this area, but it is home to one of the city's best Ottoman restaurants, Asitane. The suburbs here are quiet at night, so you're probably best off sampling the delights of this place at lunch after visiting the Chora Church (p83).

## ASİTANE Map p84      Ottoman €€

☎ 212-635 7997; www.asitanerestaurant.com; Kariye Oteli, Kariye Camii Sokak 18, Edirnekapı; starters TL 10-18, mains TL20-32; ⏰ noon-midnight; Ⓟ Edirnekapı

It's not often that you'll get the opportunity to sample Ottoman dishes devised for the palace kitchens at Topkapı, Edirne and Dolmabahçe, but this is what's on offer here. Since 1991, the chefs here have been hunting down historic recipes and trialling them in the kitchen – only the most delicious make it onto the menu. Try the *visneli yaprak sarması* (an 1844 recipe of vine leaves stuffed with sour cherries) and *ayva kalyası* (a recipe from 1539 featuring quince, lamb and chickpeas cooked in a grape molasses syrup); we're sure the sultans would have approved of them as much as we do. The surrounds are modern and elegant, featuring a pale-green colour scheme, comfortable seating, pristine napery and an outdoor courtyard for summer dining. Vegetarians are well catered for and there's live Ottoman music on Friday and Saturday evenings.

# BEYOĞLU

The streets in the Asmalımescit district, with their raft of good-quality *meyhanes* packing the crowds in every Friday and Saturday night, are giving the famous Nevizade Sokak a run for its money these days, but they're not the only establishments off İstiklal Caddesi doing well. This is, without doubt, the best neighbourhood in town in which to eat, drink and be merry.

## CHANGA Map pp102–3 Modern International €€€

☎ 212-249 1348; www.changa-istanbul.com;
Sıraselviler Caddesi 47, Taksim; starters TL21-25,
mains TL32-49; ☷ 6pm-1am Mon-Sat Nov-Jun;
🚇 Kabataş, then funicular to Taksim

A number of eateries in İstanbul attempt
fusion cuisine, but few do it well; this
sophisticated restaurant is one that does.
Order the 12-course tasting menu (TL124
for two people) and you may score delights
such as scallops with hummus and panko
crumble, roasted salmon with coconut
sauce and a cress-coriander salad with rose
petals, or slow-cooked lamb wrapped in
vine leaves and served with sour cream and
sweet chilli sauce. In summer, the action
moves to Müzedechanga on the Bosphorus
(see p210).

## MİKLA Map pp102–3 Modern Mediterranean €€€

☎ 212-293 5656; mikla@istanbulyi.com; Marmara
Pera, Meşrutiyet Caddesi 15, Tepebaşı; starters
TL14-30, mains TL36-58; ☷ 6.30pm-1am Mon-Sat;
🚇 Karaköy, then funicular to Tünel

Among the big guns of İstanbul's top-end
dining scene, one place reigns supreme
in our minds, and that's Mikla. On the top
floor of the Marmara Pera hotel, this sleek
operation serves up excellent Mod Med
cuisine to a truly international clientele.
The chefs here embrace top-notch ingredients and simple execution and the results
speak for themselves: try the absolutely
delicious Trakya Kıvırcık lamb cutlets
and follow with the pistachio and *helva*
ice cream and you too will become fans.
Service and the wine list are impressive,
and the view is quite simply to die for. Ask
for a table with a view of the Old City and
consider arriving early to have a drink in
the bar (inside in winter, on the rooftop in
summer).

## DOĞA BALIK Map pp102–3 Fish €€

☎ 212-243 3656; www.dogabalik.com.tr; 7th
fl, Villa Zurich Hotel, Akarsu Yokuşu Caddesi 36,
Cihangir; meze plate TL10-20, mains TL25-50;
☷ noon-midnight; 🚇 Kabataş then funicular to
Taksim

There's something very fishy about this
place – and the locals love it. On the top
floor of a modest hotel in Cihangir, Doğa
Balık serves fabulously fresh fish in a dining
space with wonderful views across to the
Old City. It also has a lavish meze buffet,
which is a great idea.

## MOREISH Map pp102–3 Modern Mediterranean €€€

☎ 212-245 6089; www.moreishrestaurant.com;
Nu Pera Bldg, Meşrutiyet Caddesi 67, Tepebaşı;
starters TL17-28, mains TL25-38; ☷ 6pm-11.30pm
Mon-Sat, usually closed Jun-Sep; 🚇 Karaköy, then
funicular to Tünel

Chefs Cokşun Uysal and Esra Muslu trained
in Melbourne and London before returning to İstanbul and opening this intimate
restaurant. The sophisticated interior by
Milagard Architecture perfectly complements the ambitious menu, which comes
complete with *amuse-bouche* and splendid
home-baked bread rolls. An initial perusal
of the dishes on offer may make you fear
that there is too much happening on each
plate, but fear not – everything works
wonderfully. Highlights of our last meal
included a main course of roasted lamb
and braised lamb shank with red cabbage,
tahini humus and a cognac-plum puree
followed by a dessert of flourless chocolate
mousse cake served with rosewater ice
cream. Foodies will want to try the Thursday night degustation menu (TL100), which
includes matched glasses of wine.

## BRASSERIE LA BRISE Map pp102–3 French €€

☎ 212-244 4846; Asmalımescit Sokak 28,
Asmalımescit; starters TL14-29, mains TL24-48;
☷ noon-3pm & 6pm-midnight Mon-Fri, 6pm-
midnight Sat; 🚇 Karaköy, then funicular to Tünel

Secreted in a narrow street near the Pera
Palace Hotel (p108), La Brise leaves no Parisi-
enne cliché unexplored, with Piaf on the
sound system, a back-lit bar and mellow
lighting in the dining room and a *soupçon*
of attitude on the part of the waiters. The
perfectly cooked fillet steak with béarnaise
or pepper sauce comes with wonderfully
thick but crisp *pomme frites*.

## NU TERAS Map pp102–3 Modern Mediterranean €€

☎ 212-245 6070; Nu Pera Bldg, 7th fl, Meşrutiyet
Caddesi 149, Tepebaşı; pizza TL20-25, pasta
TL20-25, mains TL25-40; ☷ noon-11.30pm
Jul-Oct; 🚇 Karaköy, then funicular to Tünel

Nu Teras is a summer-only showcase of
casual chic and Mod Med food. On the roof
of the Nu Pera building, this terrace bar-
restaurant isn't quite as glam as it was in
its heyday, but that's good news because
it means ordinary mortals can now score
a table. The extraordinary views over the
Golden Horn should be appreciated over
a pre-dinner drink at the bar before you

move on to a table and make your choice from the menu of huge and very tasty pizzas, a wide array of pasta dishes and mains such as roasted cod with tomatoes, capers, currants and pine nuts served with potato salad. We suggest opting for the pizzas and pastas, as mains can sometimes be disappointing.

### 8 ISTANBUL Map pp102–3  International €€
☎ 0532 5564 356; www.8istanbul.com; Erol Dernek Sokak 1; starters TL14-23, mains TL23-34; ☒ 8am-1am Mon-Thu, 8am-3am Fri & Sat; ☒ Kabataş, then funicular to Taksim
Heavy on atmosphere but light on attitude, 8 Istanbul caters for all budgets and tastes. The menu is a veritable United Nations, featuring Thai soups, Indian samosas, Chinese spring rolls, Mexican guacamole, Vietnamese salads, Austrian schnitzels and Turkish kebaps. All are competently executed and attractively presented. A DJ spins mood-driven tracks later in the night.

### FLAMM Map pp102–3  Anatolian €€
☎ 212-245 7604; www.flamm-ist.com; Sofyalı Sokak 12; pastas & risotti TL19-30, mains TL22-49; ☒ 11am-midnight; ☒ Karaköy, then funicular to Tünel
A bastion of the hip Asmalımescit scene, Flamm serves a mixture of Turkish, French and Italian dishes. Pasta, risotto and grills feature on the menu. The interior dining space features exposed brick walls and subtle lighting, and the outdoor tables are perfectly positioned for those who want to watch the Sofyali Sokak promenade as they dine. There are plenty of nearby options for pre- and post-dinner drinks.

### İSTANBUL MODERN CAFE
Map pp102–3  Modern International €€
☎ 212-249 9680; İstanbul Modern, Meclis-i Mebusan Caddesi, Tophane; pizzas TL16-24, salads TL15-25, pastas TL23-29; ☒ 10am-6pm Tue-Sun, 10am-8pm Thu; ☒ Tophane
An 'industrial arty' vibe and great views over the water to Sultanahmet (when there are no moored cruise ships in the way) make the cafe at İstanbul's pre-eminent contemporary art museum a perfect place for lunch. Pasta is homemade, pizzas are Italian-style and service is slick – all of which makes for a happy lunch experience. It's a good idea to make a reservation as it can fill quickly, particularly on weekends.

### ECE AKSOY Map pp102–3  Anatolian €€
☎ 212-245 7423; www.dokuzeceaksoy.com; Otelier Sokak 9, Tepebaşı; mixed meze plate TL25-30, mains TL15-35; ☒ noon-late; ☒ Karaköy, then funicular to Tünel
The cool jazz on the soundtrack suits the warm-toned casual interior of this modern *meyhane* in trendy Tepebaşı. The lady chef/host here is a true believer in the superiority of local and organic produce, and uses this to make her flavoursome dishes. This is food like Turkish mothers make – it pleases both the heart and the belly. Don't miss the mezes – they're sensational.

### CEZAYİR Map pp102–3  Modern Turkish €€
☎ 212-245 9980; Hayriye Caddesi 16, Galatasaray; starters TL6-15, mains TL16-30; ☒ noon-11.30pm; ☒ Kabataş, then funicular to Taksim
Housed in an attractive building that was once home to an Italian school, Cezayir serves Mod Med food with Turkish influences and caters to an upmarket boho crowd. In summer, the courtyard is always packed with diners sampling dishes such as boneless lamb shank roast with rice, spinach roots and aniseed. Desserts include classics such as chocolate soufflé and ice cream.

### TARİHİ KARAKÖY BALIK LOKANTASI
Map pp102–3  Fish €€
☎ 212-251 1371; Kardeşim Sokak 30, Karaköy; fish soup TL6, mains TL20-30; ☒ noon-4pm Mon-Sat; ☒ Karaköy
Walk through the run-down quarter behind the Karaköy Balıkçılar Çarşısı (Karaköy Fish Market) and you'll come upon this utter gem, one of the few old-style fish restaurants left on the Golden Horn. With seafood being such an expensive proposition in most of İstanbul's restaurants, it's incredibly refreshing to encounter top-class, perfectly prepared dishes that are within everyone's budget – and that's what's on offer here. There's no other word for the food here except fabulous, with the dirt-cheap fish soup possibly being the best you'll ever eat. The original restaurant is only open for lunch, but the same owners have opened an evening venue, the Tarihi Karaköy Grifin ( ☎ 212-243 4080; Kardeşim Sokak 45), which has great views over the Golden Horn. It must be said, though, that this part of town is badly lit and can be a little bit scary at night.

## BONCUK RESTAURANT

Map pp102–3            Meyhane €€

☎ 212-243 1219; Nevizade Sokak 19; meze TL5-10, fish TL18-30; ☽ noon-2am; ⊠ Kabataş, then funicular to Taksim

Armenian specialities differentiate Boncuk from its Nevizade neighbours. Try the excellent *topik* (meze made with chickpeas, pistachios, onion, flour, currants, cumin and salt) and the very tasty *börek*. To ensure that you get a table on the street, where all the action is, get there early or call ahead and book.

## SOFYALI 9

Map pp102–3            Meyhane €€

☎ 212-245 0362; Sofyalı Sokak 9, Tünel; meze TL2-10, kebabs TL12-18; ☽ 11am-1am Mon-Sat; ⊠ Karaköy, then funicular to Tünel

Tables here are hot property on a Friday or Saturday night, and no wonder. This gem of a place serves up some of the best *meyhane* food in all of İstanbul, and does so in surroundings that are as welcoming as they are attractive. It's a bit like eating in a close friend's home, except here you're offered a large array of meze and a wealth of grills and fresh fried fish along with the bonhomie. The *köpeoğlu* (eggplant and tomato with yoghurt and garlic) and *semizotu* (green purslane with yoghurt and garlic) are among the best we've ever eaten and the *kaşaril börek* (cheese pastries) and *kalamar* (fried calamari with garlic sauce) are damn fine, too. Regulars swear by the *Anavut ciğeri* (Albanian fried liver).

## ZÜBEYIR OCAKBAŞI

Map pp102–3            Kebaps €€

☎ 212-293 3951; www.zubeyirocakbasi.com; Bekar Sokak 28; meze TL4-6, kebaps TL10-20; ☽ noon-midnight; ⊠ Kabataş, then funicular to Taksim

Every morning, the chefs at this popular *ocakbaşı* prepare the fresh, top-quality meats to be grilled over their handsome copper-hooded barbecues that night: spicy chicken wings and Adana kebaps, flavoursome ribs, pungent liver kebaps and well-marinated lamb *şış kebaps*. Their offerings are famous throughout the city, so booking a table is essential if you wish to sample some meat and rakı in one of the city's most friendly and boisterous eateries. A hint: order one dish at a time and share each with your dining companions.

## ISTANBUL CULINARY INSTITUTE

Map pp102–3      Modern International €€

Enstitü; ☎ 212-2512214; www.istanbulculinary. com; Meşrutiyet Caddesi 59, Tepebaşı; soup TL5, salads TL3-12, mains TL6-18; ☽ 8am-2am Mon-Sat, 7.30am-6pm Sun; ⊠ Karaköy, then funicular to Tünel

This stylish cafe would look equally at home in Soho, Seattle or Sydney. On one of the city's most happening streets, its casual but chic interior is invariably packed with ladies lunching, office workers enjoying their midday meal and businesspeople meeting over coffee and exceptionally fine cake. The menu changes daily and makes full use of seasonal products – everything is light, beautifully presented and full of flavour. Prices are a steal considering the quality of the food.

## KAFE ARA Map pp102–3    Modern International €€

☎ 212-245 4104; Tosbağ Sokak 8A; pastas TL12-14, mains TL16-20; ☽ 8am-midnight; ⊠ Karaköy, then funicular to Tünel

In the Beyoğlu popularity stakes one cafe stands head and shoulders above the rest – Kafe Ara. A converted garage with tables and chairs spilling out into a wide laneway opposite the Galatasaray Lycée, this is boho central, a casual and welcoming place where you can sample well-priced panini, salads and pastas in a convivial atmosphere. The emphasis here is on top-quality, super-fresh ingredients and simple Mediterranean-slanted dishes, though it's also possible to order Turkish favourites such as *mantı* (Turkish ravioli). There's no alcohol.

## KAHVEDAN Map pp102–3      International €€

☎ 212-292 4030; Akarsu Caddesi 50, Cihangir; www.kahvedancafe.com; sandwiches & wraps TL11-17, mains TL9-21; ☽ 9am-2am Mon-Fri, 9am-4am Sat & Sun; ⊠ Kabataş, then funicular to Taksim

This expat haven serves dishes such as bacon and eggs, French toast, *mee goreng* and falafel wraps. Owner Shellie Corman is a traveller at heart, and knows the importance of things such as free wi-fi, decent wine by the glass, keen prices and good music. It's also an extremely popular bar.

## GALATA HOUSE Map pp102–3      Georgian €€

☎ 212-245 1861; www.thegalatahouse.com; Galata Kulesi Sokak 61, Galata; starters TL10-12, mains TL15-19; ☽ noon-midnight Tue-Sun; ⊠ Karaköy

This would have to be one of the most eccentric restaurants in town. Run by the utterly charming husband-and-wife team of Nadire and Mete Göktuğ, it is housed in the Old British Jail, just down from Galata Tower. The jail functioned from 1904 to 1919, and has been sympathetically but comfortably restored by Mete, who is one of İstanbul's most prominent heritage architects. Nadire uses recipes handed down from her Georgian mother to concoct great comfort food – the *hingali* (meat-filled dumplings in tomato sauce) are absolutely delicious. She also plays the piano for guests.

### LOKAL Map pp102–3     Modern International €€
☎ 212-245 5743/4; Müeyyet Sokak 9; starters TL10-20, mains TL15-20; ⏱ noon-10.30pm; 🚇 Karaköy, then funicular to Tünel

This funky place just off İstiklal Caddesi has only seven tables inside and five outside, and these always seem to be full of bright young things ordering from the eclectic menu, drinking cocktails and flirting with the waiting staff. Some of the cooks are Asian and this is reflected in the number of curries that feature – try the Thai green chicken curry with its creamy coconut base and fragrant herbs or the succulent tandoori lamb chops with yoghurt and tamarind sauce. We concur with the restaurant's slogan: 'Think global, eat Lokal'.

### ZENCEFİL Map pp102–3     Vegetarian €€
☎ 212-243 8234; Kurabiye Sokak 8; mains TL11-14; ⏱ 10am-10pm Mon-Sat; 🚇 Kabataş, then funicular to Taksim; Ⓥ

We're not surprised that this contemporary vegetarian cafe has a loyal following. Its interior is comfortable and stylish, with a glassed courtyard and bright colour scheme, and its food is fresh, cheap and varied; we just wish that it didn't include chicken on its supposedly vegetarian menu. Proof that it's not a haven for old-style hippies lies in its drinks menu, which includes treats such as freshly made *limonata* (lemonade) with Absolut vodka.

### HACI ABDULLAH Map pp102–3     Anatolian €€
☎ 212-293 8561; www.haciabdullah.com.tr; Sakızağacı Caddesi 9a; meze TL6-9, portions TL9-13, kebaps TL11-18; ⏱ 11am-11pm; 🚇 Kabataş, then funicular to Taksim

Just contemplating the sensational *imam bayildi* ('the imam fainted') at Hacı

Abdullah's makes our tastebuds go into overdrive. This İstanbul institution (it was established in 1888) is one of the best *lokantas* in the city and is one of the essential gastronomic stops you should make when in town. You'll find all the traditional favourites, as well as a wide selection of desserts, including home-bottled fruit compote and a delicious *künefe* (shredded wheat pastry with pistachios, honey and sugar). The elegant surrounds feature bottle upon bottle of pickled vegetables and comfortable banquette seating. No alcohol is served.

### KIVA HAN Map pp102–3     Anatolian €
☎ 212-292 0037; www.galatakivahan.com; Galata Kulesı Meydanı 4, Galata; soup TL4, portions TL6-8, kebaps TL10-12; ⏱ 11am-11pm; 🚇 Karaköy then funicular to Taksim

Nestled in the shadow of Galata Tower, this simple but stylish *lokanta* specialises in seasonal dishes from the different regions of Turkey. Inspect the dishes on display before choosing, as some can be overly ambitious and others a bit confrontational for non-Turkish palates. Fortunately, sitting on the front terrace and enjoying a weekend brunch of *menemen* (eggs cooked with tomatoes, peppers and white cheese) and filtered coffee in individual plungers will please everyone. No alcohol.

### GANİ GANİ ŞARK SOFRASI
Map pp102–3     Anatolian & Kebaps €
☎ 212-244 8401; www.naumpasakonagi.com; Taksim Kuyu Sokak 13; kebaps TL8-25; ⏱ 11am-11pm; 🚇 Kabataş then funicular to Taksim

Young Turkish couples love lolling on the traditional Anatolian seating at this cheap and friendly eatery. If you'd prefer to keep your shoes on, you can claim a table and chair on the first floor to enjoy excellent kebaps, rich *mantı* and piping hot pide. No alcohol.

### MEDİ ŞARK SOFRASI
Map pp102–3     Anatolian & Kebaps €
☎ 212-244 9056; Küçük Parmak Kapı Sokak 46a; kebaps TL8-25; ⏱ 11.30am-midnight; 🚇 Kabataş then funicular to Taksim

Another excellent *kebapcı* off İstiklal, Medi specialises in meat dishes from the southeastern region of Turkey, which are served with the house speciality of *babam ekmek* ('my father's bread'). It's known

# CAFE CHAINS

In recent years, the city's fashionable streets and shopping malls have been colonised by an ever-proliferating colony of concept cafes. With designer interiors, strong visual branding, international menus and reasonable prices, these chains have been embraced by young İstanbullus with alacrity, and are great places to spend an hour or so people watching over a coffee, drink or meal. Look out for branches of:

- **The House Café** (www.thehousecafe.com.tr) The most glamorous of them all, with interiors by the uber-fashionable Autoban architectural group, menus by Australian/UK-trained chef Coşkun Uysal and prominent locations including İstiklal Caddesi, Teşvikiye Caddesi in Nişantası, Sofyalı Sokak in Asmalımescit, Cevdet Paşa Caddesi in Bebek and Ortaköy Sq. Best branch: Ortaköy Sq (Map p115) – go for the Sunday brunch.
- **Kitchenette** (www.istanbulview.com) House-baked bread and pastries are the hallmarks of these popular outfits, which are found in locations including Taksim Sq and the Kanyon shopping mall. Best branch: Bebek (p208), which occupies all three floors of a stunning art deco building opposite the ferry dock.
- **Mezzaluna** Sample *la dolce vita* İstanbul-style at one of these cheerful Italian eateries. The quality of the food is impressive, with pizzas, pastas and salads that could hold their own in *La Bella Italia*. This is also one of the few places in town where you'll score decent coffee and pork products such as prosciutto. Best branch: Abdi İpekçi Caddesi (Map p113; Nişantası), which is in the thick of the shopping action.
- **Midpoint** (www.midpoint.com.tr) A laid-back West Coast American feel is evident here, with sleek but anonymous interiors and huge menus featuring wraps, salads, crepes, burgers and quesadillas. Best branch: 187 İstiklal Caddesi (Map pp102–3), which has a terrace complete with Bosphorus view.

for its Adana and beyti kebaps, which are perfectly accompanied by a glass of *ayran* (no alcohol is served). Seating is Anatolian style.

## CANIM CİĞERİM İLHAN USTA
Map pp102–3        Anatolian €

☎ 212-252 6060; Minare Sokak 1; fixed menu TL15; ✆ 10am-midnight; ⊠ Karaköy then funicular to Tünel

The name means 'my soul, my liver', and this small place behind the Ali Hoca Türbesi specialises in grilled liver served with herbs, *ezme* (spicy tomato sauce) and grilled vegetables. If you can't bring yourself to eat offal, fear not – you can substitute the liver with lamb if you so choose. Locals rate this place highly and no wonder, as this is fabulous, cheap food served in a really friendly atmosphere. No alcohol, but *ayran* is the perfect accompaniment.

## KARAKÖY LOKANTASI
Map pp102–3        Anatolian €

☎ 212-292 4455; Kemankeş Caddesi 35A, Karaköy; meze TL5-8, portions TL7-10, grills TL10-15; ✆ noon-4pm & 6pm-midnight Mon-Sat; ⊠ Karaköy

Many travellers will have heard of the famous Pandeli restaurant in the Spice Bazaar, which is known for its gorgeous tiled interior, high prices and – alas – uninspiring food. This family-run *lokanta* across the Galata Bridge in Karaköy has an attrac-

tive tiled interior that references Pandeli's, but there the similarity ends. The food here is tasty and inexpensive, and the service is both friendly and efficient. The place functions as a *lokanta* during the day, but at night it morphs into a *meyhane*, with slightly higher prices.

## KONAK Map pp102–3      Pides & Kebaps €

☎ 212-252 0684; İstiklal Caddesi 259, Galatasaray; kebabs TL8-15, pides TL7-9; ✆ 7.30am-11.30pm; ⊠ Kabataş, then funicular to Taksim

Eateries on İstiklal are often dreadful, but this long-time favourite bucks the trend. It serves excellent kebaps and pides; try the delectable İskender kebap and follow up with a serving of Turkey's famous but hard-to-find Maraş ice cream and you'll be both happy and replete. There's another branch near Tünel, but this one is much better.

## FASULI LOKANTASI Map pp102–3   Anatolian €

☎ 212-2436580; www.fasuli.com.tr; İskele Caddesi 10-12, Tophane; beans, rice & salad TL16; ✆ 7am-11pm

There are two types of *fasulye* (bean dishes) served in Turkey: Anatolian-style Erzincan beans cooked in a spicy tomato sauce, and Black Sea–style beans cooked in a red gravy full of butter and meat. This *lokanta* next to the nargileh joints in Tophane serves its beans Black Sea–style, and they are truly delicious. You can try other Black Sea specialities here, too, including *mihlama* – a type of Turkish fondue made with corn, butter and cheese (TL6).

## GÜNEY RESTAURANT
Map pp102–3                                    Anatolian €

☎ 212-249 0393; Kuledibi Şah Kapısı 6, Tünel; soup TL3, portions TL5-8, kebaps TL7-12; ☯ 7am-10pm Mon-Sat; ⓐ Karaköy
You'll be lucky if you can fight your way through the crowds of hungry locals to claim a lunchtime table at this bustling eatery directly opposite Galata Tower. Friendly waiters will set you up with a basket of fresh bread and point you towards the array of meze and hot dishes on offer.

## HELVETIA LOKANTA
Map pp102–3                                    Anatolian €

☎ 212-245 8780; Sümbül Sokak; soup TL4, salads TL5-6; ☯ 8am-10pm Mon-Sat, 8am-11am Sun; ⓐ Karaköy, then funicular to Tünel; Ⓥ
This hip *lokanta* is popular with locals (particularly of the vegetarian variety), who pop in here for fresh, tasty and cheap-as-chips soups, salads and bean dishes. Start with a yoghurt or tomato soup and follow up with your choice from the daily salads spread.

## NAMLI Map pp102–3                           Delicatessen €

☎ 212-293 6880; www.namligida.com.tr, in Turkish; Rıhtım Caddesi, Karaköy; ☯ 7am-10pm; ⓐ Karaköy
As well as being one of the best delicatessens in the city (check out that cheese selection!), Namlı also stocks hard-to-find Asian ingredients, imported tea and other treats. Take away your choice from the impressive salad and meze selection, or grab one of the tables at the front and eat in. There's another branch in Harıcılar Caddesi next to the Spice Market.

## GALATA KONAK PATISSERIE CAFÉ
Map pp102–3                                    Pastane €

☎ 212-252 5346; www.galatakonakcafe.com; 2nd fl, Hacı Ali Sokak 2, Galata; breakfast TL5-13, sandwiches TL7-11, cakes TL6-7; ☯ 8am-11.30pm; ⓐ Karaköy
After checking out the pastries and cakes on sale in the ground-floor patisserie, make your way up the stairs to the roof terrace cafe, where you can order anything that has taken your fancy downstairs or choose from a large and varied menu. For breakfast try the excellent *menemen* or the superfresh *poğaca* (breakfast buns); there are also decadent cakes for morning and afternoon pick-me-ups and kebabs and pastas for lunch. The view, which includes the Sultanahmet skyline, down the Bosphorus and over the Golden Horn, is fabulous.

## İNCİ PASTANESİ Map pp102–3                   Pastane €
İstiklal Caddesi 124; ☯ 9am-9pm; ⓐ Karaköy, then funicular to Tünel
A Beyoğlu institution, İnci is famous throughout the city for its delicious profiteroles covered in chocolate sauce. Customers squeeze into the tiny shop and most scoff standing up.

## SARAY MUHALLEBİCİSİ
Map pp102–3                         Muhallebici & Pastane €

☎ 212-292 3434; İstiklal Caddesi 102-104; ☯ 8am-11pm; ⓐ Kabataş, then funicular to Taksim
This *muhallebici* is owned by İstanbul's mayor, no less. It's been dishing up puddings since 1935 and is always packed with locals scratching their heads over which of the 35-odd varieties of sweets they want to try this time. Try the *firin sutlaç*, *aşure* (dried fruit, nut and pulse pudding) or *kazandibi* (slightly burnt chicken-breast pudding).

---

## LOVIN' THOSE LOKANTAS

If the Turkish heart lies with the *meyhane*, its stomach rests with the *lokanta*. Serving *hazır yemek* (ready food) kept warm in bain maries, these places are where the locals come for belly fuel at lunchtime. You'll find every type in town, from no-nonsense workers places serving what can only be described as stodge, to elegant establishments offering some of the best food you'll ever sample. The etiquette is the same at all: check out what's in the bain marie and tell the waiter or cook behind the counter what you would like to eat. You can order a full *porsiyon* (portion), a half (*yarım*) *porsiyon* or a plate with a few choices – you'll be charged by the portion. After taking a seat, you'll then be served your chosen plate of food by a waiter.

The city's best *lokantas* include Çiya Sofrası (p159) in Kadıköy, Hacı Abdullah (p155), Karaköy Lokantası (opposite) and Hünkar (p158).

There are also branches in Eminönü and Nişantaşı.

## KARAKÖY GÜLLÜOĞLU

Map pp102–3      Baklava & Börek €

☎ 212-293 0910; Rıhtım Caddesi, Katlı Otopark Altı, Karaköy; baklava portion TL3-5, börek portion TL5, tea TL1 ◷ 8am-7pm Mon-Sat; 🚇 Karaköy
The Güllü family opened its first baklava shop in Karaköy in 1949 and has been making customers deliriously happy and dentists obscenely rich ever since. Go to the register and pay for a glass of tea and *porsiyon* (portion) of whatever baklava takes your fancy (*fıstıklı* is pistachio, *cevizli* is walnut and *sade* is plain). You then queue to receive a plate with between two or three pieces, depending on the type you order. The *börek* here is also exceptionally fine.

# NİŞANTAŞI & AROUND

## KOMŞU Map p113      Anatolian €€

☎ 212-224 9666; Işık Apt, Valı Konağı Caddesi 8, Nişantaşı; meze TL6-9, kebaps TL17-24; ◷ noon-midnight Mon-Sat; 🚇 Osmanbey
Powerbrokers, professionals and cashed-up local residents fill the indoor dining space and pleasant terrace of this well-regarded kebap restaurant on most nights of the week. The meat is top quality – try the meltingly tender *küşleme* kebap, which is made with lamb fillet.

## HÜNKAR Map p113      Anatolian €€

☎ 212-225 4665; www.hunkar1950.com; Mim Kemal Öke Caddesi 21, Nişantaşı; portions TL14-22; ◷ noon-midnight; 🚇 Osmanbey
After a morning spent abusing your credit card in nearby shops, you'll be ready to claim a table at this upmarket *lokanta* and enjoy a relaxed lunch. The chefs take enormous pride in cooking and presenting traditional foods supremely well – everything is delicious. The restaurant's signature dish is a wonderfully smoky and creamy version of *hünkar beğendi,* but there are at least 30 dishes on offer each day, so there truly is something to suit every palate. At the time of writing, the restaurant had been forced to temporarily relocate due to extensive works on the building it usually occupies – it should be back in situ in 2010.

## KANTIN Map p113      Modern Anatolian €€

☎ 212-219 3114; www.kantin.com; Akkavak Sokağı 30, Nişantaşı; soup TL6, salads TL9-16, mains TL11-24; ◷ 9am-11.30pm Mon-Sat; 🚇 Osmanbey
Flying the flag for the international Slow Food philosophy is Şemsa Denizsel's chic eatery, Kantin. The menu changes daily according to the availability of fresh produce and is chalked up on blackboards – ask a waiter to translate if necessary. Nişantaşı's ladies who lunch flock here to grab a flower-adorned table and enjoy the delicious and attractively presented food (the fish dishes are particularly tasty). The basement produce shop sells pre-prepared food to go, which is handy for self-caterers.

# BEŞİKTAŞ, ORTAKÖY & KURUÇEŞME

The cafes, bars and restaurants around the waterside road İskele Sq in Ortaköy form a bustling entertainment precinct that's particularly busy on Friday and Saturday evenings and on weekend days. Be aware that getting here by taxi during these times can be a nightmare due to the horrendous traffic along Çırağan Caddesi.

## VOGUE Map p115      International €€

☎ 212-227 4404; www.istanbuldoors.com; 13th fl, A Blok, BJK Plaza, Spor Caddesi 92, Akaretler, Beşiktaş; starters TL25-45, mains TL27-65, mixed sushi plate TL38; ◷ noon-2am; 🚇 Kabataş then walk or 🚢 Beşiktaş
It seems as if Vogue has been around for almost as long as the Republic. In fact, this sophisticated bar-restaurant in an office block in Beşiktaş opened just over a decade ago. It's a favourite haunt of the Nişantaşı powerbroker set, who love nothing more than enjoying a drink at the terrace bar before moving into the restaurant for pricey sushi or Mod Med dishes.

## BANYAN Map p115      Asian €€

☎ 212-259 9060; www.banyanrestaurant.com; 3rd fl, Salhane Sokak 3, Ortaköy; starters TL10-26, mains TL29-42; ◷ noon-2am Mon-Sat, 10am-2am Sun; 🚢 Ortaköy
The menu here travels around Asia, featuring Thai, Japanese, Vietnamese and Chinese dishes. The food here claims to be good for the soul, and you can enjoy it while soaking

up the exceptional views of the Ortaköy mosque and Fatih Bridge from the terrace. There's another branch in Nişantaşı (Abdi İpekçi Caddesi). There's a 20% discount at lunch.

### AŞŞK KAHVE Map p115 International €€
☎ 212-265 4734; www.asskkahve.com; Muallim Naci Caddesi 64B, Kuruçeşme; ⏰ 9am-10pm, closed Mon in winter; 🚌 Kabataş
The city's glamour set loves this garden cafe to bits, and its weekend brunches are an institution. Go early to snaffle a table by the water and don't forget to have a Botox shot before you go – that way you'll fit in nicely. It's accessed via the stairs behind the Macrocenter.

# ÜSKÜDAR
One of the city's most conservative areas, Üsküdar is not the place to come if you're looking for a boozy night on the town. During the day, the myriad kebab joints and *pastanes* in the street around the ferry terminal do a bustling trade.

### NİYAZİBEY Map p119 Anatolian €
☎ 216-310 4821; www.niyazibey.com.tr, in Turkish; Ahmediye Meydanı; perde pilavı TL7, kebaps TL10-18, pides TL4-10; ⏰ 11am-9pm; 🚇 Üsküdar
Niyazibey specialises in *perde pilavı*, a dish that it describes as hen and rooster meat

(symbolising the bride and groom) cooked with rice (for blessing) and almonds (for children) and encased in pastry sheets (symbolising the home). It also serves pides and kebaps. There's another branch in Kadıköy (Halıtağa Caddesi 5B) – neither sell alcohol.

### KANAAT LOKANTASI Map p119 Lokanta €
☎ 216-310 4821; Ahmediye Meydanı; soup TL4-5, portions TL6-10, kebaps TL9-13; ⏰ 11am-9pm; 🚇 Üsküdar
This barn-like place near the ferry terminal has been serving up competent *hazır yemek* (bistro food) since 1933, and is particularly fancied for its desserts. Its understated but pleasing decor features framed photographs of old street scenes.

# KADIKÖY
We reckon that when you add the lure of a meal at Çiya to a lovely ferry trip and a wander around one of the city's best fresh produce markets, you have the ingredients for a perfect İstanbul day.

### ÇIYA SOFRASI Map p123 Lokanta €
☎ 216-330 3190; www.ciya.com.tr; Güneşlibahçe Sokak 43; meze plate TL5-10, portion TL6-12, desserts TL3-6; ⏰ 11.30am-10pm; 🚇 Kadıköy
We're going to go out on a limb here, and say that this is the best *lokanta* in the city.

## FANCY SOME BACTERIA WITH THAT?
Street vendors pound pavements across İstanbul, pushing carts laden with artfully arranged snacks to satisfy the appetites of commuters. You'll see these vendors next to ferry and bus stations, on busy streets and squares, even on the city's bridges.

Some of their snacks are innocuous – freshly baked *simits*, golden roasted corn on the cob, refreshing chilled and peeled cucumber – but others score high on the 'you must be mad!' scale. Sample these local treats and you're risking a major dose of the sultan's revenge (diarrhoea). Major offenders:

Midye dolma (stuffed mussels) Delicious, exotic and packed with more bacteria than a Petri dish. Only for those who want to live very, very dangerously.

Pis pilav (rice and chickpeas) Displayed in a glass cabinet, this rice dish often comes with boiled chicken. The direct translation is 'dirty rice', which gains a whole new meaning when you realise that the stuff often sits in the sun all day.

Çiğ köfte (raw meatball) Raw meat kneaded by hand for hours with wheat, onion, clove, cinnamon, salt and hot black pepper and then formed into patties, usually by a profusely perspiring man with a cigarette in his other hand. Enough said.

Kokoreç (lamb's intestines cooked with herbs and spices) The Turkish version of black pudding; locals love to snack on this smelly stuff. We feel queasy even thinking about it.

Balık ekmek (fish sandwich) Best sourced on the quay at Eminönü, this is the quintessential İstanbul snack. They're innocuous and utterly delectable when freshly prepared, dangerous when not. Worth the risk.

## AN ANATOLIAN GEM

Ask any food critic to nominate the most exciting regional cuisine in Turkey and they will inevitably settle on the food of Mardin, in the country's southeast. And in Mardin, the most famous restaurant is Cercis Murat Konağı, which serves delectable dishes amid the evocative surrounds of a lavishly decorated 19th-century *konak* (mansion). Imagine, then, the excitement of İstanbullus when it was announced in 2009 that this much-admired restaurant was opening a branch in Bostancı, on the Anatolian (Asian) side of the city. The menu at the new outpost of Cercis Murat Konağı (off Map p123; ☎ 216-373 1193; www.cercismurat.com, in Turkish; Yazmacı Tahır Sk 22, Suadiye Sahil Yolu, ◷ 10am-midnight) is simply spectacular, featuring dishes that are as delectable to taste as they are gorgeous to behold. Start with the *meze tabağı*, a sample platter of 12 meze dishes, or opt for individual plates including *allucıye* (a mixture of greengage, lamb, squash, chives and parsley; TL6), *incasiye* (lamb, chickpeas, plums and pomegranate molasses; TL6) or an extraordinary *kibbe* stuffed with pomegranate, pistachio and lamb (TL5). Mains include the decadent *kaburga dolması* (lamb rib stuffed with *dolma* and slow cooked; TL50 for two people) and desserts range from homemade *dondurma* (ice cream; TL5) to a platter of unusual crystallised walnut, pumpkin, tomato and eggplant (TL7.50). Accompany your meal with the restaurant's own vintages of wine (TL7 per person) or opt for a *zencefilli limonata* (fresh lemonade with ginger and mint; TL5). Perhaps the most impressive aspect to eating here is the service – the huge space is luxuriously appointed, the staff are attentive and classy touches include finger bowls filled with water scented with fresh rose petals.

The only drawback is getting here: you'll need to take a fast ferry from Kabataş (these leave at times including 10.45am, 1pm, 6pm, 6.15pm, 6.30pm, 7pm and 7.30pm and take 25 minutes to reach Bostancı). When you arrive, walk left from the ferry dock along the coast road for 10 minutes and you will reach the restaurant. Returning to Kabataş after lunch is easy (ferries leave at 2pm and 5pm), but the ferries don't run after 8.30pm, so to get home after dinner you'll need to take a taxi to the ferry terminal at Kadıköy, where you can catch a ferry to Eminönü or Karaköy. Note that on Saturdays, the only useful ferry service to Bostancı leaves Kabataş at 6pm; the ferries don't function at all on Sundays or holidays.

We love the simple modern interior and ever-friendly staff, and we adore the food – everything from the delicious self-service meze spread to the *icli köfte* (spicy meatballs rolled in bulgar and deep fried) to the plentiful vegetarian choices. Two dishes wowed us on a recent visit: a stew of fresh apricots, chestnuts and lamb; and *katmer fıstık şeker hamun kaymak* (sweet pistachio flaky pastry with clotted cream). Next-door Çiya Kebapçı is owned and run by the same people, and is just as impressive. If these places served alcohol, we'd move in permanently.

**BAYLAN PASTANESİ** Map p123    Pastane €
☎ 216-336 2881; www.baylanpastanesi.com; Muvakkithane Caddesi 19; coffee TL5-8, cakes TL4-8; ◷ 10am-10pm; ⊛ Kadıköy
Baylan has been serving its homemade pastries, *dondurma* (Turkish ice cream) and cakes to appreciative İstanbullus since 1923. This branch dates from 1925, but had its last facelift in 1961, making it a truly funky decorative time capsule. To the rear of the shop there's a courtyard complete with astroturf and a profusion of hanging baskets – a great spot to scoff a fabulous *caffe glace* (iced coffee with *dondurma*), a top-notch espresso or a plate of profiteroles.

## top picks

- Derviş Aıle Çay Bahçesı (p163)
- Lale Bahçesı (p164)
- Set Üstü Çay Bahçesı (p163)
- Leb-i Derya Richmond (p166)
- Mavra (p166)
- Mikla (p166)
- Nu Teras (p166)
- 360 (p165)
- The raft of nargileh joints at Tophane (p168)
- Zihni (p168)

# DRINKING

It may be the biggest city in an officially Muslim country, but İstanbul's population likes nothing more than a drink or two. If the rakı-soaked atmosphere in the city's *meyhanes* (taverns) isn't a clear enough indicator, a foray into Beyoğlu's thriving bar scene will confirm this fact. If you're in the mood for a drink, we suggest you go out on the town on a Thursday, Friday or Saturday night. Alternatively, you could check out the alcohol-free, atmosphere-rich *çay bahçesi* (tea gardens) or *kahvehanes* (coffee houses) dotted around the city. These are great places to relax and sample a Turkish institution, the nargileh (water pipe), and a cup of *Türk kahvesi* (Turkish coffee) or *çay* (tea).

## DRINKS

### Nonalcoholic Drinks

Drinking *çay* (tea) is the national pastime. Sugar cubes are the only accompaniment and they're needed to counter the effects of long brewing. The sweet 'apple tea' (*elma çay*) offered to many tourists is a concoction that is packed with sugar and citric acid – no self-respecting Turk would dream of drinking it. Surprisingly, *Türk kahve* (Turkish coffee) isn't widely consumed. A thick and powerful brew, it's drunk in a couple of short sips. If you order a cup, you will be asked how sweet you like it – *çok şekerli* means 'very sweet', *orta şekerli* 'middling', *az şekerli* 'slightly sweet' and *sade* 'not at all'. Though you shouldn't drink the grounds in the bottom of your cup, you may want to read your fortune – check the website of İstanbul's longest-established purveyor of coffee, Kurukahveci Mehmet Effendi (www.mehmetefendi.com), for a guide.

Freshly squeezed *portakal suyu* (orange juice) and *nar suyu* (pomegranate juice) are extremely popular drinks. In *kebapcıs,* patrons often drink *ayran,* a refreshing yogurt drink made by whipping yogurt with water and salt; or *şalgam suyu,* sour turnip juice.

If you're in İstanbul during winter, you should try delicious and unusual *sahlep,* a hot drink made from crushed tapioca-root extract.

### Alcoholic Drinks

Rakı (aniseed brandy) is certainly the most popular of all alcoholic beverages, but *bira* (beer) claims second place. The local drop, Efes, is a perky pilsener.

Served in long thin glasses, rakı fires the passions and ensures a good evening at a *meyhane*. Its aniseed taste perfectly complements meze and fish and its powerful punch assures many a convivial evening. It's drunk with water, which turns the clear liquid chalky white.

Turkey grows and bottles its own *şarap* (wine). If you want red wine ask for *kırmızı şarap;* for white ask for *beyaz şarap*. Look for bottles with the Sarafin, Karma or Doluca Özel Kav labels to enjoy the best drinking.

# SULTANAHMET & AROUND

Sadly, there are few pleasant bars in Sultanahmet. The joints along Akbıyık Caddesi are suited to backpackers and unthinkable for everyone else. Don't despair, though. Why not substitute tobacco or caffeine for alcohol and visit one of the many atmospheric *çay bahçesi*s dotted around the neighbourhood?

### HOTEL NOMADE TERRACE BAR
Map pp50–1          Bar
☎ 212-513 8172; www.hotelnomade.com; Ticarethane Sokak 15, Alemdar; ☾ noon-11pm; ⊞ Sultanahmet
The intimate terrace of this boutique hotel overlooks Aya Sofya and the Blue Mosque (Sultan Ahmet Camii). Settle down in a comfortable chair to enjoy a glass of wine, beer or freshly squeezed fruit juice. The only music that will disturb your evening's reverie is the Old City's signature sound of the call to prayer.

### KYBELE HOTEL BAR Map pp50–1    Bar
☎ 212-511 7766; Yerebatan Caddesi 35; ☾ 8am-10pm; ⊞ Sultanahmet
The lounge bar at this charming but vaguely eccentric hotel is chock-full of antique furniture, richly coloured rugs and old etchings and prints, but its signature style comes courtesy of the hundreds of colour-

ful glass lights that are suspended from the ceiling. It's a wonderfully atmospheric spot for a pre-dinner drink.

### SOFA Map pp50–1 — Bar/Restaurant
☎ 212-458 3630; Mimar Mehmet Ağa Caddesi 32, Cankurtaran; ☯ 11am-11pm
Ten candlelit tables beckon patrons into this friendly cafe/bar just off Akbıyık Caddesi. There's a happy hour between 5pm and 6.30pm each day and a decidedly laid-back feel. The food served here is adequate rather than inspired.

### SULTAN PUB Map pp50–1 — Bar
☎ 212-528 1719; Divan Yolu Caddesi 2; ☯ 9.30am-1am; 🚇 Sultanahmet
Sultanahmet's version of Ye Olde English Pub, the Sultan has been around for years and continues to attract the crowds due to its peerless position close to Aya Sofya, the Blue Mosque and the Basilica Cistern (Yerebatan Sarnıçı). The pub grub is what you'd expect from a place like this (ie stodge), but the outdoor tables are a great spot to watch the world go by and the beer is served in iced glasses, just the way it should be.

### YEŞİL EV GARDEN BAR/CAFÉ
Map pp50–1 — Bar/Cafe
☎ 212-517 6785; Kabasakal Caddesi 5, Cankurtaran; ☯ noon-10.30pm; 🚇 Sultanahmet
Most of the bars in Cankurtaran are rowdy backpacker establishments, so the elegant rear courtyard of this historic hotel is a real oasis for those wanting a quiet drink. In spring flowers and blossom fill every corner; in summer the fountain and shady trees keep the temperature down; and in the cooler months a flower-filled conservatory provides shelter. The drinks are expensive, but as the old adage says, quality doesn't come cheaply.

### CAFÉ MEŞALE Map pp50–1 — Çay Bahçesi
☎ 212-518 9562; Arasta Bazaar 45, Utangaç Sokak, Cankurtaran; ☯ 24hr; 🚇 Sultanahmet
Meşale, located in a sunken courtyard behind the Blue Mosque, is a tourist trap *par excellence*, but we still love it. Generations of backpackers have joined locals in claiming one of its cushioned benches under coloured lights and enjoying a tea and nargileh. There's sporadic live Turkish music in the evening and a dervish performance at 7.30pm and 9.30pm.

### DERVİŞ AİLE ÇAY BAHÇESİ
Map pp50–1 — Çay Bahçesi
Dervish Family Tea Garden; Mimar Mehmet Ağa Caddesi, Cankurtaran; ☯ 9am-11pm, closed winter; 🚇 Sultanahmet
The Derviş' paved courtyard, which is superbly located directly opposite the Blue Mosque, beckons patrons with its comfortable cane chairs and shady trees. Efficient service, reasonable prices and peerless people-watching opportunities make it a great place for a leisurely tea, nargileh and game of backgammon.

### SET ÜSTÜ ÇAY BAHÇESİ
Map pp50–1 — Çay Bahçesi
Gülhane Park; ☯ 10am-11pm; 🚇 Gülhane
Those who appreciate the ceremony of proper tea service will love this terraced tea garden overlooking Seraglio Point. Here, you can watch the ferries plying the route from Europe to Asia, while at the same time enjoying an excellent cup of tea served in a teapot and accompanied by hot water (such a relief after the fiendishly strong brews that are common in Turkey). It's so pleasant that you may decide to stay for a lunch of a cheap *köfte ekmek* (meatball sandwich) or a *tost* (toasted cheese jaffle).

### TÜRK OCAĞI KÜLTÜR VE SANAT MERKEZI İKTISADI İŞLETMESI ÇAY BAHÇESİ Map pp50–1 — Çay Bahçesi
cnr Divan Yolu & Babıali Caddesis, Çemberlitaş; ☯ 8am-midnight, later in summer; 🚇 Çemberlitaş
Tucked into the rear right-hand corner of a shady courtyard filled with Ottoman tombs, this enormously popular tea garden is a perfect place to escape the crowds and relax over a *çay* and nargileh. You can even score a cheap and tasty *gözleme* (Turkish crepe filled with cheese, spinach or potato) here.

### YENİ MARMARA Map pp50–1 — Nargileh Cafe
☎ 212-516 9013; Çayıroğlu Sokak 46, Küçük Aya Sofya; ☯ 8am-midnight; 🚇 Sultanahmet
This is the genuine article: a neighbourhood teahouse packed to the rafters with backgammon-playing locals, who play while sipping tea and puffing on nargilehs. The place has bucketloads of character, featuring rugs, wall hangings, low brass tables and fasıl music on the CD player. In winter a wood stove keeps the place cosy; in summer patrons sit on the rear terrace and look out over the Sea of Marmara.

# BAZAAR DISTRICT

Like most parts of the Old City, the area around the Grand Bazaar (Kapali Çarsı) is conservative and there are few places serving alcohol. There are a number of *çay bahçesi*s that are worth checking out though, as well as a *kahvehanesi* (coffee house) or two.

### VEFA BOZACISI Map p73      Boza Bar
☎ 212-519 4922; Katip Çelebi Caddesi 104, Kalenderhane; ⊙ 7am-midnight; 🚇 Laleli-Üniversite
This famous *boza* bar was established in 1875 and locals still flock here to drink the viscous tonic, which is made from water, sugar and fermented grain. The mucous-coloured beverage has a reputation for building up strength and virility – it won't be to everyone's taste, but the bar itself, with its blue tiles, mirrored columns, marble tables and wooden bar, is worth a visit in its own right. If the *boza* is too confrontational for you, the bar also serves *şıra*, a fermented grape juice.

### AY CAFE Map p75      Cafe
☎ 212-527 9853; Takkeciler Sokak 14, Grand Bazaar; ⊙ 8.30am-7pm Mon-Sat; 🚇 Beyazıt
The Grand Bazaar isn't known for the quality of its cafes, but this atmospheric place near the Cevahir Bedesteni (aka Old Bazaar) goes some way towards bucking the trend, serving decent espresso coffee and good cakes and sandwiches.

### FES CAFÉ Map p73      Cafe
☎ 212-526 3071; Ali Baba Türbesi Sokak 25-27, Nuruosmaniye; ⊙ 9am-10pm; 🚇 Beyazıt
After an afternoon spent trading repartee with the bazaar's touts, you'll be in need of a drink. Fortunately, this stylish cafe just outside the Nuruosmaniye Gate is a wonderful place to relax over a good-quality coffee, a beer or a glass of wine. It's also home to a branch of Abdulla Natural Products (p135). There's another branch of the cafe inside the Grand Bazaar (Halicilar Caddesi 62).

### KAHVE DÜNYASI Map p73      Cafe
☎ 212-527 3282; www.kahvedunyasi.com; Nuruosmaniye Caddesi 79, Cağaloğlu; ⊙ 7.30am-9.30pm; 🚇 Çemberlitaş
The name means coffee world, and this new coffee chain has the local world at its feet. The secret of its success lies with the huge coffee menu, reasonable prices,

delicious chocolate spoons (yes, you read that correctly), comfortable seating and free wi-fi. The filter coffee is better than its espresso-based alternatives. There's another branch just near the tram stop at Kabataş ( ☎ 212-293 1206; Meclis-i Mebusan Caddesi, Tütün Han 167, Kabataş).

### ERENLER ÇAY BAHÇESİ
Map p73      Çay Bahçesi
☎ 212-528 3785; Yeniçeriler Caddesi 36/28, Çemberlitaş; ⊙ 7am-midnight, later in summer; 🚇 Çemberlitaş
Packed to the rafters with students from nearby İstanbul University who are doing their best to live up to their heritage (ie develop a major tobacco addiction), this nargileh establishment is set in the leafy courtyard of the Çorlulu Ali Paşa Medrese and has a row of carpet shops down its side.

### İLESAM LOKALI Map p73      Çay Bahçesi
☎ 212-511 2618; Yeniçeriler Caddesi 84, Çemberlitaş; ⊙ 8am-midnight, later in summer; 🚇 Çemberlitaş
This club in the courtyard of the Koca Sinan Paşa Medrese was formed by the enigmatically named Professional Union of Owners of the Works of Science & Literature. Fortunately, members seem happy for strangers to infiltrate their ranks. After entering the gate to Koca Sinan Paşa's tomb, go past the cemetery – it's the second teahouse to the right.

### LALE BAHÇESİ Map p73      Çay Bahçesi
Sifahane Sokak, Süleymaniye; ⊙ 8am-midnight; 🚇 Laleli-Üniversite
In a sunken courtyard that was once part of the Süleymaniye *külliye* (mosque complex), this charming outdoor teahouse is always full of students from the nearby theological college and İstanbul University, who come here to sit on cushioned seats under trees and relax while watching the pretty fountain play. It's one of the cheapest places in the area to enjoy a *çay* and nargileh.

### ŞARK KAHVESİ Map p75      Kahvehanesi
☎ 212-512 1144; Yaglikcilar Caddesi 134, Grand Bazaar; ⊙ 8.30am-7pm Mon-Sat; 🚇 Beyazıt
The Şark's arched ceiling betrays its former existence as part of a bazaar street; years ago some enterprising *kahveci* (coffee-house owner) walled up several sides and turned it into a cafe. The nicotine colour on the walls

is testament to its long pedigree as a popular tea and cigarette spot for the bazaar's stallholders. These days they have to fight for space with tourists, who love the quirky 'flying dervish' murals, the old photographs on the walls, and the cheap tea and coffee.

# BEYOĞLU

There are hundreds of bars in Beyoğlu. The most popular bar precincts are on or around Balo Sokak and Sofyalı Sokak, but there are also a number of sleek bars on roof terraces on both sides of İstiklal – these have fantastic views and prices to match.

Coffee culture is also something that is embraced on this side of the Galata Bridge. In fact, we will go so far as to say that Beyoğlu has gone batty over its beans, and really needs to calm down. At the time of research there were seven multinational coffee-chain franchises on İstiklal Caddesi. In our view, that's caffeine addiction that's got truly out of hand…

See the Eating chapter for reviews of cafes that serve good food.

### 5 KAT Map pp102–3     Bar
☎ 212-293 3774; www.5kat.com; 5th fl, Soğancı Sokak 7, Cihangir; ⏰ 10am-1.30am; 🚇 Kabataş, then funicular to Taksim
This İstanbul institution is a great alternative for those who can't stomach the style overload at 360 and the like. In winter, drinks are served in the boudoir-style bar; in summer, action moves to the outdoor terrace. Both have great Bosphorus views.

### 360 Map pp102–3     Bar
☎ 212-251 1042; www.360istanbul.com; 8th fl, Mısır Apartmenti, İstiklal Caddesi 311, Galatasaray; ⏰ noon-2am Mon-Thu & Sun, 3pm-4am Fri & Sat; 🚇 Karaköy, then funicular to Tünel
İstanbul's most famous bar, and deservedly so. If you can score one of the bar stools on the terrace you'll be happy indeed – the view is truly extraordinary. It morphs into a club after midnight on Friday and Saturday.

### ADA Map pp102–3     Bar/Cafe
☎ 212-251 6682; İstiklal Caddesi 158A; ⏰ 8am-midnight; 🚇 Karaköy, then funicular to Tünel
The side streets off İstiklal may be full of great cafes and bars, but the grand boulevard itself possesses a motley range of choices. Fortunately, Ada is the exception. A cavernous place that's half book-and-

music store and half bar/cafe, it has style and substance in equal measure.

### ANEMON GALATA BAR Map pp102–3     Bar
☎ 212-293 2343; cnr Galata Meydani & Büyükhendek Caddesi, Tünel; ⏰ 6pm-midnight; 🚇 Karaköy, then funicular to Tünel
Largely ignored by the İstanbul bar set, this eyrie on top of a restored Ottoman hotel is one of the best places in the city to watch the sunset while enjoying a quiet drink. Views over to Old İstanbul and across the Golden Horn (Haliç) are stunning.

### BADEHANE Map pp102–3     Bar
☎ 212-249 0550; General Yazgan Sokak 5, Tünel; ⏰ 9am-2am; 🚇 Karaköy, then funicular to Tünel
This tiny neighbourhood bar is a favourite with Beyoğlu's bohemian set because of its cheap beer. On balmy evenings the laneway is crammed with chattering, chain-smoking artsy types sipping a beer or three; when it's cold they squeeze inside. Dress down and be ready to enjoy an attitude-free evening.

### BÜYÜK LONDRA OTELİ BAR
Map pp102–3     Bar
☎ 212-245 0670; Meşrutiyet Caddesi 117, Tepebaşı; ⏰ noon-11pm; 🚇 Karaköy, then funicular to Tünel
This is a true time-warp experience. We'd hazard a guess that the decor at this historic hotel has remained untouched for close on a century, and we're pleased to report that the prices haven't hiked up much during that time.

### KAHVEDAN Map pp102–3     Bar/Cafe
☎ 212-292 4030; www.kahvedancafe.com; Akarsu Yokuşu Sokak 50, Cihangir; ⏰ 9am-2am Mon-Fri, 9am-4am Sat & Sun; 🚇 Kabataş, then funicular to Taksim
The bar de jour in trendy Cihangir when this book went to print, Kahvedan is as popular with local Turks as it is with the expat community. It has an unpretentious vibe, a good selection of wines by the glass and a sound system that is blessedly techno-free. During the day it's a popular cafe offering coffee, an international menu and free wi-fi.

### KAKTÜS Map pp102–3     Bar/Cafe
☎ 212-249 5979; İmam Adnan Sokak 4, Taksim; ⏰ 9am-2am Mon-Sat, 11am-2am Sun; 🚇 Kabataş, then funicular to Taksim

Sourcing its clientele from the arts and media industries, this longstanding favourite off İstiklal is a great spot for a coffee or beer.

### KEVE Map pp102–3
Bar

☎ 212-251 4338; Tünel Geçidi 10, Tünel; ⏰ 8.30am-2am; 🚇 Karaköy, then funicular to Tünel

Is this the most atmospheric bar in the city? In a plant-filled belle époque arcade just opposite the Tünel station, Keve is invariably full of 30-somethings who've just been to a gallery opening on İstiklal and need a drink before moving on to see a new arthouse release at the cinema. The twinkling lights and wrought-iron tables add mightily to the atmosphere. It also serves a cheap open-buffet lunch.

### LEB-İ DERYA Map pp102–3
Bar

☎ 212-244 1886; www.lebiderya.com; 7th fl, Kumbaracı Yokuşu 115, Tünel; ⏰ 11am-2am Mon-Fri, 8.30am-3am Sat & Sun; 🚇 Karaköy, then funicular to Tünel

Ask many İstanbullus to name their favourite watering hole and they're likely to nominate this unpretentious place. On the top floor of a dishevelled building off İstiklal, it has wonderful views across to the Old City and down the Bosphorus, meaning that seats on the small outdoor terrace or at the bar are highly prized. There's also food on offer.

### LEB-İ DERYA RICHMOND Map pp102–3 Bar

☎ 212-243 4375; Richmond Hotel, 6th fl, İstiklal Caddesi 445; ⏰ 7pm-2am Mon-Sat; 🚇 Karaköy, then funicular to Tünel

This sleek younger sister of perennial favourite Leb-i Derya is more restrained and decidedly more chic than her big sis. Fortunately there's no threat of sibling rivalry as the crowd here is older and more cashed-up. The views from the huge windows are just as fab.

### LITERA Map pp102–3
Bar

☎ 212-292 8947; www.literarestaurant.com; 6th fl, Yeniçarşı Caddesi 32, Galatasaray; ⏰ 11am-3am; 🚇 Karaköy, then funicular to Tünel

A new addition to Beyoğlu's world-famous rooftop bar scene, Litera occupies the sixth floor of the Goethe Institute building and revels in its extraordinary views of the Old City. It doubles as a club late on Friday and Saturday nights and as a restaurant at all

times, but our experience would suggest that you're best to avoid eating here.

### MAVRA Map pp102–3
Bar/Cafe

☎ 212-252 7488; Serdar-ı Ekrem Caddesi 31A, Galata; ⏰ 9am-2am Mon-Fri, 9am-4pm Sat & Sun; 🚇 Karaköy, then funicular to Tünel

Serdar-ı Ekrem Caddesi is one of the most interesting streets in Galata, full of ornate 19th-century apartment blocks, avant-garde boutiques and laid-back cafes and bars. Mavra is a bit of everything – during the day it functions as a cafe, serving excellent sandwiches and pastries (the poğaca are excellent); at night, it reinvents itself as a hip bar that has been wholeheartedly embraced by artists, journalists and others in the creative industries. Its decor is thrift-shop chic and its shelves are full of locally designed ceramics and craft that are for sale. Nearby Building Food Lab & Apparel (p138) offers more of the same, albeit with a hard-edged minimalist aesthetic.

### MİKLA Map pp102–3
Bar

☎ 212-293 5656; Marmara Pera, Meşrutiyet Caddesi 167-185; ⏰ noon-2am; 🚇 Karaköy, then funicular to Tünel

In winter, sink into the Alvar Aalto–designed chairs and watch the twinkling lights of Beyoğlu while you down a wonderfully dry martini or good-quality glass of house wine. In summer, the poolside bar on the roof offers truly stupendous views. After your drinks, we highly recommend that you stay for dinner. See p152 for a restaurant review.

### NU TERAS Map pp102–3
Bar

☎ 212-245 6070; www.istanbulyi.com; 6th fl, Meşrutiyet Caddesi 149, Tepebaşı; ⏰ 6.30pm-2am Mon-Thu & Sun, 6.30pm-4am Fri & Sat Jun-Oct; 🚇 Karaköy, then funicular to Tünel

This fashionable summer-only terrace bar is a great place for a sunset drink. Its view is unusual in that it focuses on the Golden Horn, but it's no less spectacular for that. See p152 for a food review.

### PANO Map pp102–3
Bar

☎ 212-292 6664; Hamalbaşı Caddesi 26, Tepebaşı; ⏰ 11am-1am; 🚇 Kabataş, then funicular to Taksim

You'll have to fight your way through the throngs at this extraordinarily popular wine bar on a Thursday, Friday or Saturday night. Serious drinkers prop themselves on the high bar tables at the front and swig the cheap house wine; others take a table at the back or upstairs and pace themselves while sampling hot and cold meze.

## PASİFİC HOUSE Map pp102–3 · Bar
Sofyalı Sokak, Asmalımescit; ☾ noon-2am; 🚇 Karaköy, then funicular to Tünel
There are loads of bars on this side of town, but not too many that are both cheap and well located. Ultra-casual Pasific scores on both of these counts, which is why it's constantly packed. The fact that it's on one of the city's most happening streets is a plus, too.

## SMYRNA Map pp102–3 · Bar
☎ 212-244 2466; Akarsu Yokuşu Sokak 29, Cihangir; ☾ 9am-2am; 🚇 Kabataş, then funicular to Taksim
Smyrna is known for its long bar, collection of antique toys, couch-filled back corner and candlelit tables. The atmosphere is laid back, the music is unobtrusive and the crowd is early-30s 'Beyoğlu Arty'. If you decide to make a night of it here (and many do) there's good simple food available, too.

## WHITE MILL Map pp102–3 · Bar/Cafe
☎ 212-292 2895; www.whitemillcafe.com; Susam Sokak 13, Cihangir; ☾ 9.30am-1.30am; 🚇 Kabataş then funicular to Taksim
White Mill's couch-filled interior and fabulous rear garden are inevitably full of 30-somethings enjoying great music and a decidedly hip ambience. It also serves food (often organic).

## LOKAL Map pp102–3 · Cafe
☎ 212-245 4028; Tünel Meydanı 4, Tünel; ☾ 7.30am-1am Mon-Thu, 7.30am-5am Fri & Sat, 10am-1am Sun; 🚇 Karaköy, then funicular to Tünel
This place is popular with locals, who monopolise its tables for long breakfasts and lingering coffees. In warmer weather, the front of the space opens to Tünel Sq and provides great people-watching opportunities; when it's cooler, the velvet-upholstered armchairs are the perfect place to curl up with a coffee and a newspaper. On Friday and Saturday night it functions as a club.

## HACO PULO
Map pp102–3 · Çay Bahçesi
☎ 212-2444210; Hacopulo Pasajı; ☾ 9am-11pm; 🚇 Kabataş, then funicular to Taksim
There aren't nearly as many traditional teahouses in Beyoğlu as there are in atmospheric Old İstanbul, so this one is treasured by the locals. Set in a delightfully picturesque cobbled courtyard, it's stool-to-stool 20- to 30-somethings on summer evenings. Walking from İstiklal Caddesi through the skinny arcade crowded with offbeat shops adds to the experience.

## CLUB 17 Map pp102–3 · Gay Bar
Zambak Sokak 17; cover charge TL10 (Fri & Sat only); ☾ 11pm-4am Sun-Thu, 11pm-5.30am Fri & Sat; 🚇 Kabataş, then funicular to Taksim
Attractive young men pack this small, narrow bar as aggressive techno beats accompany wafting sexual energies. At closing time, the crowd spills out into the street to make final hook-up attempts possible. The cover charge includes one free drink.

## BIGUDI CAFE LESBIAN PUB/CLUB
Map pp102–3 · Lesbian Pub/Club
☎ 0535-509 0922; www.bigudiproject.com; 4th & 5th fl, Balo Sokak 20, Beyoğlu; ☾ pub 2pm-2am daily, club midnight-4am Fri & Sat; 🚇 Kabataş then funicular to Taksim
The pub admits gay men, but the arty terrace club is mainly frequented by lipstick lesbians and is resolutely off-limits to non-females. The rationale for the barrier is self-defence, which hints at this country's lesbian state of affairs: invisible, often not by choice.

## PERLA KALLÂVI NARGILE CAFÉ
Map pp102–3 · Nargileh Cafe
☎ 212-245 9154; 4th to 6th fl, Kallâvi Sokak 2; ☾ 10am-2am; 🚇 Karaköy, then funicular to Tünel
Follow the scent of apple tobacco to this nargileh cafe occupying the top three floors of an ornate building on İstiklal Caddesi (enter from the side street). It's inevitably full of young people (including plenty of women) enjoying a glass of tea and a bubbling pipe in the welcoming indoor spaces or on the small terrace with its Sea of Marmara views.

## TOPHANE NARGİLEH

Map pp102–3                                    Nargileh Cafe

off Necatibet Caddesi, Tophane; ⏰ 24hr;
🚇 Tophane

This atmospheric row of nargileh cafes behind the Nusretiye Mosque is always packed with trendy teetotallers. Follow your nose to find it – the smell of apple tobacco is incredibly enticing. While there, you will get an insight into the city's favourite pastime, *keyif* (the art of quiet relaxation).

# NİŞANTAŞI & AROUND

## ZİHNİ Map p113                                    Bar

☎ 212-248 8033; Vali Konağı Caddesi 39, Nişantaşı; www.zihnibar.biz; ⏰ 6pm-1am Mon-Thu, 6pm-2am Fri & Sat Oct-April; Ⓜ Osmanbey

When antique dealer Zihni Şardağ acquired the fittings of the Park Hotel's historic American Bar in the 1980s, he found himself loathe to part with them. His solution was to open this atmospheric bar in a century-old apartment designed by the famous İstanbullu architect, Vedat Tek. The scene here is elegant and upmarket, as befits its pedigree.

# BEŞİKTAŞ, ORTAKÖY & KURUÇEŞME

## ÇIRAĞAN PALACE HOTEL KEMPINSKI

Map p115                                    Bar/Cafe

☎ 212-326 4646; www.ciragan-palace.com; Çırağan Caddesi 32, Beşiktaş; 🚇 Yıldız

This is where the Botox brigade comes to show off its bling. Nursing a mega-pricey drink at one of the Çırağan's terrace tables and watching the scene around the city's best swimming pool, which is right on the Bosphorus, will make you feel like Diane Fossey observing her chimps. Regulars here

### NARGILEHS: NAUGHTY BUT NICE

When ordering a nargileh, you'll need to specify what type of tobacco you would like. Most people opt for *elma* (when the tobacco has been soaked in apple juice, giving it a sweet flavour and scent), but it's possible to order it unadulterated (*tömbeki*). The average price is TL12 to TL15. The water pipe will be brought to your table, hot coals will be placed in it to get it started and you will be given a disposable plastic mouthpiece to slip over the pipe's stem. Just draw back and you're off. Bliss!

share some habits with we mere mortals, but are definitely a different species…

# KADIKÖY

This is where the city's grunge set comes to party, and party it certainly does. The length of Kadife Sokak is filled with unpretentious bars and cafes that are busy from late morning to late at night. During the day, coffee and games of Scrabble, Monopoly and backgammon are on the agenda; at night, cheap beer, live music and conversation take over. Karga Bar is the most famous of the street's establishments, but Bahane Kültür and Lâl are great back-ups. Dress down and don't forget that the last ferry back to Karaköy leaves at 11pm (8pm to Eminönü) – if you want to stay later, a dolmuş (minbus) to Taksim will be your only public transport option.

## KARGA BAR Map p123                                    Bar

☎ 216-449 1725; Kadife Sokak 16; ⏰ 11am-2am; 🚢 Kadıköy

Karga is one of the most famous bars in the city, offering cheap drinks, loud music and avant-garde art on its walls and in the upstairs gallery. It doesn't have a street sign – look for a green building with a wooden door. There's a small courtyard downstairs to enjoy a late-afternoon beer.

# NIGHTLIFE

## top picks

# NIGHTLIFE

There's an entertainment option for everyone in İstanbul. You can while away the night in glamorous nightclubs on the Bosphorus where you'll spend your entire holiday budget in the space of one night if you're not careful, or you can drink rakı (aniseed brandy) and burst into song at a cheap and rowdy *meyhane* (tavern) or *Türkü Evi* (Turkish music bar). With its huge array of cinemas, almost religious devotion of its people to all forms of music and their great love of dance, it's rare to have a week go by when there's not a special event, festival or performance scheduled in this town. In short, the only thing you can't do here is be bored.

## Tickets & Reservations

If you can't make it to the box office, or if there isn't one for the venue, try Biletix ( ☎ 216-556 9800; www.biletix.com). It's a major ticket seller for all kinds of events from festivals and big-name concerts to football matches. Biletix outlets are found in many spots throughout the city, but the most convenient for travellers is probably the one at the İstiklal Kitabevi (Map pp102–3; İstiklal Caddesi 55, Beyoğlu; ⏰ 10am-10pm). Alternatively, you can buy tickets by credit card on Biletix's website and collect them from a Biletix outlet or the venue before the concert.

## CLUBBING

İstanbul has a killer nightlife, and the best venues are clustered around what is known as the 'Golden Mile' between Ortaköy and Kuruçeşme on the Bosphorus. This sybaritic strip is where world-famous nightclubs such as Reina and Sortie are located, and it's also where the city's jazz scene is gravitating. Frankly, the only thing to do at night in Sultanahmet is leave.

When İstanbullus go out clubbing they dress to kill. If you don't do the same, you'll be unlikely to get past the door staff (usually buffed young hunks) at the mega-venues on the Bosphorus. Fortunately, you'll have no trouble in venues in other parts of town as these cater to the transient crowd and won't care what labels you're wearing.

Clubs are busiest on Friday and Saturday nights, and the action doesn't really kick off until 1am. If you're keen to visit a Bosphorus club, you should consider booking to have dinner in its restaurant – otherwise you could be looking for a lucky break or a tip of at least TL100 to get past the door staff. Crystal is the only exception to this rule.

Many of the Beyoğlu clubs are closed from June or July – when the party crowd moves down to Turkey's southern coasts – until the end of September. Those clubbers who stay in town tend to flock to the open-air waterfront spots such as Reina (Map p115; ☎ 212-259 5919/21; www.reina.com.tr; Muallim Naci Caddesi 44, Kuruçeşme; Fri & Sat TL50, Mon-Thu & Sun free; ⏰ 6pm-midnight dining, midnight-4am dancing; ◎ Ortaköy) and Sortie (opposite).

As well as the clubs reviewed here, Angelique (Map p115; ☎ 212-327 2844/45; www.istanbuldoors.com /en/; Salhane Sokak 5, Ortaköy; ⏰ 6pm-4am Apr-Oct; ◎ Ortaköy), Blackk (Map p115; ☎ 212-236 7256; www.blackk. net; Muallim Naci Caddesi 71, Kuruçeşme; ⏰ 10.30pm-4am; ◎ Kuruçeşme) and 360 (p165) are safe bets if you want to have dinner, a few drinks and a dance or two. You'll need to make reservations for all of them, though.

### ARAF Map pp102–3
☎ 212-244 8301; 5th fl, Balo Sokak 32, Beyoğlu; admission free; ⏰ 5pm-4am; ⊞ Kabataş then funicular to Taksim
Grungy English teachers, Erasmus exchange students and Turkish language students have long claimed this as their favoured destination, shaking their booties to the in-house gypsy band and swilling the cheapest club beer around (a mere TL5). To avoid the locals' weekend mating madness and capacity crowds, go on Tuesday or Wednesday.

### BABYLON Map pp102–3
☎ 212-292 7368; www.babylon.com.tr; Şehbender Sokak 3, Tünel; ⏰ 9.30pm-2am Tue-Thu, 10pm-3am Fri & Sat, closed summer; ⊞ Karaköy then funicular to Tünel
This venue for live performances is a city institution. Its eclectic program often features big-name international music acts, particularly during the festival season. Most of the action occurs in the concert hall but it also runs an eponymous restaurant/lounge with a DJ spinning right behind the hall. Cover charges and performance times vary; book

at Biletix or at the box office (open 10am to 6pm, longer on days of performance).

## CRYSTAL Map p115

☎ 212-261 1988 (ext 2); www.clubcrystal.org; Muallim Naci Caddesi 65, Ortaköy; cover incl 1 drink adult/student TL35/25; ⏰ midnight-5.30am Fri & Sat; ⓞ Ortaköy

A year-round venue beloved of the city's techno aficionados, who come here to appreciate the great mixes and scratches of some of the best DJs from Turkey and Europe. There's a great sound system, a crowded dance floor and a lovely covered garden bar. Customers here tend to be young and affluent.

## DOGZTAR Map pp102–3

☎ 212-244 9147; www.dogzstar.com, in Turkish; Kartal Sokak 3, Beyoğlu; cover TL5; ⏰ 6pm-3am Mon-Thu, 6pm-5am Fri & Sat; ⓡ Kabataş then funicular to Taksim

It's a three-storey affair, but the compact size (300 persons max) makes for an acoustic powerhouse. The crowd comprises budding fans or hard-core followers of featured up-and-coming musical groups or DJs. And the owners altruistically give the collected cover charges to performers. They also charge reasonable drinks prices and provide a terrace for cooling off in summer.

## GHETTO Map pp102–3

☎ 212 251 7501; www.ghettoist.com; Kalyoncu Kulluk Caddesi 10, Beyoğlu; ⏰ 8pm-4am, closed summer; ⓡ Kabataş then funicular to Taksim

Decor-wise, this three-storey club behind the Flower Passage (Çiçek Pasaji; p109) combines Renaissance-style painted high ceilings with modernist touches including a long, back-illuminated bar with bottles that seem to glow in the dark. The musical program is equally interesting, comprising creative foreign or local live acts. In summer, it hosts Peymane @ Ghetto Teras (reached via a back staircase), an open-air restaurant-cum-music lounge that 'doesn't close until the sun is up'. Check the website for schedules and cover charges.

## INDIGO Map pp102–3

☎ 212-245 1307; www.livingindigo.com, in Turkish; 1st to 5th fl, Mısır Apt, 309 Akarsu Sokak, Galatasaray; ⏰ 10pm-5am Fri & Sat only, closed summer; ⓡ Kabataş then funicular to Taksim

This is Beyoğlu's electronic music temple and dance-music enthusiasts congregate here on weekends for their energetic kicks. The program spotlights top-notch local and visiting DJs or live acts. Check the website for schedules and cover charges.

## JOLLY JOKER BALANS Map pp102–3

☎ 212-251 77 62; www.jollyjokerbalans.com, in Turkish; Balo Sokak 22, Beyoğlu; ⏰ from 10pm, closed summer; ⓡ Kabataş then funicular to Taksim

The gig-goers among the lively multinational crowd enjoy the city's best locally brewed beer (the caramel brew) and gravitate towards the upstairs bi-level performance hall, which features a balcony with glass floors. Check the website for schedules and cover charges.

## LOVE DANCE POINT Map p113

☎ 212-296 3357; www.lovedancepoint.com; Cumhuriyet Caddesi 349, Harbiye; admission free; ⏰ 11.30pm-4am Wed, 11.30pm-5am Fri & Sat; Ⓜ Osmanbey

Going into its second decade, Love DP is easily the most Europhile of the local gay venues, hosting gay musical icons and international circuit parties. Hard-cutting techno is thrown in with gay anthems and Turkish pop. This place attracts the well-travelled and the un-impressionable, as well as some straight hipsters from nearby Nişantaşı.

## ROXY Map pp102–3

☎ 212-249 1283; www.roxy.com.tr, in Turkish; Aslan Yatağı Sokak 5; cover TL25, student TL5-10; ⏰ 10pm-4am Fri & Sat, closed summer; ⓡ Kabataş then funicular to Taksim

Bright young things flock to this dance-and-performance club, off Sıraselviler Caddesi, Taksim, that includes a gallery, a party space and YAN Gastrobar ( ☎ 212-249 1283; ⏰ 4pm-1am Mon-Thu, 4pm-4am Fri-Sat). If you eat here before clubbing, you get in free via a side door, dodging the long lines outside and the possibility that you might not get past the door staff.

## SORTIE Map p115

☎ 212-327 8585; www.sortie.com.tr; Muallim Naci Caddesi 141, Kuruçeşme; cover TL50 Fri & Sat, free Mon-Thu & Sun; ⏰ 6pm-4am, dancing after midnight; ⓞ Kuruçeşme

Sortie has long vied with Reina as the reigning queen of the Golden Mile, nipping at the heels of its rival dowager. It pulls in the city's glamour-pusses and poseurs, all of whom are on the lookout for the odd celebrity or tabloid fodder.

## SUPPERCLUB Map p115

☎ 212-261 1988; www.supperclub.com; Muallim Naci Caddesi 65, Kuruçeşme; admission free; ⏲ 8.30pm-4am; ◉ Kuruçeşme

With an all-white decor and a location close to the Bosphorus, Supperclub has an unmistakable resort feel. Customers lounge or dine in oversized beach beds in lieu of tables and chairs, enjoying the atmospheric lighting, live shows, imported DJ talents and highly creative cuisine. All of this adds a multisensory approach to partying.

## TEK YON Map pp102–3

☎ 535-233 0654; Siraselviler Caddesi 63, Beyoğlu; admission free; ⏲ 10pm-4am; 🚇 Kabataş then funicular to Taksim

A phenomenal run in the popularity stakes catapulted this originally unpretentious venue to the forefront of İstanbul's gay nightlife. It has now upgraded to sleek and bigger surroundings to the delight of its core hirsute, fashion-challenged clientele. Cuddly bears abound here.

## XLARGE Map pp102–3

☎ 212-788 7372; www.xlargeclub.com; Kallavi Sokak 12, Beyoğlu; cover incl 1 drink TL25; ⏲ 11.30pm-5am Fri & Sat only; 🚇 Kabataş then funicular to Taksim

This straight-friendly gay venue melds glitz with size. Occupying a converted art deco–era cinema that Atatürk was said to have habituated, it draws in both gay and straight partyphiles, who come to be dazzled by a humungous ballroom chandelier, preserved old architectural details and possibly the longest bar (under the stage) in any local venue. On the mezzanine, two supersized beds for group cavorting flank a full-service bar; one overlooks the hunky dancers or drag artists on stage. Vodka-shot (TL5) counters have been conveniently placed near people for easy refuelling.

# JAZZ CLUBS

İstanbul has a number of dedicated jazz venues ranging from bohemian to swanky in style. During the lively International İstanbul Jazz Festival (p16), the now-traditional 'Jazz Boat' and the recently added 'Balkan Boat'

pick up passengers in Kabataş for a ride on the Bosphorus with jazz ensembles performing. Live jazz also takes centre stage at the popular Akbank Jazz Festival (p17). During the warmer months, there are often unannounced freebie concerts on Beyoğlu streets.

## İSTANBUL JAZZ CENTER Map p115

☎ 212-327 5050; www.istanbuljazz.com; Salhane Sokak 10, Ortaköy; music charge varies, set menu TL65, starters TL18-29, mains TL25-36; ⏲ dinner 7pm-midnight, sets 9.30pm-12.30am, closed Jun-Aug; ◉ Ortaköy

JC's plays regular host to members of the jazz world's who's-who. The stylish setting accounts for the steep bill for dinner plus music and drinks. It's next to the Radisson SAS Bosphorus Hotel (p200).

## JAZZ CAFÉ Map pp102–3

☎ 212-245 0516; www.jazzcafeistanbul.com; Hasnun Galip Sokak 14, Beyoğlu; cover varies, dinner per person approx TL50; ⏲ 8pm-4am Tue-Fri, sets at 10.30pm & 1am, very infrequently open Mon or Sat, closed Jun-Aug; 🚇 Kabataş then funicular to Taksim

Established by Mete Gurman and Cengiz Sanlı in 1982, this mellow two-storey place is one of the city's original jazz joints and is bathed in mood lighting. Great local jazz musicians such as Bülent Ortaçgil come here to perform to 30-something jazz-heads, and musicians from other genres also feature – funk/acid or blues are played Tuesday to Thursday, for instance. In summer, the club decamps to Bodrum.

## NARDIS JAZZ CLUB Map pp102–3

☎ 212-244 6327; www.nardisjazz.com; Galata Kulesi Sokak 14, Galata; cover varies; ⏲ 8pm-1am Mon-Thu with sets at 9.30pm & 12.30am, 8pm-2am Fri & Sat with sets at 10.30pm & 1.30am, closed Jul-Aug; 🚇 Karaköy then funicular to Tünel

Just down the hill from the Galata Tower (p105), this venue, named after a Miles Davis track, is where the real aficionados go. Run by jazz guitarist Önder Focan and his wife Zuhal, Nardis is small but big in atmosphere. Its line-up of performers is exceptionally good; some come from the winners' ranks of its yearly amateur contest and others are visiting international artists. Different daily performers make every visit fresh and serendipitous – book ahead.

## GAY & LESBIAN İSTANBUL

All gay and lesbian listings in this book (clubs, *hamams* and bars) were written by René Ames, an İstanbul resident and freelance writer for *Time Out İstanbul*. René also updated the sections on clubbing, live jazz and live Turkish Music.

Having previously lived in New York, Switzerland, London and Spain, René is well qualified to assess how the gay and lesbian scene stacks up against its equivalents in the world's other big cities. He describes it as being just as lively and energy-sapping, but adds that the current impetus towards Europe makes it even more dynamic: 'People have that feeling of liberation, knowing that the European Union is hovering and showing interest in Turkey's human rights situation. It's like being in the cusp of a major historical turnover; very similar to the *La Movida* moment before Spain joined the rest of Europe, a truly exhilarating time when you can feel and live the possibilities.'

Asked how the scene differs to those of its European sister cities, he says: 'There are more tranny bars here than in New York or London or any other European capital. Leather and fetish clubs are the only ones absent in this mosaic, except when held as party themes. And we don't have dark rooms and naughty nooks like in some Western gay venues, meaning that most action needs to be done in private. There have been some marked changes in gay interactions in recent times – for instance, all the seedy soft-porn cinemas that dabbled as daytime gay social centres for lack of alternatives have bowed to constant police monitoring, choosing to close down or convert to mainstream cinemas in the past couple of years. For some furtive moments, risk-takers and the brazen can, of course, still duck into dark alleys…'

This furtiveness may be due in part to the ambiguous legal status of homosexuality here; René points out that while Turkey has no laws against homosexuality, it has none in favour of it, either. 'In otherwords, it's neither legal nor illegal and that's where the problem is. Gays can be prosecuted or just plain harassed by the authorities under other legal statutes. Most telling is the fact that there are no anti-discrimination laws covering sexual identity in this country; this is what the EU wants changed.' René is yet to witness police action leading to a forced closure of a gay venue, but he has been present when police visit and check everyone's *kimliks* (identity cards). He also notes that the *hamam* scene is changing: 'Police have been pretty vigilant against lewdness in *hamams*, too, so much so that bathhouse habitués say that the traditional homoerotic undercurrents in these bathhouses have changed considerably.'

Unfortunately, there are few organizations fighting for gay rights in Turkey. René describes the best known of these, Lambda (www.lambdaistanbul.org in Turkish), as 'a far cry from their counterparts elsewhere'; although he notes that a 2009 move by the AKP local prosecutor to close the organisation has made its members more vocal and proactive in soliciting support from various local and international human rights groups.

# TURKISH MUSIC

Turks are proud of their traditional music (see p35) and, whether young or old, will be familiar with most popular folk and *fasıl* numbers to sing along in a *meyhane* or *Türkü Evi*.

## MEYHANES

One of the most entertaining experiences you can possibly have while visiting İstanbul is to have dinner at a *meyhane* where live *fasıl* music is being performed. Several restaurants in and around the Balık Pazarı off İstiklal Caddesi are among a number of places in Beyoğlu that now offer this type of sing-and-dance-along entertainment with their reasonably priced menus. Others have a set meal deal with either limited or unlimited drinks choices (limited will be rakı, beer or soft drinks; unlimited means that you could have all or any of these plus local spirits or wine). Make sure to tip when the musicians come to your table, nothing extravagant but substantial enough to be appreciated (TL5 to TL10 per person is about right). When

booking at a *meyhane*, try to opt for a Friday or Saturday night – on other nights restaurant management occasionally tells musicians not to come in if numbers are low.

### ALEM Map pp102–3

☎ 212-249 6055, 293 4040; www.alemrestaurant. com, in Turkish; Nevizade Sokak 8-10, Beyoğlu; set menu incl all drinks TL55; ⏰ 10am-2am, live music 8pm-midnight; 🚇 Kabataş then funicular to Taksim
The only joint on Nevizade's *meyhane* row featuring live *fasıl* (on the 2nd floor), Alem offers a well-chosen set menu of mezes, meat and fish (of which they have a choice array daily). If you're not keen on singing, stay downstairs and eyeball passers-by.

### CUMHURIYET Map pp102–3

☎ 212-293 1977; www.tarihicumhuriyetmey hanesi.com, in Turkish; Sahne Sokak 47, Beyoğlu; set menu limited/unlimited TL55/65; ⏰ 9am-2am, live fasıl 8.30pm-midnight; 🚇 Kabataş then funicular to Taksim
The atmosphere of this historic place in the Balık Pazarı reeks of nostalgia (the name is

Turkish for 'Republic' and it's been around for nearly as long). Photos of Atatürk, who was a regular customer, are a feature. Try and get a table on the 2nd floor; you'll eat basic, but always fresh, food and listen to good *fasıl*.

## DEMETI Map pp102–3

☎ 212-244 0628; Şimşirci Sokak 6, Beyoğlu; dinner approx TL40/45, set menu limited/unlimited TL55/TL65; ☽ 4pm-2am Mon-Sat; ▣ Kabataş then funicular to Taksim

Located in a Cihangir hillside apartment with street-level entrance, this recently opened *meyhane* has a friendly feel and stylish decor. A display case of meze and desserts greets you as you enter and the kitchen is open, meaning that you can check out the dinner choices as you are led to your table. Reservations are a must if you want one of four tables on the terrace, which have an unimpeded Bosphorus view. Set menus are only offered for groups of six or more. There's a live singer midweek.

## DESPINA Map pp46–7

☎ 212-247 3357; Açıkyol Sokak 9, Kurtuluş; dinner incl drinks TL50; ☽ noon-12.30am, fasıl music 8:30pm-midnight; ▣ taxi

Established in 1946 by the glamorous Madame Despina, whose faded photograph greets guests at the entrance, Despina is mainly patronised by neighbourhood locals, who come for its good Armenian/ Greek food (à la carte only) and the live *fasıl* music played by very accomplished musi-

cians. On a warm evening the garden is a great setting for musical revelry.

## GARIBALDI Map pp102–3

☎ 212-245 2522; Perukar Çikmazi (Odakule Yani) 3, Beyoğlu; www.garibaldibar.com, in Turkish; set menu limited/unlimited TL60/70; ☽ 7.30pm-12.30am Mon-Sat, fasıl music 8.30pm-close; ▣ Karaköy then funicular to Tünel

Garibaldi is tucked away in the side alley of an old Armenian Catholic church next to the Odakule complex on İstiklal Caddesi. Its dining hall has great acoustics for enjoyment of its pleasing *fasıl* group. In summer the action moves to the romantic cobbled courtyard.

## KOKOSH BY ASMALI Map pp102–3

☎ 212-293 2547/48; www.asmalikokosh.com, in Turkish; set menu incl all drinks TL90; ☽ 6pm-2am Tue-Thu, 6pm-4am Fri & Sat, live music from 8pm, closed summer; ▣ Karaköy then funicular to Tünel

This place opposite the Pera Palace Hotel (p108) is home to the well-known Cumhur Cemaat Orkestrası and the singer Cumhur Demir. The musicians rely heavily on the entrancing sounds of the zither and kettledrum, which encourages vociferous singing.

## LEVENDIZ GREEK MEYHANE Map p115

☎ 212-236 7256; www.blackk.net; Muallim Naci Caddesi 71, Ortaköy; set menu incl all drinks TL80; ☽ 8pm-1am, live music 9.30pm-midnight; ◉ Ortaköy

Part of the luxury supper club complex Blackk, Levendiz offers a great Bosphorus view to accompany its inspired Greek cui-

## NIGHTLIFE RIP-OFFS

Foreigners, especially single foreign males, are targets for a classic İstanbul rip-off that works like this:

You're a single male out for a stroll in the afternoon or evening. A well-spoken, well-dressed Turk strikes up a conversation and recommends a bar or nightclub. As he seems like a nice guy, you agree to accompany him to one of these places. You enter, sit down and immediately several women move to your table and order drinks. When the drinks come, you're presented with a huge cheque – TL500 isn't unusual. It's a mugging, and if you don't pay up scary-looking guys will suddenly appear, take you into the back office and raid your wallet. If you don't have enough cash, they may even escort you to an ATM so that you can withdraw funds.

A variation is a single foreign male having a drink and a meal in a restaurant or bar. Several Turkish friends sitting nearby strike up a conversation, then suggest you all take a taxi to another venue. In the taxi, they forcibly relieve you of your wallet. Occasionally, these guys will pretend to be policemen, accosting you on a back street, roughing you up and taking your wallet in the process.

How do you avoid such rip-offs? As many Turks are generous, hospitable, curious and gregarious, it's difficult to know whether an invitation is genuine (as it most often is) or the prelude to a mugging. Tread carefully if there's any reason for suspicion. As for nightclub recommendations, take them from a trusted source, such as this book. Avoid any bar or nightclub in Aksaray (the city's red-light district) and steer clear of Beyoğlu's backstreets late at night.

sine. It is easily the most upscale *meyhane* hereabouts. Come dressed accordingly.

### ZINDAN Map pp102–3

☎ 212-252 7340, 249 6755; Olivia Han Geçidi 13, Beyoğlu; set menu incl all drinks TL60; ✆ noon-2am Mon-Sat, fasıl music 8.30pm-2am Mon-Sat; 🚇 Karaköy then funicular to Tünel

Located in a former Genoese prison (Zindan means 'dungeon' in Turkish), the building housing this *meyhane* off İstiklal Caddesi has been mercifully spared extensive renovations. At night, merry-making with gypsy troubadours and a belly-dancer will transport you to the Pera of yore.

# TÜRKÜ EVLERI

Food, drinks and *fasıl* go hand-in-hand to create a raucously memorable night-out in a *meyhane*, but in a *Türkü Evi* only drinks are needed to fuel the enjoyment of *halk meziği* (folk music). Indeed, being inebriated seems to foster appreciation of the strong sentiments that these folk songs contain. Whether expressing lament for a lost love or a longing for freedom by a group of people, they're always heartfelt and passionate. The Kurdish owners of a dozen bars in Beyoğlu's Hasnun Galip Sokak, the city's main *Türkü Evi* strip, would scoff at any suggestion of renouncing *halk* for *sanat* (art or classical Turk) music or Arabesk – they consider the former bourgeois and the latter a frivolous import from the Middle East.

### EYLÜL Map pp102–3

☎ 212-245 2415; Erol Dernek Sokak 2, Beyoğlu; ✆ 2.30pm-4am, music from 8.30pm; beer TL6, rakı TL8; 🚇 Kabataş then funicular to Taksim

This place is popular with students and young İstanbullus wanting to listen to the musical strains of their Anatolian homeland. Until the music starts, you'd think you've walked into a Turkish rock bar.

### MUNZUR CAFE BAR Map pp102–3

☎ 212-252 7340, 249 6755; www.munzurcafebar.com, in Turkish; Hasnun Galip Sokak 21, Beyoğlu; ✆ 1pm-4am, music from 9pm; beer TL4, rakı TL7; 🚇 Kabataş then funicular to Taksim

Seventeen years old and counting, this bar has arguably the best line-up of singers in the street and also hosts expert *bağlama* (lute) players. It brings in diverse customer groups trying to connect to the lyrics of the song. Refuse plates of fruits if not ordered; they're not complimentary.

### TOPRAK Map pp102–3

☎ 212-293 4037; www.toprakturkubar.tr.gg /ana-safya.htm; Hasnun Galip Sokak 17A, Beyoğlu; ✆ 4pm-4am, show from 10pm; beer TL6, rakı TL8; 🚇 Kabataş then funicular to Taksim

The tables here are arranged facing the performance area as in a music hall, all the better to soak in the singer's pathos. The biggest venue in the neighbourhood, Toprak doubles as a restaurant (mains TL13).

# THE ARTS

## top picks

- Akbank Culture & Arts Centre (p180)
- Aya İrini (p181)
- Galerist (p178)
- Santralistanbul (p179)
- Depo (p181)
- Garajistanbul (p181)

What's your recommendation? www.lonelyplanet.com/istanbul

# THE ARTS

When the EU designated İstanbul one of its European Cultural Capitals for 2010, no-one here was surprised. Pleased, yes, but İstanbullus hadn't failed to note the fact that over the past decade their city had built considerably on its formidable cultural infrastructure and been gifted a whole new generation of museums and galleries, including the İstanbul Modern (p101), Pera Museum (p108), Sakıp Sabancı Museum (p207), Proje4L/Elgiz Museum of Contemporary Art (below) and santralistanbul (opposite). Fortunately, this proliferation of venues isn't short of exciting new work to show, with the city's contemporary arts practice going from strength to strength and its visual artists finally starting to take their place on the international stage alongside their musician, writer and filmmaker peers.

## ART GALLERIES

İstanbul has a thriving visual arts scene. As well as cultural centres (p180), most of which have excellent exhibition spaces, numerous small independent galleries exhibit the work of local and international artists. Some up-market private galleries are in the shopping areas of Teşvikiye and Nişantaşı, but most of the cutting-edge private galleries have joined the high-profile contemporary spaces funded by banks and other companies on or around İstiklal Caddesi in Beyoğlu.

For larger art museums such as the İstanbul Modern (p101) and the Pera Museum (p108), see individual entries in the Neighbourhoods chapter.

The big visual arts event on the calendar is the International İstanbul Biennial (p17). For a handy guide to what's showing in the city's galleries, pick up a free copy of the *List* brochure at cafes, restaurants and nightclubs in Beyoğlu or go to www.istanbulartlist.net.

### GALERI APEL Map pp102–3

☎ 212-292 7236; Hayriye Caddesi 5A, Galatasaray; www.galleryapel.com; ⏱ 11.30am-6.30pm Tue-Sat, closed Aug; ⓡ Kabataş, then funicular to Taksim

This long-established commercial gallery behind the Galatasaray Lycée has a large stable of Turkish artists working in a number of media. Its shows are always worth a visit.

### GALERI NEV Map p113

☎ 212-231 6763; Maçka Caddesi 33, Maçka; www.galerinevistanbul.com; ⏱ 11am-6.30pm Tue-Sat; Ⓜ Osmanbey

This highly regarded commercial gallery shows paintings, sculptures and installation works by contemporary Turkish artists. It has a second gallery ( ☎ 212-252 1525; 311 İstiklal Caddesi, Beyoğlu; ⏱ 11am-6.30pm) on the 5th floor of the fashionable Mısır Apartmentı building.

### GALERIST Map pp102–3

☎ 212-244 8230; www.galerist.com.tr; 4th fl, İstiklal Caddesi 311, Galatasaray; ⏱ 10am-6pm Mon-Fri, noon-6pm Sat; ⓡ Karaköy, then funicular to Tünel

The most fashionable of the city's commercial galleries, Galerist shows young Turkish artists living at home and abroad and working in a variety of media. It's located on the 4th floor of the Mısır Apartmentı Building. Look out for its (excellent) free magazine, edited by cultural commentator Ferhan İstanbulu (see the interview p137).

### PROJE4L/ELGIZ MUSEUM OF CONTEMPORARY ART Off Map pp46–7

Elgiz Çağdaş Sanat Müzesi; ☎ 212-290 2525; www.elgizmuseum.org; Meydan Sokak, Beybi Giz Plaza B Blok, Maslak; ⏱ 10am-5pm Wed-Fri, 10am-4pm Sat; Ⓜ ITU Ayazaga

Proje4L was the first of the crop of new, privately endowed museums in the city. Established by local architect and property developer Can Elgiz, it aims to further the understanding and appreciation of international contemporary art in the city and facilitate the globalisation of contemporary Turkish art. The gallery recently moved to its new premises in Maslak, the city's financial hub. When you exit ITU-Ayazaga metro station, take the underpass and walk towards the plazas (the gallery is in the office development behind the Ziraat Bankası and Sheraton Hotel, accessed via a road to the left of these buildings).

## SABANCI ÜNIVERSITESI KASA GALERI Map pp102–3

☎ 212-292 4939; Bankalar Caddesi 2, Karaköy; http://kasagaleri.sabanciuniv.edu; ⏲ 10am-6pm Mon-Sat; 🚇 Karaköy

Kasa Galeri is located in the basement vault of the Minerva Han, formerly the Greek-owned Bank of Athens. Karaköy was once the city's main financial centre, full of handsome bank buildings, and this splendid Islamic Eclectic–style building dating from the early 20th century is one of the many impressive buildings along Voyvoda Caddesi/Bankalar Caddesi dating from this time. Part of Sabaci University's Communication Centre, the gallery shows works by young Turkish and international artists.

## SANTRALİSTANBUL Map pp46–7

Eski Silahtarağa Elektrik Santrali; ☎ 212-311 5000; www.santralistanbul.com; Kazım Karabekır Caddesi 1, Eyüp; admission adult/student/child under 12yr TL7/3/free; ⏲ 10am-8pm Tue-Sun; 🚌 44B, 47, 47C, 47E, 399B (Bilgi Üniversitesi)

İstanbul's version of the Tate Modern, santralistanbul is a contemporary art gallery housed in a converted power station on the campus of the private Bilgi University. Exhibitions are as big in ambition as they are in size. Get there by bus from Eminönü or catch the free shuttle bus from the Atatürk Cultural Centre in Taksim; these leave every 30 minutes between 8.30am and 9pm.

## SCHNEİDERTEMPEL ART CENTER
Map pp102–3

Schneidertempel Sanat Merkezi; ☎ 212-249 0150; www.schneidertempel.com; Felek Sokak 1, Karaköy; ⏲ 10.30am-5pm Mon-Fri, noon-4pm Sun; 🚇 Karaköy

Housed in an old synagogue, the Schneidertempel exhibits work by local Jewish artists, as well as frequent exhibitions from abroad. Quality varies, but we've seen some excellent photographic exhibitions here, as well as extremely moving exhibitions of historical work from the Holocaust.

## YAPI KREDİ CULTURAL CENTRE
Map pp102–3

☎ 212-252 4700; www.ykykultur.com.tr; İstiklal Caddesi 161, Galatasaray; ⏲ 10am-7pm Mon-Fri, noon-6pm Sat, 1-6pm Sun; 🚇 Karaköy, then funicular to Tünel

This centre has a prominent location on İstiklal Caddesi and an eclectic exhibition program including everything from retrospectives of 20th-century Turkish painters to spotlights on contemporary photographers working in İstanbul. It's funded by the Yapı Kredi bank, which has a long history of supporting Turkish literature and art.

# CINEMAS

İstiklal Caddesi is the centre of İstanbul's cinema *(sinema)* district. During April's International İstanbul Film Festival (p16) every corner of Beyoğlu is filled with enthusiastic cinema-goers. Tickets to this festival are hot numbers – you will need to book in advance.

During the rest of the year, the enthusiasm for the silver screen remains. Films are mostly shown in English with Turkish subtitles, but double-check at the box office in case the film has Turkish *(Türkçe)* dubbing, as this sometimes happens with blockbusters. For movie listings, see the *Hürriyet Daily News*.

When possible, buy your tickets a few hours in advance. Depending on the venue, tickets cost between TL9 and TL15 – many places offer reduced rates before 6pm, to students, and all day once a week (usually Wednesday).

## AFM AKMERKEZ

☎ 444 1 AFM; www.afm.com.tr; Akmerkez Shopping Centre, Nispetiye Caddesi 76, Etiler; 🚇 Akmerkez

This multiplex is pricey, but its comfortable surrounds are a good place to rest after a big day shopping.

## AFM FİTAŞ Map pp102–3

☎ 444 1 AFM; www.afm.com.tr; İstiklal Caddesi 24-26, Fitaş Pasajı, Beyoğlu; 🚇 Kabataş, then funicular to Taksim

This multiplex has 11 screens and all the Hollywood trimmings.

## ALKAZAR SİNEMA MERKEZİ Map pp102–3

☎ 212-293 2466; İstiklal Caddesi 179; 🚇 Kabataş, then funicular to Taksim

First a porn cinema, then an art-house joint, Alkazar has now given in to Hollywood, though it still occasionally programs an art-house hit. There are three screens and a plush and cosy interior.

## ATLAS SINEMALARI Map pp102–3

☎ 212-252 8576; İstiklal Caddesi 209, Atlas Pasajı; Ⓜ Kabataş, then funicular to Taksim
On the 1st floor of one of the historic arcades along İstiklal, Atlas is always bustling. There are three screens and the programming is eclectic. International İstanbul Film Festival screenings also happen here.

## CITYLIFE CINEMA Map p113

☎ 212-373 3535; wwwcitylifecinema.com, in Turkish; 6th fl, City's Nişantaşİ, Teşvikiye Caddesi 162, Teşvikiye; Ⓜ Osmanbey
The bar with its magnificent Bosphorus view makes this multiplex in the City's Nişantaşı Mall one of the most popular cinemas in town. It screens a mixed program of art-house and blockbuster flicks.

## EMEK Map pp102–3

☎ 212-293 8439; Yeşilçam Sokak 5, Beyoğlu; Ⓜ Kabataş, then funicular to Taksim
Functioning since the 1920s, this barn of a cinema is one of the oldest in the city. It's not the most comfortable on offer, but has managed to retain a bit of the glamour it had during Pera's heyday. It's another venue for the International İstanbul Film Festival.

## KANYON MARS CINEMA

☎ 212-353 0814; www.marssinema.com, in Turkish; Kanyon Shopping Mall, Levent; Ⓜ Levent
In the city's most glamorous shopping mall, this multiplex is a comfortable place to enjoy a flick. It screens some, but not all, films in original languages.

## REXX Map p123

☎ 216-336 0112; www.rexx-online.com; Sakızgülü Sokak 20-22, Kadıköy; Ⓜ Kadıköy
We've sheltered here from bad weather before risking a ferry back to town more than once. On the Asian side of İstanbul, the Rexx's program usually lacks surprises. The only exception is in April, when it screens part of the International İstanbul Film Festival.

## ŞAFAK SİNEMALARI Map pp50–1

☎ 212-516 2660; Divan Yolu Caddesi 134, Çemberlitaş; Ⓜ Çemberlitaş
This seven-screen cinema is the closest to Sultanahmet, only a 10-minute walk along Divan Yolu. It screens Hollywood blockbusters.

# CLASSICAL MUSIC, OPERA & BALLET

İstanbul has a lively Western classical-music scene and its own headline act, the İstanbul State Symphony Orchestra. There are also regular visits by international orchestras and chamber ensembles.

In summer, occasional concerts are also held in the atmospheric amphitheatre at Rumeli Hisarı (p205), at Yedikule Zindanları (p125) and in the watery cavern of the Basilica Cistern (p54).

During the International İstanbul Music Festival (p16) there is a wealth of classical music and opera on offer, including performances in the extraordinarily atmospheric Aya İrini (opposite).

The İstanbul State Opera and Ballet (www.idobale.com) has a season running from October to May, with some extra performances during the International İstanbul Music Festival. Most performances take place at the Süreyya Opera House (Kadıköy Süreyya Operası; Map p123; ☎ 216-346 1531/2/3; www.sureyyaoperasi.org; Bahariye Sokak 29, Kadıköy).

# CULTURAL CENTRES & PERFORMANCE VENUES

There's big money behind the arts in İstanbul, with banks leading the way in funding the major arts companies and festivals. There are also plenty of impressive venues around town where the sponsors can schmooze and the dignitaries can party after the performance. Most of these venues are cultural centres – hosting a number of different art forms – it's not unusual for these places to host an opera one night, a jazz performance the next, a ballet on the night after that and an exhibition in the foyer the whole time.

To get an overview of what's on where, refer to the monthly listings in *Time Out Istanbul*. Tickets are usually available through Biletix ( ☎ 216-556 9800; www.biletix.com).

## AKBANK CULTURE & ARTS CENTRE
Map pp102–3

☎ 212-252 3500; www.akbanksanat.com; Zambak Sokak 1, Beyoğlu; ☻ 10.30am-7.30pm Tue-Sat; Ⓜ Kabataş, then funicular to Taksim
This excellent small venue, funded entirely by the Turkish bank of the same name, hosts classical and jazz music recitals,

dance performances, film screenings and exhibitions of the work of local artists.

## ATATÜRK CULTURAL CENTRE Map pp102–3
AKM, Atatürk Kültür ve Sanat Merkezi; ☎ 212-251 5600; Taksim Sq; Ⓜ Kabataş, then funicular to Taksim

At night the lights of the city's major cultural centre glow behind its stylised steel grill, providing a welcome sight in the otherwise unprepossessing Taksim Sq. Unfortunately, the building isn't quite as beguiling during the day. The centre is usually home to the İstanbul State Symphony and Choir, İstanbul State Modern Folk Music Ensemble and İstanbul State Classical Turkish Music Choir as well as being a major venue for the İstanbul State Opera and ballet, but was closed for a major restoration when this book went to print. It was due to re-open in 2010.

## AYA İRİNİ Map pp50–1
Haghia Eirene, Church of Divine Peace; First Court of Topkapı Palace; Ⓜ Sultanahmet

Big-name classical events make the most of the acoustics in this ancient venue (see p59), particularly during the International İstanbul Music Festival. During the festival a board outside lists upcoming events and contact details; tickets are available through Biletix or at the festival ticket box at the Atatürk Cultural Centre.

## CEMAL REŞİT REY CONCERT HALL
Map p113
Cemal Reşit Rey Konser Salonu; ☎ 212-232 9830; www.crrks.org in Turkish; Gümüs Sokak, Harbiye; Ⓜ box office 10am-7.30pm; Ⓜ Kabataş, then funicular to Taksim

With its great acoustics and comfortable chairs, this concert hall is a popular venue for dance and music performances. Its handy monthly guides list upcoming events and prices in English, and are available around town (they're everywhere on İstiklal Caddesi).

## DEPO Map pp102–3
☎ 212-292 3956; www.depoistanbul.net; Lüleci Hendek Caddesi 12, Tophane; Ⓜ 11am-7pm Tue-Sun; Ⓜ Tophane

This cultural centre in a former tobacco warehouse has been set up by Anadolu Kültür (www.anadolukultur.org), a not-for-profit cultural organisation. It hosts talks, exhibitions,

films and video screenings involving artists from Turkey, the South Caucasus, the Middle East and the Balkans, and its aim is to facilitate artistic collaboration, promote cultural exchange and stimulate reflection on social and political issues relevant to the region. Rodeo (www.rodeo-gallery.com), a commercial contemporary art gallery, is also located here.

## GARAJISTANBUL Map pp102–3
☎ 212-244 4499; www.garajistanbul.org; Kaymakem Reşet Bey Sokak 11A, Galatasaray; Ⓜ Kabataş, then funicular to Tünel

This performance space occupies a former parking garage in a narrow street behind İstiklal Caddesi and is about as edgy as the city's performance scene gets. There are usually contemporary dance performances on Monday and Tuesday, poetry readings or improvisations on Wednesday, and theatrical performances on Thursday, Friday and Saturday.

## İŞ ART & CULTURAL CENTRE Off Map pp46–7
İş Sanat Kültür Merkezi; ☎ 212-316 1083; www.issanat.com.tr; İş Kuleleri 4, Levent; Ⓜ box office 9am-6pm; Ⓜ Levent (Plazalar exit)

This sleek venue in the İş Towers hosts high-profile international musicians (mainly jazz and classical), local theatre and children's pantomimes. A free shuttle service to here leaves from the front of the parking lot at the Atatürk Cultural Centre in Taksim Sq at 6.30pm on performance days.

## LÜTFI KIRDAR CONCERT HALL Map p113
Convention Centre, Lütfi Kırdar Kongre ve Sergi Salonu; ☎ 212-296 3055; www.icec.org/en; Darülbedai Sokak, Harbiye; Ⓜ Kabataş, then funicular to Taksim

Originally built for the 1948 World Wrestling Championships, this huge refurbished concert hall hosts conferences, performances by the Borusan İstanbul Philharmonic Orchestra and the Efes Pilsen Blues Festival (p17).

## PLATFORM GARANTİ CONTEMPORARY ART CENTRE Map pp102–3
☎ 212-293 2361; www.platformgaranti.blogspot.com; İstiklal Caddesi 115, Beyoğlu; Ⓜ offices & library 10am-6pm Tue-Sat; Ⓜ Kabataş, then funicular to Taksim

Funded by the Garanti Bank, this space has traditionally encompassed a library, gallery and studios for visiting artists. It aims to (in its own words) '...act as a dynamic catalyst for dissemination, research and practice of contemporary art in the city, as well as providing an exchange point for exchange between contemporary artists, curators and critics'. When this book went to print, there was talk of the centre moving location to Bankalar Cadddesi in Karaköy.

# DANCE

Many people immediately think of belly dancing when they hear the term 'Turkish folk dance', but there are other, far more authentic, traditional dance forms in the country. Although belly dancing has a long history here, it's not strictly a Turkish dance, having been brought here during the Ottoman Empire. These days it's mainly tourist fodder, and although it can be entertaining, the dancers in İstanbul are usually second-rate.

The touristy 'Turkish Shows' around town provide a snapshot of Turkey's folk dances (with belly dancing), usually accompanied by dinner. Beloved by package-tour operators, they are expensive and the food is usually mediocre at best. We suggest giving them a miss, but if you are intent on spending a night this way check www.orienthouseistanbul.com and www.kervansaray.com.tr.

### DANCE OF COLOURS Map p73
☎ 554 797 2646; www.dancesofcolours.com; FKM (Firat Culture Centre), Divan Yolu Caddesi, Çemberlitaş; adult/student/child under 8yr TL40/30/free; ⏱ 7.30pm Thu; 🚇 Çemberlitaş
This popular two-part performance features a whirling dervish and Sufi music segment followed by dances from 10 different regions of Turkey. Colourful costumes and professional dancers make for a good evening's fun, with the added bonus that you don't have to fork out for an indifferent meal.

# SPORTS & ACTIVITIES

## top picks

- **Four Seasons Istanbul at the Bosphorus** (p184) Top spa
- **Çırağan Palace Kempinski İstanbul** (p184) Best pool
- **The Ambassador Hotel Spa Center** (p185)
- **Çemberlitaş Hamamı** (p186) Top hamam
- **Yeşildirek Hamamı** (p186) Top gay hamam

What's your recommendation? www.lonelyplanet.com/istanbul

# SPORTS & ACTIVITIES

There's plenty to do in İstanbul when you want a break from the sights. You can check out the summer social scene beside a five-star hotel swimming pool, succumb to steam and a soapy scrub in one of the city's historic *hamams* (bathhouses), or scream yourself hoarse with the rest of the crowd at a Super League soccer match. Whichever you choose, you will enjoy yourself.

## HEALTH & FITNESS

In summer, going to a swimming pool here is more about seeing and being seen than getting fit, which is why the pools at the five-star hotels are so popular with locals. These hotels probably offer the best options for those travellers craving a gym workout, too.

## GYMS

Many of the local gyms are testosterone-packed joints full of muscles and attitude. The equipment is usually fairly limited too, so it's probably worth forking out a bit more and paying for a day pass at one of the big international hotels.

### ORSEP ROYAL HOTEL Map pp50–1

☎ 212-5118585; www.orseproyalhotel.com; Nöbethane Caddesi 10, Sirkeci; day pass TL30; ⏰ 10am-10pm; 🚇 Sirkeci
Conveniently located behind Sirkeci train station, this hotel has an excellent gym and wellness centre with an indoor pool, *hamam*, sauna, steambath, Jacuzzi and exercise equipment. There's also a small rooftop pool with fabulous panoramic views.

## SPAS

İstanbul's five-star hotels vie with each other to offer the most luxurious spa experience in town. All have *hamams* offering a sybaritic alternative to the traditional bath experience.

### CAUDALIE VINOTHÉRAPIE SPA

Off map p115
☎ 212-359 1533/34; www.lesottomans.com; Muallim Naci Caddesi 68, Kureçeşme; massage TL120-200, treatments & packages TL120-390; ⏰ 7am-10pm Mon-Fri, 8am-10pm Sat & Sun; 🚇 Kureçeşme
If you ask the local ladies who lunch to recommend the best spa in town, many will nominate this luxurious place in the

basement of the Hotel Les Ottomans. The surrounds are exquisite and the therapists are top-notch. A day pass to use the indoor/outdoor pools, *hamam*, adventure showers, heated ceramic lounges, whirlpool, sauna, ice fountain and oxygen room costs TL130.

### FOUR SEASONS ISTANBUL AT THE BOSPHORUS Map p115

☎ 212-381 4160; www.fourseasons.com/bosph orus; Çırağan Caddesi 28, Beşiktaş; massage TL170-260, 45min hamam experience TL180, treatments TL75-650; ⏰ 9am-9pm; 🚇 Beşiktaş
The spa at this recently opened luxury hotel has the wow factor in spades. Features include a stunning indoor pool area, steam room, spa, sauna, treatment rooms and meditation areas. The gorgeous marble *hamam* is the perfect choice if you're looking for an indulgent – rather than utilitarian – Turkish bath experience. A day pass with access to all spa facilities costs TL150.

### LAVEDA SPA AT THE RITZ-CARLTON ISTANBUL Map p113

☎ 212-334 4444; www.ritzcarlton.com; Suzer Plaza, Elmadağ; hamam treatment TL110; ⏰ 7am-10pm; 🚇 Kabataş, then funicular to Taksim
Luxurious Laveda offers Ottoman bathing rituals juxtaposed with modern wellness procedures. As well as the basic 'Traditional Hamam' treatment (given by an attendant who doesn't hurry through the soaping, skin-peeling and water massage), there's also a long list of spa therapies and massages, including a Sultan's six-hands massage. The *hamam*, which is authentically set up, sports rich marble and soothing piped-in ambient music.

## SWIMMING

Swimming in the Bosphorus is only an option for those who have a death wish. Those with a hankering for the water can head to the beaches at Yeşilköy and Florya (you can get to these by train from Sirkeci train station) – but only to paddle. The water around the Princes' Islands is relatively clean, though the tiny beaches are crammed bottom-to-bottom in summer. The best option, if you really want to go to the beach, is to visit Kilyos, Şile or Ağva on the Black Sea coast; all are day trips by bus – Kilyos from Sariyer on the Bosphorus and Şile and Ağva from the bus stand south of the Şemsi Paşa Mosque in Üsküdar.

Most of İstanbul's pool facilities are privately owned and open to members only. However, it's possible to organise a pricey day pass to use the leisure facilities at many of the city's luxury hotels, and there's much to be said for the idea of spending a day poolside at one of these places, particularly when good eateries, a health club and Bosphorus views come as part of the package.

The best outdoor pools are found in the following hotels and are open from late May to early October.

Çırağan Palace Kempinski İstanbul (Map p115; ☎ 212-326 4646; www.kempinski-istanbul.com; Çırağan Caddesi 32, Beşiktaş; Mon-Fri €118, Sat & Sun for 2 persons €189; ☼ 7am-7pm; Ⓜ Yıldız)

Hotel Les Ottomans (off Map p115; ☎ 212-359 1500; www.lesottomans.com; Muallim Naci Caddesi 68, Kuruçeşme; TL100; ☼ 9am-6pm subject to hotel events; Ⓜ Kuruçeşme)

İstanbul Hilton (Map p113; ☎ 212-3156000; www1.hilton.com; Cumhuriyet Caddesi, Harbiye; Mon-Fri TL60, Sat & Sun TL95; ☼ 8am-8pm; Ⓜ Kabataş then funicular to Taksim)

Swissôtel İstanbul the Bosphorus (Map p115; ☎ 212-326 1100; www.swissotel.com; Bayıldım Caddesi 2, Maçka; Mon-Fri TL90, Sat TL120, Sun incl barbecue lunch TL160; ☼ 7am-10pm; Ⓜ Maçka)

# ACTIVITIES

Sightseeing is the activity you'll indulge in most while in İstanbul, but while you're here it's worth forgoing the sights for a few hours and surrendering your body to the steamy environs of a *hamam*. If you're here over a weekend, it's also worth thinking about attending a football match. Just try to make sure it's one where Galatasaray, Fenerbahçe or Beşiktaş are playing, because these are the most exciting.

## HAMAMS

We run the danger of sounding like your mum here, but frankly, we just don't think it's advisable for you to leave İstanbul without having a bath. A Turkish bath, that is…

## AĞA HAMAMI Map pp102–3

☎ 212-249 5027; Turnacıbaşı Sokak 48B, Çukurcuma; bath TL20, oil massage TL30, skin-peeling scrub TL5, soap massage TL5; ☼ 9am-11pm; Ⓜ Kabataş then funicular to Taksim

Built for the private use of Fatih Sultan Mehmet in 1454, this is one of the oldest *hamams* in town and has been restored to retain its Ottoman glory. Providing an authentic Turkish bath experience (mainly for tourists), it has a low-key ambience and allows communal bathing for both genders (male masseur only). Prices are surprisingly reasonable when compared with the historic *hamams* in the Old City.

## AMBASSADOR HOTEL SPA CENTER
Map pp50–1

☎ 212-512 0002; www.hotelambassador.com; Ticarethane Sokak 19, Sultanahmet; Turkish bath with soap & oil massage 60/75min €50/60; ☼ 8am-10pm; Ⓜ Sultanahmet

There's no atmosphere to speak of at the spa centre of this shabby modern hotel just off Divan Yolu, but all treatments are private, meaning that you get the small and pretty *hamam* all to yourself. Best of all is the fact that the 60- or 75-minute Turkish massage treatment here (bath, scrub and soap massage) includes a 30-minute oil massage given by Zeki Ulusoy. Zeki is trained in sports, remedial and aromatherapy massage and he really knows his stuff – you'll float out of here at the end of your session. You can also book the *hamam* for private use (€20 per person per hour) or book a 45-minute Turkish bath treatment without the oil massage (€35).

## CAĞALOĞLU HAMAMI Map pp50–1

☎ 212 522 2424; www.cagaloglu hamami.com. tr; Yerebatan Caddesi 34, Cağaloğlu; bath, scrub & massage standard/luxury €40/55, bath €20; ☼ men 8am-10pm, women 8am-8pm; Ⓜ Sultanahmet

The most beautiful of the city's *hamams*, historic Cağaloğlu Hamamı offers separate baths for men and women and a range of bath services. You'll find a pleasant cafe as well as a shop selling quality soaps and other *hamam* accessories (the pistachio-oil soap is particularly fine). You don't need to purchase a bath mitt unless you want to – as at most tourist *hamams*, the attendants will supply one if you haven't brought your own.

## ÇEMBERLİTAŞ HAMAMI
Map pp50–1
☎ 212-522 7974; Vezir Hanı Caddesi 8, Çemberlitaş; bath, scrub & soap massage TL55, bath TL35, 30-minute oil massage TL40; ☯ 6am–midnight; 🚇 Çemberlitaş
There won't be too many times in your life when you'll get the opportunity to have a Turkish bath in a building dating back to 1584, so now might well be the time to do it. Commissioned by Nurbanu Sultan, wife of Selim II and mother of Murat III, this *hamam* was designed by the great architect Sinan and is among the most beautiful in the city. Just off Divan Yolu near the Grand Bazaar, it's a double *hamam* (separate baths for men and women) that's particularly popular with tourists. The original (and splendid) *camekan* (entrance hall) is for men only, but an impressive new version for females has recently opened within the walls of the original building. Tips are covered in the treatment price and there's a 20% discount for ISIC student-card holders.

## SÜLEYMANİYE HAMAMI Map p73
☎ 212-519 5569; www.suleymaniyehamami.com; Mimar Sinan Caddesi 20, Süleymaniye; bath, scrub & soap massage TL75; ☯ 10am-10pm; 🚇 Beyazıt
Another *hamam* designed by Sinan, though this one's not as impressive as the Çemberlitaş and is a mixed bath with only male masseurs, meaning that some women will not feel comfortable here. The price includes bath, scrub and soap massage, as well as a free pick-up and drop off from your hotel (Old City only) for groups of two or more if you book in advance.

# GAY HAMAMS & SAUNAS
Due to recent determined efforts by the police not to tolerate any hanky-panky, there's been a major change in how these steamy establishments are run. But boys being boys (particularly in a naked environment), many habitués seem to be able to find ways to enjoy themselves.

## AQUARIUS Map pp102–3
☎ 212-251 8925; Sadri Alisik Sokak 29, Beyoğlu; admission TL30, massage per hr TL50; ☯ 24hr; 🚇 Kabataş then funicular to Taksim
Unabashedly proclaiming itself as 'the only gay sauna in İstanbul', Aquarius can also lay claim to being the only one with a swimming pool in its premises, which means it comes closest to what most Western gay sauna habitués are used to – most notably a clean environment. An added attraction is the stable of 15 hunky delicious masseurs who take you into the private cubicles for a massage – be sure to negotiate the price and the service parameters clearly. Note: what goes on here should remain here.

## ÇEŞME HAMAMI Map pp102–3
☎ 212-252 3441; Yeni Çeşme Sokak 9, off Perşembe Pazari Caddesi, Karaköy; bath TL20, bath with massage TL50; ☯ 7am-7pm; 🚇 Karaköy
Its maze-like location in a backstreet behind the hardware stores that litter this part of town often discourages non-local bathhouse action seekers. But this favourite *hamam* of bears and pot-bellied moustachioed types is worth finding because of the relaxed attitude of the management. Just be careful you don't stick out like a pink thumb or you'll incite a feeding frenzy.

## CIHANGİR SAUNA Map pp102–3
Sadri Altipatlar Sokak 8, Cukurcuma; admission TL20, with locker TL25, 30min massage TL40; ☯ noon-9pm Mon-Fri, noon-10pm Sat & Sun; 🚇 Kabataş then funicular to Taksim
This undeclared gay sauna hosts closeted neighbourhood and visiting types. The sauna facilities are clean, if somewhat threadbare. The proudly gay masseur is not only expert in the use of his hands, but generous in doling out local gay info when asked. Weekends can be crowded, and it's busiest between 3pm and 7pm.

## YEŞILDIREK HAMAMI Map pp102–3
Tersane Caddesi 74, Azapkapi; bath TL20, bath with massage TL30; ☯ 6am-9pm; 🚇 Karaköy
This spacious, well-maintained *hamam* is located across from Azapkapı Sokollu Mehmet Paşa Mosque at the base of the Atatürk Bridge. It has all the traditional trappings and is crowded with testosterone-laden bathhouse lovers – among them expats and in-the-know tourists – who have been

## HAMAMS

The concept of the steam bath was passed from the Romans to the Byzantines and then on to the Turks, who named it the *hamam*. They've even exported the concept throughout the world, hence the term 'Turkish bath'. Until recent decades, many homes in İstanbul didn't have bathroom facilities and, due to Islam's emphasis on personal cleanliness, the community relied on the hundreds of *hamams* that were constructed throughout the city, often as part of the *külliye* (mosque complex) of a mosque. Of course, it wasn't only personal hygiene that was attended to in the *hamam*. It was the perfect place for a prospective mother-in-law to eye off, pinch and prod a prospective daughter-in-law, for instance, and it was equally good for catching up on the neighbourhood gossip. Now that most people have bathrooms in İstanbul, *hamams* are nowhere near as popular, but some carry on due to their roles as local meeting places. Others have become successful tourist attractions.

The city's *hamams* vary enormously. Some are dank dives where you may come out dirtier than you went in (remember – Turks call cockroaches '*hamam* insects'); others are plain and clean, servicing a predominantly local clientele. An increasing number are building a reputation as gay meeting places (we're talking truly steamy here) and a handful are geared exclusively towards tourists. If you're only going to visit one or two when you're in town, we suggest you choose the 'Big Two' – Cağaloğulu and Çemberlitaş. Sure, they're touristy, but they're also gorgeous historic buildings where most of the clientele will be having their first experience of a *hamam*, so you won't feel out of place. They're also clean and have some English-speaking staff.

### Bath Procedure

Upon entry you are shown to a *camekan* (entrance hall or space) where you will be allocated a dressing cubicle (*halvet*) or locker and given a *peştemal* (bath-wrap) and *plastik çarıklar* (plastic sandals) or *takunya* (wooden clogs). Store your clothes and don the *peştemal* and footware. An attendant will then lead you through the *soğukluk* (intermediate section) to the *hararet* (steam room), where you sit and sweat for a while, relaxing and loosening up, perhaps on the *göbektaşı* (central, raised platform atop the heating source).

Soon you will be half-asleep and as soft as putty from the steamy heat. The cheapest bath is the one you do yourself, having brought your own soap, shampoo and towel. But the real Turkish bath experience is to have an attendant wash, scrub and massage you.

If you have opted for the latter, an attendant douses you with warm water and lathers you with a sudsy swab. Next you are scrubbed with a *kese* (coarse cloth mitten), loosening dirt you never suspected you had. After a massage (these yo-yo between being enjoyable, limp-wristed or mortally dangerous) comes a shampoo and another dousing with warm water, followed by one with cool water.

When the scrubbing is over, relax in the *hararet* or head for the cool room and grab a towel. You then go back to your locker or cubicle to get dressed – if you've been given a *halvet* you can even have a rest or order something to drink. If you want to nap, tell the attendant when to wake you. The average *hamam* experience takes around one hour.

### Modesty

Traditional Turkish baths have separate sections for men and women, or have only one set of facilities and admit men or women at different times. Bath etiquette requires that men remain clothed with the bath-wrap at all times. Women either bare all or wear their underwear (but not their bra) – either is fine. During the bathing, everyone washes their private parts themselves, without removing the bath-wrap or underclothes.

In touristy areas, some baths now accept that foreign men and women like to bathe together. No Turkish woman would let a masseur touch her (it must be a masseuse), but masseurs are usually the only massagers available in these foreign-oriented baths. We suggest that women willing to accept a masseur should have the massage within view of male companions or other friends.

displaced from other bathing areas in the city where vigilance has become the norm. The need for discretion cannot be overemphasised here.

# SPECTATOR SPORTS

In İstanbul, there's only one spectator sport worth mentioning, and that's soccer. If you're a football fan, attending a match here will

be one of the highlights of your stay. And even if you're not sport-mad, these events can provide a fascinating insight into the city's psyche.

## FOOTBALL

The Big Three (*Üç Büyükler*) teams in the national Super League (*Turkcell SüperLig*) are Galatasaray, Fenerbahçe and Beşiktaş. All are

## Practicalities

Soap, shampoo and towels are provided at all of the *hamams* we've reviewed; if you're just having a bath you'll need to pay for the soap and shampoo separately – it's usually included in the cost of full treatments. Çemberlitaş is the only *hamam* where the price includes tips; at others, tipping is at your discretion. You'll get drenched, so make sure you take a comb, toiletries, make-up and (if you choose to wear underwear during the massage) a dry pair of replacement knickers (underpants). There are usually hair-dryers available for customer use.

based in İstanbul, and locals are extravagantly proud of them. Indeed, when Galatasaray became the first Turkish team to win a UEFA Cup (in 2000), locals went wild with excitement – in many eyes it was probably the most significant event since the Conquest. In 2008, Fenerbahçe reached the quarter final in the UEFA Champions League, causing great excitement throughout the country.

There are two other teams based in the city: Kasımpaşa SK and İstanbul Büyükşehır Belediyespor.

Many of the İstanbul teams have strong roots in local or ethnic communities. Translated, Fenerbahçe means 'Garden of the

## İSTANBUL'S MAJOR FOOTBALL TEAMS

- Beşiktaş (www.bjk.com.tr) Home stadium: İnönü Stadyumu, Beşiktaş, which is slated for a major renovation. Colours: black and white. Nickname: The Black Eagles.
- Fenerbahçe (www.fenerbahce.org.tr) Home stadium: Rüştü Saraçoğlu Stadyum, Kadıköy. Colours: yellow and blue. Nickname: The Golden Canaries.
- Galatasaray (www.galatasaray.org.tr) Home stadium: Currently Ali Sami Yen Stadı, Mecidiyeköy (about 3km northeast of Taksim), but soon to move to a new stadium in Seyrantepe near Maslak. Colours: yellow and red. Nickname: The Lions.

Lighthouse', a clear reference to the Greek community in old Phanar (today's Fener); and Galatasaray was formed by Muslim students of the French-run Galatasaray Lycée.

For the 24 hours preceding a big match, team scarves are worn, flags are aflutter and hotted-up testosterone-motors bounce up and down at red lights before screeching off dragging team colours behind them. At the end of the game, traffic around Beyoğlu crawls to a halt as merrymakers head to Taksim Sq (p109) to celebrate. Here, the crowds sway, chant club anthems, wave club flags and clamber all over each other, while many still find time to ogle passing women (football is strictly a male concern).

Eighteen teams from all over Turkey compete from August to May. Each season three move up from the second league into the first and three get demoted. The top team of the first league plays in the UEFA Cup. Matches are usually held on the weekend, often on a Saturday night. Tickets are sold at the stadium (*stadyum*) on the day of the match, but most fans purchase them ahead of time through Biletix ( ☎ 216-454 1555, 216-556 9800; www.biletix.com). Open seating is affordable; covered seating – which has the best views – can be very pricey.

Although violence at home games is not unknown, most matches are fine. If you're worried, avoid the Galatasaray and Fenerbahçe clashes, as the supporters of these arch-rivals can become overly excited and throw a few punches around.

# SLEEPING

# top picks

- **Eklektik Guest House** (p198) Top gay-friendly sleep
- **Four Seasons Istanbul at the Bosphorus** (p199) Top luxury hotel
- **Hanedan Hotel** (p195) Top value for money in Sultanahmet
- **Hotel Empress Zoe** (p192) Top Ottoman boutique hotel
- **Hotel Peninsula** (p195) Top cheap sleep
- **Santa Ottoman Hotel** (p198) Top value for money in Beyoğlu
- **İbrahim Paşa Oteli** (p192) Top boutique hotel
- **Sarı Konak Oteli** (p192) Top midrange hotel
- **Witt İstanbul Suites** (p196) Top apartment hotel

# SLEEPING

## ACCOMMODATION STYLES

Every possible accommodation style is available in İstanbul. You can live like a sultan in a world-class luxury hotel, doss in an anonymous hostel dorm or relax in a simple but stylish boutique establishment. We've labelled each hotel's type next to its name to assist in your choice. By 'Ottoman Boutique Hotel' we mean a small-to-medium-sized hotel, usually but not always in an old building, that places great emphasis on decor (usually with Ottoman or Anatolian touches) and friendly service. By 'Boutique Hotel' we mean a stylish modern hotel with great service and amenities. The 'Hotel' tag alone means that the place would be at home in any international city, and doesn't make any real gestures to traditional Turkish decoration or services.

With the exception of the hostels listed, all hotels reviewed offer rooms with en suite bathroom. The prices we've given include breakfast, usually of the Turkish variety (fresh bread, jams, sheep's milk cheese, olives, tomatoes, cucumber and tea or coffee). Exceptions to these norms are noted in the reviews.

## ROOM RATES

You can bag a mattress on a roof terrace for as little as €10 per night or splurge on the Grand Sultan Suite at the Çırağan Palace Kempinski Istanbul for €50,000 (yes, you read that correctly). Most of us will opt for something between the two.

A double room in an Ottoman boutique hotel in Sultanahmet will cost anywhere from €35 to €500; you'll pay a bit more to sleep on the other side of the Galata Bridge (Galata Köprüsü) and lots more to luxuriate on the Bosphorus.

All prices in this book include the 8% value-added tax (katma değer vergisi, KDV). We have cited the price range from low season to high season – during the low season (October to March, but not the Christmas period) rooms can be up to 50% cheaper. Be warned that during the Formula 1 Grand Prix (June) and in the Christmas to New Year week prices often skyrocket.

Recent years have seen significant fluctuations in tourist numbers in İstanbul, meaning that most hotels now use yield management systems when setting their rates. This means that in quiet times prices can drop dramatically. The same applies when a hotel isn't fully booked – bargains can be had if you leave your reservation until the last minute. That said, the city's hotels can also get very busy; at these times most rooms are claimed by those who have reserved well in advance of their stay. All of this means that you should treat the prices in this book as a guide only – it is highly likely that the price you are quoted will be quite different.

If booking direct, ask if the hotel will give you a discount for a cash payment (this will usually be 10%), whether a pick-up from the airport is included (it often is if you stay more than three nights) and whether discounts are offered for extended stays. Many of the luxury hotels offer special packages; ask when you make reservations.

We recommend that you refrain from booking accommodation at the airport hotel booking desks, as you'll inevitably pay a premium.

Note that all hotels in İstanbul set their prices in euros, and we have listed them as such here.

## SULTANAHMET & AROUND

The Sultan Ahmet Camii, more commonly known as the Blue Mosque, gives its name to the quarter surrounding it. This is the heart of Old İstanbul and the city's premier sightseeing area, so the hotels here, and in the adjoining neighbourhoods to the east (Cankurtaran), west (Küçük Aya Sofya) and north (Binbirdirek), are supremely convenient. The area's only drawbacks are the number of carpet touts and the lack of decent places to eat and drink.

### PRICE GUIDE

For a double room:

| | |
|---|---|
| €€€ | over €200 per night |
| €€ | €81 to €200 per night |
| € | under €80 per night |

Akbıyık Caddesi in Cankurtaran is the backpacker hub, home to raucous bars at night and street cafes during the day. Other streets in the area are low key. Küçük Aya Sofya is a charming, old-fashioned and quiet area, just downhill from the southwestern end of the Hippodrome, while just uphill and to the west, Binbirdirek is a quiet residential district named after the Byzantine cistern of that name.

Every imaginable hotel type can be found around this neighbourhood: one of the city's best luxury hotels (the Four Seasons); innumerable boutique Ottoman hotels decorated in a pleasing style that we've dubbed 'Cankurtaran Modern'; comfortable but relatively characterless midrange options; and a host of budget choices, including most of the city's hostels. Almost every place has a roof terrace with views of the Blue Mosque, Aya Sofya and/or the Sea of Marmara.

## FOUR SEASONS HOTEL ISTANBUL

Map pp50–1                    Luxury Hotel €€€
☎ 212-638 8200; www.fshr.com; Tevkifhane Sokak 1, Cankurtaran; r €280-610; 🚇 Sultanahmet; 🚫 🖥 🛜 ♿

This used to be the infamous Sultanahmet prison (remember *Midnight Express*?), and boy oh boy, we couldn't imagine anything better than being forced to do some serious time here these days. A regular entry in 'Best Hotel in the World' lists, this place oozes quality and comfort. Rooms are country-club elegant, with king-sized beds, enormous marble bathrooms and antique-style work desks. Location is ideal – the hotel is literally in the shadow of the Blue Mosque and Aya Sofya – but the fact that an extension is currently being built at the rear of the hotel site (on top of an important archaeological site – how on earth was that approved?!) means that building noise could be a slight problem until completion. Breakfast costs an extra €30 per person.

## YEŞİL EV  Map pp50–1   Ottoman Boutique Hotel €€€
☎ 212-517 6785; www.istanbulyesilev.com; Kabasakal Caddesi 5, Cankurtaran; s €180, d €250-500; 🚇 Sultanahmet; 🚫 🖥 🛜

Depending on your point of view, this place has either a proud history or a lot to answer for. The model for hundreds of Ottoman boutique hotels across Turkey, it has been one of the city's most famous places to sleep since it opened in 1984.

Brass beds and chintz furnishings feature, as do cramped bathrooms. Despite adoring its idyllic rear courtyard, overall we prefer the slightly cheaper Ayasofya Konakları (below), which was restored by and is run by the same organisation.

## SİRKECİ KONAK

Map pp50–1              Ottoman Boutique Hotel €€€
☎ 212-528 4344; www.sirkecikonak.com; Taya Hatun Sokak 5, Sirkeci; r €150-340; 🚇 Gülhane; 🚫 🖥 🛜 ♿

The owner of this terrific hotel overlooking Gülhane Park (p68) runs other hotels in the Sirkeci neighbourhood and knows what keeps guests happy – rooms are all large and well equipped, with extras such as tea- and coffee-making equipment, satellite TV, quality toiletries and luxe linen. There's also a wellness centre with pool, gym and *hamam* in the basement – a rarity on this side of town. Top marks go to the complimentary afternoon teas and incredibly helpful staff.

## OTTOMAN HOTEL IMPERIAL

Map pp50–1              Ottoman Boutique Hotel €€
☎ 212-513 6150/1; www.ottomanhotelimperial.com; Caferiye Sokak 6/1; s €120-200; d €150-240; 🚇 Gülhane or 🚇 Sultanahmet; 🚫 🖥 🛜

This four-star hotel is in a wonderfully quiet location just outside the walls of Topkapı Palace (Topkapı Sarayı; p59). Once the city's main youth hostel, the building has been extensively renovated and features large rooms decorated with Ottoman-style ceramics, textiles and *ebru* (traditional Turkish marbling). Comfort and amenity levels are high, and some rooms have Aya Sofya views (try to snaffle number 406). There's a lift, a lovely rear garden with restaurant and bar, and excellent levels of service.

## AYASOFYA KONAKLARI

Map pp50–1              Ottoman Boutique Hotel €€
☎ 212-513 3660; www.ayasofyakonaklari.com; Soğukçeşme Sokak; s €120-140, d €170-200; 🚇 Gülhane; 🚫 🖥 🛜

If you're keen to play out Ottoman fantasies, come here. A row of 19th-century wooden houses occupying an entire cobbled street abutting Topkapı Palace (p59), Ayasofya Konakları is about as authentic as the Ottoman boutique hotel comes and it's picturesque to boot. The 63 rooms are charmingly decorated and breakfast is served in a glass conservatory complete with chandeliers.

## ERTEN KONAK

Map pp50–1　　　　Ottoman Boutique Hotel €€

☎ 212-458 5000; www.ertenkonak.com; Akbıyık Değirmeni Sokak; r deluxe €100–175, executive €120–225; ⬚ Sultanahmet; 🖳 🖵 📶

Lovers of antiques and collectables will adore this historic wooden konak (mansion), which has been completely rebuilt in recent years and converted into a charming boutique hotel. The 16 rooms are beautifully decorated and wonderfully comfortable – the difference between the deluxe and executive is size (although they are all spacious) and the fact that the executive rooms have a Jacuzzi. There are top-quality rugs and luxurious fabrics galore, as well as objets d'art and antique furniture. No roof terrace, but the glassed winter garden provides a welcome haven and breakfast location.

## İBRAHİM PAŞA OTELİ

Map pp50–1　　　　Boutique Hotel €€

☎ 212-518 0394; www.ibrahimpasha.com; Terzihane Sokak 5, Binbirdirek; r standard €89–129, deluxe €129–179; ⬚ Sultanahmet; 🖳 🖵 📶

The owners of this small designer hotel just off the Hippodrome have managed to straddle the divide between sleek modernist and antique Ottoman with great success. Parquet floors, crisp white linen, marble bathrooms and gold mirrors make the well-equipped rooms distinctive, and the building's common areas ooze class. After enjoying the excellent breakfast, guests often have to be encouraged to leave the building – the alternative option of sinking into one of the foyer lounge's leather couches or claiming a chair on the rooftop terrace with its Blue Mosque view is just too tempting. It's worth paying for one of the 12 deluxe rooms, as they offer better value than the 12 standard options.

## DERSAADET OTELİ

Map pp50–1　　　　Ottoman Boutique Hotel €€

☎ 212-458 0760; www.dersaadethotel.com; Kapıağası Sokak 5, Küçük Aya Sofya; s €70–105, d €80–125, ste €140–280; ⬚ Sultanahmet; 🖳 📶

Roughly translated, the name of this comfortable mid-sized hotel means 'The Place of Happiness' in Turkish – and you will indeed be happy if you stay here. In a painstakingly restored Ottoman wooden house, the interior features exquisitely painted ceilings and custom-designed wooden furniture throughout. Rooms, which have four-star amenities, are extremely comfortable, sporting a gold and russet-red colour scheme that gives a sense of luxury. Those with sea views cost a little bit extra. There's a lift, a roof terrace with Sea of Marmara and Blue Mosque views, and a charming breakfast cafe.

## SARI KONAK OTELİ

Map pp50–1　　　　Ottoman Boutique Hotel €€

☎ 212-638 6258; www.istanbulhotelsarikonak.com; Mimar Mehmet Ağa Caddesi 42-46, Cankurtaran; standard r €79–109, deluxe r €99–149, ste €139–239; ⬚ Sultanahmet; 🖳 🖵 📶

The type of place that could fit just as easily in Washington as in this city of sultans, the Sarı Konak is a truly classy joint. The spacious deluxe rooms are beautifully decorated with soothing colour schemes, top-notch linens and attractive prints, embroideries and etchings on the walls; try to get number 303, which is pretty as a picture. The standard rooms are considerably smaller, but are just as attractive, and the suites are total knockouts – perfect for families. Guests enjoy relaxing on the roof terrace with its Sea of Marmara and Blue Mosque views, but seem to be equally partial to hanging out in the downstairs lounge and courtyard.

## HOTEL EMPRESS ZOE

Map pp50–1　　　　Ottoman Boutique Hotel €€

☎ 212-518 2504; www.emzoe.com; Akbıyık Caddesi 4/1, Cankurtaran; s €80, d €120, ste €140–240; ⬚ Sultanahmet; 🖳 📶

Named after the feisty Byzantine Empress whose portrait adorns the gallery at Aya Sofya, this fabulous place is owned and managed by American Ann Nevens and her sister Cristina, who really know their stuff when it comes to running a hotel. The prototype for 'Cankurtaran Modern', the now almost ubiquitous decorative style utilised in myriad Sultanahmet boutique hotels, the Empress Zoe is unusual in that it is constantly being changed and improved. The garden suites here are particularly enticing, overlooking a gorgeous flower-filled courtyard where breakfast is served in warm weather. Equally impressive are the Special Double with Terrace (€140) or the

Penthouse Suite (€220), which has a private terrace and views over the Blue Mosque. All rooms are individually and charmingly decorated, and although some rooms in the main building are tiny, these are available at discounted rates (single/double €55/65). The rooftop lounge-terrace has excellent views. Rates are discounted from mid-November to mid-March.

## HOTEL ARMADA Map pp50–1 Hotel €€
☎ 212-455 4455; www.armadahotel.com.tr; Ahırkapı Sokak 24, Cankurtaran; r €75-200; ⓢ Sultanahmet; ⊠ ▣ 🛜 ♿

Fresh flowers and a pond full of tortoises greet guests when they check in to this comfortable hotel. Rooms feature pale-green furnishings and are very well equipped; superior ones come with a sea view. Though the location – very near the Cankurtaran suburban train station and a few steps from the Bosphorus shore – isn't great, it's only a 10-minute walk uphill to Sultanahmet. The hotel's major selling point is the Teras Restaurant (p147), with its wonderful view and very pleasant surrounds. Check the website for special offers, as room rates can vary wildly.

## KYBELE HOTEL
Map pp50–1 Ottoman Boutique Hotel €€
☎ 212-511 7766; www.kybelehotel.com; Yerebatan Caddesi 35, Alemdar; s €80, d €110-140; ⓢ Sultanahmet; ⊠ ▣ 🛜

The gilded exterior of this small hotel (peacock blue with loads of gold) reflects the decor inside, which features hundreds of coloured lights, wooden floors covered in rugs, and antique furniture and curios. Run by three brothers in a personable and professional style, it's got bucketloads of charm and lots of added extras, including a great cafe and bar, a charming rear garden patio and a library for guests. The location near Aya Sofya is central, and the rooms, which feature cute marble bathrooms, are smallish but comfortable.

## TRIA HOTEL İSTANBUL
Map pp50–1 Ottoman Boutique Hotel €€
☎ 212-518 4518; www.triahotelistanbul.com; Turbıyık Sokak 7, Cankurtaran; s €59-99, d €79-149; ⓢ Sultanahmet; ⊠ ▣ 🛜

The old adage that handsome is as handsome does certainly applies to the Tria. Extremely comfortable rooms offer tea- and

coffee-making equipment, satellite TV, work desk and large bed; all are attractively decorated with polished floorboards, silk curtains, embroidered bedspreads and objets d'art. There's a comfortable lounge on the ground floor and a wonderful roof terrace furnished with cane armchairs and huge umbrellas – a perfect spot to view the Sea of Marmara, Aya Sofya and the Blue Mosque.

## HOTEL NOMADE Map pp50–1 Boutique Hotel €€
☎ 212-513 8172; www.hotelnomade.com; Ticarethane Sokak 15, Alemdar; s €85, d €100-120; ⓢ Sultanahmet; ⊠ 🛜

Mega style and budget pricing don't often go together, but the Nomade bucks the trend. A few years ago the owners brought in French designer Dan Beranger to give the place a total overhaul and all we can say is 'ooh la la'. Just a few steps off busy Divan Yolu, the hotel's 16 small rooms and three suites are très, très chic, with great bathrooms, stylish bed linen and satellite TV. With one of the best roof-terrace bars in town (smack-bang in front of Aya Sofya) and a designer feel, this place is about as hip as Sultanahmet gets.

## TAN HOTEL Map pp50–1 Hotel €€
☎ 212-520 9130; www.tanhotel.com; Dr Emin Paşa Sokak 20, Alemdar; s €79-99, d €89-109; ⓢ Sultanahmet; ⊠ ▣ 🛜

This well-run hotel off Divan Yolu showcases understated modern style and high-level service. Rooms are large, with satellite TVs and excellent bathrooms (all have whirlpools) and the location is extremely convenient. The lavish breakfast buffet is served on the terrace, which sports views of the Blue Mosque, Aya Sofya and the Sea of Marmara.

## EMINE SULTAN HOTEL Map pp50–1 Hotel €€
☎ 212-458 4666; www.eminesultan.com; Kapıağası Sokak 6, Cankurtaran; s €70-85, d €95-105; ⓢ Sultanahmet; ⊠ 🛜

Solo female travellers and families will feel particularly at home at the Emine Sultan. Manager Özen Dalgın is as friendly as she is efficient, and the rest of the staff (mainly family members) follow her lead. Rooms have a pretty cream-and-pink decor; all come with satellite TV/DVD and squeaky-clean bathrooms and some have sea views. A delicious breakfast is served in an upstairs room overlooking the Sea of Marmara and the roof terrace overlooks the Blue Mosque.

## HOTEL TURKOMAN
Map pp50–1     Ottoman Boutique Hotel €€
☎ 212-516 2956; www.turkomanhotel.com; Asmalı Çeşme Sokak 2, Binbirdirek; s €59-89, d €99-119; ⓘ Sultanahmet; ✕ ▯
In a fantastic position up the hill a few steps off the Hippodrome, this renovated 19th-century building features rooms that are simply but tastefully decorated with kilims, reproduction antique furniture and brass beds. Ask for room 4A (€109 to €169), which has a balcony and Blue Mosque view. The roof terrace is looking a bit worn, but has good views.

## HOTEL ŞEBNEM
Map pp50–1     Ottoman Boutique Hotel €€
☎ 212-517 6623; www.sebnemhotel.net; Adliye Sokak 1, Cankurtaran; s €70, d €90-100; ✕ ▯ ; ⓘ Sultanahmet
Simplicity is the rule at the Şebnem, and it works a treat. Run by a friendly young team, its rooms have rose-pink walls, wooden floors and comfortable canopy beds. The large terrace upstairs has views over the Sea of Marmara (as do the more expensive double rooms), and the downstairs rooms, though a tad dark, have a private courtyard garden. Our only quibble is that its prices are a bit high when compared with the competition.

## HOTEL UYAN İSTANBUL
Map pp50–1     Ottoman Boutique Hotel €€
☎ 212-518 9255; www.uyanhotel.com; Utangaç Sokak 25, Cankurtaran; s €50-60, standard d €75-99, deluxe d €95-140; ⓘ Sultanahmet; ✕ ▯ ⓦ
Like its competitors in the Cankurtaran boutique Ottoman stakes, the Uyan offers comfortable and attractive rooms with a good range of amenities. The elegant decor nods towards the Ottoman style, but never goes over the top – everyone will feel comfortable here. The view from the spacious roof terrace is one of the best in the area and the breakfast spread is generous.

## HOTEL ALATURKA
Map pp50–1     Hotel €€
☎ 212-458 7900; www.hotelalaturka.com; Akbıyık Caddesi 5, Cankurtaran; s €50-70, d €65-105; ✕
Large rooms with amenities such as minibars and satellite TVs are the hallmark of

this immaculately maintained hotel on Cankurtaran's main drag. The decor is conservative, but pleasantly so, and the roof terrace has one of the best views in the area. A safe if unexciting choice.

## HOTEL POEM
Map pp50–1     Hotel €
☎ 212-638 9744; www.hotelpoem.com; Terbıyık Sokak 12; s €45-55, d €70-80; ⓘ Sultanahmet; ✕ ▯ ⓦ
Many guests end up waxing lyrical about their stays in this cute hotel. Rooms are named after poems by well-known Turkish poets, and the tranquil rear garden is a perfect spot to linger over an anthology and a glass of tea. Book into the 'All of a Sudden' room (€120 to €150) and you'll be able to sit on a private balcony looking towards the Princes' Islands; score 'Listening to İstanbul' (€100 to €130) and you'll appreciate its large windows, sea views and king-sized bed. Other rooms are on the small side and lack style, but they're clean and have amenities such as satellite TV and hairdryer. There's also a terrace with good views.

## ARTEFES HOTEL
Map pp50–1     Hotel €
☎ 212-516 5863; www.artefes.com; Çayıroğlu Sokak 25, Küçük Aya Sofya; s €39-65, d €49-75; ⓘ Sultanahmet; ✕ ▯ ⓦ
A large wooden house adorned with flower-filled window boxes, the Artefes is almost a prototype of a safe midrange accommodation choice. It offers clean, sun-drenched rooms featuring amenities such as satellite TV and hairdryer. The foyer and roof terrace are impressive and the location is blissfully quiet.

## HOTEL ERBOY
Map pp50–1     Hotel €
☎ 212-513 3750; www.erboyhotel.com; Ebussuut Caddesi 32, Sirkeci; r €43-100; ⓘ Gülhane; ✕ ▯ ⓦ
The Vegas-style furniture and marble floors in its lobby are the Erboy's only attempts at glamour. The rest of the place is resolutely mom-and-pop style, with 120 decent-sized rooms that come equipped with satellite TV and bathrooms that are so clean they gleam. The location near Topkapı is central and quiet, and the rooms are comfortable and reasonably priced. There's a roof terrace with views of Aya Sofya, Topkapı and the Bosphorus, as well as a pleasant restaurant spilling into the cobbled street.

## HOTEL ALP GUESTHOUSE

Map pp50–1                    Ottoman Boutique Hotel €

☎ 212-517 7067; www.alpguesthouse.com;
Adliye Sokak 4, Cankurtaran; s €35-55, d €55-70,
tr €80-100; 🚇 Sultanahmet; ✗ 🔅 🛜

The Alp lives up to its location in Sultanahmet's premier small-hotel enclave, offering
a range of attractive and well-equipped
rooms at reasonable prices, including
rooms large enough for families of three
to four. Rooms have four-poster beds with
white linen and gold hangings, wooden
floorboards scattered with rugs, and extras
such as satellite TV and work desks. The
spacious front rooms are the pick of the
bunch (ask for 301 or 401) because though
some rear rooms have sea views, they also
look onto the minaret of a local mosque,
meaning that early-morning noise can be
a problem. The roof terrace is lovely, with
great sea views and comfortable indoor
and outdoor set-ups.

## HOTEL ARARAT

Map pp50–1                    Ottoman Boutique Hotel €

☎ 212-516 0411; www.ararathotel.com;
Torun Sokak 3, Cankurtaran; s & d €45-80;
🚇 Sultan-ahmet; 🔅 🖳 🛜

Decorated by Nikos Papadakis, who did
such an inspired job with the initial rooms
at the Hotel Empress Zoe (p192), the Ara-
rat is tiny, but its charming host Haydar
Sarigul and cosy rooftop terrace-bar in
the shadow of the Blue Mosque make it a
popular choice. Dark wooden floors, textile
bedspreads and clever space-enhancing
mirrors are the decorative hallmarks; quality linen and homemade *börek* (savoury
pastry) for breakfast are quality touches.
It's not worth paying the extra euros for a
view. Larger rooms sleeping three or four
are available (€65 to €100),

## HOTEL HALI

Map pp50–1                                    Hotel €

☎ 212-516 2170; www.halihotel.com; Klodfarer
Caddesi 20, Çemberlitaş; s €35-45, d €60-75;
🚇 Sultanahmet; 🔅 🛜

All the rugs in Turkey couldn't hide this hotel's institutional feel. That said, it's worth
considering due to its roof terrace (which
has amazing views), its huge bathrooms,
its quiet position and its reasonable rates.
Third- and 4th-floor rooms have views of
the Sea of Marmara and Aya Sofya.

## HANEDAN HOTEL

Map pp50–1                    Ottoman Boutique Hotel €

☎ 212-516 4869; www.hanedanhotel.com; Adliye
Sokak 3, Cankurtaran; s €30-40, d €40-60;
🚇 Sultanahmet; 🔅 🖳 🛜

Pale lemon walls and polished wooden
floors give the rooms at this small and very
clean hotel a light and elegant feel, as do
the white marble bathrooms (with hairdryer) and the firm beds covered with crisp
white linen. The huge Byzantium Room
with its Sea of Marmara views (€75 to €90)
is perfect for families. A pleasant roof terrace overlooks the sea and Aya Sofya.

## HOTEL PENINSULA

Map pp50–1                    Ottoman Boutique Hotel €

☎ 212-458 6850; www.hotelpeninsula.com; Adliye
Sokak 6, Cankurtaran; s €30-40, d €35-65;
🚇 Sultanahmet; 🔅 🛜

The management of this unassuming hotel
could quite possibly be the friendliest
we've ever encountered. And we're talking
friendly in a good, non-pushy, we-really-
like-meeting-people type of way, not the
hi-I'm-your-new-best-friend-please-visit-my-
carpet-shop type of way. Rooms are simple
but comfortable, and there's a lovely terrace
with sea views and comfortable hammocks.
The owners have recently opened a sister
hotel, the Grand Peninsula ( ☎ 212-458 7710; www.
grandpeninsulahotel.com; Cetinkaya Sokak 3, Cankurtaran;
s €35-60, d €45-80; 🔅 ♿ ) a few streets away.

## SİDE HOTEL & PENSION

Map pp50–1                    Hotel & Apartments €

☎ 212-517 2282; www.sidehotel.com; Utangaç
Sokak 20, Cankurtaran; hotel s €40-50, d €60-70,
pension without bathroom s €25-30, d €35-40;
🚇 Sultanahmet; 🔅 🖳

A sprawling place that has a long-standing
reputation for cheap, clean and comfortable
accommodation, the Side has overpriced
hotel rooms with TV, air-con and en suite;
well-priced pension rooms with shared bathrooms and fans; and fully equipped but dark
apartments sleeping one to six people (€70
to €110). There are also some pension rooms
with private bathrooms but no air-con.

## BAHAUS GUESTHOUSE   Map pp50–1  Hostel €

☎ 212-638 6534; www.travelinistanbul.com;
Kutlugün Sokak 3, Cankurtaran; dm €12-16, d €50,
without bathroom €34-40; 🚇 Sultanahmet; 🖳 🛜

When it comes to hostels, word of mouth
is the most reliable gauge of quality. And

this place generates great word of mouth. Friendly and knowledgeable staff run a professional operation that's miles away from the institutional feel of some of its nearby and much larger competitors. Dorms (some female-only) have bunks with good mattresses and curtains to provide a skerrick of privacy. Top marks go to the downstairs area with Anatolian seating and the summer rooftop terrace.

### SULTAN HOSTEL Map pp50–1      Hostel €
☎ 212-516 9260; www.sultanhostel.com; Akbıyık Caddesi 21, Cankurtaran; dm €11-17, d €50, without bathroom €42; 🚇 Sultanahmet; 🖥 🛜
Next door to – and clearly in hot competition with – the Orient, this place has been renovated in the past couple of years and rooms are cleaner and better maintained than those next door. Shared bathrooms are clean and there's unlimited free tea and coffee on offer. The pick of the rooms on offer is number 403, a double with lovely Sea of Marmara views and its own cubicle bathroom. Views from the terrace bar aren't as impressive as those at the Orient. There's a 10% discount for HI cardholders. Rooms with bathroom are overpriced – you'll be better off trying one of the small boutique hotels in the area.

### ORIENT INTERNATIONAL HOSTEL
Map pp50–1      Hostel €
☎ 212-518 0789; www.orienthostel.com; Akbıyık Caddesi 13, Cankurtaran; dm €10-15, s €45, d €55-70, s/d without bathroom €33/40; 🚇 Sultanahmet; ✖ 🖥 🛜
Always packed to the rafters with backpackers, the Orient should only be considered if you're young, don't care about creature comforts and are ready to party.

There's a shower for every 12 guests and an array of dorms, some of which are light and relatively quiet and others that are unpleasantly dark and have the most uncomfortable mattresses that we've ever encountered (and considering our job, that's really saying something). There is one female-only dorm for those gals who want to steer clear of smelly socks. The cheapest option is a barracks-style 32-bed dorm. The rooftop terrace bar has fabulous views and is a good place to relax, unlike the noisy cafeteria and internet area (they're great meeting places, though). The private, deluxe and 'Suite' rooms are ludicrously overpriced for what they offer.

## BEYOĞLU

Most travellers to İstanbul stay in Sultanahmet, but Beyoğlu is becoming a popular alternative. Stay here to avoid the touts in the Old City, and because buzzing, bohemian Beyoğlu has the best wining, dining and shopping in the city. Unfortunately there isn't the range or quality of accommodation options here that you'll find in Sultanahmet – the exception being an ever-increasing number of stylish apartment hotels and apartment rentals. These often command spectacular Bosphorus and Golden Horn views – something you pay for by having to climb six or seven floors of stairs.

### WITT ISTANBUL SUITES
Map pp102–3      Boutique Apartment Hotel €€€
☎ 212-393 7900; www.wittistanbul.com; Defterdar Yokuşu 26, Cihangir; ste €199-329; 🚇 Sultanahmet; ✖ 🛜
Showcasing nearly as many designer features as an issue of *Wallpaper* magazine, this

---

### ENERGISING EMINÖNÜ

Hotelier Faruk Boyacı is passionate about the Eminönü area and excited about the rapid changes that are occurring in its hitherto scruffy streets. 'This is the real İstanbul', he says, 'not a tourist enclave. Our markets and our university give this area great vitality, and we want to share this with visitors to our city and with other İstanbullus.' The owner of five hotels on and around Hüdavendigar Caddesi in Sirkeci, Faruk is nothing short of a human dynamo. He's an active member of the Eminönü Platform, a group of local businessmen, politicians and professionals who are working to revitalise this part of town. One of the project he is currently involved in aims to improve housing, roads and services in this part of town and encourage a healthy balance of residential and tourism infrastructure: 'There are currently only 15,000 residents living here in Eminönü — we want to bring local people back to live in this historic part of the city,' he says. Faruk and his Eminönü Platform colleagues have been working with the Ministry of Culture and Tourism to commission a heritage master plan for the area, and have facilitated projects such as the restoration of the walls of Gülhane Park, once part of the Topkapı Palace complex. 'This part of the city is much more than a transport hub,' he says. 'It's the hub of the entire city.'

---

stylish apartment hotel in the trendy suburb of Cihangir has 15 suites with fully equipped marble kitchenettes, seating areas with flat-screen satellite TVs, CD/DVD players, iPod docks, espresso machines, king-sized beds and huge bathrooms (Molton Brown toiletries). Penthouse and Sea View suites have fabulous views. The location is conveniently close to the Tophane tram stop, and weekly and long-term rates are available.

## MİSAFİR SUITES

Map pp102–3                    Boutique Apartment Hotel €€

☎ 212-249 8930; www.misafirsuites.com; Gazeteci Erol Dernek Sokak 1; ste per night €135-200; ⓡ Kabataş then funicular to Taksim; ✕ ▣ 🛜

A labour of love designed, built and furnished by Joost Rooijmans, Misafir Suites offers seven rooms sleeping two or three people and is perfect for families as it will organise everything from Playstations to babysitters. Couples will be impressed with the downstairs 8 Istanbul (p153) restaurant and bar, the delicious breakfasts in bed and the luxe bathrooms (complete with L'Occitane toiletries). The decor is characterised by Asian artefacts, deeply coloured Turkish textiles and quality fittings. All windows are double-glazed, meaning that getting a good night's sleep isn't a problem despite the close proximity of İstiklal Caddesi.

### MARMARA PERA Map pp102–3 Luxury Hotel €€

☎ 212-251 4646; www.themarmarahotels. com; Meşrutiyet Caddesi 1, Tepebaşı; s €90-350, d €100-240; ⓡ Karaköy then funicular to Tünel; ▣ 🛜 ♿

This funky little sister of the landmark hotel on Taksim Sq opened in 2004 and has been a popular choice with glam globetrotters ever since. Rooms are smallish but extremely well appointed, featuring quality touches such as a magazine selection, pillow menu and stylish white linen. Standout amenities include one of the best restaurants in the city, Mikla (p152), a rooftop pool bar with spectacular views, and a 24-hour fitness centre. It's worth paying extra for a room on a higher floor with a sea view.

## BÜYÜK LONDRA OTELİ

Map pp102–3                              Historic Hotel €€

☎ 212-245 0670; www.londrahotel.net; Meşrutiyet Caddesi 117, Tepebaşı; unrenovated s €35-60, d €50-80, renovated s €120, d €150-175; ⓡ Karaköy then funicular to Tünel; ✕

The Büyük's 'gothic house of horrors' feel may not be for everyone. Dating from the same era as the nearby Pera Palace Hotel (p108), it is looking decidedly worse for wear these days. The good news is that its run-down rooms are slowly being renovated – we'd suggest making a booking only if you are guaranteed one of these (try to score room 201). The remaining rooms are musty and very scuffed around the edges, with tiny bathrooms and no aircon. Fortunately, you can always escape them and park yourself at a table in the atmospheric foyer bar (p165).

### LUSH HIP HOTEL Map pp102–3 Boutique Hotel €€

☎ 212-243 9595; www.lushhiphotel.com; Sıraselviler Sokak 12, Taksim; s €120-160, d €130-170; ⓡ Kabataş then funicular to Taksim; ✕ ▣ 🛜

One of a fast-sprouting crop of boutique hotels around town, this self-consciously hip place has 35 attractive rooms of varying sizes, all of which are individually decorated and full of amenities. You can enjoy a big night in the downstairs brasserie and recover in the fitness centre and sauna the next day. It's on a busy street near Taksim Sq, so front rooms can be a tad noisy.

### RICHMOND HOTEL Map pp102–3 Hotel €€

☎ 212-252 5460; www.richmondhotels. tr; İstiklal Caddesi 445; r €99-199, ste €155-399; ⓡ Karaköy then funicular to Tünel; ✕ ▣

The Richmond has a fabulous location right next to the palatial Russian consulate on the city's major boulevard. Behind its 19th-century facade, the place is modern, quite comfortable and well run. Standard rooms are comfortable if characterless, but the suites are knockouts with modernist decor, excellent views, great workstations, whirlpools and plasma TVs. Best of all is the fact that one of the best bars in the city, Leb-i Derya Richmond (p166), is on the top floor, meaning that your bed will only be a short stagger away. A mainly business clientele keeps the place busy so book ahead.

## ANEMON GALATA

Map pp102–3                    Ottoman Boutique Hotel €€

☎ 212-293 2343; www.anemonhotels.com, in Turkish; cnr Galata Meydani & Büyükhendek Caddesi, Karaköy; s €100-140, d €110-140; ⓡ Karaköy then funicular to Tünel; ✕ ▣

Located on the attractive square that's been built around Galata Tower, this wooden building dates from 1842 but has been almost completely rebuilt inside. Individually decorated rooms are elegant, featuring ornate painted ceilings, king-sized beds and antique-style desks. Large bathrooms have baths and marble basins. Frankly, we're not sure which of the hotel's features is the best. Is it the classically beautiful foyer with its chandeliers, marble floors and luxurious rugs? Or the stylish modern bar-restaurant sheathed in glass that's been built on the rooftop? Ask for a room with a view.

### GALATA ANTIQUE HOTEL
Map pp102–3                                    Hotel €€

☎ 212-245 5944; www.galataantique.com; Meşrutiyet Caddesi 119, Galata; s €86-125, d €96-125; ⓐ Karaköy then funicular to Tünel; ⊠ ⌨

In the up-and-coming Şişhane neighbourhood, this somewhat fusty place has some contradictory elements. Rooms feature a bland, old-fashioned decor that staid couples from central Anatolia would like, but the roof terrace hints at boutique aspirations, featuring plastic coloured furniture, groovy light fittings and a small bar. Those self-same Anatolian couples mustn't approve at all! Views from the 4th and 5th floors and the terrace are impressive and everything's clean and comfortable, with extras such as tea- and coffee-making facilities in some rooms. The location, which is close to the Tünel station and a growing number of stylish cafes and boutiques, is excellent.

### EKLEKTİK GUEST HOUSE
Map pp102–3              Ottoman Boutique Hotel €€

☎ 212-243 7446; www.eklektikgalata.com; Kadrıbey Cıkmazi 4, Galata; r €85-115; ⓐ Karaköy then funicular to Tünel; ⊠ ⌨

Advertising itself as offering 'the first and only gay accommodation in İstanbul', this gay-owned-and-managed place offers seven individually decorated rooms with TV. You can enact fantasies in the Pasha Room, chill out after a big night in the Zen Room or just feel funky in the Retro Room. There's a small roof terrace with great views.

### THE PEAK
Map pp102–3                                    Hotel €€

☎ 212-252 7160; www.thepeakhotel.com.tr; Meşrutiyet Sokak 1-3, Tepebaşı; standard s €75-85, d €95-105, deluxe s €95-105, d €120-130; ⓐ Karaköy then funicular to Tünel; ⊠ ⌨ 🛜 ♿

You could do a lot worse than book into one of the deluxe rooms here, which are large and comfortable, with good bathrooms and lots of amenities. Their major downside is a lack of natural light. The exterior is unprepossessing, but the interior can hold its own with most of the city's business hotels and has pretensions towards boutique status. There's an English-style pub/restaurant downstairs that's often crowded with noisy Russian guests.

### SANTA OTTOMAN HOTEL
Map pp102–3              Ottoman Boutique Hotel €

☎ 212-252 2878; www.santaottomanboutique hotel.com; Zambak Sokak 1, Taksim; s €60-70, d €70-80; ⓐ Karaköy then funicular to Taksim; ⊠ 🛜

Opened in 2009, this excellent-value mid-range option is a real find. Overlooking an Armenian Catholic church, it's close enough to the main strip to catch some of the Beyoğlu buzz, but far enough away that noise shouldn't be too much of a problem. Rooms come with a beige colour scheme, framed Ottoman prints, comfortable beds with embroidered bedspreads, a work desk, satellite TV and well-equipped bathrooms. They're smallish, but not to a significant degree (ask for room 303). There's even a roof terrace (with elevator) and a downstairs guest lounge.

**WORLD HOUSE HOSTEL** Map pp102–3 Hostel €
☎ 212-293 5520; www.worldhouseistanbul.com; Galipdede Caddesi 85, Tünel; dm €12-14, d €43; 🚇 Karaköy then funicular to Tünel; 🖳 🛜
Hostels in İstanbul are usually impersonal hulks with jungle-like atmospheres, but World House is small, friendly and calm. Best of all is the fact that it's located close to Beyoğlu's restaurant, bar and club scene, but not *too* close – meaning that it's possible to grab a decent night's kip here. The small dorms are clean and light, with decent mattresses and linen. Bathrooms are in plentiful supply and there's a cheerful cafe on the ground floor. The same crew run a second hostel in the thick of the nighttime action off İstiklal Caddesi.

# NİŞANTAŞI & AROUND

Take the metro to Osmanbey, one stop from Taksim Sq (or walk 30 minutes), and you'll find the upmarket shopping district of Nişantaşı, home to two impressive boutique hotels.

**BENTLEY HOTEL** Map p113  Boutique Hotel €€€
☎ 212-291 7730; www.bentley-hotel.com; Halaskargazi Caddesi 75, Harbiye; s €240, d €280, ste €400-800; 🚇 Kabataş then funicular to Taksim; 🗙 🖳 🛜
The Bentley features luxurious rooms that look as if they're straight from the pages of *Monacle*, sleek suites for those in the mood to splurge, and location close to the Osmanbey metro station. If you overindulge in the classy foyer bar, don't worry – the health club and sauna will help you recover. The only drawback is the lack of work desk or wi-fi in rooms (there's wi-fi in the foyer area and bar).

**SOFA HOTEL** Map p113  Boutique Hotel €€€
☎ 212-368 1818; www.thesofahotel.com; Teşvikiye Caddesi 41, Nişantaşı; s €140-220, d €152-240, ste €380-1030; 🚇 Osmanbey; 🗙 🖳 🛜
The Sofa has got lots going for it – extremely comfortable rooms packed with amenities, a spa (with dipping pool) and the fashionable Longtable restaurant – but what makes this place truly distinctive is its service. Put simply, the staff here are the most friendly and efficient we have encountered in the city. Business travellers and families should consider the suites, which come with a large sitting area and small kitchenette equipped with toaster, microwave and fridge. Be warned that the street-facing rooms can be a bit noisy. Breakfast costs €24.

# BEŞIKTAŞ, ORTAKÖY & KURUÇEŞME

If you have cash to spare and don't mind being away from the centres of Sultanahmet and Taksim Sq, the suburbs along the Bosphorus could be just what you're looking for. One thing is sure: the views and hotel facilities in this golden strip are the best in town.

**ÇIRAĞAN PALACE KEMPINSKI İSTANBUL** Map p115  Luxury Hotel €€€
☎ 212-326 4646; www.kempinski-istanbul.com; Çırağan Caddesi 32, Beşiktaş; r €505-1350, ste €1375-50,000; 🚇 Yıldız; 🗙 🗙 🖳 🛜 🚐
Housed in a palace constructed by Sultan Abdül Aziz and rebuilt as a hotel in the 1980s, most of the guest rooms in this five-star place are in a modern annexe next door. The recently renovated wedding cake–style palace holds meeting rooms, posh 'palace suites', a ballroom and restaurants. The best things about the place are its location right on the Bosphorus and its amazing infinity pool. If you've got deep pockets, opt for a sea-facing room with balcony – they're much nicer than the park-view alternatives. Breakfast costs €48. Check hotel-booking websites for more-affordable deals.

**FOUR SEASONS ISTANBUL AT THE BOSPHORUS** Map p115  Luxury Hotel €€€
☎ 212-381 4000; www.fourseasons.com/bosphorus; Çırağan Caddesi 28, Beşiktaş; s €370-540, d €400-570, ste €600-18,000; 🗙 🖳 🛜 🚐 ♿
This recently opened hotel incorporates an Ottoman men's guesthouse called the Atik Paşa Konak, which was built around the same time as Çırağan Palace. Its interiors and new wings were designed by fashionable İstanbullu architect, Sinan Kafadar. It's

## BOSPHORUS NIGHTS

If you're in İstanbul to relax rather than indulge in an orgy of sightseeing, you should consider staying in one of a growing number of glam boutique hotels in the Bosphorus suburbs. Most of these are housed in painstakingly restored *yalıs* (traditional wooden houses), have chic fitouts and offer excellent restaurants. They're a long way from the sights of Sultanahmet and the entertainment district of Beyoğlu, but are perfect places for a romantic retreat. Our two favourites are the elegant Sumahan on the Water (Map p204; ☎ 216-422 8008; www.sumahan.com; Kuleli Caddesi 51, Çengelköy; r €240-345, ste €380-490; 🛇 Kandilli; ▨ ▢ ⬥ ) and stylish Ajia (Map p204; ☎ 216-413 9300; www.ajiahotel.com; Cubuklu Caddesi 27, Kanlıca; r €225-500; 🛇 Kanlıca; ▨ ▢ ⬥ ). Both are located on the Asian side of the strait and have waterside terraces, excellent restaurants and hotel launches to transport guests across the water; Sumahan also has a *hamam*.

difficult to overpraise this place – service is exemplary, rooms are wonderfully comfortable and the setting on the Bosphorus is truly magical. Add to this its excellent spa (see p184), fitness centre, restaurant, marble terrace (complete with bar/cafe) and huge outdoor pool overlooking the Bosphorus and you are left with a package that's almost impossible to improve upon. Staying in one of the Atik Paşa suites here is a once-in-a-lifetime experience.

### RADISSON SAS BOSPHORUS HOTEL
Map p115                                                        Hotel €€€

☎ 212-310 1500; www.radissonsas.com; Çırağan Caddesi 46, Ortaköy; standard r €180-215, superior r €230-265, ste €470-505; ▨ ▢ 🛜 ⬥
Stay here if you're in town to party at the Bosphorus superclubs. Prominently located on the Golden Mile, it offers 120 well-sized and very comfortable rooms, some of which have Bosphorus views and all of which share the modern style that the Radisson chain is known for. There's a spa and wellness centre on site (no pool,

though) as well as a branch of the London-based Japanese restaurant, Zuma. Breakfast costs an extra €20.

### W ISTANBUL  Map p115                    Boutique Hotel €€€

☎ 212-381 2121; www.whotels.com/istanbul; Suleyman Seba Caddesi 22, Akaretler; r €300-432, ste €560-10,590; ▨ 🛜 ⬥
Opened in 2008, this uber-stylish 'design hotel' is located between the glam shopping district of Nişantaşı and the party precinct along the Bosphorus. Though the setting is historic (the 1890s building housed domestic staff working at Dolmabahçe Palace), the renovation here is unrelentingly modern and highly theatrical. Rooms have good work desks, comfortable beds, iPod docks and fabulous bathrooms with *hamam*-influenced showers, but are expensive considering their lack of Bosphorus views. There's an Estee Lauder day spa, a fitness centre, a branch of New York's Spice Market restaurant and the trés fashionable W Bar. Breakfast costs around €20.

# FERRY TRIPS

İstanbul is a maritime city, and many travellers find that climbing aboard one of its famous flotilla of ferries ends up being a highlight of their stay.

In the 18th and 19th centuries, the Bosphorus and Golden Horn (Haliç) were alive with *caïques* (long, thin rowboats), their oars dipping rhythmically into the currents as they carried the sultan and his courtiers from palace to pavilion, and from Europe to Asia. The *caïques* are long gone, but in their place are the sleek speedboats of the monied elite and the much-loved public ferries used by the rest of İstanbul's population.

There are a number of public ferry trips to choose from. You can flit between Europe and Asia by hopping onto a ferry from Eminönü to Üsküdar (p118) or Kadıköy (p122); take the ubiquitous (but no less fabulous) ferry trip along the Bosphorus; or embark upon a day trip to the summer playground of the Princes' Islands. From the ferry you'll see minarets and mansions galore and garner an appreciation of how busy the city's waterways are – full of decrepit fishing boats, tugboats, dredges, tankers and cargo ships. Best of all is life on deck, with commuters chewing *simits* (bread rings), slurping tea, trading gossip and enjoying naps or flirtations.

At sunset, when the grandiose silhouette of Old İstanbul is thrown into relief against an orange-red or dusky pink sky, approaching Eminönü by ferry is a truly magical experience. Don't miss it.

See p200 for some accommodation options if you decide to spend a night (or more) on the Bosphorus.

## A DAY ON THE BOSPHORUS

A trip along the Bosphorus offers treats galore. See how many times you can make your way from Asia to Europe and back again! Highlights include Beylerbeyi Palace (p205), Küçksu Kasrı (p205), Rumeli Hisarı (p205), Hıdıv Kasrı (p205), the Sakıp Sabancı Museum (p207) and the Sadberk Hanım Museum (p207).

We suggest two itineraries to make the most out of your day on the water.

Catch the 10.35am Bosphorus excursions ferry to Anadolu Kavağı (p208). After admiring the Black Sea view from the ruined castle on the hill, take the 15A bus down to Kanlıca (p205). Wander around the main square and walk up to the art nouveau Hıdıv Kasrı with its gorgeous gardens. Have a light lunch here before walking down the hill to Kanlıca's main street and catching a bus south to Küçüksu Kasrı or Beylerbeyi Palace. After that, you can continue on to Üsküdar (p118) and catch a commuter ferry back to Eminönü or Beşiktaş.

A second possibility is to take the 10.35am ferry as far as Sarıyer and visit the Sadberk Hanım Müzesi. After this, take a bus south to Emirgan (p207), where you can visit the Sakıp Sabancı Museum and have lunch at Müzedechanga (p208) or Sütiş (p208). Continue back to town by bus, stopping along the way at Rumeli Hisarı to clamour over the castle's ramparts and at Bebek (p205) for an afternoon coffee or drink.

## EXPLORING THE GOLDEN HORN

A jaunty ferry plies the waters of the Golden Horn (p210) between Üsküdar and Eyüp, bringing the pious to the Eyüp Sultan Mosque (p89) and carrying *Haliç* locals to Eminönü and then over to Asia. Highlights along its shores include the suburbs of Balat and Fener (p83), which are home to synagogues, mosques and churches; the Rahmi M Koç Industrial Museum (p126) in Hasköy; and the Eyüp Sultan Mosque & Tomb.

## PRINCES' ISLAND ESCAPE

There are few more idyllic escapes than jumping on a ferry to the tranquil Princes' Islands (p212). Most day-trippers stay on the ferry until Heybeliada, stop there for an hour or so and then catch another ferry to Büyükada, where they catch a *fayton* (horse-drawn carriage) to the Monastery of St George (p213), have lunch at Yücetepe Kır Gazinosu (p214) and spend the rest of the afternoon admiring the island's many mansions and gardens on the walk back to the ferry terminal.

## BOSPHORUS CRUISE

Divan Yolu and İstiklal Caddesi are always awash with people, but neither is the major thoroughfare in İstanbul. That honour goes to

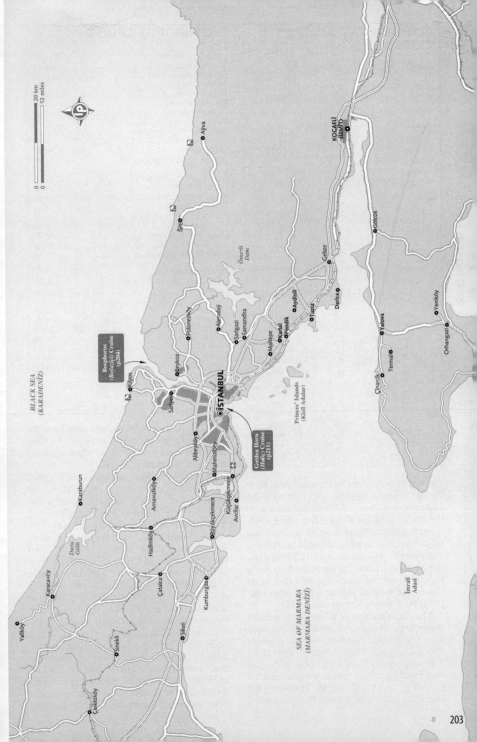

BLACK SEA
(KARADENİZ)

Bosphorus
(Boğaziçi) Cruise
(p204)

Golden Horn
(Haliç) Cruise
(p211)

●İSTANBUL

KOCAELİ
(İZMİT)

SEA OF MARMARA
(MARMARA DENİZİ)

Prince' Islands
(Kızıl Adalar)

İmralı
Adası

Ömerli
Dam

Duru
Gölü

20 km
12 miles

Ağva
Şile
Kilyos
Beykoz
Polonezköy
Alemdağ
Sarigazi
Samandıra
Maltepe
Kartal
Pendik
Aydınlı
Tuzla
Darıca
Gebze
Göltezik
Yalova
Termali
Çınarcık
Yeniköy
Orhangazi
Şahyer
Alibeyköy
Mahmutbey
Küçükçekmece
Avcılar
Büyükçekmece
Anavutköy
Hadımköy
Kumburgaz
Çatalca
Silivri
Karaburun
Karacaköy
Yalıköy
Sinekli
Çerkezköy

203

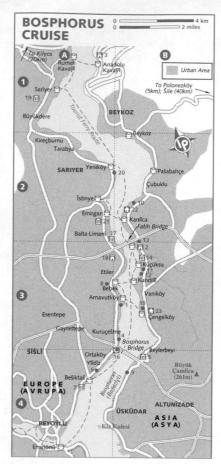

# BOSPHORUS CRUISE

0 ——— 4 km
0 ——— 2 miles

Urban Area

To Kilys (20km)

Rumeli Kavağı · Anadolu Kavağı

Sarıyer · 19

Büyükdere

Tourist ferry Route

BEYKOZ

To Polonezköy (5km); Şile (40km)

Kireçburnu · Beykoz

Tarabya

SARIYER · Yeniköy · 20 · Paşabahçe

Çubuklu

İstinye

Emirgan · 10 · 22 · Kanlıca · Fatih Bridge

21

Balta Limanı · 17

13

18 · 14 · Küçüksu

Etiler

8 · Bebek · Kandilli

Arnavutköy · 15 · Vaniköy

Esentepe · 23 · Çengelköy

Gayrettepe · Kuruçeşme

ŞİŞLİ · Bosphorus Bridge · Beylerbeyi

Ortaköy · 16 · Büyük Çamlıca (261m)

Yıldız

Beşiktaş · 7 · 9

EUROPE (AVRUPA)

ALTUNİZADE

ÜSKÜDAR

BEYOĞLU · Kız Kulesi · ASIA (ASYA)

Eminönü

the mighty Bosphorus Strait, which runs from the Sea of Marmara (Marmara Denizi) at the Galata Bridge (Galata Köprüsü) all the way to the Black Sea (Karadeniz), 32km north. Over the centuries the Bosphorus has been crossed by conquering armies, intrepid merchants and many an adventurous spirit. These days, thousands of İstanbullus commute daily along its length, fishing vessels try their luck in its waters and tourists ride its ferries from Eminönü to Anadolu Kavağı and back.

The strait's name is taken from ancient mythology. Bosphorus roughly translates from the ancient Greek as the 'place where the cow crossed'. The cow was Io, a beautiful lady with whom Zeus, king of the gods, had an affair. When his wife Hera discovered his infidelity, Zeus tried to atone by turning his erstwhile lover into a cow. Hera, for good measure, provided a horsefly to sting Io on the rump and drive her across the strait. Proving that there was no justice in Olympus, Zeus managed to get off scot-free.

In modern Turkish, the strait is the Boğaziçi or İstanbul Boğazı (from boğaz, throat or strait). On one side is Asia, on the other Europe. Both shores are densely populated and have attractions galore for the day visitor.

The Bosphorus has certainly figured in history. According to myth, both Jason of the Argonauts and Ulysses sailed up the Bosphorus, followed by Byzas, legendary founder of Byzantium. Two millennia later, Mehmet the Conqueror built the mighty fortress of Rumeli Hisarı at the strait's narrowest point to close the vital supply route to allies of the Byzantines. After İstanbul fell to the Turks, enormous Ottoman armies would take several days to cross the Bosphorus each spring on their way to campaigns in Asia. At the end of WWI, the defeated Ottoman capital cowered under the guns of Allied frigates moored here; and when the republic was proclaimed, the last Ottoman sultan walked down to the Bosphorus and sailed into exile.

For millennia, crossing the strait meant a boat trip – the only exceptions were the few occasions when it froze. Late in 1973, on the 50th anniversary of the founding of the Turkish Republic, the Bosphorus Bridge was opened. For the first time there was a physical link across the straits from Europe to Asia. Traffic was so heavy over the bridge that it paid for itself in less than a decade. Now there is a second bridge, the Fatih Bridge (named after Mehmet the Conqueror, Mehmet Fatih), just north of Rumeli Hisarı. A third bridge, even further north, is planned.

For pleasant places to eat and drink, see p208; and for details on boat and ferry services, bus connections and fares, see the boxed text, p209.

## Departure Point: Eminönü

Hop onto the boat at the *Boğaz Iskelesi* (Bosphorus Public Excursion Ferry Dock) on the Eminönü quay near the Galata Bridge. It's always a good idea to arrive 30 to 45 minutes or so before the scheduled departure time so as to be sure of getting a seat with a view. The Asian shore is to the right side of the ferry as it sails down the strait, Europe to the left. When you start your trip, watch out for the small island of Kız Kulesi, just off the Asian shore near Üsküdar. Just before the first stop at Beşiktaş, you'll pass the grandiose Dolmabahçe Palace (p114), built on the European shore of the Bosphorus by Sultan Abdül Mecit between 1843 and 1854.

## Beşiktaş to Kanlica

After a brief stop at Beşiktaş, Çırağan Palace (p116), once home to Sultan Abdül Aziz and now a luxury hotel, looms up on the left. On the Asian shore is the Fethi Ahmet Paşa Yalı, built in the late 18th century. The word *yalı* comes from the Greek word for 'coast', and describes the waterside wooden summer residences along the Bosphorus built by Ottoman aristocracy and foreign ambassadors in the 17th, 18th and 19th centuries, now all protected by the country's heritage laws. This one is known as the 'pink *yalı*'. To your left a little further on is the pretty Ortaköy Mosque (p117), its dome and two minarets dwarfed by the adjacent Bosphorus Bridge, the symbol of modern İstanbul.

Under the bridge on the European shore is the green-and-cream-coloured Balyan Usta Yalı,

built in the 1860s by architect Sarkis Balyan. Balyan built his seaside shack here so as to enjoy an unimpeded view of the imposing Beylerbeyi Palace (Beylerbeyi Sarayı; ☎ 216-321 9320; Abdullah Ağa Caddesi, Beylerbeyi; admission TL8, camera TL6, video TL15; ☑ 9.30am-5pm Tue, Wed & Fri-Sun Apr-Oct, 9.30am-4pm Tue, Wed & Fri-Sun Nov-Mar), which he had designed for Sultan Abdül Aziz on the opposite shore. Look for the palace's whimsical marble bathing pavilions on the shore; one was for men, the other for the women of the harem.

Every sultan needed a little place to escape to, and the 30-room Beylerbeyi Palace was the place for Abdül Aziz (r 1861–76). An earlier wooden palace had burned down here, so Abdül Aziz wanted stone and marble. He ordered Sarkis Balyan, brother of Nikoğos (architect of Dolmabahçe), to get to work. Balyan came up with a building that delighted the many foreign dignitaries who visited, including Empress Eugénie of France; Nasruddin, shah of Persia; and Nicholas, grand duke of Russia. The palace's last imperial 'guest' was the former sultan, Abdül Hamit II, who was brought here to spend the remainder of his life (1913–18) under house arrest. He had the dubious pleasure of gazing across the Bosphorus and watching the empire he had ruled for over 30 years crumble before his eyes.

A visit to Beylerbeyi is an attractive alternative to visiting the grander but much more crowded Dolmabahçe. The compulsory guided tour whips you past room after room of Bohemian crystal chandeliers, French (Sèvres) and Ming vases and sumptuous carpets. There's a grand *selamlik* (private quarters) and a small but opulent harem. Highlights include the music room, with its inlaid walnut walls; a sitting room with parquet floors and walls inlayed with ebony and wood; and a dining room with chairs covered in gazelle skin. After the tour you can enjoy a glass of tea in the pretty garden cafe.

Unfortunately, this ferry doesn't stop at Beylerbeyi. You can either visit at another time or alight at the ferry's last stop in Anadolu Kavağı and make your way back here by bus along the Asian shore (see the boxed text, p209).

Past the small village of Çengelköy on the Asian side is the imposing Kuleli Military School, built in 1860 and immortalised in İrfan Orga's wonderful memoir, *Portrait of a Turkish Family* (see p30). Look out for its two 'witch-hat' towers.

Almost opposite Kuleli on the European shore is Arnavutköy, a village boasting a number of frilly Ottoman-era wooden houses and one of the city's most famous *köfte* (meatball) restaurants, Ali Baba Köftecisi (p208). On the hill above it are buildings formerly occupied by the American College for Girls. Its most famous alumni was Halide Edib Adıvar, who wrote about the years she spent here in her 1926 autobiographical work, *The Memoir of Halide Edib*.

Arnavutköy runs straight into the glamorous suburb of Bebek, known for its upmarket shopping and chic cafes such as Mangerie (p208), Lucca (p208) and Kitchenette (p208). It also has the most glamorous Starbucks in the city (right on the water, and with a lovely terrace). Bebek's shops surround a small park and the Ottoman Revivalist–style Bebek Mosque; to the east of these is the ferry dock, to the south is the Egyptian consulate building, designed by Raimondo D'Aronco. This gorgeous art nouveau mini-palace was built by the last khedive of Egypt, Abbas Hilmi II, who also later built Hıdiv Kasrı (p205) above Kanlıca on the Asian side of the Bosphorus. You'll see its mansard roof and ornate wrought-iron fence from the ferry. It was closed for renovation when this book went to print.

Opposite Bebek on the Asian shore is Kandıllı, the 'Place of Lamps', named after the lamps that were lit here to warn ships of the particularly treacherous currents at the headland. Among the many *yalıs* (waterside wooden residence) here is the small Kırmızı Yalı (Red *Yalı*), constructed in 1790 and one of the oldest mansions still standing; Pierre Loti stayed here when he visited İstanbul in the 1890s. A bit further on, past Kandıllı, is the long, white Kıbrıslı Mustafa Emin Paşa Yalı, which dates from 1760.

Next to the Kıbrıslı are the Büyük Göksu Deresi (Great Heavenly Stream) and Küçük Göksu Deresi (Small Heavenly Stream), two brooks that descend from the Asian hills into the Bosphorus. Between them is a fertile delta, grassy and shady, which the Ottoman elite thought perfect for picnics. Foreign residents referred to it as 'The Sweet Waters of Asia'.

If the weather was good, the sultan joined the picnic, and did so in style. Sultan Abdül Mecit's answer to a simple picnic blanket was Küçüksu Kasrı ( ☎ 216-332 3303; Küçüksu Caddesi; adult/student TL4/1; ☯ 9.30am-5pm Tue, Wed & Fri-Sun Apr-Oct, 9.30am-4pm Tue, Wed & Fri-Sun Nov-Mar), an ornate lodge built in 1856–7. Earlier sultans had wooden kiosks here, but architect Nikoğos Balyan designed a rococo gem in marble for his monarch. You'll see its ornate cast-iron

fence, boat dock and wedding-cake exterior from the ferry.

Just before the Fatih Bridge are the majestic structures of Rumeli Hisarı (Fortress of Europe; ☎ 212-263 5305; Yahya Kemal Caddesi 42, Rumeli Hisarı; admission TL3; ☯ 9am-noon & 12.30-4.30pm Thu-Tue) and Anadolu Hisarı (Fortress of Anatolia). Mehmet the Conqueror had Rumeli Hisarı built in a mere four months in 1452, in preparation for his siege of Byzantine Constantinople. For its location, he chose the narrowest point of the Bosphorus, opposite Anadolu Hisarı, which Sultan Beyazıt I had built in 1391. By doing so, Mehmet was able to control all traffic on the strait, cutting the city off from re-supply by sea.

To speed Rumeli Hisarı's completion (he was impatient to conquer Constantinople), Mehmet ordered each of his three viziers to take responsibility for one of the three main towers. If the tower's construction was not completed on schedule, the vizier would pay with his life. Not surprisingly, the work was completed on time. The useful military life of the mighty fortress lasted less than one year. After the conquest of Constantinople, it was used as a glorified Bosphorus tollbooth for a while, then as a barracks, a prison, and finally as an open-air theatre. Its amphitheatre still functions as an occasional performance venue during the summer months.

Within Rumeli Hisarı's walls are parklike grounds, an open-air theatre and the minaret of a ruined mosque. Steep stairs (with no barriers, so beware!) lead up to the ramparts and towers; the views of the Bosphorus from here are magnificent. Just next to the fortress is a clutch of cafes and restaurants, the most popular of which is Sade Kahve (p208).

The ferry doesn't stop at Rumeli Hisarı; you can either leave the ferry at Kanlica and catch a taxi across the Fatih Bridge (this will cost around TL20 including the bridge toll) or you can visit on your way back to town from Sariyer (see the boxed text, p209). Though it's not open as a museum, visitors are free to wander about Anadolu Hisarı's ruined walls.

Past Anadolu Hisarı (before the Fatih Bridge) is Köprülü Amcazade Hüseyin Paşa Yalı, built right on the water in 1698. Built for one of Mustafa II's grand viziers, it is the oldest *yalı* on the Bosphorus. Directly under the bridge is the huge Palace of İmer Faruk Efendi, built in the late 19th century and once home to Prince İmer Faruk Efendi, the grandson of Sultan Abdül Aziz, and to his wife Sabiha Sultan, daughter of Mehmet VI, the last of the Ottoman sultans. When the sultanate was abolished in 1922, Mehmet walked from this palace onto a British warship, never to return to Turkey.

Past the bridge, still on the Asian side, is Kanlıca, the ferry's next stop. This charming village is famous for the rich and delicious yoghurt produced here, which is sold on the ferry and in two cafes on the shady waterfront square. The small Gâzi İskender Paşa Mosque in the square dates from 1560 and was designed by Sinan.

High on a promontory above Kanlıca is Hıdıv Kasrı (Khedive's Villa; ☎ 216-413 9644; Çubuklu Yolu 32, Kanlıca; admission free; ☉ 9am-10pm), a gorgeous art nouveau villa built by the last khedive of Egypt as a summer residence for use during his family's annual visits to İstanbul. You can see its square white tower (often flying a Turkish flag) from the ferry.

Having ruled Egypt for centuries, in 1805 the Ottomans lost control to an adventurer named Muhammed Ali (also known as Mehmet Ali), who defied the sultan in İstanbul to dislodge him. The sultan, unable to do so, gave him quasi-independence and had to be satisfied with reigning over Egypt rather than ruling. This was left to Muhammed Ali and his line, and the ruler of Egypt was styled hıdıv, 'khedive' (not 'king', as that would be unbearably independent). The khedives of Egypt kept up the pretence of Ottoman suzerainty by paying tribute to İstanbul.

The Egyptian royal family, which looked upon itself as Turkish, often spent its summers in a traditional yalı at Bebek (now the Egyptian consulate; p205), but in 1906, Khedive Abbas Hilmi II built himself this palatial villa on the most dramatic promontory on the Bosphorus. In the 1930s it became the property of the municipality.

Restored after decades of neglect, Hıdiv Kasrı now functions as a restaurant and garden cafe (p208). The building is an architectural gem and the extensive garden is superb, especially during the İstanbul International Tulip Festival (p16) in April.

The villa is a 20-minute walk from the ferry dock. Head north up Halide Edip Adivar Caddesi from Kanlıca's main square and mosque and turn right at the second street (Kafadar Sokak). Turn left into Hacı Muhittin Sokağı and wind up towards the villa car park. Shortly you'll come to a fork in the road. Take the left fork and follow the 'Hıdiv Kasrı' signs to the villa's car park and garden.

# Kanlica to Yenıköy

On the opposite shore is the wealthy suburb of Emirgan, home to the impressive Sakıp Sabancı Museum (Sakıp Sabancı Müzesi; ☎ 212-277 2200; www.muze.sabanciuniv.edu; Sakıp Sabancı Caddesi 22; admission varies according to exhibition; ☉ 10am-6pm Wed-Sat), which hosts international travelling art exhibitions. The museum is home to one of İstanbul's most stylish eateries, Müzedechanga (p208), which has an extensive terrace and magnificent Bosphorus views. North of Emirgan, there's a ferry dock near the small yacht-lined cove of İstinye. Just north of here, on a point jutting out from the European shore, is Yenıköy, the ferry's next stop.

# Yenıköy to Sariyer

First settled in classical times, Yenıköy became a favourite summer resort for the Ottomans, as indicated by the cluster of lavish 18th- and 19th-century yalıs around the ferry dock. These are in varying states of (dis)repair – one of the best maintained is the Sait Halim Paşa Yalı, built in 1770–80 and enlarged at the end of the 19th century for a one-time grand vizier. Look for its two small stone lions on the quay. On the opposite shore is the village of Paşabahçe, famous for its glassware factory. A bit further on is the fishing village of Beykoz, which has a graceful ablutions fountain, the İshak Ağa Çeşmesi, dating from 1746, near the village square, and several fish restaurants. Much of the land along the Bosphorus shore north of Beykoz is a military zone.

Originally called Therapia for its healthy climate, the little cove of Tarabya on the European shore has been a favourite summer watering place for İstanbul's well-to-do for centuries, though modern developments such as the horrendous multistorey Grand Hotel Tarabya right on the promontory have poisoned some of its charm. For an account of Therapia in its heyday, read Harold Nicolson's 1921 novel Sweet Waters. Nicolson, who is best known as Vita Sackville West's husband, served as the third Secretary in the British Embassy in Constantinople between 1912 and 1914, the years of the Balkan wars, and clearly knew Therapia well. In the novel, the main character, Eirene, who was based on Vita, spent her summers here.

North of the village are some of the old summer embassies of foreign powers. When the heat and fear of disease increased in the warm months, foreign ambassadors would retire to palatial residences, complete with lush gardens, on this shore. The region for such embassy residences extended north to the village of Büyükdere, notable for its churches, summer embassies and the Sadberk Hanım Museum ( ☎ 212-242 3813; www.sadberkhanimmuzesi.org.tr; Piyasa Caddesi 25-29, Büyükdere; admission TL7; ☒ 10am-5pm Thu-Tue). To get here, alight from the ferry at Sariyer and walk south from the ferry dock for approximately 10 minutes. Named after the wife of the late Vehbi Koç, founder of Turkey's foremost commercial empire in 1926, the museum is a showcase for her extraordinary private collection of antiquities and Ottoman heirlooms. Labels are in English and Turkish.

The original museum building is a graceful old yalı, once the summer residence of Manuk Azaryan Efendi, an Armenian who was speaker of the Ottoman parliament. It houses artefacts and exhibits such as beautiful İznik and Kütahya tiles and ceramics, and Ottoman silk textiles and needlework. A number of rooms in the great old house have been arranged and decorated in Ottoman style.

The collections in the new building, which is beside the original yalı, trace the waves of colonisation in Anatolia (Hitttite, Hellenistic, Roman etc) and feature some amazing artefacts, including an exquisite collection of diadems from the Mycenacan, Archaic and Classical periods.

The museum's gift shop sells quality souvenirs, including bags, hamam (bathhouse) kits, scarves and tea towels featuring attractive reproduction Ottoman fabrics.

The residents of Sarıyer, the next village up from Büyükdere on the European shore, have traditionally made a living by fishing, and the area around the ferry terminal (the next stop) is full of fish restaurants.

## Sariyer to Anadolu Kavaği

From Sariyer, it's only a short trip to Rumeli Kavağı, a sleepy place where the only excitement comes courtesy of the arrival and departure of the ferry. To the south of the town is the shrine of the Muslim saint Telli Baba, reputed to be able to find suitable husbands for young women who pray there.

Anadolu Kavağı on the opposite shore is where the Bosphorus excursions ferry finishes its journey. Once a fishing village, its local economy now relies on the tourism trade and its main square is full of mediocre restaurants and their touts.

Perched above the village are the ruins of Anadolu Kavağı Kalesi (Yoros Kalesi), a medieval castle that originally had eight massive towers in its walls. First built by the Byzantines, it was restored and reinforced by the Genoese in 1350, and later by the Ottomans. Two more fortresses built by Sultan Murat IV in the 17th century are north of here. To enjoy the spectacular Black Sea views from the castle, walk for 25 minutes up steep Caferbaba Sokağı. You'll see signs indicating the way.

# EATING & DRINKING

There are places to suit every taste and budget along the shores of the Bosphorus. Many day-trippers choose to organise an itinerary around their choice of lunch venue, and there's a lot to be said for following their example. For options in Ortaköy, see p158.

Ali Baba Köftecisi ( ☎ 212-265 3612; 1 Caddesi 104, Arnavutköy; ☒ noon-10pm) İstanbullus cross town for the tasty köfte served at this ever-busy eatery. Enjoy them with piyaz (white beans), pide (Turkish-style pizza) warm from the oven and a dusting of dried crushed chilli.

Mangerie ( ☎ 212-263 5199; 3rd fl Cevdet Paşa Caddesi 69, Bebek; breakfast TL11-30, sandwiches TL26-31, salads TL26-30, burgers TL33-37; ☒ 8am-midnight) Effortlessly chic, Mangerie is the prototype for the rapidly proliferating number of glam cafes in Bebek. The interior is light and white, and there's a terrace with terrific Bosphorus views. The food looks away from Turkey for its inspiration, and is simple but refined. To find it, go up the steep stairs next to the florist.

Poseidon ( ☎ 212-263 3843; Cevdet Paşa Caddesi 58, Bebek; starters TL5-25, fish by kg TL65-120; ☒ noon-midnight) This place evokes class with a capital 'C' – for credit-card danger. If you want some of the best seafood in the city served on a stylish deck overlooking the bobbing boats of Bebek Bay, it's the perfect place. You'll be in the company of beautifully groomed women who dote on designer handbags and are often mistaken by their businessman dining partners as said fashion accessory.

Kitchenette ( ☎ 212-287 1161; www.kitchenette.com.tr; Ipek Sokak 1, Bebek; ☒ 7am-2am) Notable for its huge terrace, club-like bar and buzzing upstairs brasserie, this branch of the Kitchenette chain offers decent but unexciting food, expensive coffee and a moneyed clientele – all of which is expected in this privileged part of town. Look for the elevated grey art deco building on the main road opposite the park and ferry dock.

**Lucca** ( ☎ 212-257 1255; www.luccastyle.com; Cevdet Paşa Caddesi 51B, Bebek; tapas TL8-20, pastas TL16-24, burgers TL24; ☼ 10am-2am) Ecstatically embraced by the in-crowd when it opened back in 2005, Lucca's star shows no sign of waning. Glam young things flock here on Friday and Saturday nights to see and be seen, but the mood is more relaxed during the week. The caffè latte (TL9) reigns supreme during the day but at night cocktails claim the spotlight, accompanied by your choice from the 'Mediterranean World Kitchen'.

**Rumeli İskele** ( ☎ 212-263 2997; Yahya Kemal Caddesi 1, Rumeli Hisarı; meze TL5-20, mains TL35-65; ☼ noon-1am) Businessmen (sometimes with girlfriend, sometimes with colleagues) are a permanent lunchtime fixture at this old timber fer̄ minal building right on the water, ord delectable meze such as *levrek marine* bass in a creamy but piquant lemon sauce) or *çıroz* (salted and dried thin mackerel). The catch of the day is priced by the kilo (prepare yourself for a hefty outlay) and there are good wine choices by the glass and bottle.

**Sade Kahve** ( ☎ 212-358 2324; Yahya Kemal Caddesi 36, Rumeli Hisarı; breakfast plate incl tea TL14; ☼ 8am-2am) Cheap and cheerful it may well be, but this terrace cafe near the fortress of Europe is also a favourite weekend brunch spot for powerbrokers, celebrities and their entourages. It serves soup and an array of sandwiches at lunch.

## TRANSPORT: BOSPHORUS

The most popular way to explore the Bosphorus is by ferry. Most day-trippers take the Eminönü-Kavaklar Boğaziçi Özel Gezi Seferleri (Eminönü-Kavaklar Bosphorus Special Touristic Excursions) ferry up its entire length, a 90-minute one-way trip. This ferry departs from the Boğaz İskelesi (Map pp50–1) at Eminönü daily at 10.35am. From mid-June to mid-September, there are usually extra services at noon and 1.35pm. A ticket costs TL17.50 return, TL10 one way. The ferry stops at Beşiktaş, Kanlıca, Yeniköy, Sarıyer, Rumeli Kavağı and Anadolu Kavağı (the turnaround point). It is not possible to get on and off the ferry at stops along the way using the same ticket.

The boats fill up early in warm weather – especially on weekends – so buy your ticket and walk aboard at least 45 minutes prior to departure to get a seat outside or next to a window. During the trip waiters will offer you fresh orange juice, tea and other drinks (at standard cafe prices).

Most day-trippers take the ferry all the way to Anadolu Kavağı and stay there until the ferry returns at 3pm (and 4.15pm, 5pm weekdays and 6pm weekends mid-June to mid-September). In fact, it's much better to follow one of the itineraries outlined on p202 or alight at Kanlıca, explore Hıdiv Kasrı and Küçüksu Kasrı, and then go back to Kanlıca to reboard the ferry on its return trip.

You can also alight at Kanlıca, visit Hıdiv Kasrı or Küçüksu Kasrı and then catch a 1.05pm ferry across the Bosphorus to Bebek, where you can have lunch before making your way back to town via Yıldız Park (p116) or Dolmabahçe Palace (p114).

From Sarıyer, 🚌 25E and 40 head south to Emirgan. From Emirgan, 🚌 22, 22RE and 25E head to Kabataş and 🚌 40, 40T and 42T go to Taksim. All travel via Rumeli Hisarı, Bebek, Ortaköy, Yıldız and Beşiktaş.

If you decide to catch the ferry to Anadolu Kavağı and make your way back to town by bus, catch 🚌 15A, which leaves from just east of the ferry terminal en route to Kavacık Aktarma. Get off at Kanlıca to visit Hıdiv Kasrı or to transfer to 🚌 15, 15F or 15P, which will take you south to Üsküdar via the Küçüksu stop (for Küçüksu Kasrı) and the Çayırbaşı stop (for Beylerbeyi).

From Kanlıca it's also possible to catch a passenger ferry back towards İstanbul. These stop at Anadolu Hisarı, Kandilli, Bebek and Arnavutköy. Afternoon departures from Kanlıca are at 1.05pm, 2.35pm, 4.20pm and 5.55pm. The trip to Bebek takes 20 minutes.

There is also a passenger ferry service between Sarıyer and Anadolu Kavağı, with 15 ferries a day from 7.15am to 11pm; seven of these ferries stop at Rumeli Kavağı on the way.

Other Bosphorus ferries include the commuter services to and from Eminönü. Most of these are of little use to travellers, although there are Eminönü-Beylerbeyi services at 11.30am and 1.10pm, as well as Eminönü-Ortaköy services at 5.50pm, 6.30pm and 6.40pm.

Yet another option is a private Bosphorus boat tour. Ticket touts are always to be found around the Boğaz dock at Eminönü flogging the tickets for these – chat with them about what's on offer (it's almost always a 1½-hour cruise to Rumeli Hisarı and back), when the boat is leaving and how much the ticket costs (usually TL20).

All bus trips mentioned in the text cost TL1.50.

Finally: a warning. All times given above were correct when this book went to print, but they could well change. Check at the ferry docks or online at www.ido.com.tr.

**Hıdiv Kasrı Café** ( ☎ 216-320 2036; Çubuklu Yolu 32, Kanlıca; sandwiches TL5-6.50, salads TL5-9, pasta TL6-6.50; ☺ 8am-11pm) Choose from the simple menu at the charming garden cafe or from the more extensive choice in the grand dining room and adjoining marble terrace. The food is average but the surroundings are drop-dead gorgeous. No alcohol is served.

**Sütiş** ( ☎ 212-323 5030; Sakıp Sabancı Müzesi, 3rd fl Sakıp Sabancı Caddesi 1, Emirgan; ☺ 6am-1am) The Bosphorus branch of this popular chain has an expansive and extremely comfortable terrace overlooking the water. It's known for serving all-day breakfasts and milk-based puddings – we recommend the *simit* with honey and *kaymak* (clotted cream).

**Müzedechanga** ( ☎ 212-3230901; Sakıp Sabancı Müzesi, Sakıp Sabancı Caddesi 22, Emirgan; starters TL13-24, mains TL22-40; ☺ 10am-1am Tue-Sun) Operated by one of the city's top restaurants, Changa (p152), this stylish eatery in the Sakıp Sabancı Museum is popular for weekend lunch or brunch – a favourite menu combo is *katmer* (local flaky pastry with goat-cheese cream and marinated green olives with preserved lemons) accompanied by a wasabi Bloody Mary. If you don't feel like visiting the museum, door staff will waive the entry fee and point you to the restaurant.

# GOLDEN HORN CRUISE

Most visitors to İstanbul know about the Bosphorus boat trip, but not too many have heard about the Golden Horn (*Haliç*) trip. Until recently, this stretch of water to the north of the Galata Bridge was heavily polluted and its suburbs offered little to tempt the traveller. All that's changing these days, though. The waters have been cleaned up, beautification works are underway along the shores, and a new culture and congress centre has opened in the trendy suburb of Sütluce. Spending a day hopping on and off the ferry and exploring will give you an insight into a very different – and far less touristy – İstanbul.

## Departure Point: Eminönü

These ferries start in Üsküdar on the Asian side, and stop at Karaköy before taking on most of their passengers at the *Haliç Iskelesi* (Golden Horn Ferry Dock) on the far side of the Galata Bridge at Eminönü. The *iskelesi* is behind a car park next to the Storks jewellery store. The ferry then sails underneath the Atatürk Bridge and stops at Kasımpaşa on the

opposite side of the Golden Horn. This area is where the Ottoman imperial naval yards were located, and some of the original building stock is still evident.

## Fener

The next stop is on the opposite shore, at Fener. This area is the traditional home of the city's Greek population, and although few Greeks are resident these days, a number of important Greek Orthodox sites are located here. The prominent red-brick building on the hill is the Greek Lycee of the Fener (Megali School or Great School), the oldest house of learning in İstanbul. The school has been housed in Fener since before the Conquest – the present building dates from 1881. Next to it (not visible from the ferry) is the Byzantine Church of St Mary of the Mongols (p87).

Closer to the shore, to the left of the ferry stop and across Abdülezel Paşa Caddesi, is the Ecumenical Orthodox Patriarchate (p89). To the right of the ferry stop, in the waterside park, is the attractive gothic revival Church of St Stephen of the Bulgars (p88).

## Balat

Staying on the western side of the Golden Horn, the ferry's next stop is Balat, once home to a large proportion of İstanbul's Jewish population and now crowded with migrants from the east of the country. The oldest synagogue in İstanbul, Ahrida Synagogue (p87), is located here.

## Hasköy to Sütlüce

Passing the derelict remains of the original Galata Bridge on its way, the ferry then crosses to the opposite shore and stops at Hasköy, home to the fascinating Rahmi M Koç Industrial Museum (p126). The museum is directly to the left of the ferry stop.

After stopping at Ayvansaray on the opposite shore (where our walking tour of the historic city walls, p90, starts), the ferry crosses back to Sütlüce. Art lovers could consider getting off the ferry here and catching 🚌 36T, 47, 47C or 47E north to Bilgi Üniversitesi, home to the cutting-edge santralistanbul (p179).

## Eyüp

The ferry's last stop is at Eyüp. This conservative suburb is built around the Eyüp Sultan Mosque & Tomb (p89), one of the most important reli-

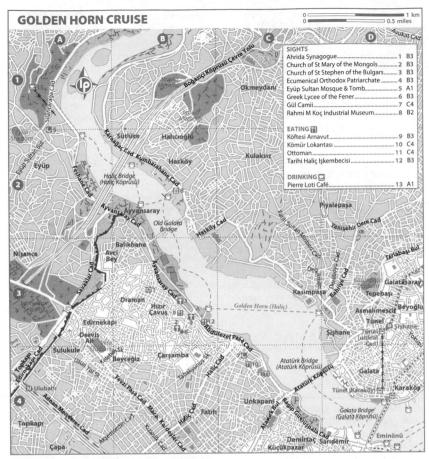

| SIGHTS | | |
|---|---|---|
| Ahrida Synagogue | 1 | B3 |
| Church of St Mary of the Mongols | 2 | B3 |
| Church of St Stephen of the Bulgars | 3 | B3 |
| Ecumenical Orthodox Patriarchate | 4 | B3 |
| Eyüp Sultan Mosque & Tomb | 5 | A1 |
| Greek Lycee of the Fener | 6 | B3 |
| Gül Camii | 7 | C4 |
| Rahmi M Koç Industrial Museum | 8 | B2 |

| EATING | | |
|---|---|---|
| Köftesi Arnavut | 9 | B3 |
| Kömür Lokantası | 10 | C4 |
| Ottoman | 11 | C4 |
| Tarihi Haliç İşkembecisi | 12 | B3 |

| DRINKING | | |
|---|---|---|
| Pierre Loti Café | 13 | A1 |

gious sites in Turkey. After visiting the complex, many visitors head north up the hill to enjoy a glass of tea and the wonderful views on offer at the Pierre Loti Café.

From Eyüp, you can catch a return ferry to Eminönü, Karaköy or Üsküdar, or catch a bus to Edirnekapı to visit the magnificent Chora Church (p83). See the boxed text p212 for bus details.

## EATING & DRINKING

Despite the inexorable creep of gentrification across the Golden Horn suburbs, it can still be difficult to find a decent place to eat, particularly on a Sunday. Fortunately, there are a few exceptions to the rule.

Ottoman ( ☎ 212-631 7567; www.halicottoman.com; Kadir Has Caddesi 9; meze TL3-8, kebaps TL10-25; 🕙 noon-midnight Tue-Sun) Featuring regional specialities from Turkey's east as well as Ottoman dishes, this restaurant – which has a roof terrace and top-floor dining room overlooking the Golden Horn – is as excellent as it is affordable. We've eaten here a fair few times with Turks who, after their first mouthful, have immediately called the waiter back to order extra dishes – always a good sign. It's a 15-minute walk back towards Eminönü from the Fener *iskelesi.*

Kömür Lokantası ( ☎ 212-631 0192; www.komurlokan tasi.com; Mustantik Sokak 33, Balat; portions €4-10; 🕙 lunch Mon-Sat) The best *lokanta* (restaurant serving ready-made food) on the Golden Horn, Kömür is frequented by students from the Kadir Has Üniversitesi, who come here to choose from the array of dishes based on recipes from the Laz region on the Black Sea.

## TRANSPORT – GOLDEN HORN

Golden Horn ferries leave Eminönü every hour from 8.50am to 8.10pm; the last ferry returns to Eminönü from Eyüp at 7.45pm. The ferry trip takes 35 minutes and costs TL1.50 per leg (slightly cheaper if you use a travel card or Akbil). Check www.ido.com.tr for timetable and fare updates.

If you wish to return from Eyüp by bus rather than ferry, 🚌 36CE, 399B/C/D, 44B & 99 travel from outside the ferry stop at Eyüp via Balat and Fener to Eminönü. 🚌 39 and 39C travel to Beyazıt via Edirnekapı, allowing you to stop and visit the Chora Church on your way back.

To return to Taksim from Hasköy or Sütluce by bus, catch 🚌 36T or 54HS/HT. For Eminönü, catch 🚌 47, 47C/E. All bus tickets cost TL1.50.

Tarihi Haliç İşkembecisi ( ☎ 212-534 9414; www.halic iskembecisi.com; Abdülezel Paşa Caddesi 315, Fener; soup TL5; ⏰ 24hr) Locals swear by the hangover-fighting properties of *işkembe* and often make late-night pilgrimages to this, the most famous *işkembecisi* (tripe soup shop) in the city. It's on the main road opposite the ferry stop.

Köftesi Arnavut ( ☎ 212-531 6652; Mürsel Paşa Caddesi 139, Balat; köfte TL8, piyaz TL5; ⏰ 8am-4pm) Unsigned and unassuming, this famous *köftecisi* first opened in 1947 and is a safe spot to scoff *köfte* and *piyaz*. It's to the left of the ferry stop on the opposite side of the main road.

# PRINCES' ISLANDS CRUISE

Most İstanbullus refer to the Princes' Islands (Kızıl Adalar, or 'Red Islands'; Map p203) as 'The Islands' (Adalar), as they are the only islands around the city. They lie about 20km southeast of the city in the Sea of Marmara, and make a great destination for a day escape from the city.

In antiquity the islands were known as Demonisia, the People's Islands. In Byzantine times, refractory princes, deposed monarchs and troublesome associates were interned here in convents and monasteries, hence the name the 'Princes' Islands'. A steam-ferry service from İstanbul was started in the mid-19th century and the islands became popular summer resorts for Pera's Greek, Jewish and Armenian communities. Many of the fine Victorian villas built by these wealthy merchants survive, and make the larger islands, Büyükada and Heybeliada, charming places to explore.

You'll realise after landing that there are no cars on the islands, something that comes as a welcome relief after the traffic mayhem of the city. Except for the necessary police, fire and sanitation vehicles, transportation is by bicycle, *fayton* (horse-drawn carriage) and foot, as in centuries past.

All of the islands are busy in summer, particularly on weekends. For that reason, avoid a Sunday visit. If you wish to stay overnight during the summer months, book ahead. Many hotels are closed during winter.

There are nine islands in the Princes' Islands group and the ferry stops at four of these. Year-round there are 15,000 permanent residents scattered across the six islands that are populated, but numbers swell to 100,000 or so during summer when İstanbullus – many of whom have holiday homes on the islands – escape the city heat. The small islands of Kınalıada and Burgazada are the ferry's first stops; frankly, neither offers much reward for the trouble of getting off the ferry.

## Heybeliada

The charming island of Heybeliada (Heybeli for short and Halki in Greek) has much to offer the visitor. It's home to the Deniz Lisesi (Turkish Navel Academy), which was founded in 1773, and which you'll see to the left of the ferry dock as you arrive. There are a number of restaurants and a thriving shopping strip with bakeries and delicatessens selling picnic provisions to day-trippers, who come here on weekends to walk in the pine groves and swim from the tiny (but crowded) beaches. The island's major landmark is the hilltop Haghia Triada Monastery ( ☎ 216-351 8563). Perched above a picturesque line of poplar trees in a spot that has been occupied by a Greek monastery since Byzantine times, this building dates from 1896. It functioned as a Greek Orthodox theological school until 1971, when it was closed on the government's orders. The monastery is best known for its internationally renowned library, which is home to many old and rare manuscripts. You may be able to visit if you call ahead.

The delightful walk up to the Merit Halki Palace hotel (p214) at the top of Refah Şehitleri

Caddesi passes a junk shop and a host of large wooden villas set in lovingly tended gardens. Many laneways and streets leading to picnic spots and lookout points are located off the upper reaches of this street. To find the hotel, turn right as you leave the ferry and head past the waterfront restaurants and cafes to the plaza with the Atatürk statue. From here walk up İsgüzar Sokak, veering right until you hit Refah Şehitleri Caddesi. If you don't feel like walking up to the hotel (it's uphill but not too steep), you can hire a bicycle (TL2 to TL3.50 per hour) from one of the shops in the main street or a *fayton* to take you around the island. A 25-minute tour (*küçük tur*) costs TL20 and a one-hour tour (*büyük tur*) costs TL30; the *fayton* stand is behind the Atatürk statue. Some visitors spend the day by the pool at the Merit Halki Palace, which is a good idea, as the waters around the island aren't very clean. Towels and chaise lounges are supplied, and there's a pleasant terrace restaurant for meals or drinks. The charge for nonguests to use the pool is TL50 on weekdays and TL60 on weekends.

## Büyükada

The largest island in the group, Büyükada (Great Island), is impressive from the ferry, with gingerbread villas climbing up the slopes of the hill and the bulbous twin cupolas of the Splendid Otel providing an unmistakable landmark. It's a truly lovely spot to spend an afternoon.

The ferry terminal is an attractive building in the Ottoman kiosk style; it dates from 1899. Inside there's a pleasant tile decorated cafe with an outdoor terrace. Eateries serve fresh fish to the left of the ferry terminal, next to an ATM.

The island's main drawcard is the Greek Monastery of St George, in the 'saddle' between Büyükada's two highest hills. Walk from the ferry straight ahead to the clock tower in İskele Sq (Dock Sq). The shopping district (with cheap eateries) is left along Recep Koç Sokak. Bear right onto 23 Nisan Caddesi, then head along Çankaya Caddesi up the hill to the monastery; when you come to a fork in the road, veer right. The walk, which takes at least one hour, takes you past a long progression of impressive wooden villas set in gardens. About a quarter of the way up on the left is the Büyükada Kültür Evi, a charming spot where you can enjoy a tea or coffee in a garden setting. The house itself dates from 1878 and was restored in 1998. After 40 minutes or so you will reach a reserve called 'Luna Park' by the locals. The monastery is a 25-minute walk up an extremely steep hill from here. Some visitors hire a donkey to take them up the hill and back for TL10. As you ascend, you'll sometimes see pieces of cloth tied to the branches of trees along the path – each represents a prayer, most made by female supplicants visiting the monastery to pray for a child.

There's not a lot to see at the monastery. A small and gaudy church is the only building of note, but there are fabulous panoramic views from the terrace, as well as the highly regarded Yücetepe Kır Gazinosu (p214), a restaurant with outdoor seating. From its tables you will be able to see all the way to İstanbul and the nearby islands of Yassıada and Sivriada.

Bicycles are available for rent in several of the town's shops, and shops on the market street can provide picnic supplies, though food is cheaper on the mainland. Just off the clock tower square and opposite the Splendid Otel there are *fayton* stands. Hire one for a long tour of the town, hills and shore (one hour TL45) or a shorter tour of the town (TL35). It costs TL16 to be taken to Luna Park. The *fayton* stand is to the left of the clock tower.

## TRANSPORT – PRINCES' ISLANDS

At least eight ferries run to the islands each day from 6.50am to 7.50pm (midnight mid-June to mid-September), departing from the Adalar İskelesi dock at Kabataş. The most useful departure times for day-trippers are 9.10am, 10.40am and noon (9.20am, 10.10am and 11.35am mid-June to mid-September). On summer weekends, board the vessel and grab a seat at least half an hour before departure time unless you want to stand the whole way. The trip costs TL3 to the islands and the same for each leg between the islands and for the return trip (cheaper using Akbil or İstanbulkart). To be safe, check the timetable at www.ido.com.tr, as the schedule often changes.

The ferry steams away from Kabataş and on its journey treats passengers to fine views of Topkapı Palace, Aya Sofya and the Blue Mosque on the right, and Üsküdar and Haydarpaşa on the left. After 20 minutes the ferry makes a quick stop at Kadıköy on the Asian side before making its way to the first island, Kınalıada. This leg takes 30 minutes. After this, it's another 15 minutes to Burgazada; another 15 minutes again to Heybeliada, the second-largest island; and another 15 minutes to Büyükada, the largest island in the group.

Ferries return to İstanbul every 1½ hours or so. The last ferry of the day leaves Büyükada at 7.35pm and Heybeliada at 7.50pm (10pm and 10.15pm mid-June to mid-September).

A shop just near the *fayton* stand hires out bicycles (TL2.50 to TL3 per hour).

## SLEEPING & EATING

There aren't many eateries of note on the islands, particularly on Heybeliada. A picnic is often your best bet.

**Merit Halki Palace** ( ☎ 216-351 0025; www.halkipalace hotel.com; Refah Şehitleri Caddesi 94, Heybeliada; s/d Sun-Thu €65/85, Fri & Sat €85/135; ☒ ) Heybeliada has a couple of hotels, including this comfortable place, perched at the top of Refah Şehitleri Caddesi and commanding wonderful water views.

**Mavi Restaurant** ( ☎ 216-351 0128; Yalı Caddesi 29, Heybeliada; mains TL14-24; ☒ 24hr) This fish restaurant on the main waterfront promenade is popular with locals and has loads of outdoor seating.

**Büyükada Kültür Evi** ( ☎ 216-382 8620; Çankaya Caddesi 21, Büyükada; sandwiches TL6-12, grills TL14, beer TL8; ☒ Apr-Oct, Sat & Sun only Nov-Mar) Set up by the Turing Association in 1998, this garden cafe serves breakfast, lunch and dinner in its terraced garden. Service can be desultory and the food's not up to much, but it's an undeniably pretty setting and a great spot for a morning glass of tea or a late-afternoon beer.

**Yücetepe Kır Gazinosu** (Monastery of St George, Büyükada; mains TL8-9; ☒ Apr-Oct, Sat & Sun only Nov-Mar) At the very top of the hill where the Monastery of St George is located, this simple place has benches and chairs on a terrace overlooking the sea and İstanbul. Dishes are simple but delicious – the *köfte* is particularly tasty. You can also enjoy a beer here.

## THINGS CHANGE...

The information in this chapter is particularly vulnerable to change. Check directly with the airline or a travel agent to make sure you understand how a fare (and ticket you may buy) works and be aware of the security requirements for international travel. Shop carefully. The details given in this chapter should be regarded as pointers and are not a substitute for your own careful, up-to-date research.

As it's the national capital in all but name, getting to İstanbul is easy. There are two international airports, two *otogars* (bus stations) from which international services arrive and depart, and two international rail stations.

Flights, tours and rail tickets can be booked at www.lonelyplanet.com/travel_services.

## AIR
### Airlines

Most of İstanbul's airline offices are in the streets around Taksim Sq, particularly Cumhuriyet Caddesi (see Map p113), but Turkish Airlines has offices around the city. Travel agencies can also sell air tickets and make reservations. The two major airlines flying domestic routes are Turkish Airlines (www.thy.com) and Onur Air (www.onurair.com.tr), though Atlasjet (www.atlasjet.com), Sun Express (www.sunexpress.com) and Pegasus Airlines (www.flypgs.com) also fly routes.

### Airports

The city's main airport, Atatürk International Airport (Atatürk Hava Limanı; ☎ 212-465 5555; www.ataturkairport.com), is in Yeşilköy, 23km west of Sultanahmet. The international terminal (Dış Hatlar) is polished and organised. Close by, the domestic terminal (İç Hatlar) is smaller but no less efficient. The city's second international airport, Sabiha Gökçen International Airport ( ☎ 216-585 5000; www.sgairport.com) at Pendik/Kurtköy on the Asian side of the city, is popular with low-cost European airlines, but is not as conveniently located.

There are car-hire desks, exchange offices, stands of mobile-phone companies, a 24-hour pharmacy, ATMs and a PTT (post office) at the international arrivals area at Atatürk International Airport. There is also a Tourist Information Desk ( ☎ 212-465 3451; ◷ 9am-11pm) supplying maps, advice and brochures. A 24-hour supermarket is at the walkway to the metro. The 24-hour left-luggage service ( ☎ 212-465 3442) charges TL15 to TL20 per suitcase per 24 hours; you'll find the booth to your right as you exit customs.

One of the few annoying things about Atatürk airport is that travellers must pay to use a trolley on either side of immigration. You can pay in lira (TL1) or euros (€1), which you get back when you return the trolley.

There's a bank, mini-market and PTT at Sabiha Gökçen airport. Use of trolleys there is free of charge.

## BOAT
### Cruise Ships

Cruise ships arrive at the Karaköy International Maritime Passenger Terminal (Map pp102–3; ☎ 212-249 5776), just near the Galata Bridge.

### Ferries & Seabuses

The most enjoyable way to get around town is by ferry. Crossing between the Asian and

## FERRY TRAVEL

Ferries ply the following useful two-way routes:
- Beşiktaş-Kadıköy
- Beşiktaş-Üsküdar
- Eminönü-Anadolu Kavağı (Bosphorus Excursions Ferry)
- Eminönü-Kadıköy
- Eminönü-Üsküdar
- İstinye-Emirgan-Kanlıca-Anadolu Hisarı-Kandilli-Bebek-Arnavutköy-Çengelköy
- Kabataş-Kadıköy
- Kabataş-Kadıköy-Kınalıada-Burgazada-Heybeliada-Büyükada (Princes' Islands ferry)
- Kabataş-Üsküdar
- Karaköy-Kadıköy (some stop at Haydarpaşa)
- Karaköy-Üsküdar
- Sarıyer-Rumeli Kavağı-Anadolu Kavağı
- Sirkeci-Harem
- Üsküdar-Karaköy-Eminönü-Kasımpaşa-Fener-Balat-Hasköy-Ayvansaray-Sütlüce-Eyüp (Golden Horn Ferry)

## CLIMATE CHANGE & TRAVEL

Climate change is a serious threat to the ecosystems that humans rely upon, and air travel is the fastest-growing contributor to the problem. Lonely Planet regards travel, overall, as a global benefit, but believes we all have a responsibility to limit our personal impact on global warming.

### Flying & Climate Change

Pretty much every form of motorised travel generates carbon dioxide (the main cause of human-induced climate change) but planes are far and away the worst offenders, not just because of the sheer distances they allow us to travel, but because they release greenhouse gases high into the atmosphere. The statistics are frightening: two people taking a return flight between Europe and the US will contribute as much to climate change as an average household's gas and electricity consumption over a whole year.

### Carbon Offset Schemes

Climatecare.org and other websites use 'carbon calculators' that allow travellers to offset the level of greenhouse gases they are responsible for with financial contributions to sustainable travel schemes that reduce global warming – including projects in India, Honduras, Kazakhstan and Uganda.

Lonely Planet, together with Rough Guides and other concerned partners in the travel industry, support the carbon offset scheme run by climatecare.org. Lonely Planet offsets all of its staff and author travel.

For more information check out our website: www.lonelyplanet.com.

European shores, these vessels are as efficient as they are popular with locals. The İstanbul Deniz Otobüsleri (İDO; ☎ 212-444 4436; www.ido.com.tr) has fare and timetable information or you can pick up a printed timetable at an *iskelesi* (ferry dock).

On the European side, the major ferry docks are at the mouth of the Golden Horn (Eminönü, Sirkeci and Karaköy), at Beşiktaş and at Kabataş, 2km past the Galata Bridge, at the end of the tram line from the airport and Sultanahmet.

Information regarding ferry service times is found here and in the Ferry Trips chapter (p202). The ferries run to two annual timetables: winter (mid-September to mid-June) and summer (mid-June to mid-September). Tickets (*jetons*) are cheap (usually TL1.50) and it's possible to use an Akbil, İstanbulkart or beşiBiryerde card (see the boxed text p220) on most routes.

There are also *deniz otobüsü* and *hızlı feribot* (seabus and fast ferry) services, but these ply routes that are of less interest to the traveller; they are also more expensive than the conventional ferries. The most useful of these routes are Bostancı-Karaköy-Eminönü, Yenikapı-Bandırma (for İzmir), Sarayburnu-Avşa, Kadıköy-Kabataş-Sariyer and Kabataş-Princes' Islands-Bostancı.

## BUS

The Büyük İstanbul Otogarı (Big İstanbul Bus Station; ☎ 212-658 0505; www.otogaristanbul.com, in Turkish) is the city's main bus station for both inter-city and international routes. Called simply the *otogar* (bus station), it's in the western district of Bayrampaşa, just south of the expressway and about 10km west of Sultanahmet. There's an ATM here, a few cafes and unspeakably filthy toilets. The LRT service from Aksaray stops here (Otogar stop) on its way from the airport; you can catch this to Aksaray and then connect with a tram to Sultanahmet. If you're going to Beyoğlu, bus 83O leaves from the centre of the *otogar* every 15 minutes between 5.50am and 8.45pm and takes approximately one hour to reach Taksim Sq. Bus 91O leaves for Eminönü every 15 to 25 minutes between 6am and 8.45pm; the trip takes approximately 50 minutes. Both trips cost TL1.50. A taxi will cost approximately TL25 to Sultanahmet, TL30 to Taksim.

Some bus companies offer a free *servis* (shuttle bus) between the *otogar* and Taksim Sq. If you're booking a ticket out of İstanbul from a bus office in Taksim (or elsewhere), ask about this service. You'll be asked to front up at the bus office around an hour before your bus is due to leave and a minibus will pick you up and take you from the office to your bus at the *otogar*. If you've just arrived by bus in İstanbul, ask your bus driver about a *servis* to the company's bus office in Taksim or elsewhere.

There's a smaller bus station on the Asian shore of the Bosphorus at Harem (Map pp46–7;

☎ 216-333 3763), south of Üsküdar and north of Haydarpaşa train station. If you're arriving in İstanbul by bus from anywhere on the Anatolian side of Turkey, it's always quicker to get out at Harem and take the car ferry to Sirkeci/Eminönü (TL1.50; every 30 minutes from 7am to 10.30pm); if you stay on the bus until the *otogar*, you'll add at least an hour to your journey. If you're going the other way, you may want to catch your bus here, instead of at the *otogar*; if your destination is serviced by frequent buses (eg Ankara or Antalya) you should have no trouble arriving at the Harem *otogar* and buying a ticket on the spot; if there are fewer services (eg Cappadocia) you should reserve your ticket by calling the bus line ahead of time, requesting that you board at Harem instead of the Büyük *otogar*.

## City Buses

The bus system in İstanbul is extremely efficient, though traffic congestion in the city means that bus trips can be very long. The introduction of Metrobüs lines (where buses are given dedicated traffic lanes) aims to relieve this problem, but these tend to service residential suburbs out of the city centre and are thus of limited benefit to travellers. The major bus stands are at Taksim Sq, Beşiktaş, Aksaray, Eminönü (Rüstempaşa), Kadıköy and Üsküdar, and most services run between 6.30am and 9pm. Destinations

## GETTING INTO TOWN

### Atatürk International Airport

A taxi from the airport to Sultanahmet or Taksim Sq costs around TL30, more if it's between midnight and 6am or if there's heavy traffic.

There's a quick, cheap Light Rail Transit (LRT) service from the airport to Zeytinburnu, from where it's easy to connect with the tram to Sultanahmet, Eminönü and Kabataş (for Taksim Sq). The LRT station is on the lower ground floor beneath the international departures hall – follow the 'Rapid Transit' signs down the escalators and through the underground walkway. A ticket costs a mere TL1.50 and services depart every 10 minutes or so from 5.40am until 1.40am. When you get off the LRT, the tram platform is right in front of you. You'll need to buy another ticket (TL1.50) and pass through the turnstiles to board the tram. If you miss the stop at Zeytinburnu (try not to), you can continue on the LRT to Aksaray and then walk to the Yusufpaşa tram stop. To find this, exit the station, cross over busy Adnan Menderes Bulvarı and turn right at the Murat Paşa mosque. A short walk will bring you to another major street, Turgut Özal Caddesi (Millet Caddesi), where the tram stop is located. Walk onto the overpass and down the steps in the middle of the road to access the stop (direction: Kabataş). Ticket kiosks are located at the stop. The tram makes its way down Divan Yolu to Sultanahmet and Eminönü, across the Galata Bridge and on to Kabataş, from where you can change to a funicular running uphill to Taksim Sq. The entire trip from the airport takes around 50 to 60 minutes to Sultanahmet, 60 to 70 minutes to Eminönü and 85 to 95 minutes to Taksim.

If you are staying near Taksim Sq, the Havaş airport bus ( ☎ 212-444 0487; www.havas.com.tr) from Atatürk International Airport is even more convenient. This departs from outside the arrivals hall. Buses leave every 15 to 30 minutes between 4am and 1am; the trip takes between 40 minutes and one hour, depending on traffic. Tickets cost TL10 (25% more after midnight or before 6am) and the bus stops outside the Havaş ticket office (Map p113) on Cumhuriyet Caddesi, just off Taksim Sq.

Many hotels will provide a free pick-up service from Atatürk airport if you stay with them for three nights or more. There are also a number of cheap (but very slow) shuttle-bus services from hotels to the airport for your return trip. Check details with your hotel.

### Sabiha Gökçen International Airport

Taxis from this airport to the city are expensive. To Taksim you'll be looking at between TL60 and TL70; more if it's after midnight or if the traffic is heavy. To Sultanahmet you'll be looking at anywhere between TL80 and TL90 depending on the time of day and the traffic conditions.

The Havaş airport bus ( ☎ 212-243 3399; www.havas.com.tr) travels from the airport to Taksim Sq 25 minutes after flights land. Tickets cost TL12 and the trip takes approximately one hour. If you're heading towards the Old City, you'll then need to take the funicular to Kabataş and the tram from Kabataş to Sultanahmet.

Hotels rarely provide free pick-up services from Sabiha Gökçen. Shuttle-bus services from hotels to the airport for return trips are infrequent – check details with your hotel.

## PUBLIC TRANSPORT OPERATORS

İstanbul Elektrik Tramvay ve Tünel (İETT) is responsible for running public buses, funiculars and historic trams in the city. Its excellent website (www.iett.gov.tr) has useful timetable and route information in Turkish and English. Metro, tramvay and LRT services are run by İstanbul Ulaşım (www.istanbul-ulasim.com.tr) and the ferries are run by İstanbul Deniz Otobüsleri (İDO; www.ido.com.tr).

and main stops on city bus routes are shown on a sign on the right (kerb) side of the bus (*otobüs*) or on the electronic display at its front.

İETT buses (www.iett.gov.tr) are run by the city and you must have a ticket (TL1.50) before boarding. Buy tickets from the white booths near major stops and bus, tram and metro stations, or from some nearby shops for a small mark-up (look for 'İETT *otobüs bileti satılır*'). Think about buying a beşiBiryerde card, which will cover five trips. You can also use an İstanbulkart and save some money. Private buses regulated by the city called *Özel Halk Otobüsü* often run the same routes; these accept cash (pay the conductor) and some accept İstanbulkarts.

## Intercity & International Buses

Many bus offices are in Beyoğlu, near Taksim Sq, on Mete and İnönü Caddesis, as well as at the Büyük *otogar* (see p216). This is a list of the top national lines:

Kamil Koç (Map pp102–3; ☎ 444 0562 or otogar 212-658 2000; www.kamilkoc.com.tr in Turkish; İnönü Caddesi 31, Taksim) Services most major cities throughout Turkey.

Metro Turizm ( ☎ 444 3455 or Sultanahmet 212-513 7119; www.metroturizm.com.tr; Divan Yolu Caddesi 16, Sultanahmet) Services most major cities and towns throughout Turkey.

Ulusoy (Map pp102–3; ☎ 444 1888; www.ulusoy.com.tr; İnönü Caddesi 59, Taksim) Ulusoy runs twice-weekly buses to and from Greece, Germany and France, as well as services to most major cities in Turkey.

Varan Turizm (Map pp102–3; ☎ 212-251 7474; www.varan.com.tr; İnönü Caddesi 19B, Taksim) Varan is a premium line with routes to major Turkish cities and to Greece, Austria and Bulgaria.

# CAR
## Driving

It makes no sense to drive in İstanbul. The traffic is hectic, free parking is scarce and drivers can be aggressive. If you have a car, we suggest leaving it at your hotel or in a car park (*otopark*) and using public transport, except perhaps for excursions out of the city.

Drivers must have a valid driving licence. An International Driving Permit (IDP) is required for stays of more than three months, or if your licence is from a locality that a Turkish police officer is likely to find obscure. Drive on the right-hand side of the road. When this book went to print, speed limits were 50km/h in urban areas, 90km/h on highways and 120km/h on motorways, but the Interior Ministry had announced plans to raise the two lower limits to 55 km/h and 110 km/h.

The Türkiye Turing ve Otomobil Kurumu (TTOK, Turkish Touring & Automobile Club; ☎ 212-282 8140; www.turing.org.tr; Oto Sanayi Sitesi Yanı 4, Levent) can supply licence, insurance and other information you'll need to hire a car or bring your own vehicle into the country.

## Hire

You need to be at least 21 years old, with a year's driving experience, to be able to rent a car. You must pay with a major credit card, or you will be required to make a large cash deposit. Most rental cars have standard gearshift;

## MARVELLOUS MARMARAY

Marmaray (www.marmaray.com) is an ambitious public transport infrastructure project aimed at relieving İstanbul's serious traffic congestion. It involves rebuilding the rail line that currently stretches between Yeşilköy on the coast and Sirkeci train station on the Golden Horn (Haliç; the stretch between Yedikule and Sirkeci will go underground, and Yedikule will become the major transport hub on the European side of the city. The line will continue from Sirkeci via a tunnel underneath the Bosphorus to another new underground station in Üsküdar, which will become the major hub on the Asian side of the city, before terminating at Söğütlüçesme, past Kadıköy.

The project's completion date was originally slated as 2010, but important archaeological finds made during excavation works have slowed the process down. These include the site of a Byzantine harbour complete with boats at Yenikapı and an ancient port and bazaar at Üsküdar. It's now thought that the new rail line will open in 2012.

you'll pay more to have automatic transmission and air-conditioning.

Rental cars are moderately expensive in Turkey, partly due to huge excise taxes paid when the cars are purchased. A week's rental will be between TL500 and TL1000, depending on the type of car and the time of year. Child safety seats are usually available for an extra charge (around TL15 per day).

Mandatory third-party liability insurance and KDV (value-added tax) are included in the standard charge. Optional collision damage waiver, theft protection and SOS personal accident and health insurance are also offered by all companies for an extra cost.

If your car incurs any accident damage, or if you cause any, do not move the car before finding a police officer and asking for a *kaza raporu* (accident report). The officer may ask you to submit to a breath-alcohol test. Contact your car-rental company within 48 hours. Your insurance coverage may be void if it can be shown that you were operating under the influence of alcohol or other drugs, were speeding, or if you did not submit the required accident report within 48 hours.

The agencies listed below are among many with 24-hour booths at the arrivals hall at Atatürk International Airport:

Avis (www.avis.com.tr) Atatürk International Airport ( ☎ 212-465 3455/56); Sabiha Gökçen Airport ( ☎ 216-585 5154); Taksim ( ☎ 212-297 9610; Abdülhakhamit Caddesi 72a)

Budget (www.budget.com.tr) Atatürk International Airport ( ☎ 212-663 0808); Sabiha Gökçen Airport ( ☎ 216-444 4722); Taksim ( ☎ 212-297 4393; Abdülhakhamit Caddesi 68a)

Hertz (www.hertz.com.tr) Atatürk International Airport ( ☎ 212-465 5999); Sabiha Gökçen Airport ( ☎ 216-588 0141); Taksim ( ☎ 212-225 6404; 1st fl, Yedikuyular Caddesi 4, Elmadağ)

National (www.nationalcar.com) Atatürk International Airport ( ☎ 212-465 3546); Taksim ( ☎ 212-254 7719; Aydede Sokak 1/2)

## DOLMUŞ

A *dolmuş* is a shared minibus; it waits at a specified departure point until it has a full complement of passengers (in Turkish, *dolmuş* means full), then follows a fixed route to its destination. Destinations are displayed in the window of the *dolmuş*. Passengers flag down the driver to get on and indicate to the driver when they want to get off, usually

by saying '*inecek var!*' (someone wants to get out!). Fares vary (pay on board) but are usually the same as municipal buses. *Dolmuşes* are almost as comfortable as taxis, run later into the night in many instances and often ply routes that buses and other forms of transport don't service.

## FUNICULAR & CABLE-CAR

There are two funiculars (*funiküleri*) and one cable-car (*teleferic*) in the city.

An antique funicular called the Tünel carries passengers between Karaköy, at the base of the Galata Bridge (Galata Köprüsü), to Tünel Sq, the southwestern end of İstiklal Caddesi. A fare costs TL1.

The second funicular carries passengers from Kabataş – at the end of the tramline from Zeytinburnu, through the Old City and over the Galata Bridge – to Taksim Sq in Taksim, where it connects to the metro. It runs every day between 6.10am and 12.50am and a fare costs TL1.50.

A cable-car runs between the waterside at Eyüp to the Pierre Loti Café (TL1.50).

All are short trips (approximately three minutes). Transport cards or Akbil can be used.

## LIGHT RAIL TRANSIT (LRT)

The excellent LRT service connects Aksaray with the airport, stopping at 16 stations, including the *otogar*, along the way. Trains leave every 10 minutes or so from 5.40am to 1.40am. There are plans to extend the service to Yenikapı. Tickets cost TL1.50 and Akbil and transport cards can be used.

## METRO

A modern metro system connects Şişhane, near Tünel Sq in Beyoğlu, and Atatürk Oto Sanayi in Maslak, the city's financial centre. Unfortunately, it's not possible to travel between the two points in one trip – one metro runs between Şişhane and Taksim Sq; another runs between Taksim and Levent 4, stopping at Osmanbey, Şişli, Gayrettepe and Levent en route; and a third runs between Levent 4 and Atatürk Oto Sanayi, stopping at Sanayi Mahallesi and İTÜ Ayazağa. The full trip takes 30 to 40 minutes. Services run every five minutes or so from 6.15am to 12.30am Monday to Thursday, 6.15am to 1am on Friday and Saturday and 6.30am to 12.20am on Sunday. Tickets cost TL1.50 and transport cards or Akbil can be used.

## TRANSPORT CARDS

İstanbul's public transport system is excellent, and for many years the Akbil system was one of its best features. These small electronic tags could be purchased with a refundable deposit of TL6, recharged with cash and then used to access easy discounted travel across the system. The Akbil system is in the process of being slowly phased out, and will be replaced by two transport cards that can be used on the city's ferries, İETT buses, LRT, trams, metro and funiculars:

- **İstanbulkart** Similar to London's Oyster Card, Hong Kong's Octopus Card and Paris' Navigo, the İstanbulkart offers a considerable discount on fares (TL1.30 as opposed to the usual TL1.50, with additional transfers within a two-hour journey window being only TL0.65). The cards can be purchased and recharged at machines at ferry docks, metro stations and bus stations. They're simple to operate: as you enter a bus or pass through the turnstile at a ferry dock or metro station, swipe your card for entry and the fare will automatically be deducted from your balance.

- **beşiBiryerde Card** Named after traditional Turkish jewellery consisting of five pieces of gold, this nonrecharge-able five-fare card costs TL7.50 and is available from machines and ticket booths at ferry docks, metro stations, some tram stops and bus stations.

Works are currently underway to extend the Taksim-Şişhane route over the Golden Horn via a new metro bridge and under the Old City to Yenikapı via stops at Unkapanı, and Şehzadebaşı. It will then connect with the LRT to Aksaray and with a transport tunnel being built under the Bosphorus as part of the Marmaray project (boxed text p218). This tunnel will include a metro connection between Yenikapı, Sirkeci, Üsküdar and Söğütlüçesme. Other works underway include construction of a 16-stop metro line running between Kadıköy and Kartal on the Asian side of town.

See p219 for details of the one-stop Tünel underground system between Karaköy and Tünel Sq and the funicular from Kabataş to Taksim Sq.

## TAXI

İstanbul is full of yellow taxis. Some drivers are lunatics, others are con artists; most are neither. If you're caught with the first category and you're about to go into meltdown, say 'yavaş!' (careful/slow down!). Drivers in the second of these categories – the con artists – tend to prey on tourists. All taxis have digital meters and must run them, but some of these drivers ask for a flat fare, or pretend the meter doesn't work so they can gouge you at the end of the run. The best way to counter this is to tell them no meter, no ride.

A base rate (drop rate, flag fall) is levied during the daytime (gündüz); the nighttime (gece) rate, from midnight to 6am, is 50% higher. Meters, with LCD displays, flash 'gündüz' or 'gece' when they are started. Occasionally, drivers try to put the nighttime (gece) rate on during the day, so watch out.

During the day a taxi from Beyoğlu to Sultanahmet costs around TL12; from Sultanahmet to Beyoğlu expect to pay TL14.

Few taxis have seatbelts. If you catch a taxi over either of the Bosphorus Bridges, it is your responsibility to cover the toll. The driver will add this to your fare.

## TRAIN
### Long-Distance Trains

When this book went to print, all trains from Europe were terminating at Sirkeci Train Station (Map pp50–1; Ankara Caddesi, Sirkeci), right next to Eminönü. Outside the station's main door there's a convenient tram up the hill to Sultanahmet, Beyazıt and Zeytinburnu and across the Galata Bridge to Kabataş, from where you can catch a funicular to Taksim Sq. Note that after the Marmaray Project (boxed text p218) is finished, trains will terminate at Yenikapı.

International services from Sirkeci include the Bosfor Ekspresi service leaving at 10pm daily going to Bucharest, Romania (TL107 to TL330 depending on which class you travel, 19½ hours). There is also a slow daily sleeping-car service (the Dostluk/Filia Ekspresi) to Thessaloniki (TL123 to TL196, 11 hours) departing at 9pm, where you can connect with trains to Athens. To book seats, call the reservation office at Haydarpaşa Railway Station.

Trains from the Asian side of Turkey, and from points east and south, were terminating at Haydarpaşa Train Station (Map p123; ☎ 216-336 4470; Haydarpaşa İstasyon Caddesi, Kadıköy), on the Asian shore of the Bosphorus close to Kadıköy. After the Marmaray Project (boxed text p218) is finished, trains will terminate at Üsküdar.

Ignore anyone who suggests you should take a taxi to or from Haydarpaşa; it's expensive and slow whereas the ferry from the station to Karaköy is cheap, convenient, pleasant and speedy. From Karaköy you can catch a tram to Sultanahmet or to Kabataş (for Taksim Sq).

Services from Haydarpaşa include regular departures to Ankara (TL15 to TL120, 5½ hours). The first stage of a new high-speed service between the two cities opened in 2009 and the second and final stage is expected to be completed by the end of 2010. The new service will cut the trip time to slightly over three hours.

International services from Haydarpaşa have traditionally included the *Transasya Espress* to Tehran and the *Toros Espress* to Aleppo, but both services have been halted while the Ankara-İstanbul high-speed train line is completed.

Haydarpaşa contains a left-luggage room (*emanet*), a restaurant that serves alcoholic beverages, numerous snack shops, left-luggage lockers, ATMs and a small post office (PTT).

## Local Trains

There are two suburban train lines (*banliyö treni*) in İstanbul. The first rattles along the Sea of Marmara shore from Sirkeci Train Station, around Seraglio Point to Cankurtaran,

Kumkapı, Yenikapı and a number of stations before it terminates past Atatürk International Airport at Halkalı. This is currently being rebuilt (see the boxed text, p218) and parts of it will be incorporated into the metro system. The second line runs from Haydarpaşa railway station to Gebze, via Bostancı and will also be rebuilt as part of the Marmaray Project. When this book went to print the trains were dirty and decrepit but reasonably reliable (nearly every half-hour) and cheap (TL1.50). Travel cards and Akbil could be used.

## TRAM

An excellent tramway (*tramvay*) service runs from Zeytinburnu (where it connects with the airport LRT) to Sultanahmet and Eminönü. It then crosses the Galata Bridge to Karaköy (to connect with the Tünel) and Kabataş (to connect with the funicular to Taksim Sq). In the near future, it will be extended from Kabataş to the ferry dock at Beşiktaş. Services run every five minutes from 6am to midnight. The fare is TL1.50 and travel cards can be used.

A two-stop antique tram runs along İstiklal Caddesi between Tünel Sq and Taksim Sq in Beyoğlu (TL1); travel cards and Akbil can be used.

A tram also runs between Kadıköy Sq on the Asian side and the exclusive residential suburb of Moda.

# DIRECTORY

## BUSINESS HOURS

Opening hours vary wildly across businesses and services in İstanbul. Actual opening hours are cited with every restaurant, bar, shop and museum listing throughout this book. The following is a very general guide:

**Banks** 8.30am to noon and 1.30pm to 5pm Monday to Friday.

**Grocery shops** 6am or 7am to 7pm or 8pm.

**Offices** Government and business hours are usually 8am or 9am to noon and 1.30pm to 5pm Monday to Friday; however during Ramazan (p225) the work day is shortened.

**Post Offices** 8.30am to 12.30pm and 1.30pm to 5.30pm.

**Shops** 9am to 6pm or 7pm Monday to Saturday; some shops close for lunch (noon to 1.30pm or 2.30pm); some stay open late and others are open seven days.

## CHILDREN

Your child (*çocuk*) or children (*çocuklar*) will be treated indulgently in İstanbul. Given the high Turkish birth rate, they'll have lots of company, too. The larger hotels can arrange for day-care (*kreş*) and baby-sitting services. Charges are usually negotiated directly with the childcare centre or babysitter. Chains including Mothercare have opened large stores in major shopping malls such as Cevahir and Akmerkez (p142), and stock everything you could possibly need. Disposable nappies (*bebek bezi*), formula and fortified rice cereal are sold at supermarkets. Highchairs in restaurants and cafes are the exception rather than the rule.

Lonely Planet's *Travel with Children* offers useful general advice for families travelling with children.

## CLIMATE

The best times to visit İstanbul are during spring and autumn, roughly from April to May and from September to October, when the climate is perfect. During July and August it is hot and steamy; a lot of İstanbullus head for the west and south coasts over these months. Chill winter winds and snow are common in winter.

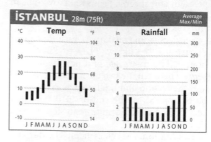

## CONSULATES

Embassies (*büyükelçiliği*) are in Ankara, the national capital. The following countries are among many who have consulates (*konsolosluğu*) in İstanbul; for other consulates check the Embassy & Consulate finder at www.yellowpages.com.tr.

**Australia** ( ☎ 212-243 1333; www.turkey.embassy.gov.au; Asker Ocağı Caddesi 15, Suzer Plaza Kat 16, Elmadağ)

**Canada** (Map pp102–3; ☎ 212-251 9838; www.canada international.gc.ca/turkey-turquie; İstiklal Caddesi 189/Kat 5, Beyoğlu)

**Egypt** ( ☎ 212-324 2133; Akasyalı Sokak 26, 4 Levent) This is a temporary office while the consulate's building in Bebek is being renovated.

**France** (Map pp102–3; ☎ 212-334 8730; www.consul france-istanbul.org, in French; İstiklal Caddesi 4-8, Taksim)

**Germany** (Map pp102–3; ☎ 212-334 6100; www.istan bul.diplo.de, in German; İnönü Caddesi 16-18, Gümüşsuyu)

**Greece** (Map pp102–3; ☎ 212-393 8291; Turnacıbaşı Sokak 22, Galatasaray)

**Iran** ( ☎ 212-513 8230; Ankara Caddesi 1/Kat 2, Cağaloğlu)

**Israel** ( ☎ 212-317 6500; http://istanbul.mfa.gov.il; Büyükudere Caddesi, Yapı Kredi Plaza, Blok C, Kat 7, Levent)

**Italy** (Map pp102–3; ☎ 212-243 1024; www.consistan bul.esteri.it; Palazzo di Venezia, Tomtom Kaptan Sokak 5, Galatasaray)

**Japan** ( ☎ 212-317 4600; www.istanbul.tr.emb-japan.go.jp, in Japanese; Büyükdere Caddesi 2-9, Tekfen Tower Kat 10, 4 Levent)

**Netherlands** (Map pp102–3; ☎ 212-393 2121; www.mfa.nl/ist; İstiklal Caddesi 197, Tünel)

New Zealand ( ☎ 212-244 0272; İnönü Caddesi 92, Kat 3, Gümüşsuyu)

Syria (Map p113; ☎ 212-232 6721; Maçka Caddesi 59, Ralli Apt Kat 3, Teşvikiye)

UK (Map pp102–3; ☎ 212-334 6400; Meşrutiyet Caddesi 34, Tepebaşı)

USA ( ☎ 212-335 9000; http://istanbul.usconsulate.gov; Kaplıcalar Mevkii 2, İstinye)

# COURSES
## Belly & Gypsy Dance

Les Arts Turcs (Map pp50–1; ☎ 212-527 6859, 638 1215; www.lesartsturcs.com; İncili Çavuş Sokak 37, Kat 3, Sultanahmet; ✆ 10am-8pm) can organise private lessons in Turkish-style belly dancing or Rom (Gypsy) dancing for TL55 per 1½ hours.

## Cooking

See p146 for details of cooking courses in İstanbul.

## Handicrafts

The historic Caferağa Medresesi (p69; ☎ 212-513 3601; www.tkhv.org; Caferiye Sokak, Sultanahmet) is the home of the Turkish Cultural Services Foundation, which runs courses for locals and travellers in techniques such as calligraphy, miniature painting, ecru (paper marbling), binding and glass painting. Courses are organised into 2½-hour sessions one day per week over three months and cost approximately TL400. It also occasionally organises shorter courses costing TL120.

Les Arts Turcs (see above) runs workshops with artisans specialising in calligraphy, henna design, carpet design, ecru and textile and ceramic design. These cost TL40 for a two-hour class.

## Language

The best-known Turkish-language courses for native English speakers are run by Taksim Dilmer (Map pp102–3; ☎ 212-292 9696; www.dilmer.com; Tarık Zafer Tunaya Sokak 16, Taksim). On offer are eight-week courses (96 hours total) costing €384; four-week courses (80 hours total) costing €320; eight-week evening courses (72 hours total) costing €288; and 12-week weekend courses (72 hours total) costing €288. Classes have a maximum of 14 students.

# CUSTOMS REGULATIONS

İstanbul's Atatürk International Airport uses the red and green channel system, randomly spot-checking passengers' luggage. Items valued over US$15,000 must be declared and may be entered in your passport to guarantee that you take the goods out of the country. You're allowed to bring one 100cc bottle or two 75cc bottles of alcohol, one carton (200) of cigarettes, 1kg of coffee and 10 cigars. There's no limit to the amount of Turkish liras or foreign currency you can bring into the country, but you must declare any amount over €10,000. It's illegal to take antiquities out of the country. Check www.gumruk.gov.tr for more information.

# ELECTRICITY

Electricity in İstanbul is supplied at 220V, 50Hz, as in Europe. Plugs (fiş) are of the European variety, with two round prongs. There are infrequent power cuts across the city, so it's a good idea to travel with a torch (flashlight) in your bag or pocket.

# EMERGENCY

Ambulance ( ☎ 112)

Fire ( ☎ 110)

Police ( ☎ 155)

Tourism police ( ☎ 212-527 4503)

# GAY & LESBIAN TRAVELLERS

Homosexuality isn't illegal in Turkey, but neither is it officially legal. There's an ambivalent attitude towards it among the general population, though there are sporadic reports of violence towards gay people, and conservative İstanbullus frown upon open displays of affection between persons of the same sex.

Lambda (Map pp102–3; ☎ 212-245 7068; www.lambda istanbul.org; Tel Sokak 28/Kat 5, Beyoğlu; ✆ 3-8pm) is the Turkish branch of the international Gay, Lesbian, Bisexual and Transgender Liberation Group.

The monthly Time Out İstanbul magazine includes gay and lesbian listings. The quarterly Kaos GL (www.kaosgl.com) is the country's only gay and lesbian magazine. The printed edition is in Turkish only, but articles in the free web edition are also in English.

Pride Travel Agency (Map pp50–1; ☎ 212-527 0671; www.travelagencyturkey.com; İncili Çavuş Sokak 33/11, Ateş

Pasajı Kat 2, Sultanahmet) is a well-regarded gay-owned and gay-run travel agency specialising in booking accommodation and tours for gay travellers.

Mehmet Murat Somer's Hop-Çıkı-Yaya series of gay crime novels feature a transvestite amateur sleuth and are entertaining reads. They include *The Prophet Murders* (2008), *The Kiss Murders* (2009) and *The Gigolo Murders* (2009).

For more information about gay and lesbian issues in the city, see the boxed text, p173.

# HEALTH
## Food & Water

Travellers in Turkey experience a fair amount of travellers diarrhoea (the sultan's revenge) and it's possible that you'll pick up a bout in İstanbul, particularly if you eat street food (see the boxed text p159).

### DINING PRECAUTIONS

In *lokantas* (restaurants) choose dishes that look freshly prepared and sufficiently hot.

Beware of milk products and dishes containing milk that have not been properly refrigerated. If you want a rice pudding (*sütlaç*) or some such dish with milk in it, choose a shop that has lots of them in the window, meaning that a batch has been made recently. In general, choose things from trays, pots etc that are fairly full rather than almost empty. Eating some fresh yogurt every day can also help to keep your digestive system in good condition.

### DRINKING PRECAUTIONS

Tap water in İstanbul is chlorinated, but is still not guaranteed to be safe (many locals don't drink it). Spring water is sold everywhere in 0.33L, 1.5L and 3L plastic bottles and is very cheap.

## Illnesses
### FOOD POISONING
### & TRAVELLERS DIARRHOEA

Food-poisoning symptoms are headaches, nausea and/or stomachache, diarrhoea, fever and chills. If you get food poisoning, go to bed and stay warm. Drink lots of fluids; preferably hot tea without sugar or milk. Chamomile tea (*papatya çay*) can ease a queasy stomach.

Simple things like a change of water, food or climate can all cause a mild bout of diarrhoea, but a few rushed toilet trips with no other symptoms is not indicative of a major problem.

Dehydration is the main danger with any diarrhoea, particularly in children or the elderly, as dehydration can occur quite quickly.

Gut-paralysing drugs such as loperamide or diphenoxylate can be used to bring relief from the symptoms, although they do not actually cure the problem. Only use these drugs if you do not have access to toilets, eg if you *must* travel. Note that these drugs are not recommended for children under 12 years.

If you experience diarrhoea with blood or mucus (dysentery), any diarrhoea with fever, profuse watery diarrhoea, persistent diarrhoea not improving after 48 hours or severe diarrhoea, antibiotics may be required. These symptoms suggest a more serious cause of diarrhoea and in these situations gut-paralysing drugs should be avoided. A stool test may be necessary to diagnose what bug is causing your diarrhoea, so seek medical help urgently.

Fluid replacement is important. Weak black tea with a little sugar, soda water or soft drinks allowed to go flat and diluted 50% with bottled water are all good. You need to drink at least the same volume of fluid that you are losing in bowel movements and vomiting. Urine is the best guide to the adequacy of replacement – if you have small amounts of concentrated urine, you need to drink more. Keep drinking small amounts often. Stick to a bland diet as you recover.

## Other Health Risks

Turks smoke like chimneys. Even though non-smoking areas in public places are starting to be introduced, you'll find İstanbul challenging if you are asthmatic or allergic and have difficulty coping with cigarette smoke.

## Vaccinations

You need no special inoculations before entering Turkey unless you're coming from an endemic or epidemic area. However, do discuss your requirements with a doctor. Consider typhoid fever and hepatitis A and B vaccinations if you plan to travel off the beaten track in Turkey; also make sure that your tetanus/diphtheria and polio vaccinations are up to date (boosters are necessary every 10 years).

A rabies vaccination should be considered for those who plan to stay for a month or longer in Turkey, where rabies is common. Rabid dogs have been a problem in İstanbul in the recent past, but the council now vaccinates dogs (the yellow tag on the ear shows they've been vaccinated) and the danger seems to have been alleviated somewhat.

# HOLIDAYS

The official Turkish calendar is the Gregorian (Western) one. Friday is the Muslim holy day, but it is not a holiday. The day of rest, a secular one, is Sunday.

## Religious Holidays

Religious festivals, two of which (Şeker Bayramı and Kurban Bayramı) are public holidays, are celebrated according to the Muslim lunar Hejira calendar. As the lunar year is about 11 days shorter than the Gregorian one, Muslim festivals occur 11 days earlier each year.

Muslim days begin at sundown. Thus a Friday holiday will begin on Thursday at sunset and last until Friday at sunset.

For major religious and civic holidays there is also a half-day vacation for preparation, called *arife*, preceding the start of a festival; shops and offices close about noon, and the festival begins at sunset.

Day-to-day business in İstanbul shuts down during religious holidays, and roads and flights out of town are full of locals escaping to the coast or mountains. Hotels in town and flights into the city can be busy with people from other parts of Turkey and the Middle East who have decided to escape to İstanbul.

### RAMAZAN (RAMADAN)

During the Holy Month of Ramazan, called Ramadan in other Muslim countries, a good Muslim lets *nothing* pass the lips during daylight: no eating, drinking or smoking.

The fast is broken traditionally with flat *pide* (bread). Lavish *iftar* (breaking of the fast) dinners are given and may last far into the night. Before dawn, drummers circulate throughout the town to awaken the faithful so they can eat before sunrise.

Although many İstanbullus observe the fast, most restaurants and cafes open to serve non-Muslims and locals who are not fasting. However, it's polite to avoid ostentatious public smoking, eating, drinking and drunkenness during this period.

Ramazan starts on or near 11 August 2010, 1 August 2011 and 20 July 2012. The 27th day of Ramazan is *Kadir Gecesi* (Night of Power) when the Quran was revealed and Mohammed appointed the Messenger of God.

Also see the boxed text p59.

### ŞEKER BAYRAMI

This is a three-day festival at the end of Ramazan. *Şeker* (shek-*ehr*) is sugar or candy. During this festival children traditionally go door to door asking for sweet treats, Muslims exchange greeting cards and pay social calls, and everybody enjoys drinking lots of tea in broad daylight after fasting for Ramazan. The festival is a national holiday when banks and offices are closed, and hotels, buses, trains and planes are heavily booked.

### KURBAN BAYRAMI

Called Eid al-Adha in Arabic countries, this is the most important religious holiday of the year. Meaning Sacrifice Holiday, it is a four-day festival commemorating Abraham's near-sacrifice of his son on Mt Moriah (Genesis 22; Quran, Sura 37). Right after the early-morning prayers on the actual day of Bayram, the head of the household sacrifices a sheep. A feast is prepared, with much of the meat going to charity. Almost everything closes, including banks, and public transport is crowded with families heading for their ancestral homes, usually in the country.

## Secular Holidays

Banks, offices and government services close for the day on the following secular public holidays:

New Year's Day 1 January

National Sovereignty & Children's Day 23 April

May Day 1 May

Youth & Sports Day 19 May

Victory Day 30 August

Republic Day 29 October

# INTERNET ACCESS

There are internet cafes all over İstanbul, usually filled with young men playing computer games and using Facebook. Look for internet cafes that advertise having an ADSL connection; other places can be frustratingly slow. Most hostels and hotels now also offer wi-fi internet access for their guests.

When in a local internet cafe, you may have to use a Turkish keyboard, in which case you need to be aware that Turkish has two 'i's: the familiar dotted 'i' and the less familiar dotless 'ı'. Unfortunately the one in the usual place is the dotless 'ı' on a Turkish keyboard; you will need to make sure you use the correct dotted 'i' when typing in a web or email address. To create the @ symbol, hold down the 'q' and the right-hand ALT keys at the same time.

The following places have relatively fast connections and staff who know what they're talking about.

Café Turka Internet Café (Map pp50–1; ☎ 212-514 6551; Divan Yolu Caddesi 22/2, Sultanahmet; per hr TL2; ☾ 9am-2am) This place is always full of backpackers and Sultanahmet locals. It's on the 2nd floor above SDC Turizm.

Robin Hood Internet (Map pp102–3; ☎ 212-244 8959; Yeniçarşı Caddesi 24/4, Galatasaray; per hr TL2; ☾ 10am-10pm Mon-Sat, noon-9pm Sun) Opposite the Galatasaray Lycée, this friendly place has lots of terminals inside and wi-fi access on its balcony. It's on the 4th floor up a steep flight of stairs.

## MAPS

Free maps in several different languages are usually available from tourist information offices, including the desk at the arrivals hall at Atatürk International Airport. For more detailed guidance, look for MepMedya's two-volume İlçe İlçe A'dan Z'ye İstanbul city plan and map; TL75). You can find it at Türkiye Diyanrt Vakfı (Map pp50–1; ☎ 212-511 4432; Baniali Caddesi 40, Cağaloğlu; ☾ 9am-7pm Mon-Sat) or İstanbul Kitapçsi (Map pp102–3; ☎ 212-292 7692; İstiklal Caddesi 379, Beyoğlu; ☾ 10am-6.45pm Mon-Sat, noon-6.45pm Sun).

## MEDICAL SERVICES

Turkey doesn't have reciprocal health-care arrangements with other countries, so having travel insurance is highly advisable.

For minor problems, it's customary to ask at a chemist/pharmacy (eczane) for advice. Sign language usually suffices to communicate symptoms and the pharmacist will prescribe treatment on the spot. Drugs requiring a prescription in Western countries are often sold over the counter (except for the most dangerous or addictive ones) and will often be cheaper, too. Ensure you know the generic name of your medicine; the commercial name may not be the same in Turkey. See the Language chapter for a list of medical terms; for a more comprehensive list, get a copy of Lonely

Planet's Turkish Phrasebook. The word for hospital is hastanesi.

Most doctors in Turkey speak English and half of all the physicians in İstanbul are women. If a woman visits a male doctor, it's customary to have a companion present during any physical examination or treatment, as there is not always a nurse available to serve in this role.

If it's an emergency and you want to try a public hospital, consider Taksim Hastanesi (Emergency Hospital; Map pp102–3; ☎ 212-2; Sıraselviler Caddesi, Cihangir; ☾ 24hr) The doctors speak English, and charges are the same whether you're a foreign visitor/resident or a Turkish citizen.

Though they are expensive, it's probably easiest to visit one of the private hospitals listed below if you need medical care when in İstanbul. The standard of care given by these places is generally quite high and you will have no trouble finding staff who speak English. Both accept credit-card payments and charge around TL180 for a standard consultation.

Alman Hastanesi (German Hospital; Map pp102–3; ☎ 212-293 2150; www.almanhastanesi.com.tr, in Turkish; Sıraselviler Caddesi 119, Taksim; ☾ 8.30am-6pm Mon-Fri, 8.30am-5pm Sat) This hospital is a few hundred metres south of Taksim Sq on the left-hand side. It has eye and dental clinics and English-speaking staff.

Vehbi Koç American Hospital (Amerikan Hastenesi; Map pp46–7; ☎ 212-44 3777, 212-311 2000; Güzelbahçe Sokak 20, Nişantaşı; ☾ 24hr emergency department) About 2km northeast of Taksim Sq, this hospital has English-speaking staff and a dental clinic.

## MONEY

The unit of currency is the Türk Lirası (Turkish Lira; TL). Coins come in amounts of 1, 5, 10, 25 and 50 kuruş and 1 lira, and notes in 5, 10, 20, 50, 100 and 200 lira. In 2003 the Turkish Government passed a law that allowed for the removal of six zeros from the lira. Don't accept any notes that have lots of zeros on them as this old currency is no longer valid.

In this book, we have cited prices for hotels and organised tours in euros, as this reflects the reality on the ground. All other prices are in TL.

Also see the exchange-rate table in the Quick Reference section on the inside front cover.

## ATMs

Automated teller machines (ATMs, cashpoints) are common in İstanbul. Virtually all of them offer instructions in English, French and German and will pay out Turkish liras when you insert your bank debit (cash) card. ATMs will also pay cash advances on Visa and MasterCard. The limit on cash withdrawals is generally TL600 to TL800 per day, though this varies from bank to bank.

All of the major Turkish banks and some smaller banks have ATMs; Akbank and Yapı Kredi are the most common. The specific machine you use must be reliably connected to the major ATM networks' computers via telephone lines. Look for stickers with the logos of these services (Cirrus, Maestro, Plus Systems etc) affixed to the machine. If the connection is not reliable, you may get a message saying that the transaction was refused by your bank (which may not be true) and your card will (hopefully) be returned to you.

## Changing Money

There are 24-hour exchange bureaux (*döviz bürosu*) in the arrivals hall at Atatürk International Airport that offer rates comparable to those offered by bureaux in the city. Count the money you're given carefully and save your currency-exchange receipts (*bordro*), as you may need them to reconvert Turkish liras at the end of your stay.

US dollars and euros are easily changed at exchange bureaux. They are also often accepted as payment without being changed. Rates are similar whichever bureau you go to, with the possible exception of those in the tourist precinct of Sultanahmet. Bureaux are open long hours (at a minimum, between 9am and 7pm). You will usually need to show your passport when changing cash.

As Turkish liras are fully convertible, there is no black market.

## Credit Cards

Most hotels, car-rental agencies, shops, pharmacies, entertainment venues and restaurants will accept Visa and Mastercard; Amex isn't as widely accepted as the others and Diner's is often not accepted. Budget hostels and hotels, and basic eateries such as *lokantas*, *pidecis*, *kebapçıs* and *börekçis*, usually accept cash only.

## Travellers Cheques

If you have travellers cheques, you will have to change them at a bank or post office. Exchange bureaux do not handle them. You'll need to show your passport.

# NEWSPAPERS & MAGAZINES

Of prime interest to visitors are two English-language newspapers that have print and on-line versions: the Hürriyet Daily News (www.hurriyet dailynews.com) and Today's Zaman (www.todayszaman. com). Both cost TL1.50 on the newsstands.

*The Guide İstanbul* is published bi-monthly and runs listings of restaurants, shops and other services. Features can be interesting, but often read as advertorial. It costs TL6.50.

There are monthly Turkish and English editions of the Time Out İstanbul (www.timeoutistanbul. com/english) magazine. Like *The Guide İstanbul*, this has a large listings section. Its features are much more readable than those in the *Guide*, and it is the best source of details about upcoming events in town. It costs TL5.

The glossy magazine *Cornucopia* runs articles on Anatolian arts, culture, history and literature. It's published three times per year and costs TL24.

You can also buy the big international papers such as the *International Herald Tribune*, *Le Monde* and the *Guardian* from newsstands. Be sure to check the date on any international paper before you buy it. The best selection of international magazines can be found at the Remzi Kitabevi bookshops at Akmerkez and Kanyon (see the boxed text p142).

# ORGANISED TOURS

The following small companies offer tours of the city:

Kirkit Voyage (Map pp50–1; ☎ 212-518 2282; www. kirkit.com; Amiral Tafdil Sokak 12, Cankurtaran; half-day tours per person €45-70; ☾ 10am-8pm) This small agency in the middle of the main hotel district in Sultanahmet specialises in tailoring walking tours for groups of two or more. You can choose from its 'Classic İstanbul', 'Ottoman İstanbul', 'Byzantine İstanbul' and 'Old Pera: The Hills of Beyoğlu' tours, as well as specialised tours such as 'İstanbul: The Unusual Way', which explores *hans* (caravansaries) around the Grand Bazaar. Other tours visit sights by public transport and minibus. It can also organise private guides (€125/85 per full/half day).

Les Arts Turcs (Map pp50–1; ☎ 212-527 6859; www. lesartsturcs.com; İncili Çavuş Sokak 37, Kat 3, Sultanahmet; half-day tours per person €55-70, full day €60-85; ☾ 10am-8pm) This friendly company has a strong arts and culture bias. It organises a wide range of off-the-beaten-path walking tours of neighbourhoods around the city, including special tours of Jewish, Armenian and Greek neighbourhoods and to the Princes' Islands. It also runs highly recommended visits to Sufi ceremonies at *tekkes* in Fatih and Silivrikapı (see the boxed text p107). The company has a second office in Cankurtan (Map pp50–1; ☎ 212-638 1215; İshakpaşa Caddesi 6), next to the entrance to Topkapı Palace.

## POST

Post offices, marked by black-on-yellow signs, are traditionally known as PTTs (peh-teh-teh; *Posta, Telefon, Teleğraf*). İstanbul's Central Post Office (Merkez Postane; Map pp50–1; Şehinşah Pehlevi Caddesi, Eminönü) is several blocks southwest of Sirkeci train station. It has a section open 24 hours a day, where you can make phone calls, buy stamps and send and receive faxes.

There are PTTs in the law courts (Map pp50–1) on İmran Öktem Caddesi in Sultanahmet; off İstiklal Caddesi at Galatasaray Sq (Map pp102–3); near the Galata Bridge (Map pp102–3) in Karaköy; and in the southwestern corner of the Kapalı Çarşı (Map p75) near the Havuzlu Restaurant on Gani Çelebi Sokak. Note that when this book went to print, the Galatasaray branch had temporarily relocated to İstiklal Caddesi while the Yeniçarşı Caddesi building was being renovated.

The *yurtdışı* slot is for mail to foreign countries, *yurtiçi* is for mail to other Turkish cities, and *şehiriçi* is for mail within İstanbul. Mail delivery is fairly reliable. Postcards to international destinations cost between TL1 and TL1.10; an airmail letter of up to 50g costs TL1.40.

If you decide to ship something home, don't close your parcel before it has been inspected by a customs official. Take packing and wrapping materials with you to the post office. Parcels sent by international express mail to most European destinations cost TL33 for the first kilogram, then TL12 for every extra kilogram; mailing to the US and Australasia is more expensive. For more information on PTT services go to www.ptt.gov.tr.

The easiest way to send a parcel is by courier; there are DHL offices in Sultanahmet ( ☎ 212-512 5452; Yerebatan Caddesi 15/2; ☣ 10am-6pm Mon-Sat) and just north of Taksim Sq (Map p113; ☎ 212-445 5850; Cumhuriyet Caddesi 20, Beyoğlu; ☣ 10am-6pm Mon-Fri, 10am-5pm Sat). Be prepared for a hefty charge, though.

## SAFETY
### Pedestrian Safety

As a pedestrian, give way to cars and trucks in all situations, even if you have to jump out of the way. The sovereignty of the pedestrian is recognised in law but not out on the street.

## Police

Blue-clad officers are part of a national force designated by the words *polis* or *emniyet* (security). Under normal circumstances you will have little to do with them. If you do encounter them, they will judge you partly by your personal appearance. If you look tidy and 'proper', they'll be on your side. If you're dressed carelessly they may not be as helpful.

Other blue-clad officers with peaked caps are market inspectors *(belediye zabıtası)*. You won't have much to do with them.

## Racial Discrimination

Turkey is not ethnically diverse. This means that travellers who are Asian or black stand out as being different and can be treated unacceptably as a consequence. As well as harassment, there have been isolated incidents of violence towards blacks, allegedly at the hands of individual members of the police force.

## Theft & Robbery

Theft is not generally a big problem and robbery (mugging) is comparatively rare, but don't let İstanbul's relative safety lull you. Take normal precautions. Areas to be particularly careful in include Aksaray/Laleli (the city's red-light district); the Grand Bazaar (pickpocket central); the streets off İstiklal Caddesi in Beyoğlu; and Galipdede Caddesi in Tünel, where bag-snatching sometimes occurs.

## Traffic Accidents

It's worth mentioning that Turkey has one of the world's highest motor-vehicle accident rates. Drive very defensively.

## TELEPHONE

If you are in European İstanbul and wish to call a number in Asian İstanbul, you must dial 0, followed by ☎ 216. If you are in Asian İstanbul and wish to call a number in European İstanbul use ☎ 212. Do not use a prefix (that is, don't use the 0 or 212/6) if you are calling a number on the same shore.

Country code ( ☎ 90)

European İstanbul ( ☎ 212)

Asian İstanbul ( ☎ 216)

Code to make an intercity call ( ☎ 0 + local code)

International access code ( ☎ 00)

Türk Telekom (www.telekom.gov.tr) has a monopoly on landline services, and it provides an efficient if costly service. You can direct-dial within Turkey and overseas with little difficulty.

The best places to make phone calls are in PTTs or at Türk Telecom Offices. There will usually be card (*telekart*) phones and *köntürlü* (metered and attended) phones at both.

Public phones are located outside PTTs, in most major public buildings, in public squares and in train and ferry stations. You'll usually need to buy a phonecard to use one (see below), but an increasing number of these phones accept international credit cards.

International calls are expensive; try to call between 10pm and 9am or on Sundays, when rates halve.

## Mobile Phones

Mobile reception is very good in İstanbul and locals have embraced the technology wholeheartedly. All mobile numbers start with a four-figure code beginning with ☎ 05.

If you want to use your home phone here you should note that Turkey uses the standard GSM network operating on 900Mhz or 1800Mhz (US phones won't work here). There are three networks: Turkcell (www.turkcell.com.tr), Vodafone (www.vodafone.com.tr, in Turkish) and Avea (www.avea.com.tr), all of which offer prepaid SIM cards (*kontürlü SIM karts*). At Atatürk International Airport, Avea and Vodafone booths are in the international arrivals hall and the Turkcell booth is in the domestic arrivals hall.

Prepaid SIM cards cost approximately TL40 for 170 credits (1 local minute = 1 credit). To buy a SIM card you'll need to show your passport to the dealer and register your phone. The dealer will then send this information through to the network provider so that your account can be activated, a process that can take up to three days.

## Phonecards

There are two types of phonecard (*telefon kartı*): the regular floppy version (*manyetik kart*) or a rigid 'smart kart'. They cost about the same and are both available at telephone shops or centres. To use these cards you call the national toll-free number, put in the PIN number on the card and make your call. Readily available phonecards usually come

in denominations of 50-*kontör* (TL3.75), 100-*kontör* (TL7.50), 200-*kontör* (TL15) and 350-*kontör* (TL19). You'll need a 350-*kontör* card to make an international call. You can't use these cards with mobile phones.

## TIME

İstanbul time is East European Time, two hours ahead of Coordinated Universal Time (UTC, alias GMT), except in the warm months, when clocks are turned ahead one hour. Daylight-saving (summer) time usually begins at 1am on the last Sunday in March and ends at 2am on the last Sunday in October. Turks use the 24-hour clock.

## TOILETS

In most public toilets you must pay around TL0.50. Instead of providing toilet paper, these toilets are equipped with a tap and receptacle for water or a little copper tube that spurts water where needed. Some toilets are tiled holes in the ground rather than sit-down numbers.

Basic public toilets can be found near the big tourist attractions and transport hubs. Some are dirty, others quite acceptable. Every mosque also has a toilet.

## TOURIST INFORMATION

The Ministry of Culture & Tourism (www.kultur.gov.tr) runs the following tourist information offices or booths:

Atatürk International Airport ( ☎ 212-573 4136; ☉ 8.30am-11pm) In the international arrivals hall.

Beyazıt Sq (Hürriyet Meydanı; Map p73; ☎ 212-522 4902; ☉ 9am-11pm Mon-Sat)

Elmadağ (Map p113; ☎ 212-233 0592; ☉ 9.30am-4.30pm Mon-Sat) In the arcade in front of the İstanbul Hilton Hotel, just off Cumhuriyet Caddesi near Taksim Sq.

Sultanahmet (Map pp50–1; ☎ 212-518 8754; ☉ 9am-5pm) At the northeastern end of the Hippodrome.

## TRAVELLERS WITH DISABILITIES

İstanbul can be challenging for mobility-impaired travellers. Roads are potholed and pavements are often crooked and cracked. Fortunately, the city is making attempts to rectify this state of affairs.

Government-run museums are free of charge for disabled visitors and many have wheelchair access. Airlines and most four- and five-star hotels have wheelchair access and at least one room set up for disabled guests. All public transport is free for the disabled and the LRT, metro and *tramvay* can be accessed by people in wheelchairs.

## VISAS

At the time of research, nationals of the following countries (among others) could enter Turkey for up to three months with only a valid passport (no visa required): Denmark, Finland, France, Germany, Greece, Italy, Israel, Japan, New Zealand, Sweden and Switzerland.

Nationals of the following countries (among others) could enter for up to three months upon purchase of a visa sticker at their point of arrival (ie not at an embassy in advance): Australia, Belgium, Canada, Greece, Ireland, Italy, Netherlands, Norway, Portugal, Spain, UK and USA.

Nationals of Russia, Hungary and many Eastern European and Central Asian countries could enter for up to either one or two months upon purchase of a visa sticker at their point of arrival.

Your passport must have at least three months' validity remaining, or you may not be admitted into Turkey. If you arrive at Atatürk International Airport, get your visa from the booth to the left of the 'Other Nationalities' counter in the customs hall before you go through immigration. You can pay in Turkish lira, euros, pounds sterling or US dollars; customs officials sometimes insist on correct change. An ATM dispensing Turkish liras is next to the counter, but it's not always working. The fees change, but at the time of research Australians, Americans, Britons and most other nationalities paid €15 (US$20, £10); for some reason Canadians paid €45 (US$60). See the website of the Ministry of Foreign Affairs (www.mfa.gov.tr) for the latest information.

## Visa Extensions

There are single- and multiple-entry visas. Single-entry visas are valid for three months from the day of entry; multiple-entry visas are valid for three-month blocks during a one-year period. Depending on your nationality, you may be able to extend your visa. Most visitors wanting to extend their stay for a few months avoid bureaucratic tedium by taking a quick overnight trip to Greece (Thessaloniki or Rhodes), returning to Turkey the next day with a new three-month stamp in their passports.

## WOMEN TRAVELLERS

Travelling in İstanbul as a female is easy and enjoyable provided you follow some simple guidelines. Tailor your behaviour and your clothing to your surrounds – outfits that are appropriate for neighbourhoods such as Beyoğlu and along the Bosphorus (skimpy tops, tight jeans etc) are not appropriate in conservative suburbs such as Balat and Fener, for instance. In general, we suggest you dress in a reasonably demure fashion; showing lots of bare leg and cleavage can lead to attention and occasional lewd behaviour on the part of local men.

Women should be careful when walking alone at night, especially in Aksaray/Laleli, Eminönü and Karaköy. It's a good idea to sit in the back seat of taxis rather than next to the driver. If approached by a Turkish man in circumstances that upset you, try saying *Ayıp!* (ah-*yuhp*), which means 'Shame on you!'

You'll have no trouble finding tampons, sanitary napkins and condoms in pharmacies and supermarkets in İstanbul. Bring a shawl to cover your head when visiting mosques.

## WORK

After sampling the manifold delights of İstanbul, many travellers decide to stay. Jobs aren't all that easy to find (Turkey has a very high unemployment level) and most of these people end up teaching English at one of the many private colleges or schools; others get work as nannies (check www.anglonannies.com) or in the tourism industry.

If you want to get a job at one of the well-paid private language schools, you'll need to have a Teaching English as a Foreign Language (TEFL) certificate or equivalent, and a graduate degree (it doesn't matter what it's in).

For loads of practical information and advice about information on living, buying real estate, working and doing business in Turkey, get yourself a copy of Pat Yale's excellent *A Handbook for Living in Turkey,* published by İstanbul-based Çitlembik Publications and available in most of the city's English-language bookshops.

DEIK (www.deik.org.tr) is the Foreign Economic Relations Board of Turkey. Its website has useful links and economic and business information.

# LANGUAGE

Turkish is the dominant language in the Turkic language group, and is distantly related to Finnish and Hungarian. In 1928, Atatürk did away with Arabic script and adopted a Latin-based alphabet. He also instituted a language-reform process to purge Turkish of Arabic and Persian borrowings, returning it to its 'authentic' roots. The result is a logical, systematic and expressive language with only one irregular noun, *su* (water), one irregular verb, *olmek* (to be) and no gender. It's so logical, in fact, that Turkish grammar formed the basis for the development of Esperanto, an ill-fated artificial international language. Word order and verb formation in Turkish are very different from what you'll find in Indo-European languages like English. Words

are formed by agglutination, meaning that affixes are joined to a root word – one scary example is *Avustralyalılaştıramadıklarımızdanmısınız?*, which means 'Are you one of those whom we could not Australianise?' This makes it somewhat difficult to learn at first, despite its elegant logic.

In Istanbul's tourist areas you'll usually have little trouble finding someone who speaks English, but a few words in Turkish will be very well received and bring just reward for your having made the effort. If you want to learn more Turkish than we've included here, pick up a copy of Lonely Planet's comprehensive and user-friendly *Turkish Phrasebook*.

## PRONUNCIATION

Once you learn a few basic rules, you'll find Turkish pronunciation quite simple to master. Despite oddities such as the soft 'g' (ğ) and undotted 'i' (ı), it's a phonetically consistent language – there's generally a clear one-letter/one-sound relationship.

It's important to remember that each letter is pronounced; vowels don't combine to form diphthongs and consonants don't combine to form other sounds (such as 'th', 'gh' or 'sh' in English). It therefore follows that h in Turkish is always pronounced as a separate letter. For example, your Turkish friend Ahmet is 'ahh-met' not 'aa-met', and the word *rehber* (guide) is pronounced 'reh-ber' not 're-ber'.

Here are some of the letters in Turkish that may cause initial confusion:

| | |
|---|---|
| â | a faint 'y' sound in the preceding consonant |
| İ, i | a short 'i', as in 'hit' or 'sit' |
| I, ı | a neutral vowel; as the 'a' in 'ago' |
| Ö, ö | as the 'e' in 'her' said with pursed lips (but with no 'r' sound) |
| U, u | as the 'oo' in 'book' |
| Ü, ü | an exaggerated rounded-lip 'you' |
| C, c | as the 'j' in 'jet' |
| Ç, ç | as the 'ch' in 'church' |
| G, g | always hard as in 'go' (not as in 'gent') |
| Ğ, ğ | silent; lengthens preceding vowel |
| J, j | as the 'z' in 'azure' |
| Ş, ş | as the 'sh' in 'show' |

## SOCIAL
### Meeting People

Hello.
Merhaba.
Goodbye.
Hoşçakal. (said if leaving)
Güle güle. (said if staying)
Please.
Lütfen.
Thank you (very much).
(Çok) Teşekkür ederim.
Yes./No.
Evet./Hayır.
Do you speak English?
Inglizce konuşuyor-musunuz?
Do you understand?
Anlıyormusunuz?
Yes, I understand.
Anlıyorum.
No, I don't understand.
Anlamıyorum.

Could you please ...?
Lütfen ...?

| | |
|---|---|
| repeat that | tekrarlar mısınız |
| speak more | daha yavaş konuşur |
| slowly | musunuz |
| write it down | yazar mısınız |

## Going Out

What's on ...?
... görülecek neler var?

| locally | Yerel olarak |
| this weekend | Bu hafta sonu |
| today | Bugün |
| tonight | Bu gece |

Where are the ...?
... nerede?

| clubs | Klüpler |
| gay venues | Gey klüpleri |
| places to eat | Yemek yenilebilecek yerler |
| pubs | Birahaneler |

Is there a local entertainment guide?
Buranın yerel eğlence rehberi var mı?

## PRACTICAL
## Question Words

| Who? | Kim? |
| What? | Ne? |
| When? | Ne zaman? |
| Where? | Nerede? |
| How? | Nasıl? |
| Do you have ...? | ... var mı? |
| How much is it? | Ne kadar? |

## Numbers & Amounts

| 1 | bir |
| 2 | iki |
| 3 | üç |
| 4 | dört |
| 5 | beş |
| 6 | altı |
| 7 | yedi |
| 8 | sekiz |
| 9 | dokuz |
| 10 | on |
| 11 | on bir |
| 12 | on iki |
| 13 | on üç |
| 14 | on dört |
| 15 | on beş |
| 16 | on altı |
| 17 | on yedi |
| 18 | on sekiz |
| 19 | on dokuz |
| 20 | yirmi |
| 21 | yirmi bir |
| 22 | yirmi iki |
| 30 | otuz |
| 40 | kırk |
| 50 | elli |
| 60 | altmış |
| 70 | yetmiş |
| 80 | seksen |
| 90 | doksan |
| 100 | yüz |
| 1000 | bin |
| 2000 | iki bin |
| 1,000,000 | milyon |

## Days & Time

| Monday | Pazartesi |
| Tuesday | Salı |
| Wednesday | Çarşamba |
| Thursday | Perşembe |
| Friday | Cuma |
| Saturday | Cumartesi |
| Sunday | Pazar |

| What time is it? | Saat kaç? |
| It's (ten) o'clock. | Saat (on). |

## Banking

I'd like to ...
... istiyorum.

| cash a cheque | Çek bozdurmak |
| change money | Para bozdurmak |
| change a travellers cheque | Seyahat çeki bozdurmak |

Where's the nearest ...?
... nerede?

| ATM | Bankamatik/ATM |
| currency-exchange office | Döviz bürosu |

## Post

Where is the (main) post office?
(Merkez) Postane nerede?

I want to send a ...
Bir ... göndermek istiyorum.

| fax | faks |
| parcel | paket |
| postcard | kartpostal |

I want to buy ...
... satın almak istiyorum.

| an aerogram | Telsiz telgraf |
| an envelope | Zarf |
| a stamp | Pul |

## Phones & Mobiles

I want to buy a phone card.
Telefon kartı istiyorum.

I want to make ...
... istiyorum.
a (local) call  (Yerel) Bir görüşme
yapmak
reverse-charge/  Ödemeli görüşme
collect call  yapmak

I'd like a/an ...
... istiyorum.
charger for my  Cep telefonum için
phone  şarj aleti
mobile/cell  Cep telefonu kiralamak
phone for hire
prepaid mobile/  Kontörlü cep telefonu
cell phone
SIM card for  Buradaki şebeke için
your network  SİM kart

## Internet
Where's the local internet cafe?
En yakın internet kafe nerede?

I'd like to ...
... istiyorum.
check my email  E-postama bakmak
get internet  İnternete girmek
access

## Transport
What time does the ... leave?
... ne zaman kalkacak?
bus  Otobüs
ferry  Feribot
plane  Uçak
train  Tren

What time's the ... bus?
... (otobüs) ne zaman?
first  İlk
last  Son
next  Sonraki

Is this taxi free?
Bu taksi boş mu?
Please put the meter on.
Lütfen taksimetrcyi çalıştırın.
How much is it to ...?
... ne kadar?

Please take me to (this address).
Lütfen beni (şu adrese) götürün.

## EMERGENCIES
It's an emergency!
Bu acil bir durum!
Could you please help?
Yardım edebilir misiniz lütfen?
Call the police/a doctor/an ambulance!
Polis/Doktor/Ambulans çağır(ın).
Where's the police station?
Polis karakolu nerede?

## HEALTH
Where's the nearest ...?
En yakın ... nerede?
chemist (night)  (nöbetçi) eczane
dentist  diş hekimi
doctor  doktor
hospital  hastane

I need a doctor (who speaks English).
(İngilizce konuşan) bir doktora ihtiyacım
var.

## Symptoms
I have (a) ...
... var.
diarrhoea  Ishalim
fever  Ateşim
headache  Ibaş ağrısı
pain  Ağrım/Sancım

## FOOD
Can you recommend a ...
İyi bir ... tavsiye edebilir misiniz?
bar  bar
cafe  kafe
restaurant  restoran

Is service included in the bill?
Hesaba servis dahil mi?

For more information on food and dining
out, see p144.

# GLOSSARY

Below are some useful Turkish words and abbreviations.

ada(sı) – island
aile salonu – family room; for couples, families and women in a Turkish restaurant
altgeçidi – pedestrian subway/underpass
arabesk – music that's a mix of folk, classical and fasıl traditions
aşik – Turkish troubadours
Asya – Asian İstanbul
Avrupa – European İstanbul
ayran – a yogurt drink

bahçe(si) – garden
balık – fish
banliyö treni (s), banliyö trenleri (pl) – suburban (or commuter) train
belediye – town hall
bey – 'Mr'; follows the name
birahane – beer hall
boğaz – strait
bordro – exchange receipt
börek – flaky pastry that can be sweet or savoury
börekçi – place selling pastries
büfe – snack bar
bulvarı – often abbreviated to 'bul'; boulevard or avenue
büyük tur – long tour

caddesi – often abbreviated to 'cad'; street
caïque – long, thin rowboat
çalışma vizesi – work visa
çamaşır – laundry; underwear
cami – mosque
çarşı(sı) – market, bazaar
çay bahçesi – tea garden
cicim – embroidered mat
çift – pair
çocuk – child
çorba – soup

darüşşifa – hospital
deniz – sea
deniz otobüsü – catamaran; sea bus
Dikkat! Yavaş! – Careful! Slow!
dolmuş – shared taxi (or minibus)
döner kebap – meat roasted on a revolving, vertical spit
dondurma – ice cream
döviz bürosu – currency-exchange office

eczane – chemist/pharmacy
ekmek – bread
emanet – left luggage
emniyet – security

eyvan – vaulted hall opening onto a central court in a medrese or mosque
ezan – the Muslim call to prayer

fasıl – energetic folk music played in taverns or meyhanes
fasülyeci – restaurant serving cooked beans
fayton – horse-drawn carriage
feribot – ferry
fiş – electricity plug

gazino – open-air Turkish nightclub (not for gambling)
gece – night
gişe – ticket booth
göbektaşı – hot platform in Turkish bath
gözleme – Turkish pancake
gündüz – daytime

hamam(ı) – Turkish steam bath
harem – family/women's quarters of a residence
hat(tı) – route
hazır yemek lokanta – ready-made-food restaurant
hisar(ı) – fortress or citadel

ikamet tezkeresi – residence permit, known as 'pink book'
imam – prayer leader; Muslim cleric; teacher
imaret – soup kitchen
iskele(si) – landing place, wharf, quay

jeton – token (for telephones)

kadın – wife
kale(si) – fortress, citadel
kapı(sı) – door, gate
karagöz – shadow-puppet theatre
kat – storey (of a building)
KDV – katma değer vergisi; value-added tax (VAT)
kebapçı – place selling kebaps
kilim – pileless woven run
köfte – Turkish meatballs
köftesi – place selling grilled meatballs
köprü – bridge
köy(ü) – village
küçük tur – short tour
kürsü – prayer-reader's platform
kuru temizleme – dry cleaning

lahmacun – Arabic soft pizza
liman(ı) – harbour
lokanta – restaurant serving ready-made food
lokum – Turkish delight

mahalli hamam – neighbourhood Turkish bath
mahfil – high, elaborate chair
Maşallah – Wonder of God! (said in admiration or to avert the evil eye)
medrese – theological school
menba suyu – spring water
merkez postane – central post office
mescit – prayer room/small mosque

Mevlevi – whirling dervish
meydan(ı) – public square, open place
meyhanes – taverns
müezzin – the official who sings the *ezan*
müze(si) – museum

nargileh – water pipe

ocakbaşı – grill
oda(sı) – room
otel – hotel
otogar – bus station
otopark – car park
otostop – hitch
otoyol – multilane toll highway

padişah – Ottoman emperor, sultan
pastane – also pastahane; pastry shop, patisserie
pazar(ı) – weekly market, bazaar
pide – Turkish pizza
pideci – pizzeria
polis – police
PTT – Posta, Telefon, Telğraf; post, telephone and telegraph office

rakı – aniseed-flavoured grape brandy

saz – traditional Turkish long-necked string instrument
sebil – fountain
sedir – low sofa
şehir – city; municipal area
sema – Sufic religious ceremony
servis ücreti – service charge

servis yolu – service road
sıcak şarap – mulled wine
şile bezi – an open-weave cotton cloth with hand embroidery
sinema – cinema
şiş kebap – grilled, skewered meat
sokak, sokağı – often abbreviated to 'sk' or 'sok'; street or lane
su – water
Sufi – Muslim mystic, member of a mystic (dervish) brotherhood
sultan – sovereign
sumak – flat-woven rug with intricate detail
sünnet odası – circumcision room

tabhane – hostel
tarikat – a Sufic order
tatıcı – specialist dessert place
TC – Türkiye Cumhuriyeti (Turkish Republic); designates an official office or organisation
telekart – telephone debit card
tuğra – sultan's monogram, imperial signature

ücretsiz servis – free service

valide sultan – queen mother

yardımcı – assistant
yeni otogar – new bus station
yıldız – star
yol(u) – road, way

## THIS BOOK

This 6th edition of *İstanbul* was researched and written by Virginia Maxwell, who also authored the 4th and 5th editions. Verity Campbell revised and updated the 3rd edition, and Tom Brosnahan wrote the 1st and 2nd. The guide was commissioned in Lonely Planet's London office and produced by the following:

Commissioning Editor Clifton Wilkinson

Coordinating Editors Kate James, Justin Flynn

Coordinating Cartographer Jolyon Philcox

Coordinating Layout Designer Cara Smith

Senior Editor Helen Christinis

Managing Editor Laura Stansfeld

Managing Cartographer Herman So

Managing Layout Designer Laura Jane

Assisting Editor Holly Alexander

Assisting Cartographers Khanh Luu, Valentina Kremenchutskaya

Cover Naomi Parker, lonelyplanetimages.com

Internal image research Aude Vauconsant, lonelyplanetimages.com

Project Manager Anna Metcalfe

Language Content Laura Crawford

Thanks to Lucy Birchley, Sally Darmody, Trent Paton, Indra Kilfoyle, Jane Hart, Michelle Lewis, Lyahna Spencer, Wayne Murphy

Cover photographs Blue Mosque (top), Nicholas Pitt/Getty Images; traditional coloured stained-glass Turkish lamp in the Grand Bazaar (bottom), Jen Judge.

Internal photographs All images are copyright of the photographer unless otherwise indicated. Many of the images in this guide are available for licensing from Lonely Planet Images: www.lonelyplanetimages.com.

## THANKS
### VIRGINIA MAXWELL

Many thanks to Pat Yale, René Ames, Tahir Karabaş, Saffet Tonguç, Ercan and Şenay Tanrıvermiş, Ann and Tina Nevens, Özlem Tuna, Shellie Corman, Mehmet Umur, Emel, Faruk Boyacı, Pelin Nasöz, Ferhan İstanbullu, Profesor Ahmet Emre Bilgili, Eveline Zoutendijk, Lora Sarıaslant, Aslı Kıyak İngin, Anke van Lenteren and the many locals who shared their knowledge and love of the city with me. At Lonely Planet, thanks to Clifton Wilkinson, Herman So, Anna Metcalfe, Kate James, Jolyon Philcox and Justin Flynn.

## OUR READERS

Many thanks to the travellers who used the last edition and wrote to us with helpful hints, useful advice and interesting anecdotes:

Roshan Abraham, Hendrik Auf'Mkolk, Barbara Barrow, Chris Blacklock, Peter Bloecher, Alan Blythin, John Broughton, Jim Broughton, Sayan Bulent, Angelita Carpentero, Cristovao Cunha, Emrah Demir, Ben Edwards, Rossi Gianluca, Richard Hodges, Graham Hopley, Lynne Humphreys, Jaesuk Hwang, Winnifred Jelier, Keith Kenney, Anne Marijn Koppen, Gretchen Lane, Blank Leonard, Marco Maragliulo, Noel Marchiandi, Elena Martini, Elizabeth Matharu, Petra Meier, Olivier Meunier, Dom Moisen, Ali Mumtaz, Eric Neemann,

## THE LONELY PLANET STORY

Fresh from an epic journey across Europe, Asia and Australia in 1972, Tony and Maureen Wheeler sat at their kitchen table stapling together notes. The first Lonely Planet guidebook, *Across Asia on the Cheap*, was born.

Travellers snapped up the guides. Inspired by their success, the Wheelers began publishing books to Southeast Asia, India and beyond. Demand was prodigious, and the Wheelers expanded the business rapidly to keep up. Over the years, Lonely Planet extended its coverage to every country and into the virtual world via lonelyplanet.com and the Thorn Tree message board.

As Lonely Planet became a globally loved brand, Tony and Maureen received several offers for the company. But it wasn't until 2007 that they found a partner whom they trusted to remain true to the company's principles of travelling widely, treading lightly and giving sustainably. In October of that year, BBC Worldwide acquired a 75% share in the company, pledging to uphold Lonely Planet's commitment to independent travel, trustworthy advice and editorial independence.

Today, Lonely Planet has offices in Melbourne, London and Oakland, with over 500 staff members and 300 authors. Tony and Maureen are still actively involved with Lonely Planet. They're travelling more often than ever, and they're devoting their spare time to charitable projects. And the company is still driven by the philosophy of *Across Asia on the Cheap*: 'All you've got to do is decide to go and the hardest part is over. So go!'

## SEND US YOUR FEEDBACK

We love to hear from travellers – your comments keep us on our toes and help make our books better. Our well-travelled team reads every word on what you loved or loathed about this book. Although we cannot reply individually to postal submissions, we always guarantee that your feedback goes straight to the appropriate authors, in time for the next edition. Each person who sends us information is thanked in the next edition and the most useful submissions are rewarded with a free book.

To send us your updates – and find out about Lonely Planet events, newsletters and travel news – visit our award-winning website: lonelyplanet.com/contact.

Note: We may edit, reproduce and incorporate your comments in Lonely Planet products such as guidebooks, websites and digital products, so let us know if you don't want your comments reproduced or your name acknowledged. For a copy of our privacy policy visit lonelyplanet.com/privacy.

Kathleen Neumann, Ramiz Polat, Isabelle Rouleau, Michael Schoberth, Thomas Schroder, Martijn Smelt, Graham Symonds, Ciska Tillema, Jon Tydeman, Jayda Uras, Ward Van Alphen, Alexander Van Der Graaf, Leonie Van Der Kolk, Christoffer Von Sabsay, Edward Wendt, Sean Windsor, Hui Yeoh

# INDEX

238

# MAP LEGEND
## ROUTES

| | |
|---|---|
| Tollway | Mall/Steps |
| Freeway | Tunnel |
| Primary | Pedestrian Overpass |
| Secondary | Walking Tour |
| Tertiary | Walking Tour Detour |
| Lane | Walking Trail |
| Under Construction | Walking Path |
| Unsealed Road | Track |
| One-Way Street | |

## TRANSPORT

| | |
|---|---|
| Ferry | Rail |
| Metro | Rail (Underground) |
| Bus Route | Tram |

## HYDROGRAPHY

| | |
|---|---|
| River, Creek | Water |

## BOUNDARIES

| | |
|---|---|
| International | Ancient Wall |
| State, Provincial | Cliff |

## AREA FEATURES

| | |
|---|---|
| Airport | Land |
| Area of Interest | Mall |
| Beach, Desert | Market |
| Building | Park |
| Campus | Reservation |
| Cemetery, Christian | Rocks |
| Cemetery, Other | Sports |
| Forest | Urban |

## POPULATION

| | |
|---|---|
| CAPITAL (NATIONAL) | CAPITAL (STATE) |
| Large City | Medium City |
| Small City | Town, Village |

## SYMBOLS

**Information**
- Bank, ATM
- Embassy/Consulate
- Hospital, Medical
- Information
- Internet Facilities
- Police Station
- Post Office, GPO
- Toilets

**Sights**
- Beach
- Castle, Fortress
- Christian
- Islamic
- Jewish
- Monument
- Museum, Gallery
- Point of Interest
- Ruin

**Shopping**
- Shopping

**Eating**
- Eating

**Drinking**
- Drinking
- Café

**Nightlife**
- Nightlife

**Arts**
- Arts

**Sleeping**
- Sleeping

**Transport**
- Airport, Airfield
- Border Crossing
- Bus Station
- General Transport
- Taxi Rank

**Geographic**
- Lighthouse
- Lookout
- Mountain, Volcano
- National Park
- Picnic Area
- River Flow

**Published by Lonely Planet**
ABN 36 005 607 983

**Australia** (Head Office)
Locked Bag 1, Footscray, Victoria 3011,
☎ 03 8379 8000, fax 03 8379 8111,
talk2us@lonelyplanet.com.au

**USA** 150 Linden St, Oakland, CA 94607,
☎ 510 250 6400, toll free 800 275 8555,
fax 510 893 8572, info@lonelyplanet.com

**UK** 2nd fl, 186 City Rd, London, EC1V 2NT,
☎ 020 7106 2100, fax 020 7106 2101,
go@lonelyplanet.co.uk

© Lonely Planet 2010
Photographs © as listed (p236) 2010

Printed by Fabulous Printers Pte Ltd
Printed in Singapore

**Mixed Sources**
Product group from well-managed
forests and other controlled sources
www.fsc.org Cert no. SGS-COC-005002
© 1996 Forest Stewardship Council

FSC